BOOKS BY JOHN EDWARD WEEMS

DREAM OF EMPIRE

MEN WITHOUT COUNTRIES

PEARY: THE EXPLORER AND THE MAN

RACE FOR THE POLE

THE FATE OF THE MAINE

A WEEKEND IN SEPTEMBER

DREAM of EMPIRE

A Human History of the
Republic of Texas
1836-1846

BY JOHN EDWARD WEEMS

with Jane Weems

SIMON AND SCHUSTER

NEW YORK

First Printing

SBN 671-20972-8
Library of Congress Catalog Card Number: 78-159140
Designed by Jack Jaget
Manufactured in the United States of America
Printed by Mahony & Roese Inc., New York, N.Y.
Bound by American Book–Stratford Press Inc., New York, N.Y.

For Mary E. Homeyer of Austin, Texas,
whose ancestors fought at San Jacinto,
and for some men in the world of books
who have been encouraging and helpful in past years:
Carl Brandt, Paul Brooks, Howard Cady,
Jacques de Spoelberch, George Garrett, Richard Kluger,
Robert Lescher, and Walter Lord.

CONTENTS

IX

REPUBLIC IN FLAMES

1842   219

X

THE PRISONERS

1843   249

XI

END OF THE REPUBLIC

1844 to February, 1846   297

WYOMING

COLORADO

KANSAS

ARKANSAS R.

N

Santa Fe

PECOS R.

RIO GRANDE

W MEXICO

OKLAHOMA

ARK.

Halted at Cap Rock ✕

SANTA FE EXPEDITION

RED R.

Pecan Point

Potter's Point

RED R.

LA.

BRAZOS R.

SABINE R.

GAINES'S FERRY

Nacogdoches

COLORADO R.

FALLS OF THE BRAZOS

TRINITY R.

NECHES R.

BRAZOS R.

SAN JACINTO R.

San Jacinto

MEXICO

RIO GRANDE

Austin

GUADALUPE R.

Bastrop

Washington

Houston

San Antonio de Béxar

Columbus

San Felipe

Columbia

Anahuac

Galveston

Gonzáles

SAN ANTONIO R.

Victoria

Linnville

Velasco

Brazoria

Matagorda

Goliad

Refugio

NUECES R.

LAVACA BAY

San Patricio

ARANSAS PASS

CORPUS CHRISTI BAY

Laredo

Monclova

Guerrero

Mier

GULF OF MEXICO

Monterrey

Matamoros

Saltillo

THE
REPUBLIC OF
T E X A S

0   MILES   200

UNITED STATES

Santa Fe

T E X A S

Austin

New Orleans

GALVESTON BAY

MEXICO

GULF OF MEXICO

Telchac

Campeche

YUCATAN

Mexico City

Veracruz

PACIFIC OCEAN

PROLOGUE

In the pleasant afternoon of Thursday, February 19, 1846, Dr. Anson Jones, the last President of the Republic of Texas, sat at his desk in Austin composing a letter to his wife. At a time when many men in his position would have been otherwise engaged, perhaps drinking and reminiscing with friends, Anson Jones was instead writing Mary, whom he had left at their plantation home near Washington-on-the-Brazos while he traveled to the capital to turn over the government of recently annexed Texas to the United States.

Already he was the former President Jones. At noon that day cannon had boomed a salute as the changeover occurred. That night—he mentioned in his letter—an inaugural ball was to be held honoring Governor James Pinckney Henderson and, indirectly, Jones. This was Henderson's day, not Jones's, but Anson Jones was glad to give it away. "My health is first rate and I never felt better or happier than I have today," he wrote Mary. "I am indeed relieved from a vast and distressing burthen."

That burden would be someone else's now—passed on to Henderson, and eventually to the United States. A wonder it was that the Republic of Texas had existed at all, and more wondrous that it had survived for nearly ten years. Internally, the Texas Republic was for most of its life a house badly divided. Externally, the world often seemed to be in conspiracy against it.

Several apparent paradoxes marked its founding. Many of the people who fought against Mexico to bring the Republic of Texas into being originally had sought only a greater degree of self-government for Texas as a Mexican state, not independence at all. A flag displayed by some of them early in the rebellion demonstrated this. They flew Mexican colors, except for the elimination of the golden eagle and substitution therefor of the figures "1824"—for the liberal Mexican Constitution of 1824, which the Mexican government itself had nullified and to which many Texas colonists wanted to return.

The Texas paradox and the internal dissension continued after that, creating controversies that are still being debated today. The small Texas Army retreated into its decisive San Jacinto victory over a large pursuing force—only one of three Mexican armies operating in Texas to quell the rebellion, but that force happened to have been led by the dictator of Mexico, Antonio López de Santa Anna, who was captured and was easily prevailed upon to send out orders ending the fighting. But then the general who had directed Texas to its triumph, Sam Houston, found himself treated almost like an enemy because of a previous feud with ad-interim President David G. Burnet. The government denied Houston passage aboard a Texas Navy vessel to New Orleans for treatment of battle wounds. Houston and his friends arranged his own transportation there.

Sam Houston figured further in the Texas anomaly. His fame as a military commander won him election twice as president of the struggling Republic, but during both terms "Old Sam Jacinto," as he was sometimes called, concentrated his primary effort on keeping Texas at peace—and actually on the defensive against Mexico, which never recognized the independence of Texas and frequently sought to harass it by raids and talk of reconquest. As president, Houston strove to forestall Texan counteroffensives against Mexico—something not easily accomplished in the seething Republic—reasoning that his country had neither men nor money for the war effort and concluding that such military operations would only drop the weight of world opinion on Texas anyway. So "Old Sam" the general, the veteran of the 1812 war against the British, and a participant in other battles, determined to fight Mexicans in the future only when essential, and sometimes—said his critics—he avoided conflict even then.

Much Texas Republic history sounds like comic opera, as a few random paragraphs demonstrate:

Texas claimed as its territory a huge chunk of land that included parts of what are now New Mexico, Oklahoma, Kansas, Colorado, and Wyoming, as well as Texas, and many citizens dreamed of an empire and a manifest destiny all their own, yet officials could never govern effectively and efficiently the settled areas of East Texas and the coastal plains.

"Texians"—as citizens of the Republic called themselves—could be described as a fanatically democratic lot, much like the Jacksonian Democrats of the United States, yet they loved titles before names. This elicited a pithy comment from an observer: "If there were more *Misters* and fewer titles, it would not be so ludicrous. A lady asked me if the gentlemen of Texas were not *generals generally*. I told her the *Major* part of them were quite *Captains* in their own way. I *Judge* she would think so if she was in at a party at Congress time . . ."

The first official "Executive Mansion" was in fact a double log cabin that some twentieth-century sharecroppers would shun, but inside it visitors met an imposing President Houston who was sometimes dressed in "velvet coat and trousers trimmed with broad gold lace," as one guest recalled.

Another President of the tumultuous Republic was a poet: Mirabeau Buonaparte Lamar, who, like many others, saw an empire instead of a frontier, then imagined a treasury to match and spent poor Texas into near-extinction in pursuit of his magnificent dreams. Meanwhile, hard-won Texas relations with France, achieved during Lamar's term, were broken off temporarily after a row involving an Austin resident, his pigs, and the French chargé d'affaires.

The Republic of Texas actually owed its continued existence to even greater turmoil in Mexico, where conflicts internal and external also raged, and of course to the tenacity of its own people. This narrative is a story of those people—not a catalog of names, dates, and statistics; those can be found in the chronology at the end. Particularly is it a story of twelve individuals whose accounts of vanished days have been relied on primarily for the narration. Many other persons are mentioned, but the twelve listed below have been selected to serve as what might be described as major characters. Each of these persons left behind diaries, journals, memoirs, or letters—or some of each—in which he or she recorded detailed observations of life in the Republic of Texas. Not even one record was truly complete, unfortunately, and the remaining information often departed this world along with the individual concerned, but no attempt has been made to fill in blank spots by use of imagination. For this reason physical descriptions of some characters are absent, something that would not be excusable in most stories.

Occasionally these eyewitness accounts showed obvious mistakes, usually because of a time lapse between the event and the recording of it, or because of a restricted vantage point on the part of the viewer. Corrections have been made to make the narrative consistent with the facts, but without changing the substance of the person's story. In these few instances a brief explanation has been inserted in the Notes on the Text section.

Many small details of Texas history are unverifiable today, more than most other history. Some vital records have been lost. Some that do exist—even official reports—contain obvious errors, too, possibly because many people of that lively time detested paperwork. Whenever doubt arose, the twelve eyewitnesses were given the benefit of it, and their stories were relied upon, occasionally with comments in the Notes on the Text about deviations from other accounts.

No direct quotations have been invented, including those in dialogue. All quotations used are as they were recorded by the individuals who lived during those times, with the exception that on rare occasions punctuation and spelling have been changed for easier reading. Words have not been tampered with.

Certain famous events in Texas history have not been recounted again here. The battles of the Alamo and San Jacinto, for instance, have been narrated too often for further detailed treatment. For the same reason the careers of renowned men like Sam Houston and Stephen F. Austin have not been retold in detail, although they figure prominently in parts of the narrative, of necessity.

The twelve persons used as major characters are these, listed here in alphabetical order and not in order of appearance in the story:

Joseph Henry Barnard, a Massachusetts native devoted to the care of his fellow man, who left medical practice in cool Canada to venture into torrid Texas, and arrived in time to witness a horrible massacre.

Barnard E. Bee, a staunch South Carolinian whose seriousness of purpose brought him to Texas at the age of forty-nine for the opportunity of public service after he had become disgusted with a political situation at home.

Thomas W. Bell, a young Southerner with an introspective bent who came to Texas to recoup after a business failure but found even greater frustration in the new land.

Charles G. Bryant, a Maine native who devoted his military temperament to a continuing fight for the liberty of people he felt to be oppressed, first against the English in Canada—where he was captured and sentenced to death, but escaped—then against the Mexicans in Texas.

His son Andrew Jackson Bryant, who inherited something of a rebellious spirit from somewhere, probably from his father, and as a midshipman in the Texas Navy exasperated both peers and superiors with it, but who eventually won respect and even acclaim.

William Fairfax Gray, nearly fifty years old when he came to Texas, a perceptive man who mixed Old Virginia propriety with an affinity for seeing new places and faces, and who was ever alert for a good business deal—revealing this characteristic by looking with a buyer's eye at lands around what became only a few days later the San Jacinto battlefield.

Moses Johnson, a native of New York who felt compelled to give Texas his services as a physician and a public administrator.

George Wilkins Kendall, a venturesome newspaperman who studied printing under Horace Greeley in New York and later went west—first to New Orleans, where he founded the *Picayune,* then to Texas, where he accompanied an exciting expedition against Mexico and recorded its activities.

Samuel A. Maverick, a gentle but resolute South Carolinian who took part in many events of pre-Republic days and later—Indian fights, encounters with Mexicans, a march of Texan captives into Mexico.

His wife, Mary Maverick, a tall woman who retained her Alabamian charm and femininity on the Texas frontier, yet who could look threatening Indians eye to eye while holding her baby and force their retreat.

Z. N. Morrell, a Southerner, friend of Sam Houston and David Crockett, and a man afire with the ambition to preach Jesus to lost souls, of whom he found plenty in Texas, but at the same time a man who could substitute rifle for Bible when he felt the occasion demanded.

Harriet Moore Page, a pretty young woman from New Orleans whose move to Texas on the eve of rebellion cast her into unexpected political troubles and whose beauty compounded her difficulties by involving her in some stormy marital situations.

The central character of this story is the Republic of Texas, but its history is told largely through these people, and some others.

I

BACKGROUND

To September, 1835

A split from Mexico became inevitable for Texas the day Anglo-Americans settled in that wilderness. The two peoples had only one common bond of any strength—a revolution to gain freedom. But the revolutions differed as much as did the people. The Anglo-Americans who revolted against English rule had a history of involvement in decision-making, however insufficient they thought it had been, and after winning their independence they established a government that showed some degree of stability, especially for a group of revolutionists.

Spain had not allowed the Mexican rebels so much involvement, with a few exceptions, and postindependence days in that new nation were marked by great instability and further violence—so much of both that the Texas settlers, even without other reasons, would have been motivated to break away, eventually, and form a government of their own. Significant racial and cultural differences hastened the rupture.

But the ultimate inevitability of rebellion by the Anglo-Americans in Texas was best stated by Mexican Secretary of War José María Tornel y Mendívil in 1837:

For more than fifty years, that is, from the very period of their political infancy, the prevailing thought in the United States of America has been the acquisition of the greater part of the territory that formerly belonged to Spain . . . It has been neither

21

an Alexander nor a Napoleon, desirous of conquest in order to extend his dominions or add to his glory, who has inspired the proud Anglo-Saxon race in its desire, its frenzy to usurp and gain control of that which rightfully belongs to its neighbors; rather it has been the nation itself which, possessed of that roving spirit that moved the barbarous hordes of a former age in a far remote north, has swept away whatever has stood in the way of its aggrandizement.

In the United States, the movement westward toward the Spanish lands was well under way many years before 1835. The new North American republic already had earned distinction as a land of opportunity, but chances in certain areas seemed more favorable for some people than for others. "Opportunity" in cities like Boston, New York, and Philadelphia was already largely controlled by a comparatively few industrialists, bankers, and businessmen who had established themselves securely, helped along by the War of 1812, which had forced the United States to develop its own manufacturing system rather than to rely on European products. This in turn had ignited a North American Industrial Revolution, which had further strengthened the position of those wealthy few. The first iron steamboat was built in the United States in 1825; the first regularly scheduled steam-powered passenger train commenced its run out of Charleston in 1830. People used the improved transportation facilities to move to cities for industrial jobs; the population of New York City jumped thirty percent—to 270,000—between 1830 and 1835.

But for many individuals city life was much too stifling, and the general lack of education prevalent during that day precluded much self-advancement there. They looked elsewhere for opportunity.

1. STEPHEN F. AUSTIN'S TEXAS

The vastness that is now Texas had attracted Anglo-Americans since the period immediately following the American Revolution. At a time when the raw wilderness just west of the Appalachian

Mountains should have offered sufficient challenge to satisfy the craving of the most audacious frontiersman, a few adventurers, with a propelling mixture of covetousness and curiosity, pressed on westward—westward across the Mississippi River, across the Sabine: westward into what was then Spanish territory, where they were not welcome, certainly not in unrestricted and unsupervised numbers. But a geographical boundary—the Appalachians—had not stopped the American frontiersmen, and neither would a political boundary.

The first Anglo-American to venture into Texas and to return to talk about it was a bold adventurer named Philip Nolan, who used his charm to wangle approval from Spanish governors at New Orleans for mustanging expeditions into the western wilds toward the end of the eighteenth century. With a few men to help him, he rounded up wild horses that roamed the Texas prairies in those days, broke them, and took them to New Orleans, where he sold them at a good profit.

But Nolan overdrew his account at New Orleans. The Spaniards heard of his boasts, spoken later on American soil, that he had made fools of them, and after Nolan visited Vice-President Thomas Jefferson in Philadelphia in 1800 they began to suspect him of having mapped their lands for United States conquest. They withdrew their approval for further expeditions, but Nolan set out anyway. The Spaniards attacked him at his crudely built fort near what is now Blum, Texas, on March 21, 1801, killed Nolan, and captured his men. In that brief fight the first shots in the American conquest of the Southwest were said to have been fired.

Nolan's death did not deter other Anglo-Americans from looking to the west for a golden fortune that shone as brightly as the sun they followed, if only in their expansive imaginations. Schemes of western empires were rumored. Some persons said Aaron Burr had in mind raising an army and using it to slice off a piece of Spanish land for himself—this possibly to be combined with a separated western portion of Burr's own United States, where he had been the nation's third Vice-President, in 1801–1805. But a trial and other publicity ended Burr's quest, whatever it was, and he never led any troops westward.

Other men did come to Texas, some with the grandiose intention of separating it from Spain or of helping Mexico win her independence. One Anglo-American came in peace, however, and if the Spanish-speaking rulers of Texas had listened more closely and sympathetically to him the Texas Rebellion would not have occurred when it did.

The man was Stephen F. Austin, a slim, young, intelligent Virginian of responsibility and gentility seldom seen on any frontier. With his father, Moses Austin, he had been engaged in mining ventures in Missouri with the approval of the Spaniards, who owned the territory then. The operation failed, and eventually Moses Austin, looking for something new, sought permission from Spain to lead a group of three hundred families in settling choice land in Texas. Before completing all arrangements Moses Austin died, and Stephen took over the project.

The Texas that appears on maps today was, when Stephen F. Austin came, an awesome expanse of land good and bad, forested and barren, wet and arid, smooth and rugged, much of it not very well known even to its owners—the Spaniards when Austin arrived in 1821, then the Mexicans, after they acquired independence that same year. Much of the interior had never been mapped. Boundaries did not correspond to present ones.

To the colonists the Texas landscape changed gradually as they traveled from east to west. A verdant eastern area, forested and adequately watered, received rainfalls of more than thirty inches annually. An undulant central section had less rain, fewer trees except in the river bottoms, but more grassland. Farther west, in the direction of the Rio Grande, an arid country of scrubby trees, short grass or none at all, and annual rainfalls of ten inches or less baked under a hot sun.

Still other distinctive areas could be found many miles inland. Far to the north lay a region Austin's colonists never saw—the high plains country of what is now the Texas Panhandle, an elevated, treeless flatland with adequate rainfall, good grass, and cold winters for such a moderate latitude. Contrasting with these plains, and to the southwest of them, rose barren mountains, all in the vicinity of what is now known as the Big Bend—ninety peaks more than a mile high, one with an elevation of 8,751 feet. More uneven land could be found west of what is now the city of Austin, where

lay a rolling, wooded hill country—as it is called today. All three of
these inland regions—high plains, mountains, hill country—were in
Stephen Austin's day in the hands of various tribes of Indians who
were mounted, powerful, and mostly courageous. Only in East
Texas and in some sections along the coast could friendly Indians
be found, but even then a settler never knew exactly how amicable
they might prove to be.

All the obstacles to colonization became quickly obvious to
Austin, who described the country in 1821 as "an entire wilderness
from the Sabine to the San Antonio River. Its civilized population
was comprised of the towns of Bexar [now San Antonio] and
Bahía [Goliad] and did not exceed 2,500 souls. The whole country
was filled with hostile and pilfering Indians. Nacogdoches was
totally destroyed and abandoned." But Austin received a large
slice of choice farming land in the east-central section, extending
well inland from along the Gulf Coast, and by the end of seven
years of what he called a laborious and slavish life he had ensured
success for his growing colony, which had increased by that time
from the original "Old Three Hundred" families to several thousand residents. He could claim to have provided abundantly for his
people—even much peace and security—more so than the ten
other important *empresarios* who by that time also had been
awarded government contracts. From his headquarters at San
Felipe de Austin, some forty miles west of present Houston, he
wrote friends and relatives in the United States letters soliciting
more immigrants, who, he said, should bring farming tools and
rifles or muskets—the first to work the land, the second to kill
deer, turkeys, and buffalo for the table. Mexican law required them
also to bring an allegiance to the Catholic Church, but this regula-
tion was not strictly enforced.

Austin also wrote letters expressing concern for his relatives'
approval of the Texas venture. He had undertaken the job with
scant enthusiasm—had taken it on at all only because of a request
by his dying father. "I have been buried for nearly ten years in this
remote wilderness," he wrote once. "The motives which brought
me here and which have governed me are such as I hope may meet
with the approbation of my family connections who care anything
about me. When I explored Texas in 1821 I was delighted and

astonished at its natural beauties and many valuable resources, [and] warmed with an ambition to try and redeem it from the wilderness." Austin thought his work would prove beneficial to mankind. "My object and ambition was to succeed with the enterprise and lay a foundation for the fortune of thousands. I have never lost sight of that main and great object, and for that reason and that alone I have succeeded."

He also wrote enticing descriptions of the country and its opportunities—not in a booster tone typical of common land speculators, but in thoughtful sentences that pointed up the opportunities for self-improvement open to individuals. In various letters he described the climate as "delightful" and "compared by some to Italy"; wrote of the unlimited opportunities for farmers and laborers in his colony, where "land is procured from the government for almost nothing"; asserted that farmers who understood "the culture of the grape" could make Texas wine an important commercial article; exulted over the fine crops already produced: sugar, cotton, indigo, tobacco, Indian corn, wheat, and "all kinds of vegetables. . . . Pasturage is inexhaustible and green winter and summer." The last statement proved especially attractive to farmers forced to contend with harsh winters.

To supplement his descriptions Austin prepared a map of Texas, based largely on his own surveys and studies, and sent it to the United States for printing. He asked that copies be sent to Governor Sam Houston in Nashville, Tennessee, and David G. Burnet in Cincinnati, Ohio. Both men, coincidentally, later became presidents of the Texas Republic.

Throughout Austin's letters is a recurrent theme: the effort of the man to subordinate his own feelings and desires for the good of his colony and its people. Especially troublesome, according to Austin himself, was his temper, but he mastered it so well that some acquaintances accused him of being weak.

A few thoughtless, disorganizing demagogues have said that I was more of a Mexican (or as they termed it) a Spaniard in heart, than an American—I have been much pestered here by bawling democrats who know nothing of liberty but licentiousness . . . but few, if any, have any idea what this country

really is, or of the influence which my labors here will one day
have upon its future destiny. . . . Many have blamed me for
being too temporizing, as they termed it. I have temporized with
the whims of the settlers, but I have never temporized with my
duty to them nor to the government.

Duty was Austin's foremost concern. This became immediately
obvious to visitors at San Felipe. Austin's austere log cabin contained two rooms, a bedchamber for himself and a land office for
his colony. He had not married, because, he said, "I have no time
to attend to the duties of a family. . . . Texas is my mistress, and
to her I am devoting all my time and affection. When I get through
with my duties to her then I may marry, but not before." His
attention to duty also indicated other character traits: temperance,
refinement, reflectiveness. Austin was a man who could become
oblivious of surroundings while pacing to and fro, in deep thought,
in front of his cabin. But at other times he could be eloquent and
persuasive, without realizing the extent of his attractiveness. He
was especially charming to the ladies, and a relative's physical
description of him told why. Austin was a slender, sinewy, graceful
man of moderate height, with small hands and feet, large hazel
eyes, fair skin when not sunburned, and dark hair inclined to curl
when damp. His normally grave, thoughtful face would become
animated when he talked to people, and it was then that his personal magnetism exerted its pull.

A combination of intelligence and sensibility supported his
charm. Once he dispatched a group of armed men after horse
thieves, presumably Indians, and ordered them to punish the
robbers, be they Indians or white, yet in the same instruction
added, "You will however be cautious of offending innocent persons, as you will be responsible for any wanton cruelty committed
by your men while acting by your orders." Austin spoke often of
"pilfering Indians" around his colony, but urged that they be
treated "with common justice." He favored giving them land and
educating the females at public expense—the females, he emphasized, because it was they who exerted the first controlling influence on children. Austin added that through such an educational
program white men might be encouraged to marry Indian women,

and this would contribute more than anything else toward extending white civilization.

But Austin also could compromise inelegantly. He declared
himself opposed to slavery—hoped it might not be formally admitted to Texas—but added, "I think it will be [admitted] finally.
. . . I doubt whether the people will be satisfied without it." For
the supposed benefit of his colony, where virtually no laborers were
available for hire, he helped to work loopholes in the Mexican law
against slavery.

Austin was a singularly reasonable man, one to whom the Mexican owners of Texas should have listened. Loyalty, not rebellion,
was inherent in him, and in 1830 he wrote, "I consider that I owe
fidelity and *gratitude to Mexico. That* has been my motto and I
have impressed it upon my colonists."

2. THE IMMIGRANTS

The Anglo-Americans who moved to Texas chose one of three main
routes for travel: river, overland (or a combination of both), or
sea.

A family from Carthage, Tennessee, that preceded even Stephen
F. Austin used a keelboat and an Indian pilot from Natchitoches to
navigate the Red River to Pecan Point, in present Red River
County, in 1816. The feat required ingenuity as well as courage. A
quarter-mile-long raft of drifted timber and other debris blocked
the river in one place, and it had become so firmly packed that an
occasional cottonwood tree grew from it. Negotiating this raft required five days. The rest of the trip proved to be almost as unpleasant. The channel wound through an interminable swamp full
of mosquitoes and alligators, and darkened by a jungle that cut
visibility even in midday to a hundred yards. Eventually, however,
the family made a home in the Texas wilderness. They arrived
without a horse, cow, or chicken, and in a country where most
neighbors were Indian. "The gun was the meat, bread, salt," said
one of the sons, ". . . and it was enough." Without a gun nothing

was possible. With it life went on, and this family managed to survive.

Other immigrants traveled overland, through forests and across deep rivers of what are now Louisiana and East Texas. Many of them stopped in Nacogdoches, a key point of land entry into Texas after the town had been rebuilt. There stood the famous Old Stone Fort, as it is now called, with walls a yard thick, built about 1779.

Most immigrants came by sea—across the Gulf of Mexico from New Orleans or another port to the mouth of the Brazos River, or to Matagorda or Aransas Bay. Despite the short distances traveled, these voyages were hazardous, because of the unseaworthiness of the vessels assigned to transport immigrants and because of the shallow water and shifting sandbars around the Texas ports.

An Irish trader who brought his bride to Texas in 1834 aboard a schooner named the *Wildcat* soon realized the danger. A storm was raging as his vessel approached narrow Aransas Pass one evening, but the captain declared he intended to cross the bar anyway. Just as the tossing schooner reached it a huge wave seized the *Wildcat* and cast her aground in five feet of water. But the ship had developed no leaks, so passengers and crew braved the rough seas and stayed aboard that night. The very next day another ship was wrecked nearby, but the Irishman and his bride reached land safely.

Another trader, an immigrant from Massachusetts, survived a Gulf voyage that also ended disastrously. Outbound from Velasco —at the mouth of the Brazos River—the vessel on which he was a passenger went aground on a sandbar. There it remained for four hours or so while the captain drank away his cares. Suddenly the vessel broke free and drifted across the bar, but none of the twenty-five passengers cared to continue the voyage, now that they had a drunken captain in command. The captain refused their request to turn back, however, and began bawling out orders that took them on a nightmarish journey.

That evening the passengers heard pumps working steadily in a rhythm that did not lull them to sleep, especially since they knew they were sailing away from land at a speed of eight knots. At ten o'clock a sailor rudely called them out of their bunks to help the exhausted crew man the pumps. The passengers nervously agreed to lend a hand, but first they accosted the captain with a demand that he head for the nearest land. Blearily he refused. Then his own men convinced him that the vessel was sinking, and he put the ship about—still drunk—and retreated to his cabin. There he slept until daylight, leaving the mate to cope with the situation. Meanwhile, passengers toiled to keep the vessel afloat, taking turns at the pumps and passing buckets of water up a companionway to the deck, where the buckets were emptied and passed down again. "Our lives was the price of our labor," said the man from Massachusetts. Throughout a chilly, dark, terrifying night they worked, hoping for a reward at daylight—the sight of land. When morning came, however, they saw only more rough seas, with no land visible even from the masthead. Finally, at three o'clock that afternoon, they sighted land. Seven hours later they had their saturated schooner safely grounded on a beach.

Even a dry arrival proved to be no harbinger of a pleasant time in Texas, however, because life for many settlers was not very comfortable, certainly not for immigrants who had become accustomed to East Coast or Southern elegance. Almost everything that afforded a fine living had to be brought in by ship. Colonial Texas manufactured practically nothing—produced only crops and cattle, and sometimes both proved to be skimpy.

Still, people came, and as long as they were under the eye of an *empresario* like Stephen F. Austin they were at first encouraged to come, to provide a buffer against wild Indian tribes and to help bring prosperity to the Texas wilderness. Most of the Anglo-Americans who ventured in were willing enough to match their lives against the dangers of a frontier existence, in a trade for the opportunity granted them. In the United States a door had been closed on many of them. In 1819 hard times had hit the country. Credit for land purchases had been restricted; debts became almost impossible to pay. Moving to Texas could solve those problems. Old debts could simply be forgotten, and new land could be obtained almost for the asking. Old crimes also could be forgotten in Texas, but an *empresario* like Austin sought respectable people for his colony. Not until later did the abbreviation "G.T.T."— "Gone to Texas"—painted on a shanty door in the United States imply that its owner had moved on to avoid some prosecution.

Many immigrants who came to colonial Texas and liked it enough to stay spoke of at least two advantages: the mild climate and an atmosphere of freedom. A man from Maine wrote home an intriguing description of easy life with a young wife and a baby daughter on Matagorda Bay, where he had built a four-room residence with large porches on two sides, only "fifty-six strides" from the water's edge. Half a mile away he could see his cattle grazing in the tall grass that provided year-round pasturage. He owned about one hundred head, including eight or ten good milk cows. Just yesterday, he wrote in his letter, he had been watching the cattle through his glass and had counted nearby sixteen deer feeding. Along with these animals, domestic and wild, his chickens, pigs, and garden furnished most of the necessities of diet, but to provide variety he had available the sea just outside his door. There he could catch fish with either hook or net, or he could wade hip deep into the surf and catch a turtle for dinner—as he reported having done during a break in his letter writing—or he could walk two miles down the beach and gather oysters from a luxuriant bed.

From his porch he could talk with men on vessels that called at Matagorda Bay. Some of them brought news from faraway places like Maine, reminding him of his once austere existence and the ridiculousness of a relative's request, "Let us know if you intend to settle in that barbarous country." He paused in his letter writing to think over that statement, then picked up his pen and wrote, "What had I when I came to Texas? Less than $40 . . ."

An enthusiastic immigrant from Massachusetts agreed with this assessment. He wrote home, "Texas has more natural advantages and in fact is superior to any other part of North America." The man added that he might return for a visit someday, but not to spend the winter. Another immigrant remembered in later years: "Texas was then a terrestrial paradise. Health, Plenty, and Good-Will teemed throughout the land. A live mastodon would not have been a greater curiosity than a tax-collector. There were no courts at law in the land, for there was no litigation. . . . The theft of cattle was an unknown crime . . . Corn-cribs knew nothing of locks. . . . In those . . . days, by tacit agreement, a cow and a calf were legal tender for ten dollars."

But the man who wrote that might have been suffering from a

severe case of nostalgia, because life in colonial Texas had its hardships. For most people the privations continued throughout the days of the Republic.

All but a few of the Anglo-American settlers lived in hurriedly built log cabins with floors of dirt or clay or, at best, split logs with the flat sides turned up. The clothes they wore were either homespun or brought from the United States, and the food most of them ate was provided by their own hands: wild game or beef or pork, coarse bread made from cornmeal, sweet potatoes but for most of them rarely any other vegetables, and strong coffee, usually black, and sometimes brewed from ground corn or some other penurious substitute. Several visitors to the Texas of that day talked about a remarkable absence of fresh milk and butter from most tables, despite the presence of cattle, but occasionally buttermilk would be available to take the place of coffee—upon request.

There were no schools. The few settlers who could afford to educate their children sent them to the United States. Absent, too, from most communities was religious training, even Catholic. Very few priests worked the Texas fields. In their absence couples felt free to live together after an informal ceremony witnessed by a few friends. Despite the shortage of priests, Stephen F. Austin would not permit itinerant Protestants to preach in his colony, because of his determination to cooperate with the Mexican government. As a result, formal religious services were rare, and Sunday in Texas became a day for play—for carousing by many—if it was not given to work. Even as late as 1845, when Texas would become the twenty-eighth state in the Union, only one of eight citizens would claim active or nominal membership in any church.

One reason for the absence of schools and churches was the scarcity of towns. Every village in the settled part of Texas was new, with the exception of San Antonio, Nacogdoches, and Goliad, and the new towns were only shabby collections of log cabins and sheds built along dirt streets that became dusty in droughts and muddy in rains. Stumps left from the recently cut trees cluttered some streets, making walking or riding at night hazardous.

The Texas of that day was a masculine world, a hard place of toil occasionally relieved by rough carousing, an uninhibited place where most men chewed and freely spat tobacco continually, and often drank too much, especially on election days, holidays, and Sundays. Drinking inevitably exaggerated the obstinate streak of argument-prone Texans, which led to further uproar. "In this vile community," one man wrote, "a boxing match is the prettiest way in the world of settling a difficulty. A victory does not draw . . . persecution . . . and a defeat is soon forgotten. Chivalry has not yet found entrance in Texas."

Besides drinking and fighting, favorite recreations were horse racing and dancing—the last a diversion made more popular, not less, by the scarcity of women. Word of an impending dance spread quickly around the country, especially to females of any age, and dancing partners for eager men sometimes included girls not yet in their teens. Steps popular then mirrored the rough existence— shuffles and stomps, not glides, which were impossible on dirt or puncheon floors.

Just as scarce as female dancing partners were competent doctors, and even when available they could be only of nineteenth-century effectiveness. Yet fevers raged in river bottoms and other stagnant areas along the low Gulf Coast—especially in the summer, when temperature and humidity soared to heights that might have caused some immigrants to remember fondly frigid winters of another day. To combat malaria and occasional epidemics of yellow fever, cholera, and other diseases brought on by inadequate food preservation and absence of sanitation, doctors relied on quinine, calomel, bleeding, and assorted patent medicines. New-comers usually fell quick victims to malaria, especially in summer, or to other ailments. Survival always was a worry.

Difficult, too, was travel—and sometimes impossible during or after heavy rains that turned normally dusty roads into brown squash and sent streams rampaging over the countryside. Partly because of these troubles mail service never got beyond being haphazard, even during the days of the Republic.

One of the two greatest inconveniences of all was the Indian threat. Most tribes became more savage as they saw more of their land falling to white men. Indians studied their enemy closely and developed effective ways of dealing with him. One Texas settler later recalled an incident that showed how cunning they could be at this. A group of Indians raiding through a region of white settlements came upon a gray mare, belled and hobbled, and realized that the animal had strayed from its owner, since they saw no houses nearby. They killed the mare, took off the bell, arranged the animal so that it appeared to be lying down, and waited behind a bush. When two horsemen appeared, obviously searching for the mare, the Indians rang the bell loudly enough to attract attention and waited for the men to find the mare. Then the Indians leaped out from their hiding place, killed one man, and sent the other—his brother—fleeing for home.

One of the ghastliest Indian attacks occurred in 1833 about four miles east of present Austin. On a late-summer day Comanche Indians attacked an immigrant from Missouri, Josiah Wilbarger, and four other members of a mounted surveying party who had halted for their noon meal near a creek. The men seized their weapons and fought back from behind a cluster of trees, but two of them soon fell wounded, one mortally. Wilbarger rushed to the aid of the other injured man, but he fell, too, when arrows tore into both of his legs. The two unharmed surveyors ran for their horses nearby and fled. Wilbarger yelled at them, begging for a ride. He even tried to hobble after them, but all his shouts went unheeded. Then he was hit again, in the back of the neck, and he collapsed on the ground. He retained consciousness, but he was unable to move or even to speak, and this saved his life. When the Indians stripped the clothes from his body he appeared to be dead. Even when they scalped him he did not move, but he recalled later that he realized what was happening. When the Indians pulled his scalp from his head he heard a sound like "distant thunder," although he felt no pain.

After the Indians had finished this grisly work they moved on to the other two men lying nearby and slit their throats. Sometime after that Wilbarger lapsed into a coma, and when he regained consciousness he realized night had fallen. He suffered agonizing thirst and crawled into the creek nearby, still bleeding. There he drank and lay in the water, chilled and numb, until he could summon the strength to crawl out.

On the following day he set out for a settlement that his group had left the morning of the attack. After staggering ahead for a quarter of a mile he fell, exhausted. Later he was found there—

blood red, looking more like an Indian than a white man—by rescuers. According to a story told by Wilbarger's brother, they had been urged on in what seemed to be a hopeless mission by a woman who said she had seen, in a dream, Wilbarger alive but seriously wounded, and greatly in need of help. Wilbarger lived eleven years after that, but the scalp wound eventually resulted in his death.

3. A GROWING THREAT

An even greater menace eventually was posed by the Mexicans. Previously they had encouraged Anglo-American settlers in several ways. A decree of September, 1823, admitted goods into Texas duty-free; the liberal Mexican Constitution of 1824, patterned somewhat after the United States document, assured reasonable government. But the Mexicans gradually moved toward an attitude of distrust and discouragement, especially after quelling a small rebellion in 1826 supporting an Anglo-American *empresario* in East Texas. About that time they realized the ultimate threat to their nation posed by the growing numbers of English-speaking colonists.

Mexico decided not to renew the free-duty privilege. Instead, the government levied a stifling tariff, which a few tactless bureaucrats sought to collect with an impunity that galled colonists. Then on April 6, 1830, the government issued a decree prohibiting further immigration into Texas from the United States—encouraging Mexican immigration instead—and applying other restrictions. This caused even the steadfast Stephen Austin some dismay, but it did not shatter his loyalty to Mexico. At the 1832 meeting in distant Saltillo of the Coahuila-Texas legislature, of which Austin was a member, he was popular and respected. Austin spoke Spanish as fluently as his native language—in an "easy, cheerful, polite way"—and he often got what he wanted. But at home Texas anger over the new restrictions grew. Compounding this displeasure were inherent cultural differences between the two peoples; frustrations engendered by an inefficient judicial system and by the great distance between Texas and its state capital, Saltillo—in Coahuila, with which Texas was combined for administrative purposes; and other grievances. These frustrations erupted in fighting. Mexican customs collectors and Mexican troops became targets of Anglo-American attacks in the coastal towns of Anahuac and Velasco. In 1832 and 1833 conventions held by the colonists listed complaints to be forwarded to the city of Mexico, where distrust of the Anglo-Americans in Texas precluded much feeling of sympathy.

Stephen F. Austin carried to Mexico the petition from the Convention of 1833, held in his headquarters town of San Felipe. In it the colonists asked for repeal of the anti-immigration law, for renewed tariff exemptions, for better protection against Indians, and, above all, for separate Texas statehood. Convention delegates had even drawn up a provisional state constitution, anticipating that the Mexican Congress would approve statehood. Austin doubted the logic and the timing of all this, because Mexico had been wracked by internal conflict and recent changes of administration. Nevertheless, he bowed to majority desire and departed for Mexico in April, against his best judgment and without the company of two hesitating men who had been selected to make the trip with him. The outcome of this journey would point up a flaw in Austin's character: his willingness to compromise his own beliefs and desires when the majority wanted something else.

At this time Austin himself was doubted by many Anglo-Americans in Texas. They felt he really did not intend to work for acceptance in Mexico of the requests; they ignored Austin's allegiance to his colony and to his people. Their doubts soared when months passed with no word of action by the Mexican Congress. But this was something Austin could not control. The Congress had ignored the petition for a time, then had been forced into recess by a cholera epidemic. The delay led Austin into frustration and an indiscreet act, something unusual for a man of his discipline. He wrote the *ayuntamiento* (local council) at San Antonio a suggestion that Texas make its plans for organizing as a separate state in the Mexican union, to avoid the "anarchy and total ruin" that seemed to impend. But when the Mexican Congress finally acted, the one major request it refused to grant was separate statehood, although other reforms were promised: repeal of the anti-immigration law, allowing an additional representative for Texas in the state legislature, and assurance against molestation of people for religious reasons so long as they did not disturb the peace. Because of these reforms Texans looked upon President Antonio López de Santa Anna as a liberator.

Austin commenced his return journey to Texas in December, 1833, but meanwhile his letter to San Antonio had come to the attention of high Mexican officials. When he reached Saltillo early in January he was arrested for inciting a rebellion and was returned to the city of Mexico. There he spent much of the next year and a half behind bars, with only a tamed jail mouse for a companion, but still he kept himself under control. He wrote letters to Texas urging calm in the wake of his arrest. "I do not in any manner blame the government for arresting me," he said in a letter to San Felipe, "and I particularly request that there be no excitement about it. I give the advice to the people there that I have always given, keep quiet, discountenance all revolutionary measures or men, obey the state authorities and laws so long as you are attached to Coahuila, have no more conventions, petition through the legal channels, that is through the ayuntamiento and chief of department, harmonize fully with the [Mexican] people of Bexar and Goliad, and act with them." Nevertheless, this harsh treatment by Mexico of a true friend eventually ended all hope for a peaceful solution of the problem, and in Texas the growing clamor of recently arrived speculators and other money-ambitious newcomers led to further complications.

Austin's place of detention for much of the time was a rambling old Inquisition prison, a dismal place haunted by the ghosts of many unfortunate men who had preceded him there. From a dungeon nearby the Mexican revolutionary leader José María Morelos y Pavón had been taken out for execution by the Spaniards. Austin himself had unpleasant memories of the prison. More than ten years earlier he had visited, in the very cell where he now found himself, a priest who had been a victim of the Inquisition. This dungeon had impressed Austin as dismal then, but the full impact had not struck him, since he had not been confined to it. Now the cell closed in on him. He saw that it was a windowless room about thirteen by sixteen feet. It was entered through a thick door that remained bolted and locked during his first three months there, when he was held in solitary confinement and his food was shoved in through a small slot in the door. "All was silent," Austin said. A small skylight in the roof admitted enough light for reading on a clear day when the sun was high—between the hours of ten and three—but for a time he could not even pass the hours in that activity, because his jailers allowed him no books.

Still, Austin's steadfastness did not desert him, and he could see beyond the blackness. His situation might have been worse, he mused. During the Inquisition prisoners frequently had been forced to wear a sacklike overgarment so that, with their heads covered, not even their guards or fellow prisoners could know their identity. "Nothing of the kind was done to us," Austin said, with charity typical of the man. In time Austin was taken daily to a roofless cell where he was allowed to sun himself, locked in and alone. Later his jailers allowed him an occasional visitor and other liberties—including books, which prompted him to say that he preferred "bread and water with books to the best of eating without them."

Contributing also to his maintenance of sanity and some strength was an absence of guilt and a realization that his imprisonment might actually benefit Texas. "My conscience told me I had committed no crime," he wrote in a letter from prison. "I was imprudent in urging the claims of Texas that were confided to me as an agent with more determination and obstinacy than was consistent with my personal security, but nothing more." As for the benefits accruing from his imprisonment, Austin listed them in the same letter. Some of the colonists who had accused him of being much too friendly toward the Mexican government would be less critical of him now and, as a side reaction, would be more calm and reasonable. His friends, who had always been in favor of peace and quiet, would continue to support him and his political philosophy. The state government at Saltillo would be stimulated to remedy some of the injustices plaguing Texas. "Thus my own principles of peace and quietness are now predominant," he said, "when had I attempted to make them prevail by direct opposition to violent measures, the reverse would have been the case. It is very certain that Texas must become a state [in the Mexican union] at some future and not very distant day. All will be in favor of it. . . . I am suffering, but the evils of Texas are remedied. This idea consoles me for my misfortunes, and enables me to bear them firmly."

Despite Austin's patience, prison took a toll. When two men from his colony visited him in October, 1834, during a journey to Mexico soliciting his release they found him so thin and his pallor so sickly that it seemed they could see through his extended hand. On this occasion Austin gave an uncharacteristic display of emotion. When he realized that his visitors were old friends from Texas, he fell upon one man's neck and wept. By then Austin had for some time assumed that people at home had forgotten him.

After having been buried alive in Mexican prisons for what seemed like years he was finally released, under bond, on Christmas Day of 1834. But more than six months passed before he was allowed to leave Mexico—in July, 1835—on board a ship bound for New Orleans. On September 1 he returned to Texas, on a vessel carrying munitions to the colonists. The ship reached Velasco that day, and people soon saw a different Austin.

A precursor of this change was an event in which Austin's vessel, the Texas schooner *San Felipe,* figured soon after landing its noted passenger. Lying near the mouth of the Brazos when the *San Felipe* arrived was a Mexican war schooner, the *Correo de Méjico,* dispatched to patrol the Texas coast to enforce compliance with more restrictions, despite the recent promises by Mexico, and at that very time involved in seizing a vessel outbound from Velasco. The *San Felipe* maneuvered as if to board, and the *Correo* fired on the ship Austin had just left. Thereafter ensued a fight that resulted in the capture of the *Correo* and gave some persons reason for calling it the first battle of the Texas Rebellion.

Austin returned to Texas at a time when another convention was planned—by colonists who believed that fighting for their rights was the only way of getting them. Opposing this war party were many peace advocates, who in the past had been led by Austin. Now they again looked to him for guidance. Austin's influence remained so great that Texas could be expected to go in whichever direction he indicated, despite the fact that the population had increased to somewhere between 25,000 and 30,000 Anglo-Americans, many of whom had entered illegally, and despite the fact that other *empresarios* had appeared on the scene as leaders.

In days past Austin would have calmed the people, but now he saw the situation through eyes opened by his jail experience and by certain recent events. The Mexican Congress had just declared itself capable of setting aside the liberal Constitution of 1824. The Mexican President, shifty and selfish Santa Anna, had thrown out promised reforms and had assumed the role of dictator, declaring that Mexico was not ready for democracy. Finally, all Texas knew that Santa Anna was sending military reinforcements to suppress for all time the Anglo-American troublemakers. Austin spoke out for the convention, which had the effect of saying that Texans should unify for war.

War was not long coming. In September Santa Anna's brother-in-law, young General Martín Perfecto de Cós, landed with an army of four hundred men at Matagorda Bay, bound for San Antonio and an overrunning of Texas. But when a Mexican detachment arrived at the town of Gonzales, sixty-five miles east of San Antonio, to reclaim a brass six-pounder cannon left there four years earlier for Indian defense, the colonists attacked the soldiers, forced their retreat, and formally began the war of the Texas Rebellion, on October 2. Stephen Austin became commander of the Texas Army—an unlikely choice—and began planning a campaign against San Antonio, where the Mexican military force was concentrated.

But when the "Consultation," or convention, that had won the backing of Austin met at San Felipe in November it declared support for the Mexican Constitution of 1824, not for a declaration of independence—largely in hope of winning the sympathy of Mexican liberals. The Consultation created a provisional state government and agreed to meet again on March 1 of the following year.

So even to the last the Anglo-Americans in Texas formally requested only more consideration and representation in exchange for a continued measure of subordination to the legal owners of their territory. But the flames had been fanned beyond any chance for control now. One member of the Consultation said, "The consequences to Texas, will differ but little, whether we fight for Independence, or State rights, for in either case we must fight and whip Mexico."

II

WAR

September to December, 1835

General Santa Anna finally had painted a true self-portrait for the Anglo-Americans in Texas. Far from being a friend, he now became known for what he was: a man who said one thing and did another. In 1835, as dictator, he had begun a reign of despotism. He saw to it that the Mexican Congress deposed the elected Vice-President, Valentín Gómez Farías, a man of too much republicanism. He hunted down political opponents and jailed them or ordered their execution. He crushed rebellions with a savagery that alienated many of his own countrymen, like the editor of the Mexican journal *El Crépusculo,* who on May 16, 1835, compared Santa Anna's personality after one of his many victories to "the tranquillity of a tiger, which, sated with the flesh of its prey, reposes on what it does not wish to devour." Santa Anna had used the army to disperse a squabbling Coahuila-Texas state legislature—an action that failed to rile Texans quite as much as might have been expected, because they looked upon the legislature as corrupt anyway. Still, the event provided more evidence of Santa Anna's unconstitutionality, and it left Texas without any government at all.

Only a privileged man—meaning a friend or supporter of Santa Anna—enjoyed a comfortable station in 1835 Mexico. In the United States, on the other hand, the "common man" had come into his own, and at this time Texas colonists had many reasons to envy his eminence. He owed it to the vigorous administration of the seventh President of the United States, Andrew Jackson, who had been inaugurated for the first of two terms in 1829.

President Jackson contended that men were wise, good, and equal—the laborer as well as the industrialist, the marginal farmer as well as the plantation owner—and that they were worthy of greater consideration than property. Imprisonment for debt became a bad memory; free public schools financed by taxes on everyone were established. Rich Americans regarded Jackson's measures as an attack on the rights of property.

In Mexico, the political situation contrasted sharply with Jackson's program to deposit a greater amount of power in the hands of the common man. In May of 1835 Santa Anna suppressed a rebellion in the Mexican state of Zacatecas, then allowed his troops to rob, rape, and murder inhabitants as punishment for the uprising. More than two thousand Zacatecans died.

After that he turned his full attention to the Texas troublemakers. An aide indicated Santa Anna's intention. "In a very short time the affairs of Texas will be definitely settled, for which purpose the Government has ordered to take up the line of march a strong division composed of the troops which were in Zacatecas. . . . These revolutionists [in Texas] will be ground down."

In Texas the colonists prepared to strike first. A San Felipe "Committee of Safety" issued a declaration on October 5: "The time has now arrived when it behooves every friend to his country to be up and doing. . . . Can we let a military despot reap the harvest . . . ?"

4. THE SIEGE OF SAN ANTONIO

At first glance Samuel Augustus Maverick's presence among frontiersmen preparing to fight for rights seemed improbable. The young man looked more like a poet than a pioneer. Two keen eyes dominated a sensitive oval face, and a small chin implied some lack of action and boldness. Fair-haired, moderately tall, slender, Maverick seemed too delicate for a frontier life, and something in his background appeared to substantiate this. He was the son of a comfortably established South Carolina planter, and he had received a college education—at Yale.

Maverick's bearing showed the gentility one would have expected of such a man. His manner was polished, but it was clearly natural rather than pretentious and ostentatious, which would have antagonized rough frontiersmen. He made no known enemies; letters written by his contemporaries to each other contain no serious criticisms of him—something that could not be said for many other Texas leaders of his day. The least favorable characteristic attributed to him apparently was a tendency to be "close and penurious," a trait indicated by a friend's obtrusive denial once that it ever existed. This same person described Maverick as quiet, sedate, dignified, and courteous, and he said further, "More eminently just and dispassionate than brilliant and captivating, mature age found him a venerated exemplar of all the highest virtues."

Closer observation of Maverick showed he was not at all out of place on the Texas frontier. His gentle appearance belied a liking for new ventures and new opportunities, and it gave no indication of a staunchness and an integrity that were remarked upon constantly by associates. Texas had in fact attracted many men like Maverick, men who lived lives of action that were enhanced in the new surroundings, not retarded, by their education and culture. Such men had been drawn to Texas by the congenial personalities of Stephen F. Austin and a few other early Texas leaders, and later by a compulsion to aid fellow men seeking liberty.

So Maverick was not a delicate man. A lingering use of his last name indicates this, if only indirectly. The word "maverick" in twentieth-century American usage describes an individualist who rejects conformity. The word came not from Sam Maverick's personality, but from a neglect once of one of his ranch hands to brand calves—not a common error in Texas before barbed-wire fencing, when cattle roamed at will. Any unbranded stock was immediately recognized as "one of Maverick's" or "a Maverick."

Although the word did not stem directly from his personality, it comes close to a description of it in twentieth-century terms.

Maverick left his native South Carolina after wounding in a duel a man who had heckled Maverick's father during a speech against John C. Calhoun's states'-rights concept of nullification. After that, at the suggestion of his father, Sam Maverick moved to northern Alabama to cool off. There he managed a plantation, but only for a brief time. He became dissatisfied with that work and left it for new chances in Texas, where he arrived in April of 1835. While exploring the coastal lowlands for possible purchase he contracted a "bilious fever," as did many other newcomers, and he sought a healthier climate inland, at a higher, drier altitude. On September 8, about a month past his thirty-second birthday, he arrived in Bexar—San Antonio—and was immediately captivated by the town. He found the Mexican inhabitants charming and the dry climate healthful.

The San Antonio that Maverick came to lay in a slight valley watered by a river that gushed out of a cluster of springs several miles above town. The river, also named San Antonio, gave life to the community, which straddled it. Along the banks lay a string of missions, all near the town. Because the river was spring-fed it provided a more reliable flow than most other Texas streams, which slowed to a trickle or dried up and cracked in torrid summer months and during droughts. This river did not. The nourishment it carried splashed the valley with green, and it gave unsophisticated Mexicans water for drinking, washing, and communal bathing.

Life in San Antonio went on at an easy pace, with no more work done than was necessary for existence. A man grew enough corn for his family, but no more. The town manufactured nothing for export, and not much for local sale. All this lassitude became most noticeable between the hours of eleven and four, when the hot, dust-powdered streets and the spacious dirt plazas lay mostly vacant while inhabitants napped.

Homes allowed for as much lazy comfort as possible. The best were built of stone and were plastered inside and out with rough coats of lime mortar, but many of them had only dirt floors and, for windows, iron-barred embrasures that reminded some Anglo-Americans of prison grates. Heavy roofs and massive walls three or four feet thick fended off the searing sun at midday and kept

interiors cool. Inside, San Antonians enjoyed their siestas sometimes stretched out on cowskins spread on floors, and many of
them ate while sitting on the same floors—often without benefit of
knives, forks, or spoons.

With late-afternoon waning of the stifling heat streets again
became crowded with a cheerful people chattering in the lilting
Spanish tongue. When last light faded, the gaiety that prevailed in
San Antonio became obvious. After dark there began spirited
fandangos. From several larger buildings came the sprightly
sounds of Spanish music played on a violin, and the rhythm of
dancing feet. The sounds proved irresistible to any man with young
blood in his veins, and as he approached the doorway he saw inside,
shaped by a flickering light, six or eight couples moving lightly and
quickly to a waltz, skimming across a level floor worn smooth by
the feet of many dancers. Their near-exhaustion rather than a
formal halt to the music usually signaled the end of the dance, and
when it came the man took his partner to a table for coffee and
cakes. The young lady sipped the coffee but often took her
mother the cakes, to help feed the family. Then she joined the
other women, all colorfully dressed, all seated on benches arranged
around the walls—watchful mothers included. There the girls once
again became visual targets of sleek males, who paraded the room
to show off bright jackets and bell-bottomed pantaloons, while their
wide-brimmed straw hats almost hid their dark, inquiring eyes.
After a few minutes the dancing would begin again.

Gaiety seemed to be in a crescendo when Sam Maverick reached
San Antonio. A week after his arrival came a noisy climax: the
September 16 independence celebration commemorating Miguel
Hidalgo y Costilla and his "Cry of Dolores" uprising in 1810 against
the Spaniards. But soon after that the dancing slowed, then
stopped—temporarily anyway. The gloom of war would accomplish what the lethargy, enervation, and indigence of workaday San
Antonio failed to do. It would smother the perpetual evening-and-
holiday blitheness.

Sam Maverick had wandered into what was soon to become the
most violent town in all of seething Texas. But he was young,
single, confident, and healthy now, and his nerves never seemed to
suffer. En route to San Antonio he had traveled through Gon-

zales—less than a month before the attack on Mexican troops caused it to become known as "the Lexington of the Texas Revolution"—but the increasing talk of war had not deterred him, and it would not send him into flight now. A month after Maverick's arrival in San Antonio General Cós reached town with the troops he had brought to crush Texas, and that same day Maverick first heard the news of the fighting at Gonzales. The colonists were gathering an army there, he heard.

Maverick and the few other Anglo-Americans in San Antonio were caught in a web. Their sympathies naturally lay with the colonists; yet here they were in a predominantly Mexican town where preparations for defense against the troublesome Anglo-Americans soon became intense. Maverick observed it all calmly and recorded events in his diary even as the excitement increased.

On Sunday, October 11, he attended a grand mass jammed with Mexican soldiers and ensouled with music more military than religious. That same day he heard news of the capture of a Mexican supply depot and thirty troops at La Bahía—Goliad—to the southeast. On the following day Mexican scouts arrived to report "great crowds" of Anglo-Americans marching toward San Antonio from the east. Military authorities pressed into service San Antonio civilians, even some Anglo-Americans, to help fortify the town. Maverick saw cannon mounted, barricades erected in the streets, and sharpshooters posted in houses.

The San Antonio excitement actually was greater than warranted. Dissension wracked the Texans' army, and, as was common among volunteer troops of that day, men felt free to return home at will, to care for affairs there, then to straggle back whenever they were ready. The army made slow progress: after leaving Gonzales on October 12 it halted several times to await reinforcements. Nevertheless, to most Mexicans this tattered army posed an immediate threat. Its numbers were reported to be large—as many as eight hundred men, with five hundred or more reinforcements on the way. Against them in San Antonio stood some six hundred troops.

General Cós made plans to use his men effectively. In addition to mounting cannon, erecting barricades, and posting sharpshooters, he put a rambling old mission once known as San Antonio de Valero—later renowned as the Alamo—into what Maverick recorded as "fort fashion." Cós ordered his men to tear out the roof of the church, build a dirt incline up to the rear top, and cover it with planks to make an artillery ramp. He planned to mount cannon at that strategic location on the east side of town. But beyond taking normal military precautions Cós was not much worried by the Texans. On October 18 he sent a courier with a letter to Stephen Austin, known by that time to be commanding the army, saying that if Austin would send his men home and come on himself to San Antonio he would "be disposed to hear him." Austin answered that he had not come to treat, but to fight. Infuriated, Cós exclaimed, "I want no more communications. Let the damn rascals come."

For security reasons General Cós placed all Anglo-Americans in town under house arrest. Sam Maverick was confined in the home of John W. Smith, a San Antonio merchant from Virginia, but despite the restrictions Maverick heard and recorded most happenings in town, and through the services of a Mexican boy he even exchanged messages later with Stephen Austin and other colonists.

Toward the end of October the Texan army encamped just outside San Antonio to await more reinforcements and other developments. The following days brought alarms and reports of skirmishes between the Texans and detachments of reconnoitering Mexicans. But in town Cós confidently completed his defenses. On October 27, Maverick recorded, soldiers took an eighteen-pounder cannon to the Alamo church and raised it to the top, using the recently built ramp. Some half-dozen smaller cannon also had been mounted in the Alamo, and still others stood ready nearby to hurl their wrath at the Texans. Cós had separated his troops into two divisions, posting one in the Alamo and the other in breastworks thrown up in the center of town.

That same October 27 Maverick heard the sounds of firing to the south. The shooting soon stopped, but it began again with greater fury the next day. Maverick learned later what had happened. A detachment of ninety Texans under Colonel James Bowie, searching for an army campsite nearer to San Antonio, were attacked by four hundred Mexican infantry and cavalry at a bend of the San Antonio River near Concepción Mission. Bowie received reinforcements and repulsed the Mexicans, inflicting sixty casualties.

After that the indecisive Texans settled down to a prolonged siege. Austin and the main part of the army encamped at an old mill on the San Antonio River a mile and a half north of town, the others at locations south, on both sides of the river.

Austin's abilities as a colonizer did not help him at all in military leadership. He proved to be too compromising to command an army—as he showed in his dealing with an old political opponent, fiery William H. Wharton, who had been an early advocate of separation from Mexico when Austin was urging cooperation. After Austin became commander of the army he appointed Wharton to his staff, in attempted conciliation, but Wharton could not mask his personal dislike of Austin nor his inability to brook anyone above him, and he fomented more trouble before resigning in a huff.

Other members of Austin's army left, too. The volunteers who had been selected previously as delegates to the Consultation left camp to return to San Felipe, where a quorum finally became available November 3. The men left behind grew more restless. Austin, Bowie, and other officers began quarreling among themselves. The remaining troops became increasingly dissatisfied because of inaction.

In San Antonio tension did not ease. Maverick observed further activity "to secure the place" and almost daily heard the sound of firing in the outskirts—more skirmishes. One day a priest sent to Stephen Austin by General Cós with repeated advice to disperse and petition the government peaceably returned with word that the Texans intended to have a fight. If Cós refused to come out they would come in—a feat that Maverick felt was becoming increasingly difficult. "The place could much easier have been taken with 200 men after the affair of Gonzales," he wrote, "than it can now with 1500 men." The Alamo had been strongly fortified, streets placed under heavy guard, and all trees, tall grass, fences, and other "lurking places" removed in order to put the Texans in plain view if or when they advanced on the town. Maverick's Anglo-American companions fell into dejection, but Maverick still voiced some confidence—especially later, when he heard rumors that four or five hundred more men were en route to join Austin's army.

Nights grew long. Often the roar of cannon not far away awoke Maverick. One early-November night he counted as the Alamo artillery hurled a hundred or more balls at something in the darkness beyond. Then the crack of small arms told him that the Texans must be probing the San Antonio defenses. Later he heard that all the firing had indeed been brought on by a party of Texans "examining the premises" and meeting the picket guard. On another night nervous Mexicans fired several signal rockets, apparently to warn of an attack, but the alarm proved false.

While the siege dragged on, balmy weather turned cool. One day Maverick noticed a twenty-degree temperature drop, from seventy-five to fifty-five degrees, in a matter of minutes because of a "norther"—a chilling wind blowing in suddenly from the north. Still the Texans did not attack.

On November 11 Maverick and his Anglo-American friends received a note from Stephen Austin, delivered by the Mexican messenger boy, giving the number of volunteers as nine hundred. Austin added that some of them had gone home. This extraordinary exchange of communications apparently never attracted suspicion, but the Mexicans were indeed wary of the Anglo-Americans in their midst—and they showed their concern that same night. When deep darkness had fallen, another alarm of attack came. Again cannon roared, and hundreds of muskets cracked defiance, including two fired from somewhere near the house where Maverick was staying. A Mexican captain and four soldiers burst into the house and accosted the occupants. The soldiers aimed their muskets at Maverick and the others, and the captain demanded to know who had fired the shots. Denials made him more furious, and he screamed in anger. He had been shot at, he yelled, and had even heard the balls whine by.

At this moment a Mexican neighbor walked in and calmed the officer. Having heard the commotion and realizing the peril faced by the Anglo-Americans, the neighbor volunteered the information that he had fired twice at enemy troops some distance away. Maverick knew the story was false, but it satisfied the officer, who ordered his men out of the house, then followed them. Without the neighborly help, Maverick mused, all of the occupants probably would have been shot without having been given any opportunity to prove their innocence. "Damn such a government," he wrote.

On the following day Maverick and his companions complained to a Mexican officer they trusted and respected, Colonel Domingo de Ugartechea, a "well-meaning" man stationed in San Antonio. Ugartechea listened sympathetically to their protests and to a request that they be allowed to leave town, then reminded them that final authority now rested with General Cós. Later Ugartechea asked the General, but Cós refused. The colonel himself called at the house to inform Maverick and the others of this decision. Then he added some advice that attested to his well-meaningness. Should any Mexican officer threaten them again, Ugartechea suggested, the Americans should "shoot such fellows." Maverick listened with amusement. It was kind assurance, he reflected, but "impractical and useless."

The siege extended into mid-November, and still the colonists did not attack. But on November 13, 14, 15, and 16 they kept the Mexicans aware of their presence with artillery bombardments. On the morning of the fifteenth—a Sunday—they commenced a brisk firing about ten o'clock. The fourth shot fell inside the Alamo and ripped off a soldier's leg. Later the balls began falling near Maverick's quarters, and he listened to them whistling loudly as if they intended to come inside. But the town suffered little damage. Maverick wrote that on the sixteenth the bombardment knocked down a hen house—the greatest damage inflicted. Often the Mexicans did not bother to reply.

By the seventeenth San Antonio was quiet again, with not even a breath of wind to rustle a sound. Some Mexicans managed to display a façade of gaiety. People talked about the approach of six hundred reinforcements being sent by Santa Anna. Ugartechea and sixty men supposedly had left town several days earlier to guide them in.

Other rumors made the rounds, including some not so pleasant to Mexican ears. The Texans also expected reinforcements, from Goliad, and they hoped to get them in time to storm the town, by night, before Ugartechea could usher in the Mexican troops. Whether or not this talk was based on reliable information, it did lead to greater precautions and some panic in San Antonio. Maverick heard sentinels challenging passing citizens in the dark street outside his quarters, then—a new development—requiring them to state their business. Maverick also heard other things: talk about shortages of ammunition and food, and growing disaffection in the Mexican ranks.

Still the Texans did not attack—and they lost their commander about this time. Stephen Austin thought over his weaknesses as a military leader and the dissension that wracked his army, and he asked to be relieved. He was replaced by a man the volunteer soldiers elected as their commander: Edward Burleson, a rough-cast man whose literacy did not extend far beyond an ability to sign his name. On November 25 Austin left his troops for San Felipe and eventually for an assignment as one of three commissioners to the United States to solicit help for Texas. By this time a number of others also had departed. Burleson could count only four hundred men willing to remain.

Cold wind and rain nipped them. Some men stoked themselves with whiskey, but for at least two volunteers this proved to be a mistake. One of them barely escaped capture when Mexican friends found him lying on damp ground south of town, put him on a horse, and sent him back to his army just before a Mexican patrol reached the spot. The other Texan was not so fortunate. The very next day the same patrol found him sleeping beside a road, woke him, and listened without sympathy to his pleas that he was their friend. One soldier shot and wounded the man while he pleaded; another killed him. Maverick heard that the soldiers were offering the man's clothes, horse, and pistol for sale.

Maverick also heard about an incident known in Texas history as the "Grass Fight." On a cold November 26 a noted Texan scout, Erasmus (Deaf) Smith, rode into the colonists' camp and reported sighting a pack train rumbling across the prairies toward San Antonio. A hundred horsemen led by nerveless Jim Bowie hurried away to mount an attack, supposing their enemy to be an advance unit of Ugartechea's reinforcements, and Burleson followed with the main army. The ensuing fight drew Mexican troops out of San Antonio to help repulse the attackers, but the Texans prevailed, forcing the Mexicans back into town with a loss of about fifty dead. Still, the pack train proved to be a disappointment. It was not Ugartechea and the additional troops, but a foraging party from San Antonio gathering grass for cavalry horses.

Maverick and his companions kept trying to get permission to leave San Antonio, and by the end of November they succeeded. Maverick and John W. Smith left town with Mexican approval, on Smith's promise that the two of them would return to the United

States. Before leaving they familiarized themselves with the Mexican defenses.

Soon after they had ridden out of San Antonio—on December 1—they heard both Mexican and Texan cannon commence firing again. That night they found food and shelter at the ranch of a Mexican friend ten miles south of town. The next morning Maverick and Smith traveled not toward the United States, but to the Texans' camp at the old mill just north of San Antonio. There the blasts of "great cannonading" shook Maverick much of that day.

They found the Texans ready to retreat to winter quarters at Gonzales or Goliad, to await spring and a more favorable time for attack. Cold weather, indecision, and a collective lack of patience had worn down any desire to assault San Antonio. Maverick and Smith described Mexican weaknesses and urged an attack, but without success. More men left camp even after their pleading.

"The spectacle became appalling," Maverick remarked, "but it was the deep darkness that foretold day." On the fourth a Mexican officer deserted to the colonists with information on dissatisfaction in his army and with other intelligence that corroborated what Maverick and Smith had said. One of Burleson's officers, Ben Milam, finally roused some men into action with an appeal for volunteers to join him in an assault on the city.

"A mere fragment" of the large army that had originally marched on San Antonio finally made the attack; Maverick estimated 250 men. The volunteers were divided into two main groups: a right division, commanded by Milam, with Maverick as a guide, and a left division, led by another officer, Francis W. Johnson, with Maverick's San Antonio host John W. Smith as a guide. A smaller group, with artillery, would attack the Alamo as a diversion. The assault would commence before daylight the next day, striking from north of the town.

Early on the morning of the fifth the roar of the cannon aimed at the Alamo signaled the start of the operation, but the Mexicans were not diverted for long from the two advancing columns. Four hours later only a few houses on the northern outskirts of town had been captured. For the next four bitter days the attackers came under the combined fire of Mexican cannon and muskets, and—when they had time to think about it—they shivered in cold,

blustery weather. But they suffered few casualties. Slowly they
forced their way into San Antonio, fighting hand to hand and from
house to house, digging through stone walls between buildings to
avoid exposure in the streets, which were commanded by Mexican
cannon in the center of town. On the seventh a rifle ball struck
Ben Milam and he fell dead in Sam Maverick's arms, in the courtyard of the Juan Martín Veramendi house. But two days later the
assault inspired by Milam and Maverick and a few others ended
successfully. Before daylight on the ninth the Mexicans hauled
down their colors and ran up a white flag. In the early morning
hours of the following day a humbled General Cós signed surrender
terms in a small stone-and-adobe residence still known as the Cós
House. Ironically, he had been reinforced at the last minute by the
expected six hundred additional troops, but the men were all released convicts and of no value in the fighting.

Maverick observed the formal surrender with satisfaction. The
Texans were awarded all public property, money, arms, and ammunition in San Antonio. Cós promised that he would withdraw his
army of more than a thousand men south of the Rio Grande and
never again fight in Texas. For protection from the Indians the
Texans gave his men muskets and one cannon, with ten rounds of
ammunition.

Gentle Sam Maverick had helped conquer the most important
Mexican military stronghold in Texas, and with a minimum of
casualties: twenty or thirty killed and wounded, compared to a
Mexican casualty count in the hundreds. When Maverick saw Cós
and his troops set out westward toward the prickly desert and
home he saw the departure of the last Mexican troops from Texas
soil. By Christmas of 1835 a few Texans felt that the war already
was over and independence had been won, but men of intelligence
and realism knew the wishfulness of this thinking.

III

INTERLUDE

Early 1836

In place of Mexican authority, which disappeared from Texas with the departure of General Cós's troops, Texans substituted their own system of law, administered by a provisional government organized by the Consultation of November, 1835—with only a few provisions, for simplicity and efficiency. Officials were few: governor, lieutenant governor, general council, judiciary, commander in chief of the military forces, and several others. During the first eight weeks of 1836 no Mexican army interfered with the administration of this provisional government, but personality clashes and the stubborn independence inherent in the men who had ventured into Texas virtually demolished it. The governor fought the council; the council voted to remove the governor and put the lieutenant governor in his office, which the governor refused to give up.

Even the military commander, Sam Houston, suffered woes. Nobody seemed to pay any attention to him. On January 17 he sent Jim Bowie and thirty men to the Alamo with orders for the commander, Lieutenant Colonel James C. Neill, to blow up the place and withdraw with the artillery, since Houston felt it could not be defended against a major attack. But instead of seeing that Houston's instructions were carried out, Bowie and his men stayed and helped Neill fortify the Alamo. Eventually Neill was replaced as commander by Colonel William Barret Travis, but not because he neglected to implement Houston's orders.

Sam Houston had other problems with his army: scant supplies, little money, halfhearted support. All these obstacles merely complicated the primary task: directing an army gathered from a population of thirty thousand colonists and some volunteers from the United States against the eight millions of Mexico. Finally Houston himself became involved in the internal disputes of the provisional government, and he left his command, on furlough, to work where he thought he could do the most good: with the Cherokees in East Texas, negotiating peace treaties with them at a time when they could hurt Texas seriously. To help persuade them he gave his assurance that Texas would honor their claims to lands long settled by them.

Despite all this commotion, immigrants continued to come to Texas, most of them from the United States. They left a country that was rapidly being divided by classes—Jackson's "common man" against the wealthy—and by sections. Although the War of 1812 had sparked a spirit of nationalism in the United States, evidenced by the Monroe Doctrine announcement of 1823 and other events, and had left citizens largely united against England, sectionalism too had grown. The North had become industrialized, through the necessity of developing home manufactures rather than relying on Europe. The South remained agricultural, slaveholding, and mostly rural, and looked to Europe as a major buyer of its cotton. That new section, the West, had sprung up beyond the Appalachians, agrarian and independent.

In Texas, people from all three sections mingled.

5. UNHAPPY MARRIAGE

Texans' willingness to serve in the army fell off momentarily. A handful of men stayed in San Antonio after the siege to help man the Alamo. Some others joined a small, poorly organized, disaster-destined expedition against the Mexican town of Matamoros. But most of the volunteers who had participated in the siege of San Antonio returned home. "The people are cold and indifferent," said

William Barret Travis, trying to enlist men for garrison duty in San Antonio. ". . . Volunteers can no longer be had." The personal feuds that shook the provisional government left Texas in turmoil on the eve of its greatest test. But this was not always obvious to immigrants.

One newcomer seeking to make a home in Texas about this time was Harriet Moore Page, a young New Orleans woman whose beauty and apparent lack of perception in romance involved her in some unfortunate liaisons.

The first had commenced before her arrival in Texas—and was one reason for her move. The man she had married, Solomon Page, had proved to be an irresponsible, improvident man who gave her little of anything besides two small children, a boy and a girl. Their life in New Orleans had created an emotional vacuum in her. Page was an incurable gambler, and at night he rarely came home before one, two, or even three o'clock. Many of their possessions vanished, gambled away, and Harriet had resigned herself to an empty destiny. Then, concluding she must make her own future, she opened a notions store in New Orleans, with success sufficient to enable her to save some money.

One night her prospects suddenly seemed to brighten further. Her husband returned home unusually early and announced they were all going to Texas. He said he had met the captain of a ship, the *Amos Wright,* and the man had described Texas so glowingly that their best hopes seemed to lie there—especially at a town called Brazoria, which the captain had described as offering great opportunity. They would get a plot of land near the town, Page declared, and he would get a job. She could set up another notions shop in Brazoria. Life would begin again.

Harriet Page had listened in silence to her ebullient husband. The last glow of faith in him had flickered out long ago, and she cared nothing for rural life anyway. But she thought of something else: her father had moved to Texas with her stepmother, and he owned a farm five miles from Brazoria. A brother also had moved there. Harriet agreed to go, and in the next few days she closed her business, packed belongings, bought staples, and boarded a ship with her husband and their two children and all their possessions. Upon arrival at Velasco, at the mouth of the Brazos River, a number of passengers disembarked before the vessel continued up the river to Brazoria. Through them Harriet sent word to her father of their arrival.

At Brazoria Dr. Anson Jones, a friend, came on board to tell her that her father was at home, ill and under his care, but that her brother would be along soon with a saddled horse to take her to her father's house. There arrangements could be made for unloading and transporting goods to a new home.

Her brother arrived, and Harriet collected the two children and a few overnight necessities and accompanied him home, leaving her husband aboard to watch their property until she returned the next day. "Knowing [his] love of gambling, I . . . begged him not to touch any of my things during my absence," she said. He promised to leave them alone.

The two children rode with her brother, the girl in front and the boy clinging on behind. After they had left the vicinity of the river Harriet saw, ahead, a level prairie. She exulted in the sounds: sprightly calls of unseen birds, a whisper of a Gulf breeze rustling the grass, the soft pat of horses' hoofs. War, if there was one, was far away. Instead, "the bonnie face of Texas smiled out."

Then in the distance she saw a log house—her father's—built just outside a thick belt of timber "curved like a great protecting arm" about the prairie. She found her father ill in bed, but over-joyed to see her. Harriet told him all about herself and about the move. She had brought a supply of staples, including flour, a scarce item in Texas. She promised him one of the two barrels.

The next morning she prepared to return to Brazoria, but her father insisted that she and the children stay with him, and he would send a wagon and driver for her husband and their posses-sions. She watched the wagon leave: it rumbled across the prairie and slowly vanished in the distance. Throughout that day she waited anxiously for its return.

Then she saw the wagon reappear, far off. As it came nearer she strained to catch a glimpse of her husband and the goods—and realized the wagon was almost empty, carrying only two men, one barrel of flour, and little else. "No one can imagine what I felt," she said. She could guess what had happened, and after the wagon had come to a halt in the yard her husband leaped down and told her. He had lost most of the things gambling the night before.

Nearby, Harriet's brother listened and exploded with anger. Page answered him roughly. Harriet pleaded for quiet, to avoid upsetting her father inside the house. She succeeded in calming the two, and her brother declared he would go to Brazoria and retrieve the lost property. The next day, with the help of Anson Jones, he got everything back but the foodstuffs. He delivered the things to her with an ultimatum: either she leave "that man" or he would never speak to her again. Silently she weighed the burdens and decided to stay with her husband. Perhaps on the Texas frontier he would not have so many chances to gamble.

Page blustered off then to look for a house for his family. After a few days he returned and moved them, first into a shack on Chocolate Bayou, a few miles distant, then into a log cabin on Austin Bayou, "twenty miles away from the nearest settler," Harriet estimated. A man Page met had convinced him that stock raising offered the best opportunity in Texas, and after Page moved his wife and two children into their Austin Bayou home he told them he was going to leave for a few days to talk with the man about a job keeping his stock. Before Page left he took ten dollars and promised to return with food as soon as he could. Harriet implored him not to be absent longer than three days.

Then she tried to make the home on the prairie as attractive as possible, although she was "heartsick and lonely," and all she had to work with was a one-room log house with a shed. "We were left alone on the desolate prairie, [with] no voice to break the stillness but the howling of wolves and panthers about our tiny home, and the cry of the wildcat after prey."

As their scant food supply diminished, her anxiety increased. On the evening of the sixth day after Page's departure Harriet stood in the doorway staring into the "limitless distance" and saw him returning. Before he reached the house she saw that he had brought no food. She asked about the money, and he answered that he had bought clothes to wear to war. Some men were volunteering to go, he said, and he did not want to be called a coward.

Harriet Page boiled over. "If you go off and leave us to starve," she told him, "I hope the first bullet that's fired will pierce your heart and just leave you time enough to think of the wife and children you left to die . . . in this wilderness."

Page left anyway.

6. LAND AGENT

The Texas turmoil did not discourage a Virginia attorney, William Fairfax Gray, from coming, as land agent for two entrepreneurs of Washington, D.C., and as a seeker on his own. None of the three men seemed at all dismayed by the threat of Mexican retaliation against Texas, least of all Gray. A veteran of the War of 1812, he nevertheless paid little attention to military activities in Texas, judging by the scarcity of references to it in a copious diary he left behind. He seemed to feel certain that events would work in favor of Texas. He wrote in his diary that an acquaintance had convinced him one of two things would happen: the United States would buy the territory, or Texas would establish its independence. On the eve of major fighting Gray would be found searching battle-fields-to-be for land purchases.

Gray left on the trip that would take him to Texas when he was in his late forties and the head of a growing family. An early picture of him once used in a book showed a handsome, dark-eyed, dark-haired man with a curl in the middle of his forehead and long, curly sideburns. He wore a ruffled shirt and a fancy pin.

Originally Gray set out with the intention of buying land around Vicksburg, Mississippi, but people he met persuaded him to go on to Texas. Like Sam Maverick, Gray seemed to be an unlikely man for the frontier. He had established a law practice, was set in his middle-aged, somewhat snobbish ways, was a domestic man forced to leave his family behind—in Fredericksburg, Virginia—while he traveled: by stage to the Ohio River and down it and the Mississippi to New Orleans, and eventually on to Texas.

He had left Fredericksburg at noon on October 6, 1835—at the time the Texas volunteers were gathering at Gonzales for their march on San Antonio. His wife, Milly, had bidden him a sorrowful goodbye. Her frail health had almost broken in June during an attack of intermittent fever. The illness, combined with childbirth, left her too weak to continue teaching music. Someone else took her students.

None of this stopped Gray. He aimed to look for fortune in the new country.

The trip downriver had tried his Virginia soul. He felt ill much of the time, with headaches, fever, and upset stomach, and he chewed rhubarb with the hope of forcing his bowels to function better and perhaps relieve his distress. His steamboat, the *Algonquin*, was "second-rate" and packed to twice its capacity. One Sunday at a landing the crew and some Kentucky roughs offended his Episcopal propriety by staging a mock religious service and inducing some imperceptive passengers to join in piously. Gambling went on continually, and a number of "very lively ladies" from Pittsburgh quickened festivities for a time until the captain ordered one of them off the ship. The "blackguardism and profanity" of some passengers convinced Gray they were fit only for the gallows.

But there had been compensations. Most of the hundred passengers aboard were "gentlemen . . . men of business." Also present were several ladies, in the finest sense of the word. Gray enjoyed meeting such people. He was a good conversationalist and a keen observer, and his affinity for people he found interesting was reciprocated. Wherever he went he made friends easily, and he listed them in his diary. He also recorded a few mild flirtations with women he found attractive, and one such dalliance—with the wife of a New Orleans man who was ailing—brightened this trip.

At Vicksburg the Mississippi lands proved disappointing, and Gray determined to go on to Texas. By the end of December he was in New Orleans, where on New Year's Day he met Stephen F. Austin and Branch T. Archer, two of the three commissioners sent to solicit money and recruits for Texas. Gray spent many hours talking with them, paying close attention to their description of the country—its character, conditions, and prospects. He found them elated over the prospects, especially because of the recent capture of San Antonio.

Gray liked Austin immediately, but Archer talked too much and too loud. "[Austin] appears to be a sensible and unpretending businessman," Gray said. A few days later, however, Gray detected a timid, troubled air about the man. "There is great kindness and affability in his manner, but an expression of anxiety pervades his features." Gray felt that this apprehension was reflected in the

Texans' first attempts at fund raising: they gave every indication of not knowing how to proceed. They sought to raise money to support an army and a fledgling government on a pledge of Texas land, but they had devised no satisfactory plan, and they failed to attract the "wealth and respectability" of New Orleans. Such ineptitude troubled Gray's orderly mind. Eventually, however, the Texans were able to obtain a $200,000 loan in the city. Gray quietly agreed to examine the Texas political situation personally for the lenders and to advise on the practicality of another loan.

Gray listened to everything and methodically sifted out every piece of information about Texas that seemed helpful: which places were sickly and which healthful; what law books he would need; the areas that seemed likely to grow—Galveston Island, where some men proposed erection of a port city, and San Antonio, where land for irrigation from the river could be bought cheaply. San Antonio residents were mostly "Spaniards," Gray heard, but very few of them were expected to remain in the country. While he was in New Orleans Gray received several offers of Texas land beginning at twenty-five cents an acre, but he was a cautious man and insisted on seeing the property before buying.

By mid-January he was ready to leave New Orleans for a look. He arranged passage on a boat bound up the Mississippi and the Red River, whence he would travel overland into Texas. His last few days were busy ones, crammed with writing letters: to his wife (from whom he had not heard since his departure), to his business associates, and to others. On the seventeenth, a Sunday, he was so busy he even neglected to go to church.

He collected letters of introduction to important Texans, written for him by New Orleans residents he had met, and he agreed to take along numerous private letters for delivery. In the early afternoon of the nineteenth, following a delay due to stormy weather, he left New Orleans on a riverboat, the *Levant,* that carried more despicable gamblers who kept him awake until the early hours while the vessel paddled its way up the broad Mississippi. At the Red River the boat angled westward into that stream, which presented to Gray "a most forbidding aspect. The color for which it takes its name is a dusky, dirty mud of brick-dust tinge, but not so bright, resembling the muddy water in which bricklayers dip their facing brick." The ugly water was in a high stage, and it swirled southward through a gloomy swamp next to the river—a swamp that had awed many immigrants. Gray estimated the width of the water as two hundred yards. "It is the dreariest region I have ever seen," he said, "—worse, even, than the Mississippi." At Natchitoches Gray left the boat, bought a horse for a hundred dollars, and on the twenty-sixth departed with two other men for Texas.

Two days later, at dusk on a damp, chilly evening, he crossed into Texas on a ferry operated by another native Virginian, James Gaines, at a location where the Old San Antonio Road met the Sabine River. That night Gray warmed himself before a fire in Gaines's tavern and listened to his host talk of the new land. Gaines had left Culpeper County thirty years earlier, had first come to Texas in 1812, and had acquired a store of experiences that fascinated Gray.

Gaines had announced as a candidate for election to what would become known as the Convention of 1836, which was to meet on March 1 at Washington-on-the-Brazos. The election had been set by the provisional government for February 1, four days away. Gaines, "much of a politician," was busy with his last-minute campaigning, standing on a platform of independence for Texas, then union with the United States. Gray listened and apparently began calculating how he could use the election and the ensuing convention to his own advantage as a land agent.

7. CONCERNED PHYSICIAN

Gray and Harriet Page came to Texas despite the turmoil, Dr. Joseph Henry Barnard because of it. He was one of numerous physicians who felt compelled to minister to Texas during this time of need.

When Barnard arrived in Texas he was thirty-one years old, an age that belied a life already full of the adventure he always sought. He followed the sea for three years; graduated from Williams College, in his native Massachusetts, in 1829; practiced medicine in Canada; moved in 1835 to Chicago, a bustling young town of promise. There he heard of the rebellion in Texas and on December 14 left to join it, traveling down the Mississippi River to New Orleans, where he arrived January 6, 1836.

Barnard's visit to New Orleans coincided with Gray's, but no records show that the two men ever met. Barnard did meet Stephen Austin, about the same time Gray met him, and Austin encouraged him to go on to Texas. Further inspiration for Barnard, who could mix romanticism with realism, came from a turnout on January 8 of volunteer companies "in best array" to commemorate the twenty-first anniversary of the Battle of New Orleans against an earlier enemy.

That very night another battle was celebrated in the city—the recent siege and subjection of San Antonio, an event that continued to stir New Orleans emotions. "There is very excellent spirit in favor of Texas here," a visitor wrote that January 8, "[and] they have had an overflowing benefit at the Camp Street Theatre . . . at which 'the fall of San Antonio' was presented well gotten up." That same writer saw many volunteers in the city waiting for transportation westward and wrote that Texas could expect to have an army of five thousand men in ninety days.

Barnard was one of those volunteers, and two days after the benefit performance he boarded the schooner *Aurora,* bound for Matagorda Bay in Texas. A rough passage shook him into seasickness and shattered his enthusiasm, but only temporarily. When he reached the Texas coast he was able to observe it with interest.

Matagorda, built about 1829 at the mouth of the Colorado River, looked like many other nondescript villages Barnard would see in Texas. Twenty or so scattered houses, a few stores, and two boarding houses had been built on a low prairie facing the gray-green water of the bay and extending backward to the Colorado River, which flowed into the bay at that point.

At Matagorda Barnard first heard some political talk that almost changed his mind. Governor Henry Smith, making "a great display of billingsgate," was feuding with the general council, and the provisional Texas government had almost ceased to function. It was mostly stumbling toward the February 1 election and the March 1 convention at Washington-on-the-Brazos—and hoped-for better days. Political and military matters looked discouraging to Barnard, and he "waited a while and watched events." But he was incapable of idleness, and while he mulled over his future course he and several companions explored the bay and the river in a small boat, hunting and fishing, for fun and for food.

On the second of February Barnard left the boat and rode horseback fifteen miles to Texana, a village lying near the junction of two rivers, the Navidad and the Lavaca. The place originally had been named Santa Anna when the colonists thought of the Mexican leader as their liberal supporter, but this name had been changed—with venom—a year before Barnard's visit. At a military camp near Texana Barnard found another physician volunteer, Dr. John Shackelford, who had recruited a company from Alabama, provided them with seventy-five stands of arms, clothed the men in red jeans, and brought them to Texas as "the Red Rovers." They had arrived about the same time as Barnard.

Barnard liked the Alabama doctor, and he accepted an invitation to stay in camp. Shackelford seemed to him typical of the men who appeared in Texas about this time. Riffraff did not flock in during the hard struggle for independence, although some inevitably arrived. Shackelford had left his family in Courtland, Alabama, to make the move, and he had brought with him his oldest son, Fortunatus, and two nephews. Shackelford's genial presence heartened Barnard and helped bring him out of his gloom over the Texas situation.

Two days after Barnard's arrival a horseman galloped into camp with a rumor of the approach from the west of Mexican troops, and Barnard joined the Red Rovers as a private. He embarked on his newest adventure with typical gusto, looking upon army life as a lark. Certainly the companionship was warm. Barnard discovered in the Red Rovers three men with whom he had traveled down the Mississippi to New Orleans, and he joined their mess. But during the following days he found little time for idle chat with these friends. On the afternoon of the same day he joined the Red Rovers their commander ordered them to prepare for a march to the presidio of La Bahía, at Goliad, there to join a force of several hundred men led by James W. Fannin and strengthen the resistance to any Mexican thrust that might come.

A bustle followed the order. Shackelford wanted to begin the march that same afternoon—not on the following day, which was a Friday and to him a day of bad omen. Hurriedly the men gathered up and packed their possessions and broke camp. They traveled up the Lavaca River, relishing the fresh flat scenery of coastal Texas and the excitement of their mission. Barnard noticed that a few men tried to top off their exuberance with whiskey, and they began fighting among themselves. Shackelford stopped them.

On the fifth they left the Lavaca and traveled westward toward the town of Victoria, across a grassy prairie. When they came to a creek named Garcitas they encamped; the next day about nine o'clock they took up the march again. An hour after their departure a wet norther blew up and stung their faces with cold rain, but they pressed on for Victoria, where they arrived late that day drenched, numbed, and exhausted, and with considerable loss of enthusiasm. There they camped for several days, drying clothes and baggage and waiting for the long norther to blow itself out. Then they traveled on westward, toward James Fannin, La Bahía, and their destiny.

On the twelfth—a Friday—they caught their first glimpse of the fortress of La Bahía. They saw it lying just beyond a tree-lined river some six miles distant from their vantage ground, a hill on the west bank of Manahuilla Creek, which they had just forded. A short distance northeast of the fort was the small town of Goliad.

They hurried across another stretch of level prairie, forded the river—the San Antonio—and entered the heavy gate of the presidio. They were escorted in by a joyous company of La Bahía men who had left the fort to meet them just as they crossed the river.

Barnard peered around the interior of the presidio, built at this location by the Spaniards in 1749, and wrote a description of it in his journal. He saw a huge, square plot of ground surrounded by a strong stone wall eight or ten feet high, all located for military advantage on a rocky elevation just west of the San Antonio River, which provided a water supply. Along the inside west wall of the presidio barracks had been constructed. Near the northeast corner stood a stone church, with walls three feet thick. Outside, some houses had been built comfortably near the presidio.

When Barnard and the Red Rovers arrived the garrison force

numbered about four hundred men, but La Bahía was large enough to accommodate all of them without crowding. Barnard's unit pitched tents in the presidio yard, near the gate, and he soon found the life of a private soldier novel, pleasant, and at that time well enough supplied. Most of his comrades were men of character, he noticed. They were fighters with a genuine sympathy for freedom—not mercenaries.

Barnard's professional status came to Fannin's attention, and the commander appointed him surgeon. But the garrison had only a few sick soldiers from day to day, and Barnard's duties were light. With little else to do, he helped the others strengthen the walls of the fort and build a "covered way" from the rear of the fort to the river two hundred yards distant, for safer access to water.

"Having thus prepared ourselves," he wrote, "we awaited with confidence the advance of the enemy."

8. AN ELECTION

While Barnard had been exploring the coast in a boat and thinking over what he should do, the land agent and attorney William Fairfax Gray was in Nacogdoches, deep in the pine woods of East Texas, engrossed in the February 1 election.

As the day drew nearer, the air of excitement increased. Gray, constantly curious, sampled the mood of the town and found sentiment fairly divided between a desire, even now, to adhere to the Mexican Constitution of 1824 and a demand for absolute and immediate independence. On the side of the constitutionalists, Gray recorded with a display of his snobbery, were all the "native Texans," or Mexicans, "who are a swarthy, dirty-looking people much resembling our mulattoes, some of them nearly black, but having straight hair."

On the side of the independence firebrands were some volunteer soldiers recently arrived in company strength from Kentucky. They noisily rejected a local decision denying them the right to vote and demanded that their ballots be taken and counted. When their acting commanding officer, a lieutenant, paraded the company with rifles loaded and threatened to shoot up the door of the stone house where the balloting was to take place, the citizens of Nacogdoches were called to render a final decision by show of hands whether the soldiers would be allowed to vote. When it was taken, the count gave a majority of thirty or so to the "no" side— supported, of course, by the constitutionalists—and when this was announced the Mexicans shouted triumphantly. Their glee enraged the soldiers, who seemed ready to open fire on the people.

At this moment Gray felt compelled to use his training as attorney to quiet the turmoil. He told the soldiers that since they were only recent arrivals in Texas they had no right to vote, or at best the privilege was questionable, and that their armed interference in an election was contrary to the principles of republicanism, which he supposed they had come to Texas to uphold. Gray urged the soldiers to avoid election violence and to save their fighting for the Mexican army. Another man spoke in support of Gray, and the soldiers appeared to be persuaded. But then one of the independence candidates, Robert Potter, a hothead from North Carolina, spoke to the soldiers and urged them to press for the right to cast their own ballots.

The matter reached a chaotic climax when Thomas J. Rusk, another candidate, told the soldiers that the election judges were reconsidering their decision. Soon after that the volunteers were told they might vote after all. By that time, however, Gray's argument had taken effect. The soldiers had discussed the issue among themselves and had agreed unanimously not to vote. This decision pleased Gray immensely, but then the volunteers countermarched again. "With the waywardness of children" they reconsidered, and eventually every man cast a ballot in the election, Gray said. After that, and for the rest of the day, the company marched to and fro in front of the polling place, to the music of fife and drum. But Gray found consolation: a citizen told him his speech to the men had prevented bloodshed. Furthermore, Gray was himself permitted to vote in the election, having declared his intention of becoming a Texas citizen. "I am now considered as identified with the interests of the country and entitled to all the rights of citizenship," he wrote in his diary, and he adjusted smoothly.

Even the weather pleased him. Election day was cool and clear, dry and elastic, like good autumn weather in Virginia. But he did not expect it to last. "Three white frosts and then a rain is the rule here." The rain would surely come.

9. A SOLDIER OF THE CROSS

Gray and the other politically minded men had not been the only passionate speakers in Nacogdoches during the election turbulence. Perhaps the fieriest orator of them all skipped the politics and concentrated on the sinners. While the election was in progress a lanky, sharp-faced, high-strung Baptist preacher from Tennessee, Z. N. Morrell, rode into town en route home from a look at the wild country around the falls of the Brazos River, near present Marlin. He saw the milling people and felt driven to address them in behalf of the Lord. Although he was only thirty-two, he had preached in Tennessee for nearly ten years, and with such intensity that it had almost ruined his health. But his very soul still burned within him to preach Jesus. He had forsaken his Savior as a boy, when he had given himself to the race track as a rider of such zealousness that he had earned the nickname "Wildcat." Now he yearned to make up for that neglect, so he brought the Gospel to Nacogdoches—and for a while it overshadowed the election and the coming convention.

Morrell looked around for a suitable pulpit and found one: on the foundation timbers of a large frame building under construction. He climbed onto his makeshift platform, stretched his gawky six-foot two-inch frame to full height, held his watch in his hand, and in a powerful voice developed through a decade of delivery called out, "O-yes! O-yes! O-yes! Everybody that wants to buy, without money and without price, come this way!" Then he burst into his personal battle song, "Am I a Soldier of the Cross?" His actions attracted a large crowd of curious people; the Texas of Morrell's day certainly was not known for clergymen. He took as his text the first verse of Isaiah 35, "The wilderness and the solitary place shall be glad for them; and the desert shall rejoice and blossom as the rose." He worked his theme slowly but energetically, making up for a lack of education with enthusiasm, and spoke for at least an hour. By the end of that time he hoped that the second verse of that chapter had been guaranteed: "It shall blossom abundantly, and rejoice even with joy and singing: the glory of Lebanon shall be given unto it, the excellency of Carmel and Sharon, they shall see the glory of the Lord, *and* the excellency of our God." Finally he finished, and his listeners crowded around him with congratulations and handshakes. Morrell's "soul was full to overflowing."

Some persons in Texas knew Morrell. A few had even heard him preach in Tennessee. Those who had not soon learned his background. In Tennessee he had averaged a sermon a day for that ten-year period, until his lungs had begun hemorrhaging. His doctor advised him to seek a warmer, drier climate, and he and his family—wife and four children—at first tried Mississippi, which was a mistake. The humidity there was as bad for him as the Tennessee weather. Texas would surely have suited the doctor's orders—plenty of hot, dry days there, no doubt; but the religious climate was not so suitable: "the iron arm of Catholicism was stretched over the whole land of Mexico, then embracing . . . Texas, [which] did not make it a very desirable field for a Baptist preacher, who had always been accustomed to expressing himself boldly and independently." But Morrell had heard about unrest in Texas, and he anticipated the formation soon of an Anglo-American republic that would throw off Mexican rule and the Catholic yoke at the same time. Meanwhile he waited.

Months passed. His lungs showed no improvement, and his doctor insisted that he stop preaching. It could prove fatal, said the doctor, especially since Sunday services sometimes stretched from bright morning until the sun drooped low in the west. In Mississippi Morrell had agreed to lighten his load to the extent that he served only as supply minister. But he could not abide the doctor's order for long. Burning with fire "to declare the way of salvation to the lost," he found the temptation to preach impossible to resist.

Growing increasingly impatient, he returned late in 1835 to Tennessee. There friends convinced him that Texas would be a good location for him even though it had not established its independence. Someone who knew the country suggested that the area around the falls of the Brazos could nurture a colony. When his doctor reemphasized the necessity of finding a good, dry climate soon, he was persuaded. Besides, an old hunting companion, David Crockett, and another friend, Sam Houston, had gone to Texas, and he wanted to join them there. He made a tentative agreement with Crockett to meet at the falls of the Brazos on Christmas Day for a bear hunt.

Morrell had settled his family for his absence and left, with several other men. He crossed the Sabine into Texas at Gaines's Ferry on December 21, 1835, and soon after that heard with delight of the Texans' success in capturing San Antonio. The verdant landscape cheered him also. The countryside had not yet been browned by a hard freeze, and "game of almost every description was so plentiful that it required but little more effort upon the part of man than the animal to obtain a subsistence. All these great blessings could only produce *one result* upon [a certain] class of the population . . . and that result was indolence." This would be a good field indeed for the Lord's work.

Morrell traveled by day and slept under the heavens by night, cooked bear bacon, turnip greens, and buffalo beef to appease a healthy appetite, and happily contemplated the souls he would save as if they were money in the bank. But near the falls of the Brazos his outlook dimmed. Delays had kept him from his Christmas meeting with Crockett. On the twenty-sixth Morrell figured he was still a day away from the place, but he and his companions could not hurry: their trail was crisscrossed and confused by buffalo and mustang tracks and sometimes could be followed only by looking for horseshoe prints; their horses were lame; and the entire country belonged to the Indians—something that required constant watchfulness. When Morrell finally arrived at the falls he discovered that he had beaten Crockett, who never did make an appearance.

Morrell went on his hunt anyway. It was a disappointment without the greatest bear hunter of them all, but he consoled himself by preaching on December 30 to a group of forty land hunters from Tennessee who had encamped some thirty miles away on Little River. This was his first sermon in Texas, and it inspired him perhaps more than it did his listeners. With his health on the way to restoration and his lungs again at a noticeable strength, he decided to return to Tennessee for his family and to settle at the falls of the Brazos. So it was that he hastened homeward, violating a personal custom by traveling on a Sunday, and arrived in Nacogdoches during the election to campaign as a soldier of the cross.

When his hour-long sermon from Isaiah and the handshaking had ended, he prepared to depart. He planned to ride horseback to Natchitoches, board a Red River steamboat there for Natchez, then take passage up the Mississippi to Memphis. But Morrell would be back; a harvest of souls lay waiting for him in Texas, whose fortunes he had decided to share, "good or bad."

10. LEISURELY LOOKING AT TEXAS

For a few days after the election the attorney William Fairfax Gray poked around Nacogdoches, and his business-oriented mind operated continually. He found the town to be situated in a little valley, on an uneven, sandy plain between two clear streams, the Banita to the west and La Nana to the east, which ran swiftly enough to provide power for mills or other machinery. Gray mused over that and another commercial possibility: the construction of a canal, on either creek, to run a few miles downstream to a junction with the Angelina River, which provided a water passage for some large boats to a point within eight miles of town.

Other features of Nacogdoches were less attractive to him. The town was old—its age was indicated by four aged Indian mounds that Gray found on the north side—but the population had fallen from several thousand to only four or five hundred. Most buildings were miserable, shabby structures made of logs daubed with red mud to cover openings, or of picket walls and flimsy roofs chinked with the same ugly substance. "They are scarcely equal in appearance to the Negro houses in the suburbs of Fredericksburg," he said. The stone house later called the Old Stone Fort stood as a solid exception, in the center of town.

Despite the shabbiness, Gray saw some beautiful walks and plazas in town and felt that with proper management Nacogdoches could yet enjoy a bright future. "What mighty things might here be done under a good government with wise laws and a public spirit among the people. Here might flourish a . . . city distinguished for learning, sciences, opulence, trade, health, and all the blessings and comforts of civilized life."

Some "tolerably good" society already existed among a few families of Anglo-Americans, none of whom mingled with the Mexicans. But there were also hotheads and troublemakers among the Anglo-Americans. Most notable of these, Gray thought, was the man Robert Potter, who had sought to inflame the volunteer soldiers with his election-day invective. "Potter is regarded as a disorganizer, and his coming among them is greatly deprecated by the intelligent and well disposed. He is courting popular favor with all his art and is succeeding to a wonderful degree. He can only float in troubled water."

Potter would, in time, drag others into the water with him, but Gray would not be among them. Gray avoided the company of unpleasant people. He associated instead with the "intelligent gentlemen" of Nacogdoches—he listed them in his diary—and obtained from them more information about Texas for his file on investment opportunities. Money-making seemed forever foremost in his mind (and in theirs), and many of the discussions concerned this subject. One of Gray's acquaintances suggested that to enhance the economic prospects of the area around Nacogdoches all the friendly East Texas Indians should be moved to an area just east of the region now known as the hill country, to serve as a buffer between the whites of East Texas and the fierce Comanche Indians, who roamed the wild region west and north of where the friendly Indians would thus stand. Whether the East Texas Indians would have been amicable after that move had been forced on them never seemed to concern the esteemed gentlemen with whom Gray associated, and Gray himself wrote, "This would be a most valuable step for this part of the country." Furthermore, although the local Indians were friendly, and their trade in skins, venison, "pecan nuts," and other goods helped Nacogdoches merchants, they were "a filthy bunch and unpleasant neighbors." The location of their villages, within five or six miles of town, served to "retard the settlement of the country by whites." Every day that week Gray had seen the Indians in town exhibiting their "drunkenness and bestiality."

He had seen also the "tolerably good" society making merry in a way that was demure by comparison, and he had been favorably impressed. One night he attended a ball held in shabby, crowded Brown's Tavern and was amazed at the number of well-dressed, attractive ladies, about twenty altogether, all of them well-behaved. To reach the place they had walked through red mud and a rain that had begun about noon; the town had no carriages for hire. Two violins and a triangle provided music for the dancing, which impressed Gray as being even more graceful and decorous than he had seen back home in Fredericksburg. He was especially pleased to see that the ladies and even the men returned home about one o'clock sober and in good humor.

These moments of pleasure were but interludes in Gray's business trip. On Saturday, February 6—the day when Dr. Barnard and the drenched Red Rovers were drying out at Victoria before going on to Goliad—Gray mulled over two business propositions, both concerning large tracts of land at about thirty-five cents an acre. He also began devising a plan to enhance his chances in Texas. He would offer himself as secretary of the convention scheduled to meet March 1 at Washington-on-the-Brazos. He spoke to local members-elect about this and wrote other delegates in nearby towns. Such a position, he calculated, would enable him to become better acquainted with the leading men of Texas and would be "a stepping stone to something better." That night in his diary he wrote a note to himself to learn the names of all the delegates, so that he might lobby in his own behalf. On the following day he and a companion left Nacogdoches on a trip that would allow him a close look at some of the lands he might buy.

He carried some letters addressed to Sam Houston, who was known to be in the area that Gray expected to visit, and on the second day out Gray was delighted to encounter the man and four other officers, traveling on horseback. Gray handed Houston the letters, then watched with interest as the General dismounted and sat on the ground to read them.

Some required answers. Houston wrote the replies, in pencil, in his bold, flowing hand, gave the letters to Gray for eventual delivery, and remarked that he was on his way to negotiate a treaty with the Cherokees and other tribes settled north of Nacogdoches, but that he would be in Washington-on-the-Brazos by March 1. Then Houston and the four other officers bade goodbye and rode on. Gray, scarcely able to restrain his curiosity until Houston was gone, examined the General's answers and read with elation some "highly flattering" references to himself. Then he and his companion, too, rode on.

Days they spent riding across prairies, fording streams, and always observing the countryside and its grass, water, and soil. Gray was entranced by rolling prairies so clean they looked cultivated and by the life that inhabited them: herds of grazing cattle, an occasional deer, flocks of geese and cranes, and, on ponds, ducks in large numbers. Few good farmhouses were to be found, but the countryside provided a "splendid picture of rural beauty and fertility."

At nights they put up at any settler's house they happened upon. Frequently they found that other travelers had preceded them, and they all crowded around the supper table to dine on fried pork, coarse corn bread, and miserable coffee—or sometimes buttermilk, if the hostess had any. After much talk they went to bed, wherever space permitted. This meant that some of them slept on the floor or in straw beds, but Gray often fared better because of his age. If a spare bed or cot was available it was usually given to him. Hospitality was not the sole reason for welcoming guests, because on the following morning most hosts expected to be paid—about twenty-five cents for each meal, the same amount for corn given a horse, and a dollar for the bed.

In mid-February—when Dr. Barnard, as a private soldier, had begun to enjoy the novelty of garrison life at La Bahía—Gray was in Washington-on-the-Brazos, using his critical eye to assay the town as a convention site. He found its faults dismaying: not one decent house in the whole town, which was made up of a dozen or so wretched cabins; and only one well-defined street, which had been hacked through the woods. Stumps still poked out of the ground, endangering pedestrians and horsemen. On Sunday morning, February 14, he left the town to look over more land, but he intended to return in time for the convention. Meanwhile, he was "glad to get out of so disgusting a place. . . . A rare [town] to hold a national convention in. They will have to leave it promptly to avoid starvation."

11. FOOD FOR A STARVING FAMILY

Hunger also had become a great concern to Harriet Page, left with her two children on the desolate prairie at Austin Bayou. For a time after her husband left for the army she had gathered bunches of scarlet berries from parsley haws that grew near the cabin, and she and the children had lived on them.

Each day had dawned more menacingly. The children became increasingly fretful with hunger, and the nights grew even more fearful. The rustle of wind in the trees and the calls of wild animals from somewhere outside the cabin emphasized their isolation.

Harriet Page was no frontierswoman. When she came to Texas she knew how to make a stylish dress and how to fix hair in the latest coiffure style, but life in frontier Texas was "a sealed book" to her. "I only trusted that God would help," she said, but she also hoped that her husband, thoughtless though he was, might send someone back for them.

Days passed, but Page sent no one for his family. Then one afternoon help came from another source. The man who owned the land stopped by to look in on his tenants. Harriet Page greeted him jubilantly and told him her story. He listened with consternation, then took his rifle and left to get food. He returned with a wild turkey and cooked it in a manner Harriet had never seen before: he skinned it, cut off the breast, and roasted the piece on a wooden spit over a fire. Later he killed more game for them—turkeys and deer—before leaving. Soon afterward a driver with wagon and team came for Harriet and her two children, and they left their isolation for the company of Texans who were becoming increasingly upset by rumors of approaching Mexican soldiers.

IV

FIGHT FOR INDEPENDENCE

Late February to Early June, 1836

The coming of the Mexicans in late winter of 1836 resembled the arrival of a "blue norther," a Texas cold-weather phenomenon preceded by several days of deceptively warm weather. The warmth, almost oppressive, would warn people of the coming of something different, but at the same time would leave them hoping it would not be stormy. Then they would see it: a black cloud rising above the northern horizon, "well calculated to strike terror to the newcomer, especially if he had come from a country where storms were prevalent," said a citizen of Republic days. "It had an inky blackness, its outer edges sometimes taking on a greenish cast." An observer could sometimes see rolling ahead of it a smoky blue mist, looking something like an ocean wave. "As it came bounding and leaping along it looked as if it might be carrying death and destruction to everything in its path. At its approach, loose horses, cattle, deer, and every living animal would flee . . . to the timber [or] to the south side of hills, deep valleys and ravines, or anywhere to escape its cold blast." Temperatures plummeted by tens of degrees in a very short time.

But the Mexicans came from the west. The Texans stood confidently in their path, watching their arrival. "I again express it as my opinion," one said, "that the old blood of '76 will be so hot in this country that . . . we will seek Santa Anna anywhere he may be found this side of the great desert."

77

In the United States, people followed Texas events with great interest. Some had kinfolk there; others who did not felt bound by a bond virtually as strong as blood: a love of freedom. A mark remained where the English yoke had chafed. Although the Liberty Bell had cracked a few months earlier—on July 8, 1835, while tolling for the deceased Chief Justice John Marshall—the word "liberty" still rang clear among Americans, especially among the sons and grandsons of men who had fought for their rights against the repressiveness of a king and a nation that believed colonies should exist only for the benefit of the mother country.

Appeals from Texas, at this time anyway, found emotional receptiveness in the United States among Jackson's "common men" as well as the wealthy, among many antislavery Northerners and among Southerners who contended that a state had the right to nullify an unwanted federal law, whatever it was, within its borders. Nearly everybody waited anxiously for the latest news from Texas. New York and other cities presented benefit theatricals, with the money to go to Texas. Philadelphians burned Santa Anna in effigy.

12. A JITTERY CONVENTION

Toward the end of February an unmistakable report of the arrival of Mexican troops reached the Anglo-American settlements in eastern Texas. It came from William Barret Travis, who sent a dispatch on February 23 from San Antonio saying that a large enemy force had been sighted near town and that the Alamo garrison of some 150 men urgently needed supplies and assistance. The horseman bearing this message rode from out of the darkness into the Brazos River town of San Felipe on the night of the twenty-fifth, in the wake of a crisp norther that had dropped temperatures from summertime heat during the afternoon to near freezing after sunset.

William Fairfax Gray was a visitor in San Felipe when the messenger arrived with this foreboding information, and Gray observed the excitement that ensued: "The people now begin to think the wolf has actually come at last, and are preparing for a march."

Gray had come to San Felipe—still the political and economic capital of Texas—with the intention of concluding some land business. Despite "wet and miry" weather he had called on Governor Henry Smith immediately and had been received courteously—and candidly. Smith spoke freely of the Texas situation and blamed Stephen F. Austin's pacificism for the current afflictions. Gray wrote that the Governor called Austin "Mexican in his principles and policy and that he *ought to be hung!*" But Gray had not been impressed by this diatribe. He added a candid judgment of his own: "My impression of Gov. S. is that he is a strongly prejudiced party man, too illiterate, too little informed and not of the right caliber for the station he has been placed in."

The news from the Alamo made further dealings in San Felipe impossible. Gail Borden, Jr., entrusted with Land Office papers, had begun packing them for removal eastward upon the approach of the enemy. Gray rode up the Brazos to Washington, against a cutting north wind that blew in his face during the entire trip.

A day or two after his arrival at Washington he heard about another dispatch from Travis. Dated the twenty-fourth, it told of the Alamo defenders being besieged and bombarded by an estimated one thousand or more Mexican troops commanded by Santa Anna, who had demanded surrender and had been answered by a cannon shot. ". . . I call on you," Travis pleaded, "in the name of Liberty, of patriotism & everything dear to the American character, to come to our aid, with all dispatch." Then he added grimly that, whatever the result of his appeal, he intended to defend the place until "Victory or Death."

The entreaty stirred the town, and some persons wanted to hurry off to the Alamo, but the logical leader, Sam Houston, had not yet come in from his expedition to the Cherokees. Gray recorded another reason for the lack of action: "the vile rabble here cannot be moved." Gray himself stayed in Washington. The convention was only two days away, and he had made the commitment in New Orleans to report back on the logic of another loan (which he eventually advised against).

Gray's campaign to be named secretary proved to be unsuccessful, but he recorded proceedings of the convention in his diary, and it was fuller in many places than the official journal. His account began with the last day of February, Monday the twenty-ninth— another warm day, since the norther had blown itself out. "Many . . . members are coming in . . . Gen. Houston's arrival has created more sensation than that of any other man. He is evidently the people's man and seems to take pains to ingratiate himself with everybody. He is much broken in appearance but has still a fine person and courtly manners. Will be 43 years old on [March 2]. Looks older."

The warm weather lasted only long enough to fool people. During the night they shed clothes and bedding for comfort, but before morning another gusty norther had dropped the temperature to within one degree of freezing. That chilly Tuesday about twenty delegates gathered in an unfinished frame store and shivered through opening-day organization. Their country's poverty seemed emphasized by sheets of cotton cloth stretched across openings intended for windows. A cold draft seeped into the room anyway.

The portentous news from San Antonio and other developments had wiped out all sentiment for returning to the Mexican Constitution of 1824. On the first day of the convention a committee was appointed to prepare a declaration of independence, and on the following day, within an hour of its first and only reading, this was unanimously adopted. "It underwent no discussion," Gray said, "and no attempt was made to amend it. The only speech made upon it was a somewhat declamatory address in committee of the whole by Gen. Houston." The date was March 2, a birthday for both Sam Houston and the new Republic of Texas.

Two days later the delegates named Houston commander in chief of the Texas Army, an organization that impressed Gray most unfavorably. The revolutionists were commissioning many officers for ability in enlisting soldiers, not for military proficiency, and the more the recruits, the higher the rank. One successful recruiter suggested, "Tell them our women have been insulted, our virgins defiled, and our men treated like devils instead of Christians." Other officers had been commissioned because of military experience, however unworthy, and one Texan lieutenant Gray met proved especially repulsive. The officer had served in the United

States Army for eighteen years as an enlisted man and during that time had been tried by eight courts-martial, Gray said. Now he held a commission in the Texas Army, but his conversation and manners "were [what] might be expected from such an education." Later Gray gave a franker summation of his thoughts: "What a government, what an army!"

As the convention dragged on, life in the village of Washington became even more uncomfortable. Visitors—delegates included—slept wherever they could and packed the dining tables of the few boarding houses to eat coarse meals of pork or beef, corn bread, and strong coffee. Some delegates who fared poorly in the day's debating drank away their frustrations in the evenings, making the following mornings all the more difficult. Hope flickered, alternating with black despair. A message from James Fannin at Goliad saying he had begun a march with 350 men to reinforce Travis at the Alamo inspired momentary confidence. People around Washington figured wishfully: with Fannin's troops and some others Travis might have six or seven hundred defenders now. "It is believed the Alamo is safe," Gray wrote on March 2, the day the declaration of independence was adopted. But news came on horseback, across vast distances and unbridged rivers sometimes flooded, and it did not come swiftly. Fannin had turned back to La Bahía—after barely getting out of sight of the place—discouraged by broken wagons, escaped oxen, and a general shortage of equipment and supplies. Only thirty-two volunteers ever reinforced the Alamo; they spurred their horses into the compound, from Gonzales, on March 1, and the gates that swung closed behind them doomed them as martyrs.

Work proceeded slowly on drafting a constitution. Gray watched it critically, probably reflecting on the higher quality he could have brought to the document. He settled himself as cozily as possible while awaiting the outcome. He and four other men, the others all delegates, rented a carpenter's shop, where they lodged at a total cost of only twenty-five dollars for a period to end April 1. Other expenses also were light. Board—without butter, milk, and sugar—cost $1.25 a day. Horses could be kept free, staked on a nearby plain.

Gray enjoyed his companions more than he did the quarters. His roommates were three Texans of Mexican ancestry, Lorenzo de Zavala, José Francisco Ruíz, and José Antonio Navarro, all working now with the Anglo-Texans for independence, and a North Carolinian, Jesse Badgett, who had been elected a delegate to the convention by the Alamo garrison and had left the fortress only a short time before. Nearby roomed still another delegate from San Antonio, Sam Maverick, who had left the town just before the besieging army cut it off, then had been delayed by high water and had not reached Washington until March 3, when he signed the declaration of independence.

Gray found the three Mexicans especially intriguing. Zavala, forty-six, had become an ardent liberal and an exponent of democratic reform in Yucatán when he was only eighteen. Ruíz, fifty-three, was a long-time revolutionary but could speak no English. Navarro, forty-one, nephew of Ruíz, was both a Roman Catholic and a Mason. All three men, Gray wrote, were obliging, kind, and polite. Zavala offered to teach Gray Spanish, and Gray's efforts to learn it pleased the three men—their servants too. Nevertheless, Gray could not refrain from recording a criticism: "They are a kind people but indolent. My industry in writing and studying surprises them."

Of the constitution and its framers he was even more critical. The constitution, patterned generally after that of the United States, was awkward and poorly worded, Gray thought. Furthermore, it seemed to be forever in the making. When it was finished Gray changed his opinion and called it good on the whole, but the delays still irked him. "What with . . . the Mexicans on one side and the Indians on the other, and the organization of a new government, this convention would seem to have enough on their hands to do, yet they get on slowly. The evil spirit of electioneering is among them for the *high offices* in prospect. . . . There is a great want of political philosophy and practical political knowledge in the body."

Early Sunday morning, March 6, another urgent appeal from Travis at the Alamo arrived, brought out by a horseman who had used the cover of darkness to dash past pickets. Delegates heard it read to them in a special session: Travis again mentioned Santa Anna's demand that the Alamo garrison surrender or expect death, as the blood-red banner waving from the top of San Fernando Church in San Antonio indicated, but said that he intended to fight on. He pleaded again for help, emphasizing that it must arrive soon.

Impulsive Robert Potter, a delegate, proposed immediate adjournment so that every man in town might leave at once to reinforce the Alamo. Sam Houston objected. Organizing a government was the delegates' job, Houston insisted, and he stressed the importance of completing that work. Houston said he would leave at once for Gonzales, where a group of volunteers had assembled, and assume command of them. He would relieve the men in the Alamo, if it were possible to do so. Houston then departed.

Days passed, and Washington-on-the-Brazos received no more word from San Antonio. This gave some worried people a great deal of information in itself. Travis and his men surely were surrounded and completely cut off—or captured or dead by now, although no one wanted to speculate about that.

Sam Houston's presence was missed in Washington. He was one of the few delegates who had any formal political experience. But the convention stumbled on toward its end without him and worked on Sunday, March 13, the same as any other day. This did not surprise Gray, but it did sadden him. Since coming to Texas he had seen virtually no observance of the Lord's Day, and he thought Texans an ungodly people.

"No intelligence yet from the Alamo," he wrote that day. "The anxiety begins to be intense." His roommate Jesse Badgett had left a brother in the fortress when he departed for Washington and the convention. Others in the town also had relatives with Travis. Many delegates wanted to adjourn and get out of town, but not all necessarily in the direction of the enemy.

No news came on the following day. Still the delegates tried to concentrate on their work, while perhaps envying the flocks of wild geese that flew overhead in the warming weather, bound northward.

On the next day came word that Travis had inflicted heavy casualties on a Mexican attack and had repulsed it. Few people allowed themselves to be heartened by this news, because of the circuitous route it had taken before reaching Washington, and it

was just as well they did not. Half an hour later two dispatches
arrived from Sam Houston containing the terrible news of the fall
of the Alamo and the massacre of its garrison on the morning of
Sunday, March 6. Houston had ordered his army to burn Gonzales,
where it had been encamped, and to retreat eastward.

Washington fell into complete confusion. Santa Anna was on his
way, no doubt inspired by his victory at the Alamo. Delegates
became "impatient of debate," Gray said, and they hurried completion of the constitution and other work. Frequently the convention was in complete disorder, with numerous members on the floor
at the same time, shouting questions, clapping, and being shouted
at by the chair. After hasty work on the sixteenth, however, the
constitution was finished, and after a recess for supper it was
adopted. Then the delegates elected officials to administer an ad-
interim government. They chose for President David G. Burnet, a
tactless man whose forty-seven years had been filled mostly with
adventure. Burnet had been a member of an expedition to free
Venezuela from Spain, then had lived with the Comanche Indians
in Texas for two years, and later had been an *empresario* briefly.
For vice-president the delegates chose Gray's urbane roommate,
Lorenzo de Zavala.

By the time these two men and a number of Cabinet members
had been sworn in, the hour was 4 A.M. The exhausted delegates
wearily voted adjournment until nine o'clock. Everyone was nervous about the enemy's whereabouts, and during the rest of the
night occasional alarms of Santa Anna's approach excited the town.
Patrols left to investigate, but found only black emptiness.

Sunlight of the first full day of new government, with a constitution in effect and duly elected officials in office, brought very little
satisfaction to Washington. Gray described the atmosphere: it
seemed like the approach of death. Texas was an unarmed, unpro-
visioned, invaded country, without a real army and with no money
to raise or equip one. Later that morning an eastward-bound
traveler reported the Mexican cavalry to be crossing the Colorado
River at Bastrop, seventy-five miles west of Washington. Convention delegates quickly adjourned, saddled horses, and rode off in
many directions. Robert Potter, the man who had inflamed the
volunteer troops at Nacogdoches, used his position as newly named
Secretary of the Navy to press into public service a horse belonging

to the wife of former Lieutenant Governor James Robinson, leaving the woman afoot. Elected officials of the new government hurried toward Harrisburg, near the coast, having decided that was the safest place for the present—and it allowed communication with New Orleans. Washington residents, along with most other Texans, fled eastward in what became known as the "Runaway Scrape," eastward away from the advancing Santa Anna, eastward toward the United States.

Gray described the flight.

A general panic seems to have seized [the people]. Their families are exposed and defenseless, and hundreds are moving off to the east. A constant stream of women and children and some men with wagons, carts, and pack mules are rushing across the Brazos night and day. The families of [Washington] and storekeepers are packing up and moving. I had sent some clothes to be washed by a woman who occupies a shed at the end of the town. I went this morning to get them and found the place deserted. The pots, pans, cooking ware, etc., and some bedding were left, and only the articles most easily moved were taken. But in their haste and panic they had not forgot to be honest. My clothes were washed and neatly tied up and placed in an adjoining office when I got there.

Gray packed the clothes, then he too rode off—southeastward, into a gray drizzle, across billowy grassland occasionally rimmed by woods nearly hidden behind the mist. His friend Zavala had invited him to stay at his home on Buffalo Bayou, near present Houston—directly across the bayou from a plain that in a little more than a month would become known as the San Jacinto battlefield.

On the way Gray stopped at a plantation down the Brazos called Groce's Retreat. There he found a cluster of several houses, but all were small and crowded, and he was forced to make a bed on the floor. Other temporary residents included President Burnet and the Cabinet, whose three-day visit, from March 18 to March 21, gave Groce's the distinction of being a capital of Texas, although a most unstable one.

At Groce's Gray also saw a survivor of the Alamo: William

Barret Travis's slave Joe, twenty-three, who had seen his master killed in the attack. Gray listened while Joe described the tragedy to President Burnet and his Cabinet, exactly two weeks to the day after it had occurred, and he recorded Joe's story in his diary:

The garrison had been exhausted by work and by constant watching, Joe said, so that in the early hours of Sunday morning, March 6, only one man was awake—an officer on watch atop the wall surrounding the compound. The alarm came from him, about five o'clock, and it brought Travis out of his blanket on the floor of the headquarters room. He seized his shotgun and sword and called to Joe, who had been sleeping nearby, to follow him. Joe grabbed his own weapon and ran after Travis: across the plaza and up the north wall, near a battery of cannon. "Come on, boys!" Joe heard his master yell. "The Mexicans are upon us, and we'll give them hell."

From out of the predawn gloom thousands of shouting Mexicans surged toward the Alamo, carrying muskets, swords, and scaling ladders. Travis aimed his shotgun at the enemy troops below and fired—then was tossed backward with a head wound. "He fell within the wall on the sloping ground and sat up," Gray recorded. "The enemy twice applied their scaling ladders to the walls and were twice beaten back." But Joe did not see this. As soon as his master had fallen he ran for a barracks room, where he hid during the rest of that awful morning. When Santa Anna's troops succeeded in scaling the wall and pouring into the Alamo they found Joe in the room. Two soldiers tried to kill him, but an officer intervened and sent him to Santa Anna for questioning about the numbers and types of Texas soldiers. After that Santa Anna released him.

Gray listened to Joe's account, then mused over the uselessness of the Alamo defense. Sam Houston himself had ordered the place abandoned as being defenseless against a superior force. Gray felt obliged to express his own opinion on the tragedy: "Texas will take honor to herself for the defense of the Alamo and will call it a second Thermopylae, but it will be an everlasting monument of national disgrace."

Gray continued on to Zavala's, casting appraising eyes at good land along the way. One evening during his ride down the lush

banks of Buffalo Bayou he wrote in his diary: "Passed a vacant
house, which by inquiry I learned belongs to a widow who has left
the country and resides in Cincinnati or Boston named Wilson.
There are three labors [177 acres each] attached to it. She gave
$350 for it. Pretty place. Good spring. Keep it in view."

At Zavala's comfortable home, which was attended by four or
five servants, Gray met his host's twenty-seven-year-old wife,
Emily, a beautiful black-eyed New Yorker—"too refined a lady for
this sphere"—and their three small, well-mannered children, the
youngest just beginning to crawl. "Oh, how they made me think of
my own dear ones," Gray wrote, in a rare reference to his family.
But this interlude seemed destined to be brief. During the last
week in March Gray heard from four travelers fleeing for Louisiana
that Sam Houston and his small army were in a continual retreat
some distance northwest and that nobody knew the whereabouts of
James Fannin's men, who had been at Goliad. Gray guessed that
Fannin was surrounded and unable to communicate, the same as
Travis at the Alamo.

13. GRIM PROPHECY

One of Fannin's last dispatches had seemed grimly prophetic—
although probably only coincidentally, since Fannin was not impressed by Mexican military capability. It had been written one
day after he canceled his brief attempt to aid the Alamo, and one
day after fifty members of the senseless expedition against Matamoros were attacked at San Patricio, sixty miles southwest of
Goliad, and all but five of them killed or captured. The survivors
escaped to Goliad and told Fannin of the approaching enemy.
From La Bahía—renamed Fort Defiance by the Texans—Fannin
had written a former business partner on February 28: "Hoping
for the best, and prepared for the worst, I am, in a devil of a bad
humor, Farewell, J. W. Fannin, Jr."

When the Mexican tide began rolling in, Sam Houston first had
told Fannin to reinforce the Alamo, then had canceled this order.

Now he instructed Fannin to destroy his fort and retire eastward—
an order similar to the one Houston had sent to the Alamo before
the siege. Defending the Alamo and La Bahía seemed to Houston
like building sand castles on the beach at low tide.

When Houston's order came Fannin was unable to comply immediately, because of a previous action. Two days earlier he had
sent a company of men under Captain Amon B. King to nearby
Refugio to escort some civilians out of the closing clutches of the
advancing Mexican army commanded by General José Urrea, and
to get information about the enemy force. Mexican rancheros
attacked King's men, who sent a messenger with a plea to Fannin
for help. Fort Defiance responded at once: Colonel William Ward
and a battalion of Georgia volunteers were ordered out to help.
They reinforced King, but they stayed in the area too long. Delays
and a dispute between King and Ward over which man would
command wasted too much time. King and his men were captured
and promptly executed, but Ward's battalion moved out in time to
escape with their lives.

At Fort Defiance an unknowing Fannin waited, anxious about
his men's fate and now about his own. Houston's withdrawal order
had been received; Fannin had sent a courier to Ward telling him
to return, but the messenger had been captured by the Mexicans
and his dispatch read by Urrea. Fannin waited one day, then
another. Neither King nor Ward reappeared. Finally, on the evening of March 18—the day after the delegates at Washington-on-
the-Brazos had fled after hearing the rumor of the Mexicans'
approach there—Fannin and his officers decided to begin a withdrawal eastward on the following morning. Already Mexican troops
had been seen around the fort, and some fighting had broken out.
Worse, scouts reported large enemy forces in the vicinity.

The decision to retreat cheered Dr. Barnard and most of the
other men. By this time the confinement of garrison life had become tedious and, with the arrival of the Mexicans, full of anxiety
and upsetting rumors. Physical comfort also had vanished. Food
and other supplies were nearly gone. Some men stood sentry duty
barefoot, and all with shriveled stomachs. But a retreat promised
no easy escape from their predicament. The men knew that Fannin
worried about the possibility of an ambush at the wooded San

Antonio River crossing, not even a mile away, but that he refused the advice of some officers to spike the cannon and leave them behind, for a faster withdrawal.

Before daylight the next morning Fannin sent a cavalry troop of thirty men through a black-velvet fog to reconnoiter the ford. After they had probed and reported the way clear Fannin ordered his men to commence their march. Oxen as debilitated as the troops struggled with the clumsy artillery and baggage wagons, which creaked and cracked as they rumbled down the rock-strewn road toward the river and Victoria, thirty long miles away. The cavalry went on, to scout the land ahead before rejoining later, but Fannin's caravan was slow to follow. A cart broke down, requiring a halt while its contents were reloaded on other wagons. Not until ten o'clock was the rear guard across the river. On the other side, the lately named Fort Defiance reverted to La Bahía and lay deserted. Smoke from fires set by Fannin's men sent word to waiting Mexicans to come on in and reoccupy the place.

But no Mexican soldiers could be seen. Fannin believed now that he had evacuated the fort unobserved and that the Mexicans would be satisfied not to follow him. He, his men, and his vehicles lumbered six miles farther to Manahuilla Creek, forded it, and went on some distance across a flat stretch of land toward a creek known as Coleto.

Barnard watched everything with the closeness of a physician who cared. At a point beyond the Manahuilla he saw a field of new grass, a green blanket spread by nature over the barrenness left after a recent prairie fire. He saw Fannin halt his weary men and worn animals there, three or four miles from the Coleto, despite his friend Shackelford's warning that the place was unprotected. This was true, but the grass offered grazing for oxen, and Fannin's scouts reported no enemy to be seen. As Fannin expected, the Mexicans seemed to be planning no attack, not even a pursuit. But as a precaution he left four mounted men behind to watch the rear.

After a one-hour pause Barnard heard an order to resume the march. Fannin sent his main cavalry unit ahead, to probe the crossing at the Coleto, but was forced to halt again when another wagon broke down. Cursing men reloaded supplies and recommenced the

march—and then the first Mexicans appeared: two mounted soldiers who emerged from a belt of trees about a mile to the right
rear. While the Texans stared, four more rode into view, then
others. Fannin ordered a six-pounder cannon unlimbered, and
three shots screamed toward the enemy. All three fell well short,
but the action stirred some other excitement. The horsemen Fannin had left behind suddenly galloped into view from behind the
trees, roused out of peaceful daydreaming by the activity around
them. Only one man raced toward the Texan army. The other
three spurred their mounts on past, a hundred yards to the right—
"without stopping to look at us," Barnard said. Shouted curses of
their furious comrades sped them along.

Fannin still was not greatly worried about his situation. He
ordered the march resumed—slowly, to avoid exhausting the depleted animals. He declared that the Mexicans in view were only
skirmishers and would not attack if the men acted coolly and
deliberately. He intended to go on to a dense woodland that
rimmed the Coleto, where they would be safe.

But more Mexican cavalrymen were appearing by the minute,
and soon Fannin's army was encircled. A mile or so away, the trees
along the Coleto beckoned in early-afternoon light, but the enemy
owned them. Fannin headed his army toward a second-best sanctuary—higher ground nearby. Before he could reach it, an ammunition wagon broke down. He ordered another halt, and Barnard
observed that their position was an extremely discouraging one: on
low ground several feet below a surrounding plain. His friend
Shackelford left a more vivid description: "The prairie, here, was
nearly in the form of a circle. In front was the timber of the Coleto
about a mile distant; in the rear, was another strip of timber, about
six miles distant; whilst on our right and left equi-distant, four or
five miles from us, there were, likewise, bodies of timber. But,
unfortunately for us . . . we were compelled to take our position
in a valley, six or seven feet below the mean base, of about one-
fourth of a mile in area." All around them grew tall grass—good
hiding for an attacker. They had no water and no food.

The enemy force eventually exceeded a thousand men; the
Texan numbers were about three hundred, with the cavalry absent
ahead. Fannin expected his horsemen to return as soon as they

became aware of his predicament, but they never did. When they realized that he was cut off they decided they could not rejoin him and hurried on to Victoria.

Fannin arranged his men in a hollow square, posted artillery—which the Mexicans did not have—and then ordered his troops to hold their fire. He repeated this command when blaring bugles and flying flags heralded a Mexican attack. Enemy soldiers first sent a wild volley toward them from a distance of a quarter of a mile. The Texans watched as their foe crept forward, and they heard the sputtering of another volley. Still they held their fire, until the Mexicans had advanced to within a hundred yards. Then Fannin ordered them to shoot back with everything, artillery included, and this stopped the advance. But one of the men wounded early in the fight was Fannin himself, hit in the thigh. He barely escaped death when a musket ball crashed into his rifle while he was in the act of firing.

From 1:30 P.M. until after sunset Fannin's men fought off the enemy. His artillerymen eventually were forced out of the action—not by Mexican marksmen, but by a lack of water. Without sponging, the cannon became too hot to use, and Fannin was forced to rely solely on small arms. But this fire left an awful picture on the prairie, which one of the Texans described: "Killed and maimed men and horses were strewn over the plain; the wounded were rending the air with their distressing moans; while a great number of horses without riders were rushing to and fro back upon the enemy's lines, increasing the confusion among them: they thus became so entangled, the one with the other, that their retreat resembled the headlong flight of a herd of buffaloes, rather than the retreat of a well-drilled, regular army . . ."

With darkness came a respite: General Urrea called off most of his troops. The Mexicans encamped in the woods Fannin never reached, and on every side of his beleaguered men, who spent a dismal, misty, supperless night without water and with the knowledge that at daylight their ordeal would begin again. "We was in a great fix to fight," said a fifteen-year-old volunteer. All around them sharpshooters posted by Urrea blasted away at every likely target inside the square until return fire aimed at the musket flashes finally silenced most of them.

The Texans counted their casualties: seven killed and sixty wounded. Barnard the physician could offer the wounded little more than helpless sympathy. He had virtually no medical equipment and would not have been able to use it anyway. The blackness of that night seemed "impenetrable," but the sounds came through quite clearly: cries for water and delirious shrieks from the scores of wounded. Some uninjured men dug frantically into the ground for water, but found none.

Barnard was scarcely able to help himself. Weary, thirsty, and hungry, he lay down on bare earth and tried to sleep, but the cold soon numbed him. He stood up and began exercising. Then, through the darkness, an order reached him and the others: dig a trench around the entire camp—make it several feet deep. That solved Barnard's problem of warmth, but it did nothing for his thirst, hunger, or weariness. When the trench had been dug, men brought carts, wagons, and carcasses of horses and oxen and put them atop the breastwork, with grim finality. This labor was disturbed frequently by cries of the wounded, by unnerving bugles blown in the dark distance, and by shrill Mexican screams from somewhere around them of *"centinelo alerto!"* Thus the night wore away for Barnard—damp, cold, and threatening.

In the first light of Sunday, March 20, the Texans saw a large force of men with many pack mules reinforcing the troops who surrounded them. Later they felt the effect of this: grape and canister rained on them from artillery brought up by the Mexicans. The last vestige of hope vanished. The breastworks dug during the night were meant for protection against small arms, not cannon. Fannin's men were worn, and their numbers had been reduced to little more than two hundred able men. Exercising the prerogative of volunteer troops in those days, they debated surrender, with the only apparent alternative being a dash for the woods, leaving behind their wounded. This possibility they rejected.

Fannin nevertheless sought to bolster them. Barnard listened to his talk: "We whipped them off yesterday, and we can do so again today." But an overwhelming majority supported surrender, if an "honorable capitulation" could be arranged. They felt this way, Barnard said, despite an awareness of the Mexicans' faithlessness.

Fannin ordered a white flag hoisted, and it flapped in a cold north wind. Although he suffered painfully from his thigh wound, he met the enemy commander at a point midway between the lines and there discussed capitulation. When he returned he told his men the terms offered: after surrendering arms they would be treated as prisoners of war, their private property respected, their wounded taken to Goliad and treated, and their return to the United States arranged. The date said to have been promised for their return differed among eyewitnesses, but Dr. Barnard wrote that he heard a Mexican colonel supervising the surrender of arms declare, "Well, gentlemen, in ten days liberty and home." General Urrea later refrained from mentioning these terms in his report to Santa Anna at San Antonio, merely recommending clemency for the captured men.

Prisoners able to walk marched back to La Bahía. The wounded remained on the battlefield, and Barnard, Shackelford, and two other physicians attended them as they were able, but a Mexican soldier stole Barnard's instrument case. Some of the wounded lay on the field for two days awaiting the arrival of evacuation wagons, and Barnard stayed with them. Not until Tuesday was the last wounded man carried back to La Bahía and packed into the smelly church with the rest.

Two days after Barnard returned he treated the Mexican wounded, upon the request of Mexican officers. The day after that—Friday—he saw escorted into the presidio survivors of Ward's volunteer Georgia battalion that had escaped capture temporarily after going to Captain King's assistance, but had been apprehended later. On Saturday Fannin asked Barnard to dress his wound. While Barnard worked, Fannin reminisced about his family —his wife and two daughters. He hoped to see them soon. Earlier that day he had returned from a trip with a Mexican colonel to nearby Copano Bay, to see whether a ship might be available there to return the prisoners to the United States. None was, but this promised to be only a temporary disappointment.

Barnard, Fannin, and other prisoners talked into the late hours of Saturday night, and some of the musically inclined entertained —like the man who played "Home, Sweet Home" on a flute. The happiness was contagious and the companionship warm. "I felt more cheerful this evening than I had since before our surrender,"

Barnard wrote. "We had reiterated assurances of a speedy release." Sleep came easily that night.

Barnard awoke the next morning at the summons of Colonel Francisco Garay, an urbane Greek whose quest for fortune had brought him into Mexican service. Garay had entered the officers' room where Barnard and Shackelford slept, and now, having roused both men, he asked them to dress and accompany him. Without explanation he led them to the presidio gate, where Barnard saw waiting a group of about eighty other Anglo-American volunteer soldiers and their commander, all recently captured without a fight at Copano Bay. These men were not members of Fannin's army, but Colonel Garay instructed Barnard and Shackelford to go with them, under escort, to a tent set up in a peach orchard about a hundred yards southeast of the presidio. Barnard wondered at the colonel's expression, which was grave, but he asked no questions. Instead, he and Shackelford walked along behind the other prisoners through the orchard, which had been freshly dressed in green by the young spring, and into the tent. There they saw two men lying on the ground, under sheets. The doctors presumed the two men were patients, but waited for the colonel to arrive and give instructions.

Fifteen minutes passed; twenty. Impatient of the delay, they told a guard they were returning to the presidio to wait there, but the soldier ordered them to stay. Five more minutes passed, and still the colonel had not arrived. Then a volley of small-arms fire startled them. It had been fired somewhere in the vicinity of the river, just east of the fort.

"What's that?" Shackelford asked. One of the Mexicans replied that some soldiers had fired their muskets to clean them, but the explanation was not convincing. Barnard said, "My ears . . . detected yells and shouts in the direction of the fort, which, although at some distance from us, I recognized as the voices of my countrymen. We started, and, turning my head in that direction, I saw through some partial openings in the trees several of the prisoners running at their utmost speed, and, directly after, some Mexican soldiers in pursuit. . . ." Other shots followed.

While they stared, appalled by the scene, Colonel Garay finally appeared. He assured them of their safety and expressed regret at what was happening. Even as he spoke they heard screams, and Barnard grieved silently for the plight of Shackelford, who "suffered perhaps the keenest anguish that the human heart can feel." The fate of the Red Rovers, which included his son and two nephews, had become obvious.

Later they learned what had happened. At seven o'clock the previous evening, about the time Fannin had been talking of his family and the flute player had been entertaining his listeners with "Home, Sweet Home," a courier had arrived from Santa Anna's headquarters at San Antonio with an order to execute the prisoners—something that Santa Anna thought should already have been done at the discretion of officers on the scene:

. . . As the supreme government has ordered that all foreigners taken with arms in their hands, making war upon the nation, shall be treated as pirates, I have been surprised that the circular of the said supreme government has not been fully complied with in this particular. *I therefore order that you should give immediate effect to the said ordinance in respect to all those foreigners* who have yielded to the force of arms, having had the audacity to come and insult the republic, to devastate with fire and sword, as has been the case in Goliad, causing vast detriment to our citizens; in a word, shedding the precious blood of Mexican citizens, whose only crime has been their fidelity to their country. I trust that, in *reply* to this, you will inform me that *public vengeance has been satisfied.* . . .

The order came to a flustered, faltering Colonel José Nicolás de la Portilla, left in command at La Bahía by General Urrea, who had moved on with a large detachment of troops to occupy the town of Victoria. Within an hour of the receipt of this, Portilla was reading with further dismay an instruction from Urrea himself, who had received a complaint from Fannin and in response had ordered: "Treat the prisoners with consideration, and particularly their leader, Fannin. Let them be employed in repairing the houses and erecting quarters, and serve out to them a portion of the rations which you will receive from the mission of Refugio." To Urrea's discredit, he probably realized that his instruction could not be carried out because of a shortage of troops at La Bahía for guard duty.

That Saturday evening the Anglo-American prisoners had enjoyed themselves more than had the unhappy Portilla, who said he spent a sleepless night "vacillating between these conflicting orders." But in the end Portilla was no man to challenge Santa Anna, although a few other Mexican officers dared to do so. With dawn came resolution—a safe one for Portilla. He ordered his men to rouse the prisoners, divide them into three groups, march them out of the presidio, and shoot them—all without warning, to simplify the operation. The men were to be told only some false destinations, to avoid an attempted break.

So it was done, on a sultry Palm Sunday, March 27, 1836. But Portilla displayed some humanity: he excused from execution the eighty prisoners recently captured at Copano Bay. They had not been armed when taken, and Santa Anna's death order applied specifically to foreigners captured with weapons. Colonel Garay, next in seniority to Portilla at La Bahía, was responsible for saving some men from death: Barnard, Shackelford, and a few others, including the two men Barnard and Shackelford had found lying covered in the tent. They were two of Fannin's men, Barnard discovered later, who had done some excellent carpentry work for Garay. The wife of Mexican Captain Telesforo Alavez also rescued a few of the very young Anglo-Americans, including Benjamin Hughes, a Kentucky boy who was only fifteen and undersized for his age at that. Just before Hughes's column was to commence its march out of the presidio gate Señora Alavez spotted the boy and asked a soldier to bring him to her. Then she stood with her hand on his shoulder, watched sadly as the prisoners were escorted through the gate, and tried to dispel the boy's rising confusion and fear.

On both sides of each group of doomed prisoners, who were formed in double file, marched a column of soldiers, grimly silent today instead of chattering as usual. They took one group half a mile up the sandy San Antonio road, another some distance eastward on the road to Victoria, and the third—including Shackelford's son and nephews and the rest of the Red Rovers—about half a mile down the San Patricio road, which led southwestward. The puzzled prisoners heard orders to halt and observed one guard column pass through their ranks to join the column on the other side. The soldiers raised their muskets to fire, and only then did most captives become aware of their fate. A few men yelled final words of defiance; others tried to run. Most fell at the first volley.

A prisoner in the group that had been taken up the road leading to San Antonio bolted for dense brush along the river, to his right, and managed to escape the killing behind a black smoke curtain raised by the first volley. He heard shots behind him and, in the direction of the fort, more volleys and more screams. "As I ran off," he remembered afterward, "several poor fellows who had been wounded tried to hide in the clump of weeds and grass, but were pursued and I presume killed." Virtually all of these men were run down and slain, by shot or by bayonet. But the lucky escapee reached the river, swam it, and joined two more fleeing prisoners on the other side. About twenty-five others also escaped, but the counted dead later exceeded 340.

Young Benjamin Hughes cried when he heard the shots and realized their meaning. "Immediately after, some of the Mexican soldiers coming back as they passsed me would flourish their bayonets as if my time was near at hand," Hughes recalled later, but when Señora Alavez spoke to them sternly they hurried on. For her humanity she became known as "the angel of Goliad."

The killing continued that morning. After disposing of their three groups of unwounded prisoners the Mexicans dragged about forty wounded men from the cramped, stinking hospital into the yard of the presidio and shot them. Among the last to die was Fannin. Then they carried these bodies to a location a quarter of a mile from the fort, dumped them there, and burned them. They burned the rest at the execution sites.

After the gunfire had ceased a Mexican escort took Barnard and Shackelford back to the fort, where Colonel Garay told them a story they had heard before—that they could expect transportation to the United States soon. Until then they were ordered to resume their duties, ministering to the Mexican sick and wounded in the hospital of the presidio of La Bahía.

14. FLIGHT EASTWARD

One hundred fifty miles northeast of Goliad, word of the massacre caught up with the fleeing citizens and quickly spread among them in rumors as awful as the truth. This talk diverted William Fairfax Gray's interest in land dealings—at least temporarily. For days, as guest at Lorenzo de Zavala's residence on the bank of Buffalo Bayou, he had been speculating about the absence of information from Fannin. Then the rumors had begun trickling in: word of a battle, and of mass executions. On Easter Sunday, one week after the massacre, Gray heard a new report that appeared to be authoritative: Fannin and his troops had fought the Mexicans near Coleto Creek from four o'clock one afternoon until the next morning, "when finding he had but thirty men left he hoisted the white flag and surrendered. They were taken to Goliad and shot."

Other rumors floated in, like pollen on a breeze. They came to rest momentarily, then spread farther across the country. Sam Houston's continuing retreat occupied most of the talk, and the General was the target of much abuse. Worse, he suffered straggling losses from his army, which numbered at most about a thousand men. Some left to find their families, then joined them in flight eastward. But by the end of March Houston's "retrograde movement" had halted temporarily. He reached a location on the west bank of the Brazos above San Felipe—a site across the river from Groce's Retreat, where Gray had stayed—and encamped there for a fortnight while he drilled his green troops in military fundamentals. Houston himself tapped out reveille on a drum—not trusting the instrument to anyone else—and occupied his night hours reading Caesar's *Commentaries,* enduring with silence the loneliness of a military commander under pressure and under constant criticism not only from civilians but from his own officers and men. The pestering communications from President David Burnet to engage the Mexicans and the exhortations of Secretary of War Thomas Rusk for greater determination especially pricked him.

But they only rankled, because Houston was his own man. At one point in the campaign he commented, "I consulted none—I held no councils of war—if I err the blame is mine." He had his own plan: to retreat eastward to the protection of the United States if necessary to save what army was left to him, then later to fight with additional volunteers that would probably become available. His antagonist Burnet was himself engaged in a continuing flight from the Mexicans, and these sudden shifts of the seat of government alarmed people almost as much as did Houston's retreat. So Houston never considered giving in and attempting an attack here against the strong Mexican forces, which were divided into three large armies that threatened Texas in three areas: along the coast, farther inland in a central section, and along the northern frontier.

Not even the most alarming news kept Gray's mind off land for very long. His travels took him early in April to Lynch's Ferry, a key crossing of the San Jacinto River near its junction with Buffalo Bayou, and there he saw a scene resembling a giant camp meeting. Crowding the green prairie were tents, carts, wagons, luggage, cattle, Negroes, horses, and other "moveables" of men, women, and children running from the Mexicans. Most waited for passage on the ferry, but some tried to force their cattle and horses to swim the stream. Gray did neither. He left his horse there on April 4, a Monday, and with three other speculators took a small sailboat down the river toward Galveston Island—then a barren place— leisurely observing the countryside, with his mind on money, not Mexicans. After a five-hour voyage during which the boat traveled only ten miles, Gray and his companions reached a location at the northwestern tip of Galveston Bay called Morgan's Point, about the same time a sidewheel steamer, the *Cayuga*, hove to there, crowded with refugees. The hour was late—eleven o'clock—and Gray ate a simple supper of bread and milk at the home of businessman-landowner James Morgan before going to bed.

Early the next morning Gray and the others put off in the boat again and crossed San Jacinto Bay, at the mouth of the river, to look at some land mentioned to them. After examining the property they returned to Morgan's Point in time for a late dinner, then walked around the place with their host, who had Gray's eye for trade. Morgan operated a business and a shipping company and had bought a large tract of land on which he planned to lay out a town with the name of New Washington—which Gray thought tasteless.

Galveston Island still attracted Gray, and the sidewheeler *Cayuga,* having stayed over at Morgan's Point to take on wood, was bound for that place. Early Wednesday morning he and his companions put their small boat aboard the steamer and embarked for the trip, but it seemed that the *Cayuga* would never get there. An hour after departure it was delayed by a meeting with an armed schooner, the *Flash,* belonging to James Morgan, bound from the Brazos River for Morgan's Point with an important cargo on board: two cannon nicknamed the Twin Sisters, gifts from citizens of Cincinnati, Ohio, and destined for Sam Houston's nebulous army; the newly named Secretary of the Navy, hotheaded Robert Potter—the same man Gray had predicted would "float in troubled water"; and a "number of ladies from the Brazos whose husbands were in the army."

Among the women was the pretty, abandoned Harriet Moore Page, whom Potter had met and chosen for special protection. With her two children she had commenced the flight eastward from Brazoria, dressed, for some reason, in a black silk gown, white crepe shawl, and black velvet hat with trimmings of white satin ribbons and feathers—quite a contrast to the calico, sunbonnets, home-knit stockings, and buckskin moccasins worn by most other women. Alone among strangers who gawked at her, Harriet had felt miserable and helpless until Potter, in the area on government business, noticed her pretty face in the crowd and offered to take her and her children to Velasco, where they could find a ship. He had even suggested that she ride behind him on his horse, and she had thankfully accepted his kind offer. Now they were aboard the *Flash,* but their voyage was halted momentarily: the vessel had been stopped by a sandbar.

Gray's *Cayuga* turned back to tow the *Flash* across the bar, then escorted it to Morgan's Point. Not until nine o'clock Thursday morning did Gray and his companions reach Galveston Island. Scanning the scene, Gray saw three low areas of land cradling the gray-green harbor. Immediately to the south lay the lonely marsh of Galveston Island, extending westward out of his vision. To the north, resting in Galveston Bay, was desolate Pelican Island, a sandy wilderness of use only to the gawky birds who gave their name to the land. There they laid their eggs and hatched their young. In the distance to the east, low on the horizon, lay Bolivar Point, the tip of a peninsula that closed a protective arm on Galveston Bay.

Of more immediate interest to Gray were some ships anchored nearby, and especially two 125-ton schooners of the Texas Navy: the *Independence*, a former United States revenue cutter, and the *Brutus*, fitted out as a privateer. These ships, together with the 125-ton *Invincible* and the smaller *Liberty*—all purchased by authority of the old general council—carried the Texas colors on the Gulf.

At noon that day Gray took dinner and wine aboard the neat *Independence* with her friendly officers. Then he visited the *Brutus*, which was undergoing carpentry repairs. From her cluttered deck Gray noticed two sails appear in the distance, approaching from the south. He heard one vessel fire a gun, and watched as both ships came to anchor. A boat wallowed through the whitecaps with word that the two vessels were the *Invincible* and a prize, the United States brig *Pocket*, captured while carrying dispatches, contraband cargo, and enemy officers—all under false papers—to Mexico. Gray heard also that the *Invincible* had fought a Mexican armed schooner several days earlier and had run the enemy aground.

This news sparked a celebration, and Gray joined in. They all toasted these successes of the infant Texas Navy and future ones to come, and many officers expressed wishes that they had been on board the *Invincible* for the action. But the *Pocket* capture eventually turned sour. The United States secured damages, through litigation not finally settled until three years later.

Always curious, Gray arranged a visit to the victorious ship. Before nightfall he had boarded the *Invincible*, where he met Captain Jeremiah Brown, "an exceedingly plain and unpretending man," and other officers. Then he returned to his steamer for the night.

Early the next morning Gray went sight-seeing once again, this time on Galveston Island, where he enjoyed a full view of the Gulf. "A fresh breeze from south brought the waves in with a noise resembling a great waterfall. The sight of the breakers, white crested, lofty, and angry looking, was truly grand . . . Saw a great number of birds, cranes, curlews, gulls, pelicans. The latter at a distance resemble companies of soldiers . . ." One sight Gray did not see was a town. The Gulf owned the island, and occasionally, during storms, its water swirled completely over the land. At the location of a fort once maintained by the pirate Jean Laffite (for about two years until 1820) Gray noticed an array of broken bottles, crockery, bricks, and nails. In his imagination he foresaw future use for all this vacant expanse: "A considerable city must one day spread up on this bay somewhere, but at what point is yet uncertain."

Fascinated, Gray walked beside the roaring surf on hard, clean sand. He picked seashells to box and send his children—while at the same time on the mainland a hundred miles northwest Santa Anna, fat with his Alamo victory, occupied the old Texas capital of San Felipe and thought over the best way of getting his men across the Brazos and to settlements along the coast.

Gray and his companions now struck off in that general direction, but without knowing of the momentous developments. They began their return in the small boat to Morgan's Point and Lynch's Ferry, facing the chilling blasts of a norther that lashed them with spray and seemed about to capsize them. They fled to the safety of a cove near Clear Creek, tied up the boat, and sloshed to a nearby house. There they were warmed, fed, and entertained while the cold wind blew itself out, but for Gray the hospitality was chilled somewhat by a scene outside the house. Their host dealt in slaves smuggled from Cuba, and Gray saw about fifty of them living outdoors "like cattle." All were young—from ten to twenty-five years old—and Gray thought they seeemed small and feeble. But when a beef was slaughtered, Gray observed, they "fought over the garbage like dogs and vultures" and would have torn the meat to pieces except for the presence atop the beef of an "American Negro" who lashed the others away with a cracking whip. Gray seemed to blame the Cuban slaves for their own plight, and certainly for making his stay much less enjoyable.

The next morning Gray took leave of the host who had "kindly" entertained him. He rode on a borrowed mule to Lynch's Ferry, where he arrived April 13 and learned that his horse was missing.

That same day, about fifty miles west, Santa Anna pushed his troops across the Brazos River, bound for Harrisburg, on the right bank of Buffalo Bayou. A Mexican resident had reported that the Texan government was located there—at the moment.

Gray's three companions hurried to Harrisburg, too, to get a government grant for land they had located around Galveston Bay, but Gray himself was on foot now and unable to accompany them. In his diary for the thirteenth he recorded that the "report of the near approach of the enemy is confirmed by numerous persons," but after he had found his horse he looked up President Burnet at Burnet's plantation home near Lynch's Ferry and got his signature on a Galveston Bay land grant.

By the fifteenth the situation in Gray's part of the world had become truly alarming. Shortly before midnight Santa Anna rode into Harrisburg with some chosen dragoons, but he was disappointed. Officials of the Texan government, warned just in time, had taken to the steamboat *Cayuga*—the same one Gray had boarded earlier at Morgan's Point—and had commenced a voyage to Galveston Island. There the Texan government later set up another capital—a thoroughly mobile one, aboard *Cayuga,* ready to move on at once. Frustrated, Santa Anna burned Harrisburg on the sixteenth, then sent troops to Morgan's Point—"New Washington"—to apply the torch there.

Now the time had come—finally—for Gray himself to withdraw. On the sixteenth he bought a fresh horse at Lynch's Ferry and with one of his former companions set out eastward for Anahuac, Beaumont, and Louisiana. The first night they camped with a group of refugees who shared supper with them, then they all spread cover on the ground and slept under the stars. The next day Gray and his friend stopped at the Galveston Bay home of a prosperous man whose wife pampered Gray with buttermilk and three bowls of ripe blackberries—a festive interlude that was interrupted by the arrival of a horseback rider who galloped up and reported Mexican cavalry at Lorenzo de Zavala's residence and at Lynch's Ferry and no doubt headed their way. The horseman hurried on to warn other people in the vicinity, and Gray and his companion decided to ride with him.

At an old mouth of the Trinity River water halted them. Many refugees also had stopped in the vicinity; their tents and wagons again gave the appearance of a camp meeting. Everyone sought a way across, and not patiently: by now the people were thoroughly frightened by the possibility of a sudden appearance of the Mexicans. They crowded, argued, cursed, and threatened—with pistols —while an overworked ferry crew could satisfy only a few persons every trip. "A hoary headed brute named Patton" swore at Gray, the first man in Texas to use such language on him. After waiting for three hours Gray and his friend finally swam their horses across and found more hospitality at a home on the other side.

By the eighteenth the fleeing people had become so frightened they sometimes mistook Gray and his companion for Mexicans and fled for the nearest cover. In all this excitement finding food was no problem. Everyone was leaving home and abandoning most possessions, and many departing residents offered Gray any stores he wanted—bacon, sugar, coffee, biscuit: better for him to have it than the Mexicans. But some travelers did not wait for invitations. They broke into abandoned homes and helped themselves to anything. The Runaway Scrape was known as a time of mass burglary.

On Gray traveled, across more water and poor coastal prairies, through occasional woods. At night he might kindle a fire, cook his supper, then, refreshed, roll in a blanket and sleep in the open; or, on a luckier evening, he might find the hospitality of a family who had not yet fled their home. Still he recorded in his diary an occasional reference to a plot of land that attracted him, with a notation to look into it closely at a more convenient time.

By the twenty-first, about 1 P.M., he was in Beaumont, a small cluster of crude houses and a customhouse. On eastward he rode toward the Sabine, through difficult swampland and "the worst road" encountered in Texas. Gray saw an ox bogged down in the middle of it, with only head and back above the mud. The yoke had been removed by its owner, who had left the animal to sink to a horrible death.

On the twenty-third Gray arrived at the Sabine, but again crowds of refugees ahead of him delayed a ferry crossing, so he resigned himself to spending another uncomfortable night on the precarious soil of Texas. Then, in one o'clock darkness, a horseman thundered up with astonishing information: Sam Houston had fought Santa Anna's army not far from Harrisburg, had killed five hundred of the enemy and had taken the rest prisoners. "It is likely there has been a battle and a victory, but the result is too much wholesale," Gray wrote—and he was right, in a way. There were errors in the man's report, but even its most glowing sentences failed to illumine a fact: the army commanded by Santa Anna had suffered a complete defeat, and the Mexican dictator himself was a prisoner of the Texans. The war was over.

Santa Anna had become too cocksure. One of his generals, Vicente Filisola, second in rank to him, said later that Santa Anna felt the war had been won by the victories at the Alamo and Goliad, and had made tentative plans to return to Mexico, leaving Filisola in command. Santa Anna and a comparatively small army—still plenty large enough to contend with Houston's—had raced on ahead of the other Mexican troops in that attempt of his to capture the Texan government at Harrisburg. He had failed, and in the process he had committed an error. He had pushed on so eagerly that he had isolated himself and his troops in unfavorable country. By April 16, when he entered and burned Harrisburg, he had led his men eastward so far and so fast that he was ahead of Houston's retreating army, so that Houston actually had begun chasing Santa Anna, if only accidentally, after resuming his march following the halt on the Brazos River.

Santa Anna learned of Houston's location and turned to fight him, blundering onto a battlefield now known as San Jacinto where he was virtually surrounded by water—to the northwest by Buffalo Bayou, on the east by the San Jacinto River and Estuary, to the south by marshland of Galveston Bay, and westward, behind him, by Vince's Bayou, spanned by a crude bridge that a Texan detachment confidently destroyed after Santa Anna's men had crossed over it. Having arrived at what would be the field of battle, Santa Anna camped in a grove of trees, putting prairie between himself and the Texans, who occupied a wooded position along Buffalo Bayou.

Late in the afternoon of April 21 Houston suddenly attacked Santa Anna while the Mexican dictator and some of his men were enjoying a siesta. In only eighteen minutes the furious Texans made lambs of the soldiers who had overwhelmed the Alamo, killing them with gunfire, knives, and rifles used like clubs. After the battle had ended, six hundred Mexicans lay dead and all the rest, about seven hundred, were captured—including Santa Anna him-

self and his brother-in-law, General Cós, who had promised after
the siege of San Antonio never to fight Texans again. On the Texas
side casualties were small. Of the 783 men who actually attacked,
nine died and thirty-four suffered wounds.

Santa Anna agreed to send orders to the other army commanders
to withdraw from Texas. But the significance of all this would
come to Gray only later. On the twenty-fifth, after the danger had
passed, Gray fled from Texas. That day he crossed the Sabine
River on a crowded ferry at a cost of one dollar. When he reached
the United States he felt a glow of security—as he indicated in his
diary—and again he began looking closely at the land in his path
with both eyes open for business.

15. INTO THE FIRE

The Baptist preacher Z. N. Morrell also was looking for opportunity, but in a direction opposite to Gray's. Morrell had made his
way to Tennessee, picked up his family, and set out again for
flaming Texas. While traveling in Louisiana, on his way to the
Sabine crossing, he had met a deluge of people fleeing from Texas
and the terrible Mexicans. "I was upbraided by everybody I met,
and by some cursed as a fool, declaring that my family would be
slain either by Mexicans or Indians before we would get far beyond
the Sabine." But Morrell had made up his mind: he was going to
settle near the falls of the Brazos River and save the souls there—
if there were any left. "Seldom in life had I turned back, and,
trusting in God, we travelled on." Before long he too heard of Sam
Houston's victory, with what must have been great thanksgiving.

16. FREEDOM AND MEMORIES

Dr. Joseph Henry Barnard, the survivor of Goliad, enjoyed no
such secure feeling at this time. He and Dr. Shackelford had not
been freed, as promised for a second time. Instead they had been

sent by their captors from La Bahía to San Antonio on April 16 to treat Mexican officers wounded in the Battle of the Alamo.

It had been good to get out of Goliad, even traveling as captives guarded by Mexican troops. They crossed the gloomy San Antonio, a River Styx of memory now, and rode through "delightful country" that seemed to purge them of the pall of death. Across rolling prairies in spring verdure they traveled, invigorated by the fragrance of the flowers. They reached San Antonio at sunset of the nineteenth, six weeks after the Alamo had fallen. Barnard moved into assigned quarters in a thick-walled house on the northeast corner of Commerce and Flores streets; Shackelford stayed about one block away.

Santa Anna had provided virtually no hospital facilities for his army—a flaw he did not exactly regret, since he felt that the absence of medicine would persuade officers and men it was "not so bad to die as to come out wounded." Barnard found plenty of work to keep his mind off his situation—and off the ghastly screams of Goliad that would haunt him for the rest of his life. He saw scores of wounded men walking the streets and concluded, "A pretty piece of work 'Travis and his faithful few' have made of them." From March 6 to April 20, when Barnard and Shackelford assumed their medical duties, the wounded had received little attention. No amputations had been performed; not even much lead had been cut out of the limbs of victims who still lived—something truly dismaying to professional men. Their services were obviously appreciated—both doctors received kind treatment, especially from the women—but no one would or could tell them about events beyond the Brazos. They had known as much in Goliad: "Santa Anna was ravaging the whole country and the Texans were flying before him to the Sabine . . . Matagorda was taken, and . . . San Felipe was burned by its own citizens and abandoned on the approach of the army." Barnard had taken nothing but melancholy with him to San Antonio despite the momentary fragrance of flowers on the way.

More than two weeks passed. Then, on May 6, Barnard left his quarters at Commerce and Flores for his evening walk, as he was allowed to do, and noticed at once an excitement on the streets. People huddled together and talked anxiously. Subdued inquiry brought him a bit of information: General Santa Anna had lost a battle and had been captured. Barnard at first refused to let himself believe this, as had William Gray at the Sabine, but the continued excitement convinced him. The mood reminded him of poetry he erroneously attributed to Byron:

'Twas whispered in heaven, 'twas muttered in hell
And echo caught faintly the sound as it fell.

After he had finally allowed himself to believe "it must be true, then!" he next found himself wondering about what his countrymen would do—and should do—about a reprisal for all they had suffered. He had seen too much horror recently to think they should forgive. He thought again of the Alamo, only a short distance away. "The few who fell here fell in open fight, it is true, and fighting to the last, they asked no quarter, and yet does not an order to give no quarter deserve to be retaliated? Does not . . . the massacre at Goliad in violation of pledged faith . . . deserve . . . just vengeance on the author of these enormities, and by whose special order they were perpetrated?" He realized his own predicament at this time, but his nerves had grown calluses during past weeks. "It may be dangerous for me, but I have faced too many dangers of late for that to influence any sentiments in regard to a principle of right and wrong or a matter of duty and obligation."

For days after hearing of the San Jacinto fight Barnard had no idea what the Mexicans around him in San Antonio intended to do. One day he heard that they intended to evacuate Texas; another, that they intended to fortify the town and bring in reinforcements for renewed war against the Texans. That certainly seemed to be their plan on May 15, a balmy Sunday, when Barnard strolled through full-blooming gardens over to the Alamo and watched troops strengthen defenses for what could have been still another bloody battle there. But a few days later Barnard noticed many Mexican residents packing and leaving town. Then he heard that the military commander had received orders to destroy the Alamo and join the main Mexican army near Goliad for evacuation from Texas.

By late May San Antonio was free of Mexican troops. On the day that the very last soldier crossed the river bound for Goliad, Barnard—in his journal—triumphantly called on Travis, Bowie, Crockett, and the other Alamo dead to "look down upon your enemies discomfitted and routed—retreating ignominiously from the country they entered with such bravado!" As the troops filed out, smoke boiled up from the Alamo. After the last soldier had left, Barnard and Shackelford walked over to the fortress to see how much of it remained. They soon saw that part of the church was ablaze: the wooden artillery ramp leading from the front to the top rear of the building had been set on fire by the retreating Mexicans, and it was burning too furiously now to be extinguished. Barnard observed with satisfaction that the solid masonry church walls would not be severely damaged by the fire—but much of the rest of the compound had been leveled, the water ditch filled up, artillery and ammunition dumped in the river to ruin.

Lost in reverie now, Barnard wandered about the site, "which must forever mark this spot as the Thermopylae of Texas." He gazed at the place where Travis was said to have fallen, and where other action took place. Then he and Shackelford made a pilgrimage to a location a quarter of a mile or so from the Alamo, where bodies of the defenders had been piled and burned. Except for an occasional leg or arm bone, all had been reduced to ashes.

On the following day Barnard and Shackelford left San Antonio, pausing after several miles for a last look at the town from the height of a gentle rise. Then, with thoughts each man kept to himself, they went on, to Goliad and another pilgrimage. En route, they went miles out of their way to put safe distance between themselves and an encampment of the retreating enemy; enough of the Mexicans and their empty promises of a safe passage home. On the last day of May they met the main body of the Texas Army—commanded now by General Thomas J. Rusk, since Sam Houston had gone to New Orleans for treatment of a San Jacinto wound—and they fell in with the troops, who were bound westward for Goliad to oversee the Mexicans' departure and to collect and bury the bodies of the La Bahía victims.

They had no trouble locating the remains. Most of the bodies had been burned, but not all of them. What the flames had not accomplished, vultures and wild animals had. They found bones and "entire skeletons" scattered over the plain for some distance. Much of Thursday, June 2, was devoted to gathering the remains, and they were buried on the following morning in a ceremony as formal and impressive as the makeshift Texas Army could provide.

It began soon after eight o'clock, when the troops were paraded inside the walls of Fannin's old Fort Defiance. At nine commenced a slow, solemn march to a mass grave some distance away, located not far from where Barnard and Shackelford had witnessed the massacre. The artillery led the procession, followed by a military band playing funeral music and a detachment of troops with arms reversed, then the remains of the dead, preceded and followed by groups of six commissioned officers. Later in the procession came other detachments, including five official mourners—present members of the army who had been with Fannin that dreadful Palm Sunday, had been marched out for the execution, and had miraculously escaped. While the procession made its way to the grave a gun was fired from the fort every minute. When the cortege reached its destination the gun fell silent.

Dr. Barnard heard General Rusk deliver a brief speech addressed to his "fellow soldiers":

"In the order of Providence we are this day called upon to pay the last sad offices of respect to the remains of the noble and heroic band who, battling for our sacred rights, have fallen beneath the ruthless hand of a tyrant . . . Relinquishing the peace, the ease, the comforts of home; leaving behind them all they held dear . . . they subjected themselves to fatigue and privation, and nobly threw themselves between the people of Texas and the legions of Santa Anna. There, unaided by reinforcements, and far from hope and help, they battled bravely [outnumbered] ten to one. Surrounded in the open prairie by this fearful odds, cut off from provision and even water, they were induced, under the sacred promise of receiving the treatment usual to prisoners of war, to surrender. They were marched back, and for a week treated with the utmost inhumanity and barbarity. They were marched out of yonder fort under the pretense of getting provisions, and it was not until the firing of

musketry and the shrieks of the dying were heard that they were
satisfied of their approaching fate. . . .

"But we have a consolation yet to offer them. Their murderers
sank into death on the prairies of San Jacinto under the appalling cries: 'Remember La Bahía!' We have another consolation
to offer. While liberty has a habitation and a name their tragic
fate will be handed down to remotest posterity on the brightest
pages of history . . ."

Some of the men present could not mask their tears. Others bit
their lips and gripped their weapons more tightly. Not far away,
the Mexicans even at that moment were traveling westward on
their way out of Texas, and it was well that they were: Rusk
remarked that his men had become so infuriated by the scene of
barbarism that if the Mexican army had come in sight of his troops
he could not have controlled them.

After the ceremony was over the procession marched back to the
fort and disbanded. Dr. Barnard had made that approximate walk
once before—upon his return from the peach orchard, after the
massacre, when he and Dr. Shackelford had been escorted back to
La Bahía to treat the Mexican wounded in the hospital there. No
doubt he remembered it now. Some time later he wrote:

"Strange and unaccountable have been the vicissitudes of for-
tune. Surely no mortal can tell what the morrow will bring forth.
Our disastrous battle was succeeded by the glorious one of San
Jacinto . . ."

The Republic of Texas had earned its grandiose title on the fury
born of the bloody defeats at the Alamo and at Goliad. But, as Dr.
Barnard observed, "Surely no mortal can tell what the morrow will
bring forth."

His words rang true. While many people cheered the exodus of
the last Mexican troops from Texas soil as a final solution, others
saw the situation as a problem requiring many more answers.

V

YOUNG REPUBLIC
Summer, 1836, to Autumn, 1838

Many Texans foresaw a quick solution to their country's needs: recognition by the United States and immediate annexation. Such good fortune was not forthcoming.

Even a good friend like President Jackson, the Westerner, seemed to delay a move for recognition—not the first time he had surprised some people. Jackson, born in South Carolina, a practicing politician in Tennessee as well as Washington, had been a friend of the states'-rights advocate John C. Calhoun, but Jackson had voiced fierce opposition to Calhoun's argument that a state had the right to nullify federal law. At a Jefferson Day banquet in 1830 Jackson had glared at Calhoun and had proposed a toast: "Our Federal Union—it must be preserved." This had ended a friendship, but Jackson's determination helped to prevent nullification and perhaps secession in his time.

Now Texas threatened to fan more flames. Many Americans who supported the fight for liberty there rejected the next logical step: accepting Texas as another slave state in the Union. Neither Jackson's Democratic Party nor the opposing Whigs, a party the Jacksonians said favored the wealthy and privileged, wanted to bring this question to a head. Just before Jackson left the presidency to Martin Van Buren, his own choice as a successor, he did sign a bill recognizing Texas independence. But a petition for annexation drew a firm rejection from Washington. Texas officials withdrew the request and began a flirtation with England and France, seeking recognition, trade treaties, and loans. They found both nations cool.

The ad-interim government that had come into office in Texas with the independence declaration seemed at times to be in as much turmoil as the provisional government had been. In its eagerness for recognition and annexation it had appointed two sets of commissioners to the United States, which brought not doubled effort but confusion. It named Mirabeau B. Lamar commander in chief of the Texas Army, then watched helplessly as the troops refused to accept him. It disagreed about what to do with its famous prisoner, Santa Anna, but finally signed two treaties with him, one of them kept secret at the time. In those documents Santa Anna vowed never again to fight against Texas, and to return to Mexico and persuade his countrymen to recognize Texas independence. But in Mexico Anastasio Bustamente had assumed the presidency, and his Congress had voted against approving anything done by Santa Anna while a prisoner.

Poverty and a $1,500,000 war debt faced Texas. Loans appeared to be the only way out, but little cash ever came from the United States, soon to be enfeebled by the financial Panic of 1837, and nothing came from England and France. In desperation Texas turned to Sam Houston as president, to unsupported paper-money issues, to taxes on a people unable to pay. Nothing seemed to work.

"We are in a deplorable condition Pecuniary morally & intellectually," one Texan remarked. "Yet I hope all will be well." The man who said that later committed suicide, but other men continued to try.

17. A CONTENDER

The Indians had never ceased to trouble Texans. They did pass up an opportunity to swoop down on civilians fleeing in the Runaway Scrape, largely because of the previous peacemaking by Sam Houston with the Cherokees and possibly because of the presence on Texas soil, on orders of President Andrew Jackson, of a United States Army force with instructions to keep the Indians in check during this perilous time—an action that brought protests from the Mexican minister in Washington. But Indian peace proved to be only temporary, as many Texans discovered.

One person thus enlightened was Z. N. Morrell, the Baptist preacher, who had settled at the falls of the Brazos River with his wife and four children, as he had said he would. He found six or eight other families settled there, and, nearby, a small fort erected by the new Republic, manned by about forty soldiers called "Rangers." All this offered good prospects for preaching, but the location had its disadvantages. The main one concerned the Indians: braves roamed the area, keeping the soldiers on continual alert and the families in constant anxiety. Signal smokes could be seen often, first on the west side of the river, then on the east. What the signals meant Morrell did not know. Maybe the Rangers did: they were more experienced. But even they had to go out into the wilderness and do some probing. They knew the Indians liked to come south in small groups, then join up for whatever mischief they planned, usually about full moon. Sometimes the Rangers were able to warn settlers before this happened, but not always.

Grim backdrop for this was the knowledge of what had happened recently to a colony at Fort Parker, located near the headwaters of the Navasota River, not even forty miles away from Morrell's new home. A Baptist elder, John Parker, had moved with kinfolk to Texas from Illinois before the rebellion and had chosen as the location of a private fort a rise overlooking the wooded river bottom. The territory was far removed from the safety of other settlements, but it had some advantages for the eight or nine families who inhabited it: nearby fields were fertile, winters were comparatively mild, and Mexican authority was distant, affording religious freedom.

But the isolation had not precluded involvement. When the men of Fort Parker heard reports from the settlements about Santa Anna's invasion some of them joined the Texan army. Other occupants of the fort fled eastward. In May, after Sam Houston's victory at San Jacinto, they returned to their fort—some time before Morrell settled his family at the nearby falls—to commence what appeared to be an idyllic existence, now that Texas was free. By day the men went out into the fields to work their crops. At night they herded their horses and cattle into the fort, which was walled with strong timbers and further protected by two tall watchtowers that provided a view of the surroundings. After the last chore had been completed and supper eaten, they bedded down in their comfortable log houses for the night. The walls would keep out nocturnal prowlers: with the gate closed, only the dim light from the heavens could gain entrance.

But people grew careless. Sometimes they neglected to close the gate, and it lay open on the balmy, bright morning of May 19, after some men had left for the fields. Inside, a child glanced out the entrance and saw a swarm of Indians, more than he had ever seen before. There were about five hundred, many of them the dreaded Comanches—all mounted and waiting some distance away, staring back at the fort.

The child's screams brought the occupants running. Benjamin Parker, a son of Elder John Parker, strode out to talk with the Indians, who were showing a white flag. He returned to the fort to say that they professed friendship and that they wanted beef and directions to a water hole. The last request gave them away: nearby was the Navasota River, and they surely knew it. But Parker said he would return and talk with them—possibly he could ward off an attack—and despite pleas he walked back toward the waiting Indians.

But they were finished talking. They swarmed over Parker and killed him, while horrified relatives watched. Then, screeching and shouting, they attacked the fort and ran down the occupants, spearing, stripping, and mutilating them—men, women, children. One baby they later roped and threw into a cluster of prickly pears, pulling it back and forth until the body was an unrecognizable mass. When it was over only five persons in the fort remained alive, as helpless prisoners of a tribe whose women loved to torture captives after shrieking invitations to "come to the dance." Two of the prisoners were Cynthia Ann Parker, aged nine, and her brother John, six. These two children, soon to be separated, were to grow up as Indians themselves and to become legendary in Texas history.

The fate of Fort Parker emphasized the seriousness of an ammunition shortage at the falls of the Brazos: the Rangers had left to them about five rounds of ammunition each. It was important that they stay there, to protect the families, so Z. N. Morrell volunteered to go after replenishment. But he did not undertake the journey without misgivings. At this point the Devil "sorely tried" him. Lying between him and Washington-on-the-Brazos, where powder and lead might be obtained, were more than a hundred wooded miles of danger and possible death waiting behind every tree, every bush. He thought of his recent sermon, so powerful and courageous, that he had preached at Nacogdoches: "The wilderness and the solitary place shall be glad for them; and the desert shall rejoice, and blossom as the rose." Bold, encouraging words—so easy to say then. Without admitting his doubt to anyone, Morrell asked himself now if he really did believe what he had said, and after some silent thought and prayer he decided that he did. So he saddled his horse, said goodbye to his family, and commenced the long ride down the lonely Brazos banks to Washington.

One village lay on his route—Nashville, a settlement of perhaps a dozen families, which gave him a chance to preach that night. The next morning he rose at daylight and pushed on for Washington. At sunset he arrived there and found the town not much changed from the way it had looked to the signers of the declaration of independence: a cluster of frame buildings and log cabins, and only one cleared street, where numerous stumps still stood.

Morrell found that his fame had preceded him to Washington. Tired and hungry, he asked a man for directions to a public house. The man pointed one out, then asked Morrell if he were not a Baptist preacher. "I replied that I bore the name of one in Tennessee, and would not deny it in Texas." An ensuing invitation to preach that night was something Morrell could not refuse, and a large crowd gathered to hear him. But the trip had exhausted him, and he retired as soon as he could, "having travelled entirely alone, along crooked Indian trails, one hundred and twenty miles in two days, and preached each night." He needed to buy ammunition on the following day and return without delay.

Early the next morning he began shopping, but not one store in

Washington had powder to sell. He found some lead and loaded in his saddlebags as many bars as he thought safe, then bent several others, strung them, and balanced them on his saddle horn. All this lead would be worthless without powder, but he hoped to find a supply at the village of Independence, ten miles east.

Independence had no powder, either—in fact, little of anything. "It looked more like dependence . . . than independence. Such was the appearance of all our towns." No reason to tarry there, and no time to spare anyway. Morrell rode on northeastward, to pick up the Brazos River again for his return journey. One chance for powder remained: at Jackson's store, eight miles south of Nashville, where he had preached two nights earlier. Between him and his destination lay a creek with one of those troublesome Spanish names—Yegua. He found it out of banks, ugly, and a perilous obstacle for a horse carrying a man and a supply of lead. He scanned the scene before him: "The stream was swimming, for about thirty feet, in the main channel—the whole bottom, nearly three miles wide, was a sea of water." No time to spare here either, so Morrell plunged in, and his horse carried him and the load safely across. He emerged on the other side soaked and dripping, but concentrating now on only two things: the possibility of an Indian attack, and Jackson's store.

He arrived there late in the evening, "weary and hungry and impatient," and still wet from the soaking. He entered the store, which was crowded, and asked for powder. A shipment had just come in by wagon from Columbia on the coast, he heard with delight—then learned that all of it had been spoken for by the very men who were crowded around him. They had paid in advance and were there to claim their share.

But Morrell had the gift of persuasion. He unlimbered his preacher's voice, and in a short time he depicted the perils of his people on the fringe of civilization so vividly that the men agreed to let him buy six canisters of powder, despite the fact that they too were constantly threatened by Indians. Thankfully Morrell paid for the precious supply. By evening of the following day he had returned to his family and the little colony at the falls. "The soldiers, on receiving the powder and lead, were in fine spirits. There was no danger of starvation, with plenty of ammunition, and hopes were entertained that the Indians could now be held in check."

Morrell's trip was a remarkable one. He had ridden the same horse at least 240 miles in four days and had returned with lead when it was scarce and with powder when none seemed to be available. It was almost like the story of the loaves and the fishes in Morrell's Bible—a divine comparison that probably never entered his mind. But for any doubters Morrell had identified himself as a preacher who did more than talk. On the hard frontier such a man could exert a considerable influence, and Morrell's move to Texas certainly seemed not to have been in vain.

Again settled at home, Morrell surveyed his situation and found opportunity aplenty. "There were no [other] Baptists at the Falls . . . It was thirty miles to the nearest settlement on Little River. . . . Thus cut off, I did what I could for the spiritual welfare of those by whom I was immediately surrounded." His audience must have listened intently.

18. THE NEW HOME

Like the Morrells, the recently abandoned Harriet Page and her new husband, Robert Potter, also selected a homesite far removed from the central settlements, sometime around the end of the first year of Texas independence.

Their courtship had been as confused as the times. After Potter singled her out for his protection and took her aboard the vessel at Velasco he was kind and attentive to her and her children, and apparently nothing more. When Harriet's daughter fell sick and died aboard the ship he consoled her "as a brother," and after the Battle of San Jacinto, when Harriet longed for relatives in Kentucky, he offered to accompany her there. But after arrangements for the journey had been completed Potter declared that it was impossible to go: he said a yellow-fever epidemic was sweeping Kentucky. Harriet became indignant at this obvious ruse and declared she would go on by herself. At that point Potter proposed marriage, and Harriet said coyly she had never imagined his intention. She told him she was still legally married to Solomon Page, but Potter explained that unless she had been married by a priest, as required then by Mexican law, her marriage had not been valid in Texas anyway. This seemed acceptable to her, and she and Potter were married in a simple, informal ceremony—"just as binding as if judge and clergy were present," Harriet said.

The Potters had not moved to their new homesite immediately after marriage. They had lived near the settlements for a time, and had followed with interest some early events—like the kidnaping of the famous prisoner General Santa Anna. Potter, as David Burnet's secretary of the navy, had advocated execution of the captured Mexican generals and enslavement of the rest of the prisoners, and he had much public support. But President Burnet himself, Sam Houston, and a few other officials urged a more moderate course, both in the interest of world opinion and in hope that Santa Anna would help Texas—as he promised to do—upon his return to Mexico. The moderate course had prevailed, and Santa Anna had been kept a prisoner under close guard (mostly for his own safety) until after the signing of the two peace treaties at Velasco. From there, about the first of June, President Burnet sought to send him back to Mexico aboard the Texas Navy vessel *Invincible*.

Elated, the Mexican dictator boarded the ship, wrote a farewell note to Texans, and sent it ashore: "My Friends: I know that you are valiant in war and generous after it; rely always on my friendship and you will never regret the consideration you have shown me. Upon my returning to the land of my birth, thanks to your kindness, accept this sincere farewell from your grateful Antonio López de Santa Anna."

But Santa Anna was not destined to go home so quickly. Texans remembered the Alamo and Goliad and were only enraged by his entreaty to "rely always on my friendship." Around Velasco the atmosphere became explosive. Some men even talked of arresting President Burnet and setting up a dictatorship, and almost everyone wanted to get his hands on Santa Anna. Unfortunately for the General, the *Invincible* was delayed several days in sailing, and during the wait there arrived 250 volunteers from New Orleans commanded by an incendiary from North Carolina, Thomas Jefferson Green, whose four-month West Point stint and brief service as

a Texas recruiter had given him leadership delusions. Green and
his troops craved some kind of action, and this situation offered it.
They added their noise to the din and forced Burnet to order Santa
Anna brought ashore. Green himself was one of the crowd that
fetched the hated man. Santa Anna quailed, then protested that he
was being treated more like a criminal than like a prisoner of
war.

Once ashore, Santa Anna was put under a strong guard—again,
mostly for his own safety. Months later, at his suggestion, he was
sent with three escorts to Washington, D.C., to offer himself to
Andrew Jackson for mediating peace between Mexico and Texas—
a mission that he knew would fail, but it finally got him returned
aboard a United States vessel to Mexico, where he found safety,
but no immediate power or influence.

Coupled with the Santa Anna turbulence was a new invasion
scare, ignited by the report of two Texas commissioners who had
been sent to Matamoros under a truce flag to ascertain whether all
Texas prisoners had been released. The commissioners were arrested and themselves became prisoners, but they were able to get
word back to Texas that eight or ten thousand Mexican troops
were poised and ready to strike: "They will soon be down upon
you in great numbers. . . . Fall back to the Colorado and call all
the men to the field, for if you don't Texas is lost. . . . You must
not spare any pains for the sake of saving us. We are willing to be
lost to save Texas!" Hearing this news, men and boys turned out—
more than three fourths of them, in some sections—to "teach the
audacious foe a sequel to San Jacinto." But after waiting for nearly
two months they returned home. The invasion never came, and the
imprisoned commissioners escaped and returned to Texas.

But the most momentous development in those confused months
following the victory at San Jacinto was the nomination and election of Sam Houston as President of the Republic of Texas. Probably no other man could have kept the country together. Houston
antagonized and alienated as well as charmed, but he was the
biggest man in Texas. A contemporary told why:

> He had a remarkable memory and was a good judge of human
> nature. His personal appearance was grand: standing over six
> feet in height, his body and limbs were well proportioned. His

voice was excellent; and, altogether, a more commanding figure
and effective speaker would be difficult to find. He never failed
to command attention from his audience. His was of a kindly
and generous disposition when pursuing the even tenor of its
flow, but harsh and vindictive when thwarted or opposed. Especially did those who had the temerity to cross his political
pathway become the objects of his scathing invective. His memory was equally as tenacious of the acts of an opponent as of the
kindly offices of friendship; he never forgot either, and he
seldom failed to repay his enemies in kind and with the addition
of usurious interest. . . . Sam Houston as president of Texas
was irrefragably "the right man in the right place." No other
hand [but] his could have steered the frail ship of state through
the tortuous channels . . .

In August, only a month before the election, Houston "yielded
to the wishes of my friends in allowing my name to be run for
President." The crisis required it, he added, or he would not have
agreed. He would have preferred a soldier's life.

The race was a runaway. Houston won overwhelmingly, even
against Stephen F. Austin, whom most Texans looked on as too
pacific for the times—but whom Houston chose as his first secretary of state, a position Austin held until his death in December.
Pressure from malcontents persuaded ad-interim President Burnet
to resign early to make way for a genuine winner, and Houston
took the oath as president at an improvised frame Capitol built
under some giant live-oak trees in the scraggly Brazos River village
of Columbia in late afternoon of October 22, 1836.

In his inaugural address Houston displayed a bit of the drama
for which he was famous. Near the end he stopped speaking, dis-
engaged the sword he wore, and presented it to the Speaker of the
Texas House of Representatives, who had administered the oath.
Houston explained his action: he had given up military command
for civilian administration. In the audience eyes misted, and Houston himself seemed lost in his own emotion. But one unwilted
observer thought that the gesture was entirely theatrical: Houston
already had given up command of the Army after San Jacinto,
when he had gone to New Orleans to have his wound attended to,

and now he had just taken an oath that reinvested him with command of all Texas military forces. This seemed to corroborate another description of Houston, by another contemporary: "He was a most consummate actor in the serious as well as frivolous affairs of life . . . and had ways peculiar to himself to compass his purpose, scrupulous or unscrupulous. It seemed to matter little with him, so that he achieved success. He was excessively vain—a flatterer and loved to be flattered."

Sometime after Sam Houston's inaugural Harriet Moore Page Potter and her new husband moved to their new homesite: a high promontory they called Potter's Point, overlooking blue Caddo Lake near the northern edge of the Texas-Louisiana border. Potter was no friend of Sam Houston's, and the services requested of Potter by former President Burnet no longer were in demand. Potter built his house far from the capital.

Harriet surveyed the location with delight. From the house, which had been built among the many trees bordering the lake, she could look for miles across the water to the other side—when it was not lost in distant haze. From her front door she liked to search the other side of the lake with a glass for signs of life and to examine lush islands that rose out of the blue silence nearer her.

Below, water rippled onto a clean beach at the bottom of the promontory. She could hear the gentle splashes. Halfway down the cliff, near the steep path, a spring of clear water gushed onto rocks and tumbled down in a small stream. All around her grew a forest of flowers, vines, bushes, trees, many of them bearing sweet fruit and berries. The afternoon sun poked its slanting rays through the foliage only with difficulty.

But it was evening that truly captivated her—when the sunset sky turned crimson, then purple, and the water of the lake merged with the darkness. Sometimes only the rhythmic swishing from below was left to tell her that the water was still there. On other nights Harriet sat in silent meditation and felt that the "spirits of the moon came down to woo the spirits of the lake."

She had found happiness at last, and even had she known then that she would not enjoy the company of another white woman for many months the thought probably would not have bothered her. Only later did she feel concern about her new marriage, and that only momentarily—when a newly arrived woman neighbor re-marked that she would not have married Robert Potter "for any-thing" because of the way he had treated his first wife, in North Carolina. While married to her, the woman declared, Potter had fallen in love with a beautiful heiress during a visit to Washington City and had begun seeking some way to shake loose from his marital bonds. When Potter returned to North Carolina he learned that his wife had been baptized at a church revival, and this gave him an idea. He accused his wife of misconduct with the minister. The accusation brought misery to several households, the woman told Harriet, and had led to trouble that resulted in Potter's im-prisonment and eventual move to Texas. For proof the woman gave Robert Potter's new wife a book that told all about these things.

Harriet refused to believe this, but the truth was that Potter had indeed been forced to leave North Carolina after a series of inci-dents. Once he attacked his first wife's cousin in a jealous rage and received a two-year jail sentence. After his release he was elected to the North Carolina legislature, from which he was expelled for "playing a game of cards unfairly, contrary to the rules." But some people claimed the real offense was maiming, not cheating. After that, in the summer of 1835, he had left for Texas, as had some others in trouble with the law.

Harriet Potter kept her faith in him. After her arrival at Potter's Point her only real concern had been about the isolation.

"What do you think of it?" Potter had asked when they stood for the first time on the promontory.

Harriet expressed delight with the beauty of the place, then added, "But there are no neighbors [except] the Indians. I don't see anyone living here. What are we going to do without neighbors?"

Potter reassured her. "You will find that the Indians make the best of neighbors," he replied. Thus began Harriet Potter's new life in the wilderness.

19. TRIBULATIONS

If the Indians around Potter's Point were good neighbors they were of a friendlier type than the ones around Z. N. Morrell's home. Early in 1837 Indian troubles increased there—at a time when President Sam Houston was practicing generosity to his red brothers and arousing the anger of Texans who had seen their kin tomahawked.

Tracks in a light February snowfall that powdered the ground around the falls of the Brazos first indicated that another Indian raid southward was in progress. A few Rangers from the nearby fort saw the tracks; every day some of them rode southward toward a fort on the Little River, and at a midway point they met men from the other fort and swapped information. Now here was another raiding party, but it seemed to be only a small one.

A thirty-four-year-old Ranger from Vienna, Austria, named George Erath led about fifteen men in pursuit of the Indians. They rode for miles, buttoned up against cold weather that bit even harder after sunset. Then they saw the one trail converge with a number of others: the Indians had separated into smaller groups and had met at this pre-selected spot. The Rangers' job would not be easy. Erath, in a thick accent, ordered a halt and a cautious examination of the country ahead. The evening had become quite dark, but from a rise they saw an Indian camp some distance away, in bottomland around a creek named Elm. Fires glowed—not cheerfully for these few Rangers. They tied their horses and advanced on foot. Only the dark night was on their side. They crept into Elm Creek, positioned themselves under a bank, and waited for sunrise. For a wonder, they had avoided arousing the dogs. The silent camp with its glowing timbers lay nearby. Whispering, Erath divided his men into squads of three or four, assigned them different fires to shoot at when the time came, and told them to make certain no two men shot at the same Indian. The night wore on slowly.

When predawn lightened the eastern sky the Indians began milling around the campfires. The Rangers stared, guessed their enemy must number at least 150 men, and made final plans about attacking. But they were interrupted by the camp dogs, which discovered their presence and began yelping an alert. Erath told his men to fire, and around every campfire bodies collapsed to the ground. The other Indians leaped for safety and for weapons and attacked the Rangers, who withdrew slowly to where they had left their horses. In the retreat they lost two men.

The Indians were no more eager to press the attack than the Rangers had been. They withdrew, broke camp, and fled to a safer country. When Z. N. Morrell heard about this he felt a satisfaction: "But for this engagement, the large body of Indians would very soon have been in the settlements below, killing, burning, and stealing; for they never came down in such large numbers in those days without desperate ends in view. . . . Now I felt a thousand times paid for my long ride to Washington, amid so much exposure and anxiety. This work was done with the ammunition that I procured while on that trip."

Prospects for approaching spring brightened, at least for a while. The light snow melted soon—snow rarely fell and scarcely ever stayed on the ground long in that part of Texas—and more rain came to nourish the earth and prepare it for surviving the long, hot, dry days of summer. Morrell planted corn in a twenty-five-acre fenced field that he had rented on the opposite side of the Brazos (the east side) from where he lived. He crossed the river twice a day, once in the morning and again in the evening, swimming his horses and oxen and paddling himself and his helpers over in a canoe. The Rangers stood guard "free of charge" while he planted and cultivated his crop there and, later, on a fifty-acre unfenced field at "Wild Prairie," a location not far away.

The bottomland was rich and new to cultivation. Morrell's crop sprang up in a way to gladden the heart of a farmer; later, when he harvested the corn, it would yield fifty bushels to the acre, even "with the little work we were able in primitive style to give it." Only wild bear disturbed the crop much. The few cattle owned by the settlers preferred to roam some luxuriant prairies farther back from the river.

That spring of 1837 came with warmth, a new green landscape, and the usual abundance of wildflowers that gave their fragrance to the breeze. Morrell cheerfully anticipated his first Texas crop. But then everything seemed to turn sour. The Indians came back— Morrell heard of their raids nearby. The financial condition of the Republic worsened: Texas owed money to its Army and Navy, owed for supplies and ammunition, yet "had not a dollar to pay for anything. . . . The families and the forts on the frontier had either to join hands, and farm and fight together . . . or fall back, [thereafter] leaving the people in the settlements below to be the extreme frontier on the north." Finally, and most urgent, the Ranger commander told Morrell confidentially that ammunition was almost gone again, and this time other necessities were low.

Morrell had established himself as leader of the settlement, a situation to his personal credit and to his disadvantage. The commander singled him out for an appeal, emphasizing that "secrecy was safety," and Morrell felt obliged to share his family's stores that had been hauled in by oxen from Natchitoches, nearly three hundred miles away. As they dwindled he contemplated spending part of his personal savings—several thousand dollars—acquired from land sold in Mississippi. Certainly no man would expect to be an island in this wilderness.

Eventually Morrell hitched his eight oxen to a wagon that could haul five thousand pounds of supplies (to be bought mostly with his own money) and left for the new town of Houston, to which the seat of government had recently moved. With him he took his twelve-year-old son, to help with driving during the 350-mile round trip, and two horses. He left in the waning days of March "with the probability of being captured by the [Indians], and slain by the way; or, if permitted to return, with the probability of finding my little log cabin in ashes and my family [killed]."

But the worst that happened to him was the loss of both horses, stolen while he and his son were camped on land now occupied by the present town of Bryan. The thief was not an Indian, but a fellow Texan. Morrell pursued him, recovered one horse, bought another, and pushed on, forgetful of everything except getting to Houston. When they reached the Navasota River they saw that spring rains had flooded the bottomland and left the stream nearly bank full. After a struggle through the ooze they reached the bank, and Morrell was preparing to tackle the next part of the crossing when his son interrupted him. "Pa, what are you going to do?" he asked. "You said when we got here we would get something to eat. We have had no bread since yesterday. There is no boat, no canoe. Our skillet is lost, and we can't even get a place dry enough to bake an ash cake."

The river could wait. Morrell searched for earth and wood dry enough for starting a fire. Then he cut from an ash tree a large block of wood for baking a johnnycake. Soon the odor of cooking food and boiling coffee wafted through Navasota River bottoms.

After the meal and a chat with his son Morrell turned again to the river. He had been told that a man lived near here, on a hill on the other side. He shouted in the top reaches of his preacher's voice, and after a while a man appeared on the opposite bank. "What will you have, sir?" the stranger asked.

Morrell told him: help in getting his wagon and team across the river. The man, who had plenty of experience, demanded five dollars, and the price was agreed on. Within three hours Morrell and his son stood on the other side of the flooded stream after transporting camp equipment across on a small raft, then pulling the wagon across and swimming the animals to the other side—all with the man's supervision. For another five dollars, he said, he would have a canoe ready for their return journey, and Morrell agreed, but with growing concern for the disappearance of his savings: "Here was ten dollars for crossing the Navasota twice, with great labor and peril."

Late on a Saturday afternoon, a week or so after leaving the falls of the Brazos, Morrell and his son reached Houston. To get into town they were forced to swim still another stream, Buffalo Bayou, from a location opposite the Main Street landing. Once across, they could relax a little: half of the trip had been completed. They must have made an odd appearance clattering down Main Street toward a room for the night: eight dripping oxen, whose reins were in the hands of a twelve-year-old boy; an empty freight wagon that bounced and creaked along; a tall, thin man astride a horse, with another mount in tow—the whole entourage from God knew where.

That Saturday night was lost to history. Where—or if—Morrell found a room in the capital city of Texas he did not record. Perhaps he and his son camped out again, for Houston was a crowded, bustling town with adequate facilities only for drinking—mostly in tents hurriedly thrown up. A congressman in Houston not long after this observed that "drinking, fighting, and wrangling" were the order of the day—"I never was so tired of a place in my life"—and he felt certain that the Congress then in session would reflect the spiritual emptiness of the town.

But the day after Morrell's arrival was notable. It was Sunday, March 26, 1837, and the Reverend Mr. Morrell had seen enough of Houston to realize it was a community in need of the Gospel. He dressed in presentable clothes and looked for a place to preach. Soon he discovered that no sermon had ever been delivered in Houston. A group of men helped him to improvise benches for a congregation, and in "a cool shade on that beautiful spring morning" Morrel brought the word of the Lord to town.

Monday morning Morrell and his son shopped for powder, lead, and supplies, then hurried home "as rapidly as an ox-team, heavily loaded, could carry us." At the Navasota River the canoe was ready—five dollars—and the man charged another five dollars for helping them back across the river, an expense Morrell had hoped to avoid. No matter—they had the supplies, then some good fortune. Near the place where Morrell's horse had been stolen he found the animal safe and well, in the hands of a man to whom he was glad to give a twenty-five-dollar reward. With the animals and the precious supplies they rumbled on up the east bank of the Brazos, and when they reached a site opposite their cabin and the fort they shouted across jubilantly to a welcoming party that they had brought powder, lead, and commissary stores. "Hats were waved," Morrell said, "and as loud a shout was raised as would have been during the late war on the arrival of a seventy-four-gun ship in some great emergency." Morrell himself seemed to be the singlehanded savior of this settlement.

But Morrell found that life continued to be a mixture of joys and sorrows. "The little colonies here and there were frequently greatly elated, catching eagerly at every little ray of light that made their prospects even tolerable. Oftener, however, gloom hung over the camp. From north, east and west, rumors reached us of

Indian outrages, that made our blood chill sometimes with fear, and then by turns boil with feelings of . . . revenge." The gloom increased when Morrell thought about the transience of the supplies he had brought back.

But of course he continued preaching. One Sunday he traveled to Nashville, some forty-five miles down the Brazos from the falls, to conduct a service, and almost everyone in the small settlement turned out to hear him. They crowded into a small dirt-floor log cabin, and Morrell had no trouble filling their ears. Just as the service closed, a band of Indians shrieked upon them, killed two men, and galloped off. Morrell and others seized the weapons they always kept near them, ran for their horses, and sped away in pursuit. The Indians escaped northward, and the unhappy horsemen returned to Nashville, where Morrell was expected by the tearful survivors to conduct a burial for the two victims.

For him this proved to be no routine ministerial task. He knew the Indians had fled in the general direction of the settlement at the falls of the Brazos, and he preached the funeral with the awful thought in mind that he might find his own family dead. As soon as he had brought the service to a close he mounted his horse and reined it toward home, despite enveloping darkness. "Forty-five miles to ride alone in the night, with a knowledge of the fact before me that the Indians were above and between me and my home, and that I was liable to be attacked at any moment." It was enough to make the strongest man tremble, and Morrell suffered weaknesses —as he always admitted.

While he rode alone in the blackness he found himself tested again. "Where is your faith now?" a silent voice asked him. He thought this over and reflected that it might be well after all to return to Mississippi and Tennessee and work in those fields, even if his health suffered. People there had been generous before, and he knew they would like to have him back. The voice went on: "The Indians will certainly get you yet, either on this trip or some other."

At that dark moment Morrell's faith wavered badly. Then he thought of other precarious situations he had survived, and he mused, "God sent an angel to provide food for Elijah under the juniper-tree, when he had despaired and was willing to die, and sent fire to consume the offering in the presence of the prophets of Baal. He also put into the heart of Rahab the harlot to conceal the spies while examining the city of Jericho and its fortifications, and finally caused its walls to tumble down at the sound of the rams' horns, leading Israel safely into the promised land of Canaan." In the Republic of Texas a man had to have something to cling to.

"God gave me an inward token that I should be concealed from the Indian's watchful eye," Morrell said, "and that he would recognize my offerings in years to come. The wilderness would yet blossom as the rose." Soon after sunrise he reached the falls of the Brazos and found everybody well.

20. A NEW FAMILY

Like Z. N. Morrell, Sam Maverick also had a family to worry about. The carefree days of before and after the siege of San Antonio were over for him. He had married Mary Ann Adams, a tall, fair girl from Alabama whose feminine air hid a will and a compulsion for activity that were as strong as her husband's.

They had met accidentally after Sam Maverick had returned on a visit to Tuscaloosa in 1836. One day while riding along a country road he had happened upon her—"a lovely blue-eyed blonde young woman in a green muslin dress"—and the chance meeting had flowered into friendship, then into romance. They had been married August 4, 1836, at her widowed mother's home three miles north of Tuscaloosa. She was eighteen, Sam thirty-three.

But by this time Maverick was also married to Texas. The new nation he had helped bring into being claimed him like a magnet, and he was eager to return there. Mary Maverick indicated the extent of his loyalty in a diary entry on their wedding day: "I was married to Samuel A. Maverick, late of South Carolina, now a Texan." Although the Mavericks lingered in the United States, visiting relatives and acquaintances in Alabama and, later, his father in South Carolina, Texas was continually on his mind, even in his dreams. "I must go back," he said.

Pleadings by his father failed to change his mind. In March of 1837—about the same time the Baptist preacher Z. N. Morrell was in rowdy Houston delivering the first sermon ever preached there —Sam and Mary Maverick left Alabama for his father's plantation, Montpelier, in South Carolina, for a farewell visit. At Montpelier the Mavericks, father and only son, had an emotional reunion after a separation of several years. The year before, his father had mourned Sam—or "Gus," as he always called him—as having been killed at the Alamo, not knowing that his son had been elected a delegate to the convention at Washington-on-the-Brazos and thus had escaped Santa Anna's slaughter. When Sam spoke of returning to that place, his father offered him Montpelier and its vineyards, orchards, fields, mills, and shops, or another place, if he would stay. Sam Maverick could not be persuaded to change his mind once it had been made up, but his father's sadness seemed so acute that he agreed to postpone his departure.

Not even the birth of a son, on May 14, deterred him, but it did slow him down more. Throughout the summer he and Mary and the baby, also named Sam, remained at Montpelier, with Grandfather refusing to accept their departure. But on the day the baby turned five months old—October 14, 1837—Sam Maverick decided the time had come to say goodbye. He and his young family left for a final visit to Tuscaloosa before going on to Texas. For a few hours Sam's father rode along with them, putting off the farewell as long as possible, and when he finally did turn back to Montpelier "it was dreadful to see his grief in saying farewell to his son," Mary observed. Texas was a distant land, full of unfathomable dangers.

At Tuscaloosa they stayed six weeks, making final preparations for the trip. Mary's youngest brother, Robert, slight and sickly, needed a change of climate, and his mother reluctantly consented to let him go along. Finally, early in December, they left: Sam, Mary, young Sam, Robert, and ten Negro slaves, including four children. For the trip they had a carriage, a large Kentucky wagon and team, three extra saddle horses, a blooded filly, and, in the wagon, a comfortable store of provisions: tents, bedding, food. Like Sam's father, Mary's mother put off a goodbye as long as possible. After they had started down the long road from home her mother ran after them for one more embrace. "She held me in her arms and wept aloud," Mary remembered afterward. "She said, 'Oh, Mary, I will never see you again on earth.' I felt heartbroken and often recalled that . . . cry and never beheld my dear mother again."

Southwestward through the forests of Alabama and Mississippi they traveled, occasionally camping for several days at a time to rest, wash, and let boggy roads dry after torrential rains. At Rodney, a small town north of Natchez, they crossed the Mississippi River and plunged into the Louisiana wilderness, where high-water marks on trees stood above the top of their carriage. But the river was behaving at that time and the roads were good. They pushed on across the Red River at Alexandria, then across the Sabine—"a sluggish, muddy, narrow stream"—and reached the soil of the Republic of Texas early in January, 1838.

Sam Maverick thought over the vulnerability of San Antonio to Mexican attack. He realized that no one knew what the Mexicans were doing from day to day. Certainly the Republic of Texas, even with crafty Sam Houston as President, was in a precarious position. So Maverick decided to go on to San Antonio to see for himself about the desirability of moving a family there. He left his wife, young Sam, Robert, and the Negroes at the large Navidad River home of George Sutherland, a veteran of San Jacinto, while he scouted the area.

At Sutherland's Mary Maverick had a quick introduction to the perils of life in Texas. Soon after her arrival a freezing norther caused the death of two of their horses. She heard stories almost as chilling—from Sutherland's wife, Fanny, who had seen her eldest son leave for San Antonio two years earlier, to learn Spanish, and had heard later that he had been killed at the Alamo. Mary Maverick was told that when March 6 came Fanny would stay in her room alone the entire day, grieving.

From Fanny and others Mary Maverick also heard awesome stories of the Runaway Scrape, "when women and children fled in fear before Santa Anna's advancing . . . troops . . . burning and plundering as they came, and how it rained almost every day for six weeks of that time." She talked with a fellow boarder, Captain James Austin Sylvester, one of a group of Texas soldiers who had captured a Mexican later identified as General Santa Anna himself, the day after the battle at San Jacinto.

But Mary's most traumatic experience at Sutherland's probably was an encounter with a famous chief of the Cherokees, The Bowl—"Old Bowles," she called him—a friend of Sam Houston's. The chief and a dozen or more of his tribe were returning from the town of Houston and a meeting with the President one day when they camped near Sutherland's. That afternoon the occupants, Mary included, organized an impromptu after-tea dance, and when the chief heard the gaiety he appeared at the door, dressed in breechcloth, anklets, long white linen shirt given him in Houston, moccasins, and a feather headdress. When the dancing stopped— which was not very long after the chief's sudden appearance—he announced himself as a good friend of the President of the Republic of Texas, who had lived in the Indian nation and had taken his own daughter as a wife. "Old Bowles" said that he had made Sam Houston a chief, with a title something like "Big Drunk," Mary understood.

Then the chief stopped talking and ogled the young women present. He remarked that during his visit to Houston the pretty ladies had danced with him, kissed him, and given him rings. At that moment Mary Maverick missed her husband very much. "We begged to be excused and requested him to retire, when he in great contempt stalked out and our dance broke up." Life in Texas, she learned, was indeed unpredictable.

21. SAVAGES RED AND WHITE

Unpredictability was something Z. N. Morrell had come to expect. About the only predictable part of life at the falls of the Brazos was that sooner or later ammunition and other supplies would run short, and he would have to go for more. For that reason he had been forced to make still another trip to Houston—about the time the son had been born to Sam and Mary Maverick—but this time he was not so fortunate as he had been in the past. The money left in his personal savings was declared worthless by Houston merchants. It consisted of paper from banks in the United States, and because of the Panic of 1837 many banks there had failed. The panic was making itself felt in Texas too. Business in Houston had become stagnant, and all Texas was suffering more than usual.

Morrell had gone on to New Orleans from Houston, hoping to find some way out of his money troubles, and had "walked the streets of the Crescent City for fourteen consecutive days, trying to make negotiations. It was then, with many of us, a bread and meat question." Finally he talked with a few merchants in need of cash of some kind to repay bank loans: they were willing to exchange items from their stock for his money, at sixty cents on the dollar. Morrell happily accepted—and thus drifted into merchandising.

He shipped his goods back to Houston, but his Texas homecoming was not happy. At Houston he learned that Indians had overpowered the fort at the falls and that his family had fled down the river to Nashville. "The best crop I ever made was all lost, our household furniture and farming tools all captured, and about a thousand dollars lost in the failure of the banks." Morrell had suffered his own private Panic of 1837, but still his faith held: "God be praised . . . my wife and children lived." He stored the bulk of his merchandise in Houston, shipped some of it in two wagons to Washington-on-the-Brazos, and established a store and a home there. He brought his wife and children down from Nashville—and of course he brought the Baptist Church with him.

Morrell found Washington to be as full of sinners as Houston. The moral quality of Texas inhabitants seemed to have deteriorated since the days of Stephen F. Austin's colony. The old settlers looked on many recent immigrants with embarrassment and anger, calling them adventurers and blacklegs, and reflected that although locks had been unnecessary in Texas only a few years ago, now no property was safe.

Pestering Morrell in Washington were a number of idle men, lately volunteers in the Texas Army but presently unemployed, since President Sam Houston had furloughed most of the troops to head off a rumored plot to invade Mexico—and to save money. Volunteers from Texas returned to their homes, but many from the

United States were left stranded. Their clothes disintegrated to rags. Most of them had no money, only bounty claims and land certificates, which nobody but speculators seemed to want—and could buy for a token. With no work and no hope, they turned to any form of entertainment to pass the time, including attending a weekly evening prayer meeting that Morrell had organized in Washington. The preacher at first found no fault with their behavior at the service: they "were very polite and sang elegantly all the parts of music." But their conduct after the final song, "Old Hundredth," and the benediction was not so admirable. Morrell saw them: "the . . . billiard-saloon would be lighted up, and a large crowd—God have mercy on them!—would be assembled for the night. . . . There was King John Barleycorn within, double-refined, with all his machinery propelled by the engine of hell, fed with the fire of damnation, drawn directly from the 'bottomless pit' of eternal perdition."

Then through boredom or pure meanness their behavior at services grew worse. They organized a prayer meeting of their own, which they held in a tavern immediately after attending Morrell's service. They mimicked the first service "to the best of their ability," which was very good indeed. Names of the same men called on for prayer at the first service were again called at the second, and jokesters responded with prayers and exhortations. When Morrell heard about this his reaction varied from anger to mortification to grief, then to a frank observation: "Those are fearful days for any people when an army is disbanded among them, whether that army has been successful or unsuccessful."

A revival meeting conducted by visiting ministers gave them a chance for further mischief. The first night passed by peacefully, but the second night did not. The pranksters stationed a man with a chicken behind the building (an abandoned billiard parlor) and put another man on a long porch in front, where the remaining twenty or so idlers gathered to watch the fun.

It began with the singing. Because of a shortage of hymnals the leader lined out the songs. When he did this the man at the back of the building grasped the chicken by its neck, and when the congregation began singing he made the chicken squawk. At the same time, one of the men on the porch stuck his head through a window, shouted, "Glory to God," then quickly withdrew, while the rest of the idlers on the porch responded, "Amen and amen!"

Morrell, whose seat was near the infamous window, leaped into action after the first round of this. He grabbed his walking cane, a hard Tennessee stick made of hickory with a buckhorn head, and stood poised at the window waiting for the second round. The dismayed song leader announced the next words, the congregation sang, the chicken squawked, and the man stuck his head in the window. But this time Morrell whacked him with the cane and opened a gash over his eye. The service continued without further interruption, and at the end of it Morrell asked permission to speak. He addressed his remarks to the furloughed soldiers still on the porch: "Before me are sons from the battlefield of San Jacinto. . . . For what did you charge the enemy's cannon and burn the bridges behind him, unless it was for civil and religious liberty? . . . And yet, in less than two years, you have commenced to pull down what you have built up by so much toil and sacrifice." Morrell did not make Christians of the idlers—in leathery Texas he had not converted a single soul in nearly two years of effort— but the interruptions ceased, and though some of his friends feared for his life he was not harmed.

Morrell always said God was with him. Other people claimed he was just plain lucky. Whatever it was, Morrell escaped from many perilous situations during his days in the Republic of Texas— twice, at least, in 1838.

The first came after the reopening of the Texas Land Office over the veto of President Houston, who foresaw much litigation if land certificates were located before the country had been sectioned, and who warned of attacks by the Indians on newcomers trying to take possession of their territory. Immigrants swarmed in looking for land, and Morrell fell victim to the fever. He had given up merchandising—it had taken too much time away from preaching—and had determined to locate on western lands for new opportunity and for better climate to heal lungs again ailing. But the country that attracted him, west of the Brazos, was an Indian-filled wilderness. Only a few settlements had been built there, mostly along the Colorado River. In the extreme southwest, beyond Goliad, no settlement worthy of the name could be found on

Morrell's side of the Rio Grande. Even the Mexicans refused to venture into that wild region. But this was the country Morrell and several other men chose to explore.

At Columbus, on the Colorado River fifty miles south of Washington, he met three other land seekers and rode with them across green prairies dotted with deer to Victoria, then to Goliad. There Morrell preached a sermon to a handful of listeners in the old Catholic church. Beyond Goliad, Morrell and his companions followed a compass course to a prearranged meeting with a party of eight surveyors, across prairies where trees and water became scarcer by the mile. They watched a herd of antelope that kept them entertained for a while—and they saw signs of the recent presence of Indians. These became more numerous the farther west they traveled.

At San Patricio, an abandoned Irish settlement vacated during the 1836 campaign, they met the surveyors and rode with them to the site of present Corpus Christi—then not even a settlement but "a name simply given to a locality on our southwestern coast at the mouth of the Nueces River." They arrived at that lonely spot about sunset of a March day in 1838. There they camped, after seeing entirely too many signs of Indians in the vicinity. Despite the all-night vigil of a rotated guard, none of the twelve men slept very soundly—"the nearest assistance . . . was full ninety miles away."

Next morning the surveyors took weapons along with their equipment and established a beginning corner, on the bay, then worked inland, on ground now occupied by the city. Days passed without any trouble from the Indians, and the eight surveyors became less cautious. They camped at the end of a day wherever their work had taken them. But Morrell insisted on greater caution. Every night he and his three companions sought a secluded campsite several miles distant.

Morrell's indiscretion came later. One day he and a member of his party decided to look over the country farther still to the west, believing "no Indian . . . had a horse that could run as fast and as long as ours." They rode along a small creek for six or seven miles, then left it to cross a rough prairie. Their ride was leisurely until they were startled by a yell somewhere behind them.

Urging their horses forward, they rode to a rise, looked back, and saw, about a mile away, a dozen mounted Indians watching them from a location near the creek. The Mexican lances they carried glistened in the sunlight.

Morrell and his friend realized their exposed situation. Only the shelter of trees could possibly save them, but the nearest woods they could hope to reach lay four miles distant, and the Indians were almost a mile closer to that spot than they were. "They stood perfectly still, waiting to see what course we would take. Knowing that we were cut off from our company, and feeling confident that they could reach the timber first, they considered us a sure prize."

The Indians yelled again, and this time Morrell and his companion yelled back with bravado that was all bluff, reminding Morrell of the times when, as a youngster, he whistled in the dark to keep up his courage. "Every time they screamed the war-whoop we replied. My lungs were now apparently sound, and seeing what was before me, I straightened up in my stirrups and tried to feel that I was about twenty-one years old." Between yells, Morrell and his companion had been able to reach a decision: they felt sure their own horses could win a race to the woods, but if a few Indians did get there first they would try to shoot their way through.

The two men spurred their horses, and the race began. But Morrell and his friend held their animals back, saving them for a final spurt at the finish. Before the race was half over they could see that their estimate of the Indian horses had been correct. Only four posed a real threat. All were scattered across the prairie.

Faster toward the woods they raced: "We were rapidly approaching each other in the form of an inverted V." The two men barely won. They reached the timber some distance ahead of the first Indian, leaped from their horses, took cover behind trees, and aimed their weapons at the two leading braves. As they did this the Indians threw themselves over on the opposite side of their horses, leaving exposed only an arm and a leg, and galloped out of range. But Morrell and his friend had decided to hold their fire. Even if they had shot two Indians, the rest would have been upon them before they could have reloaded.

The Indians stayed out of range, not daring to challenge firearms with bows, arrows, and lances. Morrell taunted them in

Spanish for being dogs and cowards—"knowing that an Indian trembles in the presence of a resolute spirit." Then he thought of a better bluff: he mounted his horse and rode farther into the woods, shouting orders to a pretended company of men nearby. The ruse worked: the Indians fled, and Morrell and his companion returned to the surveying party.

After such a close escape Morrell considered giving up all claims to western lands and returning home, but further reflection kept him where he was: "Texans in that day had little respect for preachers who gave any signs of cowardice; and as I desired to return home in 'good report among them that are without,' that my ministry might not be hindered, I contented myself the best I could, and hurried on the surveyors as rapidly as possible."

Days passed without further trouble. The only Indians seen were occasional friendly visitors in camp—Lipans and Tonkawas. For Morrell the terror of the recent race for the woods faded. Abject boredom with camp life replaced it. Impatiently he waited for the surveyors to finish their work. He and his friend even began talking of another westward trip, one that would take them away for several days. The friendly Indians had spoken of a salt lake that lay toward the sunset. Morrell wanted to see it, even if it was in country occupied by Karankawas, a small, decimated tribe known for past cannibalism, and by fierce Comanches, "enemies to each other and enemies to everybody else." The Comanches inflicted brutalities on other Indians as well as on white men.

Morrell and his friend used a compass to set a course south of west across another sea of coastal grass. They saw wild horses by the hundreds and game of every description, but no Indians. On the first night, forty miles out, they camped near cool fresh water and good grass. Sleep came easily.

About noon the next day they saw wild cattle grazing in the distance and determined to kill one of them for meat. Using a stretch of woods for cover, they rode toward a particularly fine animal—then saw, beyond it, a lone Indian advancing on the same animal, with the same intention. The Indian saw the two men and quickly strung his bow, but the range was too far for the primitive weapon.

Morrell's friend raised his rifle to fire, but Morrell protested. "We were in no danger, could not plead self-defense, and in the

commission of a deliberate murder I feared the judgments of God."
Morrell called out in Spanish to the Indian, declared their friendship, and, to illustrate his words, covered the end of his rifle barrel
with his hat. The Indian and the two white men rode off on courses
almost parallel, and Morrell continued to express friendship. The
Indian, a young Karankawa, replied with an invitation to visit his
camp and his chief, but Morrell politely declined. He was not all
that friendly.

After the Indian had disappeared, Morrell and his companion
determined to return to camp without delay. They deliberately
avoided their outbound trail—this might lead them now to more
unwanted meetings—and traveled about fifteen miles out of their
way. At their camp the other two members of their party joined
them, and they left to find the surveyors, about four miles away.
When they sighted the surveyors' camp they saw that it was surrounded by a party of Indians—about forty.

Morrell felt certain these were Karankawas. He halted his little
group, called to the Indians, displayed his firearms, and discovered
that they were indeed Karankawas—the lone Indian whose life he
had spared was with them and recognized him. When the chief had
been convinced that Morrell was the man who had been responsible for the generosity, he called off his braves and made a treaty.
"You are friends," the chief said.

A week or so later, after Morrell had returned home to Washington-on-the-Brazos, he mused over these happenings. "The course
that many of the . . . settlers of this country pursued, killing
every lone Indian that was cut off from his company, was a great
outrage." Besides that, it brought murderous Indian retaliation.
Morrell thought over what might have happened and concluded, "I
thank God yet that my motto ever was, even among Indians, not to
kill except in self-defense."

22. SETTLING DOWN

Spring of 1838 gave way to summer. Prairie grass that the early
rains had brought forth yellowed and wilted under a piercing Texas
sun, until refreshed by a shower, then, a day or so later, wilted

again. But Sam and Mary Maverick chose the sticky month of June to leave George Sutherland's place on the Navidad River for their new home in San Antonio.

Sam Maverick had looked elsewhere before deciding to return to the town that had attracted him three years earlier. No settlements existed between San Antonio and the Rio Grande, and the town was open to surprise assault by a Mexican force. Texans never knew when another invasion might come: rumors of impending attack seemed to be constant. So Maverick had visited Matagorda Bay—he owned land at Cox's Point there—but the mosquitoes had swarmed so thickly over him he knew the location would never do. He decided on San Antonio, then took passage to New Orleans to buy furniture and provisions for the new home.

In June he returned to Sutherland's to pick up his family and the servants. Again they rumbled westward in carriage and wagon —ten miles to Texana, three miles to Dry Branch, twelve to Hatch's, three more to De Leon's rancho on the Garcitas. On to Victoria, built in the shade of giant trees on the banks of the Guadalupe River. Slow traveling, and bumpy—the jostling broke a wagon wheel—but Mary Maverick was enthralled by the new country, although her husband and some of the Negroes suffered every other day from chills. At Goliad she lost herself in reflection over the massacre of Fannin's men, which had occurred almost on the very ground she occupied, but she mistakenly attributed the murders to Colonel "Garrie" (Garay), who, she heard, ordered the massacre when General Urrea refused to do so. "Infamous name be it forever." History harbors its mistakes.

A turn northward now up the wooded San Antonio River: nine creaking miles to Arroyo Cabeza, eighteen more to Ojo de Agua. The June days passed away—faster, it seemed, than the Maverick entourage traveled. Seventeen miles more, and the wagon broke down again. Sam Maverick looked along the river for wood to repair it and happened upon a man who was, of all things, a wheelwright. Maverick accepted an invitation to take the broken wheel to the man's house and to bring his family in the carriage. Two of the Negroes accompanied them. The others put up a tent and stayed with the wagon.

Three days later Maverick and the rest returned with the repaired wheel and put it on. They had the wagon ready for reloading when several mounted Indians suddenly appeared, declaring, *"Mucho amigo."* Mary Maverick studied them with a combination of loathing and fright: they were loud and filthy, but they seemed determined to establish intimacy. They were joined by other Indians, who appeared a few at a time until Mary Maverick counted a total of seventeen—all of them riding around and into the camp, paying particular attention to the horses. They kept repeating, *"Mucho amigo."*

Mary heard that they were Tonkawas. She was not persuaded by their friendly declarations. If they were friends their appearance belied the fact: they were well armed, wore war paint, and displayed trophies of a recent battle with Comanches—two scalps, a hand, and several pieces of putrid flesh. Mary Maverick heard that these morsels would be taken home for the squaws to dance around, then devour. "I was frightened almost to death, but tried not to show it. They rode up to the carriage window and asked to see the papoose. First one and then another came and I held my little Sam up and smiled at their compliments. I took care to have my pistol and Bowie knife visible and kept cool and refused to hand the baby out to them to see how pretty and white he was."

All the time Sam Maverick and the others—who were also armed—continued loading the wagon, saddling horses, and preparing to move on. Darkness had fallen before they were ready to leave, and when they departed every one of the seventeen Indians followed. Maverick instructed two of his mounted Negroes to act as a rear guard, and they traveled on under a bright moon—uncertain of ever seeing another sunrise, trying to ignore the Indians near them, but always aware of their presence.

About midnight some of the Indians turned back, apparently discouraged by the armed watchfulness or the obvious lack of welcome. After that others disappeared, one by one, until by sunrise only two remained. By that time everyone in the party was exhausted, and Maverick called a halt. His Negroes erected tents, but still the two Indians stayed: "They sat down in an observant attitude."

When Mary Maverick took her baby into her tent one of the Negroes, Griffin, told her, "Don't be afraid, Miss Mary, but go to sleep." Then he grasped an ax, sat down in front of her tent, shook a fist at the two Indians, and said, "Come this way if you dare, you devils, and I'll make hash of you."

Three days later Sam and Mary Maverick arrived at San Antonio, where much history remained to be made. In September they rented the Huisar house—just north of Veramendi's, where Sam Maverick had caught Ben Milam as he fell during the siege and capture of the town three years earlier.

VI

HOPES RISING AND
FALLING

1839

"How bright the horizon before you," President Mirabeau B. Lamar told the Texas Congress in his first message in December, 1838. Assumption of power inspired him and made him even more optimistic than usual. For the moment Lamar was able to overlook the condition of Texas: it was worse than ever. Sam Houston, who by law could not succeed himself, had held the fragile Republic together, a remarkable feat in itself, but his other achievements were few, and concerned with relations with the United States: recognition, agreement on the Sabine River instead of the more limiting Neches for the eastern boundary of Texas, and negotiation of a few damage claims. The Texas debt was greater than ever, Houston's popularity lower. Prices were high, the value of Texas money more depressed. Eighteen thirty-nine proved to be an up-and-down year in many ways, one of several such periods in Republic of Texas history.

Lamar saw more of the up than the down, which may have been fortunate for his mental well-being, but it was unfortunate for Texas. Lamar's first appropriation for civil purposes totaled $550,000, against Houston's last one of $192,000; for military purposes, $1,523,445, against Houston's $881,000. Lamar tried to arrange loans to finance his government, but he too failed. Then he spent money anyway, using Sam Houston's unfortunate standby, paper-money issues.

The United States also had its share of troubles, a fact that compounded Texas' problems. Andrew Jackson had left his country another legacy besides the common man and the new President, Van Buren. A depression had stemmed from the Panic of 1837, which had resulted in part from Jackson's inflationary depositing of federal funds in state banks to kill the national bank he opposed, then—to check the inflation—his order to accept only gold or silver in payment for government lands. This stifled the American economy, gave Whigs hope for the next election, and sent more land-seeking immigrants to Texas, where conditions proved to be even worse.

The United States also was beset by increasing violence over the slavery issue, and not all Northern residents were abolitionists. Four years earlier William Lloyd Garrison, who preached "All men are created equal," had been rescued from an angry Boston mob, and two years earlier the antislavery journalist Elijah Lovejoy had been killed by rioters in Alton, Illinois. Texas had no monopoly on turmoil.

On the other hand, brightening any Texan's horizon at this time was an accidental relationship with France, which had gone to war against Mexico over some brutalities and uncompensated damages concerning French nationals in that country. France forced Mexico to pay, and in the process developed a friendship with Texas because of the mutual enemy. This led to recognition and a trade treaty in the autumn of 1839.

But even the French episode had its gloomy side. In some fighting at Veracruz, Texas' old enemy Santa Anna pompously defended his country, losing a leg in the action but winning back popularity and power. Then, realizing the precarious financial and political situation of his country, he let Anastasio Bustamente fill the risky office of president while Santa Anna himself continued to run it unseen. But in time he would show his old face again.

23. A CHANGE FOR TEXAS

Z. N. Morrell, who, like most other Texans, had alternated between optimism and pessimism, saw the year 1838 go out and 1839 come in with a feeling of insecurity. Texas had made scant progress. Crops had been poor. Money was scarce. Only poverty seemed plentiful.

Sickness afflicted low areas like Houston, which was just recovering from one of the yellow-fever epidemics that periodically swept sections of Texas. "There are a fearful number of new graves," a Houston resident said during the fall of 1838. "This was the sixth today. This is an awful disease and does not seem to be understood by the physicians. It is not the usual yellow fever."

One of Morrell's own reasons for dejection was not shared by every citizen: "In the fall gloom hung heavily all over the land. The government was unsettled. Sam Houston's term of office, as president of the Republic, expired on the second Monday in December, 1838 . . . He who had so long been as it were the very soul of Texas was about to retire, and there was a general feeling of anxiety as to the result of another administration."

But many people were glad to see Sam Houston go. One man wrote to a friend about a recent occurrence: "I regret you should have accompanied the president! By no common courtesy—he is not entitled at your hands—he will *use* but not serve! I know him thoroughly—and do not speak from *feeling*—for really—personally he has treated me with great courtesy—and I have always done him that justice." Others expressed outrage over his drinking. Most of Houston's enemies ignored the possibility that some things they found offensive about him might have kept the fragile Republic from disintegrating. Nevertheless, if Houston had been a god-like creature, as one man observed, there would have been no Mirabeau Buonaparte Lamar.

Lamar, a native of Georgia, was Houston's successor as President. He possessed a temperament more suitable to a poet (which he was in fact) than to a president of a frontier republic. He had not been a good student because, some people said, he was timid and lacked confidence, but it may have been because of a lack of motivation. He could push himself to excel in some efforts, as in the role of Brutus in a school production of *Julius Caesar*. As an adult he was a quiet, somewhat diffident man until a topic close to his heart brought out his spirit and occasionally his wrath. In his young-adult days the practice of law had not interested him; neither had the operation of a general store, where the dull talk of customers bored him. He never seemed to like doing what he had to do. Politics proved more attractive. He had been introduced to the work as the confidential clerk of Georgia Governor George M. Troup. He also found the editorship of a newspaper challenging. But all these possibilities vanished for him in Georgia when his wife died, leaving him a daughter and profound grief. When his own health began to fail he left his daughter with relatives and departed, in 1835, for a new life in Texas. He threw himself into the fight for independence and distinguished himself at San Jacinto. Fame made his name well known in Texas, but not the correct pronunciation of it. Texans called him "My-ree-bo" or "Mee-ry-bo" Lamar.·

As vice-president under Houston he had liked the President less and less, but as he saw Houston's first-term popularity waning he had said nothing publicly. He chose to wait and take advantage of the situation at an appropriate time. He believed his destiny lay in leading the Republic of Texas to greatness as its president. In that task he could put his creative powers to practical use—and he would do just about everything differently from Houston.

Toward the end of Houston's term, with public credit low, money depreciating, and enemies like David Burnet calling Houston "Big Drunk" and a "half Indian," support for Lamar as President had grown. Houston saw it and resented it—the poet was not his kind of man—but his forces split over a candidate. They finally selected a man named James Collinsworth, but he committed suicide before the election, as did another nominee, Peter Grayson. Lamar had been opposed only by an unknown, self-nominated candidate, Bob Wilson, whom he swamped by a margin of better than twenty-five to one. Elected vice-president was David G. Burnet—"Davy G.," as Houston venomously referred to him.

A less likely-looking President for Texas could scarcely have been imagined. Besides being a poet, Lamar was an otherwise unusual leader for the Republic of Texas. A man who boarded with Lamar in Brazoria described him as having a dark Gallic look, accentuated by long black hair inclined to curl, and large, round, blue-gray eyes. Nor did his dress fit the Texas pattern. He wore his clothes loose, even baggy, with deeply pleated trousers—the "only person I ever saw in Texas in that style of dress," said the fellow boarder. Others were more impressed by Lamar's courtly manners and by the diffidence that lingered into manhood and left him markedly reserved, although he could be warm and witty when in the company of just a few confidants.

Once, while visiting in the home of a friend, Samuel W. Goode, in Montgomery, Alabama, Lamar gave an indication of this ability. Goode's daughter Emily asked Lamar to write in her album. When he picked up a pen to write he noticed that the last entry had been written by John Howard Payne, the minstrel author of "Home, Sweet Home," who had composed this verse:

> Lady, your name, if understood,
> > Explains your nature to a letter;
> And may you never change from *Goode,*
> > Unless, if possible, to *better*.
>
> > > > J. H. PAYNE

Lamar wrote underneath:

> I am content with being *Goode,*
> > To aim at *better* might be vain;
> But if I do, it's understood,
> > Whate'er the cause it is not *Payne.*
>
> > > > MIRABEAU B. LAMAR

Lamar's circle of friends certainly did not include Sam Houston. Houston knew it, and did not mind at all. As the day approached for Lamar's inauguration Houston began planning a trick. Some officials of the protocol-ignorant republic wondered whether an outgoing President should have any place on the platform, and others wondered whether Houston would condescend to appear at the event anyway. But Houston answered both questions without consulting anybody. At the ceremony, held on the porch of the modest frame capitol building in Houston, the outgoing President appeared dressed in a manner reminiscent of George Washington, with powdered wig and Colonial attire. He towered over Lamar and Burnet, and he took possession of the platform. For nearly three hours he delivered a farewell address. By the time he had finished, the sensitive Lamar was so distraught that he did not deliver his own address. He asked his private secretary to read it, and the man did—in a dreary monotone that clearly gave Sam Houston another triumph.

But Lamar had great plans for Texas. He would oppose annexation to the United States, would keep Texas independent and build it into a republic the whole world could look to some day as a model. Some of Lamar's visions were progressive beyond his time in Texas. One was his stand on education: "A *cultivated mind is the guardian* genius of Democracy, *and while guided and controlled by virtue, the noblest attribute of man. It is the only dictator that freemen acknowledge, and the only security which freemen desire.*" He urged the establishment of a school system, including a university, which finally came into being more than forty years after he had proposed it.

Other ideas were more practical than poetic. Lamar urged strengthening the Army and the Navy and erecting military posts for defense—or offense, as it developed—against the Indians and the Mexicans. "As long as we continue to exhibit our mercy without shewing our strength," he said in opposition to Sam Houston's policy, "so long will the Indian continue to bloody the edge of the tomahawk and move onward in the work of rapacity and slaughter." He declared that the poorest citizen "whose sequestered cabin is reared on our remotest frontier, holds as sacred a claim upon the government for safety and security as does the man who lives in ease and wealth in the heart of our most populous city."

Lamar's destiny, as he saw it, would be to lay out an empire stretching from the Gulf of Mexico to the Pacific and rivaling the United States in population, wealth, and power. This would mean taking more land from Mexico, but Lamar guessed it might be easy enough. He calculated that the people in New Mexico, for instance, would be glad to transfer themselves to Texas jurisdiction in due time.

None of Lamar's optimism lifted the veil of gloom from Z. M. Morrell, who had moved recently to La Grange, a wooded town on the Colorado River. "Long as memory holds her seat will the early settlers of Texas remember the events of 1839. Harassed by war on every hand, the unsettled state of society made our circumstances almost beyond endurance. Our currency was almost worthless, and the Republic without credit abroad." To make matters worse, the Indians grew more hostile and troublesome—especially the Cherokees, because the Texas Congress had refused to approve Sam Houston's treaty of early 1836 assuring them the lands they had settled on.

Texans talked worriedly of a plot between the Cherokees and the Mexican government. Several months earlier a rebellious Nacogdoches resident, Vicente Córdova, had led a group of Cherokee and Mexican followers in publicly disclaiming allegiance to the Republic. His forces had been routed from their sanctuary in the East Texas woods by hurriedly assembled militiamen, but Córdova was not captured. His continued presence in Texas filled some people with foreboding. Despite all the troubles, President Lamar ordered from New Orleans for his personal use a splendid carriage adorned with seal and flag, to be drawn by four horses, at a cost of $2,300.

24. RUNNING FIGHTS

The signal smokes Z. N. Morrell and his son saw from the vicinity of the Guadalupe River on a late-March afternoon in 1839 meant to Morrell one thing for sure: more danger.

For a preacher, Morrell could get himself involved in some exciting worldly affairs, and here was another instance. Morrell and his son had traveled across the prairies from La Grange to San Antonio to find a better market for some land he was forced to sell to meet expenses. At San Antonio they had stayed two days, and Morrell had devoted part of that time to visiting the site in front of the Alamo church where his friend David Crockett had fought and probably died. Now Morrell and his son were returning home, but once more prospects looked discouraging.

Morrell watched the smokes and wondered about the best course to take. "An occasional volume of smoke on the east and west of the river gave the clearest evidence that the Comanches, in detached companies, were travelling in a southeasterly direction across the country." Morrell and his son would have to cross this route, but Morrell guessed the Indians would have passed before he and his son arrived.

Nevertheless, they kept a sharp watch for stragglers. Once they came upon a pool where some Indians had watered their horses. The pool was still muddy, but the landscape was silent. They rode on cautiously, and Morrell thought to himself that they had escaped trouble at least for the moment. They crossed the Guadalupe and encountered two other white men traveling in the same direction. Together they planned to make an all-night ride to Gonzales, to avoid any more Indians, but weariness began to gnaw their bones.

In early darkness they stopped to make coffee. They started a fire, boiled the coffee, and poured steaming cupfuls. They were relaxing and enjoying their drink when they heard a gunshot to eastward, perhaps a mile away: probably a citizen of the nearby settlement of Seguin, out hunting. But then they heard more shots—two, three, half a dozen, then "platoons," and the noise became louder. Quickly they loaded campware, mounted horses, and rode toward a nearby hill for a look.

Darkness restricted vision, but they could make out groups of horsemen engaged in a running fight—right over their campfire. They watched until the ghostly riders had galloped out of sight and the firing had ceased; then they rode through the darkness toward Gonzales as fast as they could. On the way, the day's excitement and fatigue finally overtook them, and they halted on a flat mesquite prairie near the protection of some trees. Three men would sleep while the fourth, alternated every hour, would keep watch. They staked their horses, then examined weapons and placed them nearby within easy reach. A bright moon shone down on the countryside for the lonely man on watch.

Not even an hour had passed when the soft hoot of an owl alarmed the lookout. The man woke Morrell, who in turn quietly roused the others. They all lay still, peering toward their staked horses. In the moonlight they saw three mounted Indians riding toward Morrell's horse—the one on which he had outrun other

Indians to the safety of timber the year before. "Determined to sacrifice life before they should have him," Morrell waited until the Indians were within thirty feet of the animal. Then he sprang up, raised his weapon as if to fire, and loosed a terrifying Comanche yell worthy of a Baptist preacher who specialized in shouting down things like hellfire as well as mere Indians. The curdled Comanches turned and fled, and the two white men with Morrell took aim at the retreating figures. Morrell stopped them from firing, admonishing both about killing except in self-defense. But Morrell agreed with them that "this was not a good place to rest." The three men and a boy mounted their horses and rode on toward Gonzales.

There Morrell learned the details of the running fight that had snuffed out his campfire. Texas volunteers led by Edward Burleson were pursuing sixty or so Mexicans, Indians, and Negroes led by Vicente Córdova—the same man who had caused trouble among the Cherokees in East Texas. One of Córdova's followers had deserted and informed Burleson that the man was riding from East Texas southwestward to Mexico to bring back arms and ammunition for an Indian uprising against Texas. Burleson had collected sixty or so men around Austin and had hurried off after Córdova. He overtook him near the site of Morrell's camp, killed a score of Córdova's men, and wounded Córdova himself.

But Córdova escaped again, and with other survivors of the fight fled to Mexico. Morrell and all other Texans learned about two months later what happened after that.

From Matamoros the Mexicans sent an agent, Manuel Flores, to Texas with a shipment of ammunition for an Indian uprising— three hundred pounds of powder, three hundred pounds of shot and lead bars, and other supplies, all carried on one hundred mules and horses, and guarded by about thirty armed men. Flores had orders to inflame the Indians against Texas, but to avoid involvement with the United States. The Indians were expected to harass settlers constantly—"to burn their habitations, to lay waste their fields." After that preliminary work the Mexican Army would come to retake Texas.

Flores' departure from Matamoros and his specific instructions were unknown at the time to Texas officials, although the deserter had given enough warning so that patrols watched for Córdova's return. One such patrol, a company of Rangers led by a Captain Mike Andrews and a Lieutenant James Rice, operated out of Hornsby Bend, a settlement on the Colorado River nine miles east of present Austin. About the middle of May twenty-one of the Rangers, reinforced by six civilian volunteers, left on a reconnoitering expedition that took them south to Onion Creek, near its juncture with the Colorado River. There Captain Andrews ordered a halt for camp. About dusk Lieutenant Rice and one other man rode off to hunt game—the company was traveling without provisions—but when they reached the crest of a hill south of the camp they saw a sight that made them forget about the prospect of venison roasting over a fire. Far away, stretched out in a long line, they noticed perhaps a hundred horses headed northward, in their very direction. Dusk made it impossible to tell whether all the horses had riders, but some certainly seemed to. On the backs of a few white horses they could make out dark splotches—probably Córdova and his men coming back to give the Indians ammunition for razing Texas. Lieutenant Rice and his companion galloped back to camp with the news.

The Rangers broke camp indecisively. Two dozen men challenging maybe a hundred or more seemed too risky. But Captain Andrews fell in behind the mysterious caravan and began following it, while his men debated the likely strength of the force. After a while Andrews halted his men again to make camp. They left their horses saddled and slept—supperless—with weapons in easy reach. The trail would be easy enough to pick up tomorrow.

At daylight, without breakfast, they resumed their march. After a few miles the trail wound into woods and, at one point, under a "stooping tree"—too low for a man on horseback to ride under. Hoofprints told them that all but twenty-five or thirty of the horses had passed directly under the tree. Some men still were not convinced that the force might not be so large as they had feared, but they went on anyway, and soon saw that the caravan ahead had entered a dense thicket of post oak and cedar.

The Rangers were about to plunge into it when they heard the others coming out. Captain Andrews hesitated, uncertain what to do. From inside the thicket the strangers perceived his indecision and sent out a tirade of curses and taunts—all in Spanish, providing Andrews with some satisfaction: at least he knew now, beyond doubt, who these people were. But he still remained uncertain about their strength, and when one of the civilians told him, "Captain Andrews, if you take your men into that thicket it will be equivalent to leading them into a slaughtering pen," Andrews was persuaded to order a retreat.

So the Rangers headed home. But some of them became indignant about the weak showing, and after an hour or so one man asked Andrews to permit volunteers to go back after the enemy. Andrews, a shamed man now, thought that over, then consented, swore, and declared, "Yes, and I'll go back, too." All but six men (not all of the six were the civilians) rode back to the thicket, but when they arrived they found that the Mexicans had gone on northward.

The Rangers followed all day without overtaking them. By nightfall Captain Andrews' horse was so worn that he determined to return home the next morning. Two other men with exhausted mounts planned to accompany him—leaving seventeen men and Lieutenant Rice to complete the job. Republic of Texas history was forever being made by small numbers.

At daylight Rice and his men were up and about, without breakfast. Two scouts went ahead to pick out the trail. The others followed, slowly at first, across hard ground where the trail was almost lost, then faster, in a gallop, as the signs became clearer. At the South San Gabriel River they saw where the Mexicans had nooned not long before. Four fires still burned—only four fires, the Rangers saw with relief.

After another mile of riding, the two scouts ahead signaled the main body to slow down. Rice rode on to investigate and learned that the enemy had just ridden over the crest of a hill ahead. Rice ordered the men to proceed at a gallop, and soon they saw the caravan they had been following for two days and nights. After a series of skirmishes Rice put his enemy where he wanted him: on a steep bluff overlooking the North San Gabriel River—about six miles west of present Georgetown. In desperation the Mexican leader and eight or ten men turned on the Rangers and attacked, attempting to give the others time to find a crossing, and the

Rangers melted in confusion, but not for long. When the attackers wheeled and raced back to where they had come from, a Texan shot the man who had been commanding them. The man rolled off his horse and onto the ground, while his comrades sped toward the river. They found a crossing and fled into hills farther north. But they left behind the supplies and the animals, and Rice's Rangers found the powder, shot, and lead bars, and a quantity of silver.

Happily they counted the mules and horses—about one hundred in all. They examined the body of the dead Mexican leader, found it to be the agent Manuel Flores, and later discovered in his baggage official documents detailing the plot against Texas. The Mexican government had indeed agreed to support it, and these supplies suggested grimly what might have happened, except for the historic work on May 17, 1839, of a Ranger lieutenant and his handful of men.

But the gleeful Rangers had plunder, not posterity, in mind as they withdrew with their loot. Their scant numbers no longer seemed unfortunate. Shouting, joking, laughing, even able to forget their hunger for a while, they began the trip home. A few wore captured sombreros, and this almost proved fatal to them. After riding only a few miles they met a force of about thirty Rangers hurrying up as reinforcements, and nearly drew their fire because of the hats.

The two groups exchanged greetings, and Rice described the recent fight. The newcomers listened, then some of them suggested that they all share the spoils. At first Rice's men considered this request a joke, and when they realized it was not meant that way they replied that they had fought the Mexicans to get this booty and they were willing to fight thirty Rangers if necessary to keep it.

The threat won them privacy, but it also left them hungry. The reinforcing Rangers backed off sulkily and refused to share any food with Rice's starved men, who had not eaten for three days now. Furthermore, they refused to provide a camp guard so that the tired Rangers could get a night's sleep. Rice detailed his own men to stand watches over the camp and all the pillage, and the next day he led them back to Hornsby Bend, where they divided the spoils among their small number.

25. AGENT FOR PEACE

President Lamar continued to dream of a peaceful, prosperous, progressive Republic of Texas with independence acknowledged by all nations—especially by Mexico, whose recognition would be the most meaningful. If Mexico said Texas was free, no nation in the world could withhold recognition by contending that the new Republic could not stand on its own feet.

Early in his term—about the same time the specter of Vicente Córdova was haunting Texans—Lamar proposed doing something about Mexican recognition, and not so dreamily, either. He had some sound reasons for anticipating success. The war with France had weakened Mexico; a rising tide of federalism, even revolution in some sections, was threatening the established Mexican centralists; and Santa Anna had regained power and influence. Perhaps the General could be persuaded to remember the promise he had made in the Velasco treaties. But a great deal of wishfulness colored Lamar's thinking, as it always did.

Part of Lamar's dream in regard to recognition involved Barnard E. Bee, a South Carolinian whose sense of propriety was indicated by his utter disgust with the drinking habits of Sam Houston. Bee had come to Texas at the age of forty-nine, leaving behind him a clash over nullification (as had Sam Maverick). He had been attracted to the new country by what he considered a fight for freedom and by the chance to find an important niche.

After his arrival Bee had served in the Texas Army, then as secretary of treasury and state in the Burnet ad-interim government, as secretary of war under President Houston, and finally as secretary of state under President Lamar. But it was a mission to Mexico that gave him the inclusion in Lamar's dream.

Lamar chose Bee for the job of securing Mexican recognition because he had been one of the men who had accompanied General Santa Anna to Washington and the meeting with Andrew Jackson. This experience would bring Bee a more favorable reception in

Mexico, Lamar calculated, because Bee and Santa Anna had
become amiable companions.

Had Bee been less driven by public-mindedness and by that
sense of his own destiny in Texas he no doubt would have been
happier to stay at home in Velasco within the surf sounds of the
Gulf of Mexico. There, in a comfortably furnished residence, he
enjoyed the constant sea breeze that his Venetian blinds admitted
while they kept out glare. Nearby, the beach was "too inviting to
be neglected," and he enjoyed taking his wife for buggy rides on
the firmly packed sand at water's edge. The activity and the air
perked her up (her already fragile health had been impaired
further by the loss of a child), and the beach proved invigorating
also to Bee, who occasionally ailed in various middle-aged ways.
But the assignment to Mexico drew him away. He had resolved to
make Texas his home, and the prospect of being the medium for
procuring stable peace for his adopted country was compelling.
Bee, like Lamar, dreamed of a great future, one in which he would
of course figure prominently. He saw himself as vice-president of
the Republic—as he wrote friends—and probably as President.
The Mexican trip could help him tremendously.

So he read with favor a long letter from Secretary of State James
Webb appointing him minister plenipotentiary to Mexico to draw
up a peace treaty with that country. Webb's letter, written from
Houston February 20, 1839, cautioned Bee that he probably would
not be received as a minister plenipotentiary, since that in itself
would be an acknowledgment by Mexico of the existence of a
Texas Republic. But if he was not thus received, Webb added, Bee
should present himself as an agent of Texas. Webb sent separate
credentials for this contingency. While Bee worked in Mexico,
Texas representatives in Washington would urge United States
officials and the British consul to persuade their governments to
exert pressure on Mexico in Bee's favor.

There the practicality ended. The Secretary told Bee to require
unconditional recognition of Texas in any treaty drawn up, and to
insist on national boundaries as decided by the Texas Congress—in
other words, the Rio Grande. It would be permissible, Webb said,
to word the treaty so that a boundary could be decided later, and if
necessary Texas would pay five million dollars over a five-year

period to clear its claim to all land east of the Rio Grande. But much preferable, Webb reiterated, would be the immediate settlement of the boundary question.

Webb then mentioned that since Bee's old traveling companion Santa Anna had again taken the reins of Mexican government, this would be a particularly appropriate time for the trip. The Secretary reviewed with a great deal of naïveté the promises that Santa Anna had made at Velasco in 1836: never again to take up arms against Texas, and upon his return to Mexico to persuade the government to negotiate peace and formal recognition. As for the Texans' own abrogation of a section of the Velasco treaties, the agreement to send Santa Anna at once to Veracruz—which had been broken through the efforts of the men who had forced Santa Anna's removal from the *Invincible*—Bee was to point out to Santa Anna that the reasons for nonfulfillment were well known to him and involved no lack of faith on the part of the Texas government.

Webb concluded his letter with a list of seven reasons that Bee might use in persuading Mexico why she should make peace with Texas and grant recognition rather than pursue a militant course. The reasons were these: dissimilarity between the two cultures, incompatibility of political ideas, conflicts that would result from this incompatibility, worthlessness of Texas to Mexico because of its remoteness and because of its proximity to the United States, difficulty for Mexico in keeping the Indians in check at so great a distance, benefits accruing to both countries from friendly trade and travel, and the disposition exhibited by Texas since the Battle of San Jacinto to rely on friendly negotiations for settlement of differences rather than on war.

The cardinal points of the mission, Webb reemphasized, were restoration of peace, acknowledgment of independence, and recognition of the boundaries as defined by the Texas Congress. "All beyond this is left to your own judgment," he said.

This was a large task even for a former traveling companion of General Santa Anna, but Bee felt confident. "I mean to be received and to be successful," he wrote Webb.

Getting to the Mexican port of Veracruz, where Webb suggested he go, was not simple. With Texas and Mexico technically at war, no direct transportation between the two countries existed. Bee took passage out of Galveston on the steamship *Zavala* for New Orleans. On the day he sailed he observed that the new Texas port was booming: where three years earlier the attorney William Fairfax Gray had walked along empty beaches of a desolate island collecting shells, now all was bustle. A hundred or more buildings were being constructed, including a cotton compress; the busy harbor was crowded with fifteen or twenty vessels loading and unloading; and immigrants were swarming in, some to settle in Galveston, others to go on inland.

Bee arrived in New Orleans March 28, but not until May 2 did he find a vessel—the American steamer *Woodbury*—bound for Veracruz. Six days later he reached the place and immediately addressed a letter to the commandant general, Guadalupe Victoria, asking permission to see the Secretary of State in the city of Mexico with the intention of being presented to Santa Anna. Until he received an invitation ashore he would stay aboard the ship.

Bee's welcome was not warm. The editor of the Veracruz newspaper *El Censor* heard about his arrival and wrote:

> We do not know which most to admire, the audacity of those brigands in sending us their peddler to ask us to allow the peaceable possession of their robbery, or the answer the [Veracruz] commandant general gave to the individual who apprized him of the arrival of this quixotic ambassador. From the tenor of the reply, it appears that, if he lands, he will be accommodated with lodgings at the prison. Nevertheless, the supreme government will designate what ought definitely to be done. The commandant says he is not aware of the existence of a nation called the "republic of Texas," but only a horde of adventurers, in rebellion against the laws of the government of the republic.

The situation became discouraging even for an optimist like Bee. Not only did the shore look unpromising; after a few days he was on the verge of losing his quarters afloat. The *Woodbury* was preparing for departure, but Bee still had not been invited ashore. He began looking for another ship and wangled an invitation from the admiral of the French fleet, which had stayed at Veracruz following the recent war. Bee was transferring his baggage from the

Woodbury to the admiral's barge when he saw a Mexican boat approach and heard a hail. The boatman carried a letter for "Don Barnard"—an invitation to come ashore, signed by General Victoria. Bee scampered back aboard the *Woodbury* and wrote a quick but very polite answer, saying that he would pay his respects on the following day. Then he completed his move to the French ship.

When Bee called on General Victoria he found him to be a cordial man. The General said he was awaiting instructions from the capital on how to handle Bee's visit. Bee also met a man who introduced himself as a secret agent of the Mexican government detailed to make a preliminary contact with him to learn the nature of his instructions, "in order that if they prove satisfactory the cue might be given to the Mexican Congress." Bee answered that he had already communicated with the Secretary of State in Mexico City and would reserve this information for his ear.

Bee felt encouraged. "The fact is important: it proves they are disposed to listen," he wrote James Webb back in Houston. "They tell me here with money I can do everything—without it nothing." That should have been enough of a hint, naïve though Bee was in international intrigue. The thing Texas had least of was money.

A few days later General Victoria informed Bee that he had received instructions to keep him in Veracruz pending consultations in Mexico City. About that same time Bee wrote back to Texas: "The secret agent has been communicative—seems he desired to ascertain the boundary and what we were willing to pay . . . The Colorado [River], it seems, is what they supposed we would be satisfied with." In Washington, the Texan minister was writing Bee about this same time suggesting that another matter might be settled along with independence: the purchase of land all the way to the Pacific, "including California." President Lamar's enthusiasm seemed to be contagious.

For another week Bee waited aboard the French ship in Veracruz. Other communications passed between General Victoria and the capital, but none of them invited Bee to come on to Mexico City. Finally Victoria told him he might as well go home rather than wait any longer "if independence was [the] object."

Still, the General remained cordial, and on May 24 he talked with Bee for an hour. He repeated the government's decision: independence was out of the question, because if Texas were given freedom other Mexican states would demand it, too. The best course for Texas would be to request reunification, Victoria said, and she would be received gladly, like the prodigal son. The past would be forgotten.

When Bee pointed out the impossibility of this because of the cultural differences, the General assumed a sterner attitude. With the French question settled and the federalist uprising crushed, Victoria said, Mexico could devote its attention to reconquering Texas. A nation of eight million or more people would have little trouble annihilating forty or fifty thousand in Texas.

Bee refused to be bested. The conquest of Texas would offer no inducement to most Mexicans, he answered, and to induce soldiers to fight in such a remote country Mexico would have to take them there in chains. Once there they would be defeated, because Texas could count on more volunteers from the United States and other nations.

"We didn't convince each other," Bee wrote James Webb, and ended his talks. He never proposed an armistice, not even informally. He observed the Mexican elation over the conclusion of the trouble with France and the departure of their forces, and over the quelling of some federalists, and he refrained from mentioning peace, believing the Mexicans would attribute it to apprehension on the part of Texas. A chance for agreement with Mexico possibly remained, Bee said, but "the way would have to be paved with gold."

"I ought not to have come here . . . I leave by the first opportunity," he wrote Webb, and he left on May 28 for Havana aboard the French steam frigate *Phaéton*. From Havana he sailed to New Orleans, then after some delay proceeded by ship to his home in South Carolina, where his family had already gone. Travel was slow, almost as slow as negotiating with Mexico, and it was not until September that Bee could write back to Texas from Pendleton, where he had joined his family, "Oh how preferable to the politics and sickenings of public life."

26. MOVING TO MILITANTNESS

In Texas the policies of President Lamar took a more militant turn. Unlike his predecessor Sam Houston, Lamar proved willing to fight both Mexicans and Indians without much provocation—and sometimes with none at all. Now he focused on the Indians, whom he regarded as an immediate threat, considering the letters that had been found in the captured baggage belonging to the late Manuel Flores. These letters did not prove that the Indians already were involved in the plot—only that Mexico hoped they would be—but this did not deter Lamar. At first he tried to remove them peaceably—particularly the East Texas Cherokees, whom he considered most dangerous.

The preacher Z. N. Morrell could have advised Lamar against doing what he did. Never kill an Indian except in self-defense, Morrell would have said, and he probably would have avoided what ensued.

For about seventeen years the Cherokees had occupied choice land just north of Nacogdoches. They had arrived before any Anglo-American settlers. "Being an agricultural people," Morrell observed, "they had previously given no trouble." The Cherokees considered white men who began settling around Nacogdoches as the intruders. To keep the tribe peaceful during those precarious days before San Jacinto, Sam Houston had of course promised them their land. Now Lamar was insisting that these Indians move—the same as the United States had treated the Cherokees earlier—and when his commissioners failed to get an agreement for this the President ordered troops to force the Cherokees out. In two engagements on July 15 and 16, 1839, about five hundred Texas troops attacked the Indians, who were eight hundred strong. More than a hundred Cherokees were killed or wounded; among the dead was their chief—"Old Bowles," of Mary Maverick's acquaintance.

Thus the Indians were forced off their land and supposedly

vanquished. But Z. N. Morrell knew better—he knew that they were "determined to avail themselves of every opportunity in [the] future to avenge the blood of their chief and fallen warriors." An officer who participated in that campaign later attested to the truth of Morrell's statement and the logic of his frontier pacifism: "For eighteen months afterward the Indians came back in small parties, and committed fearful depredations upon the lives and property of the people on the frontiers."

27. NEW CITIZEN IN A NEW CAPITAL

One of the most exposed locations in all Texas was selected at this time as the supposedly permanent capital, upon the urging of President Lamar, and it represented an amplification of his dream. The new town by prior law received the name of Austin, in honor of the deceased father of Texas, and Lamar once said of it, "This should be the seat of future Empire." But a young immigrant from Tennessee, Thomas W. Bell, looked over the town soon after it had become the capital and seemed less optimistic about its chances. There he was in the midst of the "talented gentry of the whole nation," and yet he wrote home, "Take them generally, they are a set of gamblers and drunkards, I am inclined to think."

Gamblers and drunkards could only repel Thomas Bell, an introspective twenty-four-year-old with strict morals that came from a religious background. Bell had left his father's farm to make some money—an item always short at home—but he had failed in his first attempt: selling bacon from hogs driven from Tennessee, with his brother's help, halfway across the state of Mississippi to Grenada, where four uncles resided. Bell had heard that Grenada was prosperous and was a gathering point for men setting out to find their fortune in Texas, but by the time Bell opened up his business there prosperity had passed on. The bacon he offered for sale would not bring even eight cents a pound.

Bell went on to Texas, with an uncle and a cousin, in the summer of 1839. They crossed the Sabine River into the pine-shaded redlands of East Texas and traveled westward along a series of ridges that gave them a view of prairies inhabited only by unseen Indians and birds and animals—buffalo, deer, some bear, turkeys, herds of wild horses. They crossed the sandy Brazos River at Nashville— where Z. N. Morrell's sermon had been followed by an Indian attack—and plunged into an unmarked wilderness on the other side. For seventy miles they traveled with no road to guide them, seared by a summer sun that had allied itself with a prolonged drought to brown the prairie grass. On the evening of August 6, after a final day of torrid travel, they reached Austin, and just in time: Bell showed symptoms of sunstroke. But he recovered quickly. The Colorado River climate was fine—provided a man protected himself from the sun, which seemed to be bigger, brighter, and bolder in Texas—and once the rain had renewed the grass Bell considered this a beautiful country.

President Lamar also had been struck by its beauty the year before, and that was the reason Austin had been laid out as the new capital of the Republic despite its perilous location. During the autumn of 1838, before his inauguration, Lamar and some other men, including six Rangers, had happened upon the scene while hunting buffalo near a small village later named Waterloo. They had camped one night near the cabin of a man who lived on the north bank of the Colorado. On the following morning they had been awakened by the man's son, who told them of the presence of buffalo nearby. Lamar and the others brushed sleep aside, mounted their horses, and charged the buffalo, killing many of them. Lamar was said to have killed a bull while racing toward the river down what is now Austin's Congress Avenue. Afterward the hunting party reassembled on a hill overlooking the site—the hill where the Texas Capitol now stands. It was then that Lamar surveyed surroundings and remarked on their appropriateness as "the seat of future Empire." Later, as President, Lamar had instructed commissioners seeking a site for a permanent capital to go to the scene of his buffalo hunt. They shared Lamar's enthusiasm, and the city that was to become Austin came into being.

By May, 1839, the clatter of construction had broken the stillness around the river. Men stood guard against Indian attacks while others sawed and hammered on the seat of future empire.

Frame government buildings appeared on both sides of Congress Avenue. Nearby lay President Lamar's "palace," a frame residence whose two stories, with front and rear porticos, provided a bit of grandeur for the rustic scene. The austere buildings emitted the country smell of freshly cut wood, and Congress Avenue became a bog in wet weather, but no matter: "The city of Austin bids fair to become one of the most refined and pleasant cities in the western world." It had succeeded as the capital of Texas all these places: San Felipe, Washington-on-the-Brazos, Harrisburg, Galveston, Velasco, Columbia, and Houston—and Groce's Retreat, for those three days after the Alamo tragedy.

When Thomas Bell arrived in Austin that August he found immediate employment as a carpenter. He detested the job and resented the necessity of working for others, but he looked upon it as temporary salvation. He built one house, then went to work on Spicer's Tavern—if it could be called a tavern, he reflected. The building was a crude one constructed of pine that had been hauled in from thirty-five miles away, from an area around Bastrop. Logs covered with pine boards made up the walls; roughhewn pine planks made the floors.

Bell was in Austin when the papers and people of officialdom began arriving in October. First came the archives, books, and furniture, brought up from Houston in forty creaking wagons. Then the President and his Cabinet rode into town, heralded by blasts on a bugle whose sounds no doubt could be heard by wondering Indians lurking in the hills nearby. Not even a week before Lamar's arrival they had swooped down from their stronghold and murdered thirteen white men building homes a dozen or so miles from Austin.

Lamar himself had faced a possible encounter with Indians while riding up from Houston. After traveling about half the distance he had received an urgent message from his Secretary of State in Austin warning him of the presence of marauding Indians on his route. "Send word to Austin at what time you will come on," the man had written, "& I will meet you at Barker's five miles above Bastrop with a party of fifteen or twenty men to guard you through . . . Don't think of coming through alone." When Lamar and his Cabinet rode down Congress Avenue the armed escort accompanied them.

Austin was an unlikely national capital, and Thomas Bell an unlikely resident of it. Each summer morning as the sun rose on another day of sweaty toil, Bell thought of home and family and wished he were there enjoying the peaceful society of father, mother, brothers, and sisters, and visiting with old friends and schoolmates, "many of whom I shall never see again." Roaming was not pleasant; he called it folly. Because of his reticence and introspection he did not make new friends easily. He moved on "neither known nor knowing . . . in this dreary world of sorrow among this motley race of earthly mortals."

But an avocation seemed to keep him going—a quest for knowledge, pursued after working hours. Austin of late 1839 struck any visitor as shabby, but despite its newness and its isolation the town attracted some interesting men, and on occasion they lectured evenings to the public. Bell could almost always be found in the audience listening attentively. At first he skipped the congressional debates, partly because of work and partly because of a revulsion for the duly elected lawmakers, but later he developed an interest in Texas politics, and he exchanged this news with his father and brothers in Tennessee through correspondence and a swap of newspapers.

Despite his yearning for home, Bell realized that Trenton, Tennessee, held no future for him. So he stayed in Austin and wrote home long descriptions of the region. From the fertile valley of the Colorado the land rose in gentle swells to afford a striking view of the countryside, which resembled "one vast meadow" around the river. To the northwest rose steep hills covered by dense woods—but this was the abode of the Indians, and cautious persons stayed out of it. Throughout the area, Bell said, a thirsty man could find cool, clear springs and streams. The general appearance "is of as healthy a country as I ever saw." A few people suffered from agues and fevers, but the sicknesses that plagued lowlands along the coast skipped Austin.

Gradually Bell became acclimated in every way, and he almost considered Austin home. About the end of 1839, when the town had completed its first six months of existence, a census gave it a population of 856 souls: 145 "slaves," 61 women, 100 children, and 550 men. Seventy-three of the white men called themselves church members, but no meeting houses had been built. The town consisted of nine stores, nine drinking houses, six gambling houses, and six inns, in addition to the government buildings and private residences.

Bell was boarding at Spicer's Tavern for four dollars a day, enjoying meals of venison, plenty of bread, and coffee drunk from tin cups. Nights he would "sleep on the earth and cover with the skies like most of the Texians." The hardy life seemed to agree with him. His health improved, became as good as it ever had been in his twenty-four years. Altogether the location seemed most desirable—"I think it is destined to become a considerable place"—but in time Bell would become dissatisfied and move on, as was always his tendency. In this respect too he resembled "most of the Texians."

VII

YEAR OF
INDIAN TROUBLES

1840

In Mexico federalists replaced Frenchmen as threats to the centralist government. Revolts kept that nation occupied with internal
problems and left no time for the government to threaten Lamar's
Texas, although at the time no Texan could be certain this would
hold true for very long. By June, uprisings in the north had been
quelled, but a new revolt had broken out in Yucatán. Lamar talked
of alliance there, partly with the hope of frightening Mexico into
recognizing Texas independence. He sent the Texas Navy to aid
the rebels, but nothing resulted.

At home Lamar found troubles enough without looking elsewhere. His fiscal policies and his inability to obtain a loan from
England or France sent the Texas economy plummeting to new
depths, although late in the year his representative negotiated
treaties with England and the Netherlands that led to recognition,
but no money. Trade came to a virtual halt not only because of the
diminished value of the Texas dollar—the promissory notes issued
in 1836 had fallen to about fifteen cents—but also because of the
absence of currency. "San Luis is experiencing the terrible pecuniary depression which is every where felt . . . no sales can be
made of any property for want of Currency," one man said. Another wrote, "Times here are perfectly ruinous. Our most solvent
men are unable to meet their lightest obligations and property of
every description is unsaleable."

169

Depression in the United States was almost as severe. In New York, individuals and institutions concerned over the abject poverty of thousands of city residents organized some thirty relief agencies to help them. The ailing economy proved to be one undoing of the Democrats' President Van Buren, who saw the Whigs reverse the usual role, label him an opulent-living aristocrat, and late in the year elect their simple "man of the people," William Henry Harrison, commander of an American army that had fought Indians on the Tippecanoe River in 1811. To entice Southern voters they had chosen a Virginian, John Tyler, for his vice-president.

Not all American life was bleak. A ten-hour day newly adopted for federal employees gave some people a little more leisure time, perhaps for reading the latest books—Dana's *Two Years before the Mast*, Cooper's *The Pathfinder*, and Poe's *Tales*—or for enjoying a new sport called baseball.

Texas had a lighter side, too. Despite the economic plight, one of the most talked-about events of 1840 was a social item: the marriage of Sam Houston, which came as a general surprise. "In all my . . . life I have never met with an individual more totally disqualified for domestic happiness," Barnard Bee wrote. "He will cut her with his wraths. . . . I implored him at Austin to resort to any expedient rather than marry."

But Houston's bride, Margaret Lea, proved to be an exceptional woman. Houston ceased his notorious drinking and after election to the Texas Congress in November devoted himself to an implacable campaign against Lamar, attacking the man's harshness in Indian relations, which dominated 1840 events.

28. INTO A TIME OF HORROR

In San Antonio 1839 faded into '40 and Mary Maverick looked back on an event-filled year.

In January her husband had commenced a one-year term as mayor of the town, an honor indicative of the trust placed in him by both Mexican and Anglo-American residents.

Early in February San Antonio had lain chilled under a rumpled blanket of snow that drifted to a height of two feet on the north side of Mary and Sam Maverick's house. A group of surprised and excited young people had sleighed up and down Soledad Street, shouting and laughing. The snow had whitened the ground for almost a week—this in a town normally known for its piercing midday sun that sent people fleeing inside dank interiors for naps, to emerge again only when long shadows provided some sanctuary.

That same month Mary and Sam Maverick had moved into a new house on the northeast corner of Commerce and Soledad streets, diagonally across the street from the Main Plaza. About a month later Mary Maverick had given birth to their second child, Lewis Antonio, in that house. "Lewis was the first full-blooded American child born in San Antonio."

Eighteen thirty-nine had been a remarkable year, and for Mary Maverick, at least, mostly a pleasant one. Eighteen forty came in with promise lessened, largely because of certain government policies. But it proved to be equally noteworthy—if unpleasant—because of the brutality exhibited by both Texans and Indians.

Mary Maverick was to witness a grim display of this from their new home, a three-room stone residence with a view of the Main Plaza in front and the San Antonio River in the rear. Neither she nor her husband doubted the permanence of their location now, and they had added some outbuildings on their expansive lot—kitchen and servants' room on one side of the small stone house, a second servants' room on another side, and a stable near the river. Toward the stable Mary located her garden, dominated by sixteen large fig trees and protected by a "good ugly picket fence." A picket fence also surrounded her back yard, which was trimmed with rows of pomegranates. To one side of the yard, just across the property line and the fence, grew several china trees and a magnificent cypress, with large branches that amply shaded both lots. Mary chose the shelter afforded by the giant cypress for locating the "wash place"—her laundry—and a bathhouse.

To thwart the numerous horse thieves Sam Maverick kept a strong lock on his stable, and because he belonged to a group of volunteer Indian fighters called the Minute Men (led by a small, wiry, homely but magnetic Tennesseean named Jack Hays) he kept saddle, bridle, blanket, weapon, ammunition, and bags of provisions—sugar, salt, coffee—ready to go within fifteen minutes from the time he heard an Indian alarm rung from the bell of San Fernando Church. When this happened he changed into buckskin, gathered up his equipment, mounted his horse, and galloped off to meet the others. Together they would set off after marauding Indians, prepared to fight or to chase them back to the hills to the north and west and destroy their villages. If the campaign lasted several days Maverick and the others expected to kill game for food, as did other volunteer groups throughout the Republic.

Frequently the Indians raided almost into San Antonio. In 1839 they attacked the Mavericks' two Negro men who were planting a labor of land north of the Alamo, sent them running for the river, then took the plow animals and galloped off.

But one day in 1840 the Indians came in peace—ostensibly at least. Early that year Comanche Indians sent word to Texas officials at San Antonio that they wanted to talk about a treaty and about ransom for prisoners they held. The wary Texans replied that if the Indians would surrender all prisoners in their possession they would get a treaty. The date mutually agreed on was March 19, 1840. Then the Texans, with advice from the capital, began preparing a surprise. They would post near the meeting place three companies of infantry under the command of Colonel William S. Fisher, but the Indians would be officially received by two commissioners: General Hugh McLeod, a twenty-five-year-old graduate of the United States Military Academy, and William G. Cooke, thirty-one-year-old quartermaster general of the Texas Army.

On Tuesday the nineteenth Mary Maverick and other San Antonians peered curiously at some seventy Comanches—men, women, and children—who came into town, led by a chief, Muguara, who had a reputation of being friendly toward the whites. Accompanied by Texas officials, Muguara and a dozen other chiefs entered the courthouse, which was a short distance south of the Mavericks' home. Mary Maverick and a woman neighbor stared at the procession from behind a picket fence surrounding the neighbor's house. It was directly across Commerce Street from the Mavericks and in the direction of the courthouse.

Then they watched the feats of marksmanship performed by

some Indian women and children who had remained outside the building—the "council house," it would be called. A San Antonian set up a number of small coins as targets, and the Indian children promptly shot them down with arrows from an impressive distance. Mary saw near the courthouse a house guest of theirs, Mathew Caldwell, a renowned Indian fighter, looking on. For once he was unarmed. Near the courthouse the Texas infantrymen waited.

While Mary Maverick watched the Indians outside, the atmosphere inside the courthouse grew tense. Through an interpreter one of the commissioners asked, "Where are the prisoners you were to bring?" Maguara replied, "We have brought the only one we had; the others are with other tribes."

The prisoner the Comanches had brought was a fifteen-year-old Anglo-American girl, Matilda Lockhart, who had been captured eighteen months earlier while gathering pecans with four other children. She seemed a picture of death. Bruises and sores covered her arms, head, and face; her nose had been burned off by the Indians' method of awakening her—applying a chunk of fire to her nose and laughing when she cried.

Silence followed the chief's statement. The Texas commissioners knew of at least fifteen white prisoners held by these Indians— Matilda Lockhart said she had seen some of them. The commissioners surmised that the Indians planned to bring them in one by one, to get a greater ransom. Quiet instructions brought the infantrymen into the building.

Muguara spoke again, insolently. "How do you like the answer?" More silence followed, but when the troops were posted and ready for action one of the commissioners told the interpreter to inform the Indians they would be held as hostages until all prisoners had been safely returned. The interpreter balked, protesting that he would be killed as soon as he opened his mouth with that information, for the Indians had brought scalping knives and bows and arrows with them and had not been disarmed. The commissioner insisted, and the interpreter moved to a position near the door before he began talking.

When the Indians heard of their proposed fate they shrieked defiance with whoops that were instantly heard and evaluated by the Indians outside. Mary Maverick saw them aim their arrows at human targets instead of at the coins—and before the white victims realized what was happening. One of the first to die was the man who had been setting up the coin targets for the young Indians. Another early casualty was Mathew Caldwell, the Mavericks' house guest, who was accidentally shot by one of the soldiers. But Caldwell was not out of the fight. Some people said he threw rocks at the Indians with his back against the courthouse wall.

Inside, the chiefs sought to break out. They seized knives or strung bows and attacked. One Indian leaped for the door and stabbed a sentinel. Another slashed the troop commander with his knife. But the soldiers opened fire on the trapped Indians, and eventually most lay on the spattered council-room floor dead or dying of wounds.

Mary Maverick watched and listened in awe. "When the deafening war whoop sounded in the courtroom it was so loud, so shrill, so inexpressibly horrible and suddenly raised that we ladies, looking through the fence at the [women's] and boys' marksmanship, could not comprehend the noise. The Indians, however, knew the first note and instantly shot their arrows . . ."

Then she and the neighbor ran for cover—the neighbor for her own house and Mary for her front door across the street. The Indians around the courthouse ran, too, after shooting their arrows at the unsuspecting whites. They headed for the river, pursued by the troops. Mary Maverick's house lay between them and their destination.

Moments after she darted inside her front door an Indian ran up, intent on pushing his way inside, but she slammed the door in his face and quickly barred it. Then she noticed her husband and her brother sitting at a table in an adjoining room, poring over a survey map. She told them about the council house and the Indians and the fight—about everything they had missed while intent on their work inside the thick-walled house. After that she started for the back yard to look for her children, while the two men seized their weapons and lunged for doors—her husband for the front door and her brother for the rear.

Mary Maverick ran into the back yard, increasingly terrified for the safety of her children, and almost bumped into three Indians who had sprinted through the gate. "Here are Indians," she screamed at her brother, then gaped at the scene before her. The Comanches had come face to face with the Mavericks' Negro cook, Jinny, who was standing protectively in front of Mary's two children and her own brood with a heavy rock held in both hands above her head. "If you don't go away from here I'll mash your head with this rock," Jinny declared.

The Indians gave up any disposition toward mischief and sped on toward the river, but not quickly enough. Mary saw her brother aim, fire, and bring down an Indian in midstream. He shot a second time, and another Indian fell while climbing the opposite bank. Then her brother dashed off up Soledad Street in pursuit of other Comanches, and Mary Maverick escorted Jinny and the children safely inside the house. But Mary was incapable of shutting herself up. She opened the door fronting on Soledad, looked out, and saw across the narrow street the sprawled body of an Indian, badly wounded and obviously near death. While she watched, a man walked up, laughed at the bloody sight, and aimed a pistol at the body.

"Oh, don't," Mary called out. "He's dying."

The man laughed again and answered, "To please you I won't, but it would put him out of his misery."

Next she saw, lying farther away in the street, two dead Indians—she had not noticed them before. About that time her attention was diverted by the appearance of an elegantly uniformed cavalry officer, Lysander Wells, who rode by on a colorfully caparisoned Mexican horse. She watched him pass her house. The saddle appeared to be silver-mounted. As he rode by the Veramendi house just north of hers on Soledad she was startled to see an Indian leap behind Wells, hug him with a strong grip, and struggle to wrest the reins from Wells's hands. For agonizing minutes she watched the two men sway backward and forward and from side to side astride the horse, which stood almost still while the fight raged on its back. Then she noticed Wells work a hand free, reach for his pistol, twist around in the saddle, and fire into the Indian. The Comanche fell limp, rolled off the horse, and left Wells free to gallop up Soledad looking for more Comanches.

The deadly struggle had entranced her, and after it had ended she realized she was standing in the center of Soledad Street, entirely unconscious of where she had walked. The voice of a Texan lieutenant hurrying by roused her. "Are you crazy?" he asked. "Go in or you'll be killed."

She went back into the house, "but without feeling any fear." Next she opened the door fronting on Commerce Street and looked out on several more dead Indians.

Mary Maverick had seen most of the Council House Fight from beginning nearly to the end. She had seen the Indians run for the river along Soledad or Commerce—the very streets that lay in front of her house—pursued by armed citizens and soldiers who overtook and shot them in the streets and in the river, then, after ammunition had run out, killed them by hand. But now, while she waited in her house, the grim fascination disappeared and time passed more slowly. Streets lay silent and deserted, except for the motionless bodies. She had no idea where her husband and brother were, or whether they still lived.

The arrival of the wounded house guest, Mathew Caldwell, interrupted her thoughts. Some men brought him back to the Mavericks' house and placed him on a bed. There he lay groaning from a wound that had caused his leg to swell so much his boot could not be removed. A doctor cut away the footpiece, which was filled with blood, and dressed the wound. The rifle ball had pierced one side of Caldwell's boot and had torn through his leg, but then the leather had stopped it. When the doctor cut off the boot he found the ball inside.

Mary Maverick again visited her neighbor across Commerce Street, perhaps to relieve some of the anxiety about the safety of her husband and brother. But she found no comfort there. From inside the house she saw the doctor who had treated Caldwell's wound appear at a window, bow courteously, say, "With your permission, madam," then place a severed Indian head on the outside sill. The two women stared in horror at the sight while the doctor vanished momentarily and appeared again with another bloody head. This time he stopped to explain his purpose. He had examined all the dead Indians and had selected these two heads, male and female, to preserve as specimens. He said he had also chosen two bodies, male and female, to keep as skeletons—a treasure he had long yearned for.

"And now, ladies," he concluded, "I must hurry and get a cart to take them to my house!" Mary Maverick watched him walk away, caked with dirt and blood, "exulting for the cause of science in his magnificent specimens." Before dark he returned for his frightful load.

About that time her husband and her brother returned, and she greeted them with vast relief. They would not be added to the day's toll: thirty-three Indians killed, eight wounded, and all but two of the others run down and captured; seven Texans killed and eight wounded.

But the bloody day had not yet ended. The two Indians who had escaped capture were located inside the back-yard kitchen of the neighbor's house Mary Maverick had visited that afternoon. The Indians, both men, had shut themselves in and refused entreaties to surrender. No one seemed enthusiastic about forcing an entrance and bringing them out. Most people stayed clear of the area as the evening grew darker.

But a few men gathered nearby and discussed ways out of the dilemma. They argued without any decision until one man risked climbing on top of the structure and surveying the situation from there. In the roof he saw a hole the size of a bucket. He climbed down, reported this to the others, and suggested a plan. After a while they were ready.

The man climbed back on the roof, leaving the others stationed near the kitchen door. He lighted a turpentine-soaked candlewick ball, tossed it through the hole, and hit one Indian on the head. The two Indians opened the door to run, but both were instantly killed by the men in the yard—one with an ax to the skull before he was even out the door. The total Indian dead rose to thirty-five.

"What a day of horrors," Mary Maverick remarked. Sleep was long in coming, and she lay awake listening to cries and groans, from a nearby house, of a lieutenant who had been shot through the lungs and was vomiting blood. The doctor who had collected the Indian specimens attended him. No one thought the lieutenant would live through the night, but he eventually recovered.

Down Soledad from the Mavericks' house another group agonized through that night. In the jail adjoining the courthouse nearly thirty Comanche survivors, most of them women and children, were locked up—a terrible ordeal for those proud people. After daylight the next morning Texas officials released one of them, a woman, and gave her a horse and provisions for an assignment: to return to her people, tell them about the battle and its results, and say they must now bring in all the prisoners and exchange them for the captured Indians. The woman said she would return within four days, and the officials promised a truce, during which time they would refrain from organizing any campaign against the Comanches. But unless the captives had been returned by the end of the truce period, Mary Maverick heard, the Indian prisoners would be executed, under the assumption that the whites already had been killed.

Days passed, and no Indians returned, no released captives appeared. But on March 26 a woman who had escaped from the Indians before the Council House Fight appeared in San Antonio carrying her three-year-old child on her back and told astonished listeners a harrowing story of her nineteen-month captivity. She was a Mrs. James Webster, who had been captured with her daughter on Brushy Creek near Austin after the Indians had killed her husband and son and other members of their party. The woman looked to Mary Maverick more Indian than white, dressed as she was in buckskin, deeply suntanned, and with hair cut short—banged from ear to ear and squared over her forehead.

During her captivity Mrs. Webster had suffered daily indignities. She had been beaten continually during the idle times between her assigned chores—cooking and staking out ponies. Then one night after the chiefs had left for the council-house meeting she took her child and sneaked out of camp, trying to follow their trail to San Antonio. At daylight she found brush cover and slept, then after dusk began her long walk again—by moonlight, under stars that had long ago been voided of any romance. She kept alive only by feeding herself and her child on roots and berries and an occasional meat-encrusted bone found at an old camp. Several times she resigned herself to death, but she kept on until predawn of the twenty-sixth, when she lay down on the crest of a hill after another exhausting night. Now she could go no farther: she was "in a fog, not able to drag one foot after the other," as Mary Maverick recorded her story.

Mrs. Webster peered eastward, in the direction of San Antonio. While she watched, the rose of another dawn bloomed slowly. The sun might shine on San Antonio today, but not on her. Then far off, illuminated by the first rays of morning, appeared the top of a church that could only be San Fernando. Four years earlier General Santa Anna had used the same building for flying his deadly "no-quarter" flag, but now San Fernando meant life. Hope overcame exhaustion, and Mrs. Webster walked the remaining miles into town.

There Mary Maverick and other women cared for her. They fed her, then helped her bathe—a good deed that turned into an ordeal. The stench of Mrs. Webster's buckskin clothes overcame one woman, who swooned in nineteenth-century fashion and required urgent attention herself. Mary Maverick ran for a bottle of cologne on a shelf in the next room and sprinkled some of it under the woman's nose. This revived her, but not in the manner expected. The ailing woman pleaded, "Stop! Stop! That's pepper vinegar." Everyone laughed and accused the woman of playing possum. Then they returned their attentions to the long-suffering Mrs. Webster, who was washed—"her skin yet fair and white beneath the buckskin"—and was put to bed for a refreshing sleep.

Later the Indians brought to San Antonio a few white prisoners for exchange, but most of the captives never were heard from and were no doubt killed. The Texans refrained from executing their own prisoners—if they ever intended it—but their earlier actions already had inflamed the Indians beyond redemption. To Comanche honor this clearly required revenge, and the Indians gathered in their western fastnesses to begin planning for it.

Years later President Lamar's old foe Sam Houston, whose understanding of Indians might have avoided the tragedy, remembered these days. During his own administration, he remarked, Texas had maintained no standing army and had enjoyed a peaceful relationship with many tribes. Then Lamar's administration had come in, appropriated one and a half million dollars Texas did not have to create two regular regiments, and embarked on a continuing campaign against the Indians—first against "a friendly tribe [the Cherokees] who lived in sight of our settlements" and lived by mutually beneficial trade with Nacogdoches. Houston recalled how Texas soldiers forced the Cherokees off their prized lands, killed some of them, and sent the rest fleeing toward the Comanches. What was the consequence? Houston answered his own question: "Every Indian upon our borders from the Red River to the Rio Grande, took the alarm. They learned that extermination was the cry; and hence it was that the flood of invasion came upon our frontiers, and drenched them with blood. The policy of extermination was pursued, and a massacre of . . . chiefs at San Antonio, who came in amity for a treaty, took place."

Now it was the Indians' turn to massacre. But Houston reiterated in his remarks made years later, "The extermination policy brought it on."

29. INDIAN VENGEANCE

The Rev. Z. N. Morrell had seen enough Indians during his several years at the exposed falls of the Brazos, then at La Grange, which was also near the frontier. He traded for some rich land on the Guadalupe River thirty miles above the town of Victoria, intending this time to make his move permanent. During the summer of 1840 he was transferring household goods to his new home when he discovered that no matter where he went it seemed that Indians were destined to trouble him.

On a sweltering day in July Morrell and some helpers packed his wagons with lumber at Bastrop—located in a narrow pine belt near his La Grange home—and hauled the cargo to his place on the Guadalupe. There they unloaded it and headed back toward La Grange, early in August. After traveling only a short distance they came across the tracks of Indians—more of them than Morrell had ever seen in a group. He estimated at least four hundred Indians, probably more. They were bound southeastward in the general direction of Victoria. Considering what had just happened at San Antonio, Morrell knew that they did not have peace and tranquillity on their minds. Never before had Indians invaded in such numbers; usually their raids were carried out by small groups. He "trembled for the settlements below" and concluded that the best way to deal with the horde of Indians would be to hurry on toward

La Grange and the Colorado River Valley, where he could alert Edward Burleson and other Indian fighters. If he hurried and if Burleson hurried, they could sweep down on the Indians from the north and at least cut them off from their haunts in the western wilderness.

With these thoughts Morrell rode on with the others two more miles and came across more evidence of the recent presence of Indians: a riderless horse, which apparently had been whipped and spurred to the point of exhaustion. Then they were startled by the sudden appearance in their rear of Indians themselves—a band of twenty-five or thirty chasing a herd of mustangs. When the Indians saw that Morrell's party was well armed they turned away without coming into range, but Morrell attributed their retreat to "the providence of God . . . They could have overpowered us in a very short time." He guessed that this band of Indians represented the rear guard of their powerful army.

Not until later did Morrell become aware of still more good fortune that swung in his favor about this time. Shortly before his arrival in the area where he saw the Indians, another group of red men had attacked two Texans on horseback. They shot one of the two and left him for dead—possibly explaining the riderless horse Morrell had seen—then chased the second and captured him. They brought him back to the place where the other man had fallen, anticipating taking two scalps there, but discovered that the first man had vanished.

The frustrated Indians killed their victim on the spot and mutilated his body—in view of the survivor hidden nearby, as later became known. Then, only minutes after the Indians had left, Morrell and his companions and their wagons and horses appeared. Morrell learned about it later when he met the survivor, who had seen everything from the hiding place that he refused to abandon.

While Morrell rode on toward home the army of Indians plundered coastal settlements. Their actual numbers exceeded Morrell's estimate; later guesses ranged from five hundred to one thousand, with six hundred probably accurate. They had swooped down from the far northwest mostly undetected. The land through which they had traveled was an expanse of country mostly uninhabited, offering an easy route to the unsuspecting settlements far below.

The residents of Victoria noticed hundreds of mounted Indians just outside the town in the afternoon of August 6. "We at first supposed they were Lipans, who sometimes paid us friendly visits," one man said later. That delusion passed quickly. They could see that the Indians were busily rounding up five hundred or so horses that had been left by traders on a prairie at the outskirts of town. Thoroughly alarmed now, the men in Victoria ran for their weapons, although realizing the folly of a fight—they numbered about fifty. The town lay mostly helpless. People barricaded themselves inside the strongest buildings, waited, and watched.

No attack came. The Comanches contented themselves with rounding up all the horses and mules they could find in the vicinity—two or three thousand—and an occasional murder or capture of a Texan they happened upon. That night they withdrew to the bank of a creek three miles from Victoria, killed three men and captured a Negro girl in the vicinity, and encamped. In town, some men rode out for reinforcements from other settlements, but they figured the Indians would be gone before they could organize an effective attack. That usually happened.

But on the following day the Indians surrounded the town. They attacked four unsuspecting men riding into Victoria from the east, lanced one to death, killed another after a chase, and pursued the other two all the way into town. Then they burned a house on the outskirts and withdrew. In town the inhabitants gathered at the public square—mostly to speculate on their fate—but the Indians rode on toward Lavaca Bay, occasionally killing or capturing inhabitants and adding to their vast collection of horses and mules. That night they camped on Placido Creek, twelve miles from the small town of Linnville, which they decided to attack on the following day.

At Placido Creek the Comanches surprised two men driving freight wagons toward Victoria. One of them escaped by hiding in tall grass and later fleeing through the night to Victoria. The other man was captured and killed—his hidden friend could hear him begging for his life. Later that same night a Linnville merchant passed by the very same place on his way to Victoria, observed the two wagons and campfires on the nearby creek, presumed they belonged to traders en route to Linnville for goods, and rode on unmolested. Not until he reached Victoria did he realize what a dangerous gauntlet he had run.

In Linnville after daylight the next morning a few early-rising citizens noticed to the west a dust cloud raised by hundreds of horses. At first they presumed it to be a vast herd being brought for trade. Then they realized the danger posed by the thundering horses and shouted an alarm—with flight, not resistance, the only thought. Just before the Comanches poured into town most of the inhabitants fled to boats and lighters anchored in the shallow bay. They rowed away in terror. But not everyone was so lucky. In town some slept past salvation, and still others were killed or captured in the water while splashing wildly for the boats. Indians chased the collector of customs, H. O. Watts, into the water and killed him, then seized his young wife, a bride of only a few weeks, and dragged her screaming back to the shore.

From the boats, people watched helplessly. After the Indians had disposed of the last inhabitant they began looting Linnville storehouses. In one building they found a two-year supply of groceries, clothing, housewares, and law books recently purchased in New Orleans by Sam Maverick and intended for shipment to San Antonio. Maverick himself had planned to accompany the goods and to oversee their transportation, but he had been detained and thus missed the action. Other storehouses contained everything from staples to fancy ribbon, hats, and umbrellas. The Indians broke into everything and loaded the most attractive items on their retinue of stolen horses and mules. Then they set fire to the buildings and celebrated wildly. From the boats, onlookers could see them "dashing about the blazing village, amid their screeching squaws and little Injuns, like demons in a drunken saturnalia, with . . . hats on their heads and . . . umbrellas bobbing about on every side like tipsy . . . balloons."

One observer could stand the merriment no longer. He seized a weapon and jumped from his boat into water three or four feet deep, waded to shore, and stood there waiting for a whooping Comanche to come within range. But the Indians stayed clear, and from the boats people persuaded the man to return. When again on the boat, he discovered his weapon was not loaded.

That afternoon the Indians left Linnville with their horses and mules and all the goods they could haul. From their heads and the heads of their animals fluttered colorful ribbons, and some braves still wore hats and carried umbrellas. That night they camped on a bayou near Linnville. The next morning they met a force of Texans rallied by the Victoria men who had ridden out of town seeking help, but after a brief skirmish with few fatalities they eluded these men and continued homeward.

30. TEXAN VENGEANCE

Z. N. Morrell finally had reached his destination, the home of the Indian fighter Edward Burleson, who lived twelve miles from La Grange. Morrell had long since realized the hopelessness of helping the settlements in the path of that horde, but Burleson could summon volunteers and engage the great Indian army.

Morrell reached Burleson's house at sunrise and told him what he had seen. Burleson listened, then called for a favorite horse and his saddle; he and Morrell would ride out to summon volunteers. Before mounting, Burleson pointed to some gashes on the saddle— one inside the horn, another outside, and a third on the rear of the tree—and remarked to Morrell, "All these were made while I was in the saddle." Morrell did not doubt him. He knew enough of Burleson's biography.

Burleson and Morrell were about to leave when they saw a horseman approaching at a gallop. The man appeared to be waving in his hand a piece of paper, and when he rode up to them he handed Burleson a letter. Morrell remembered later it went something like this:

> General: the Indians have sacked and burned the town of Linnville; carried off several prisoners. We made a draw-fight with them at Casa Blanca,—could not stop them;—we want to fight them before they get to the mountains. We have sent expressmen up the Guadalupe.
>
> BEN. McCULLOCH

Morrell and Burleson rode some distance up the Colorado Valley, spreading the news as they traveled and calling for volunteers. Meanwhile, other detachments also were on the way, and they all agreed to meet at a location on Plum Creek, about twenty-five miles south of Austin, where the Indians probably would pass on their way home. Burleson asked Morrell to go on to Austin, summon volunteers there, and meet him and his men at a designated site near Plum Creek the next day.

Morrell hurried to Austin, where he spread the word. Early the next morning he and a group of Austin volunteers left for the rendezvous. But when they arrived there they discovered that Burleson and his men already had left, so they followed in the direction of the proposed interception on Plum Creek. They found Burleson, and just in time. The Comanches already had passed on their way home, and a combined Texan force led now by General Felix Huston was preparing to attack from brush along Plum Creek. With the addition of Morrell and his men from Austin the Texans numbered about two hundred, against some six hundred Indians elated by success.

When the Comanches became aware of their danger they drove their thousands of horses, mules, and pack animals loaded with plunder on ahead. The braves stayed behind to delay their enemy, while still keeping a safe distance from him. Morrell observed their tactics.

. . . During this delay several of their chiefs performed some daring feats. . . . One of these . . . chiefs attracted my attention . . . He was riding a very fine horse, held in by a fine American bridle, with a red ribbon eight or ten feet long tied to the tail of the horse. He was dressed in elegant style, from the goods stolen at Linnville, with a high-top silk hat, fine pair of boots and leather gloves, an elegant broadcloth coat, hind part before, with brass buttons shining brightly right up and down his back. When he made his first appearance he was carrying a large umbrella . . . This Indian and others would charge towards us and shoot their arrows, then wheel and run away, doing no damage. This was done several times, in range of some of our guns. Soon the discovery was made that he wore a shield, and although some of our men took good aim the balls glanced. An old Texan . . . asked me to hold his horse, and [sneaking through brush] as near the place where they wheeled as was safe, waited patiently till they came; and as the Indian checked his horse and the shield flew up, he fired and brought him to the ground. Several had fallen before, but without checking their demonstrations. Now, although several of them lost their lives in carrying him away, yet they did not cease their efforts till he was carried to the rear.

The Texans pressed an attack and sent the startled, howling Indians into a stampede. They followed vigorously, raising clouds of dust that cut vision and stung eyes. They killed and wounded many, but kept up their pursuit with hope of annihilation.

Morrell was riding with the other volunteers when a scream from a nearby clump of bushes stopped him. He investigated and found a young white woman trying to pull an arrow from her breast. He pulled the woman's hands away from the arrow and tried to calm her. She was from Linnville, he learned—Mrs. Watts, the bride of the customs collector who had been killed in the water near her. She and the other prisoners had been shot when the Texans charged. Morrell saw lying nearby a white woman dead and a Negro woman wounded.

A doctor arrived on the scene, cut away Mrs. Watts's dress and flesh from the arrow, and tried to extract it, but the woman gripped his hand and screamed so loudly he stopped. A few minutes later he tried again, and the arrow came out. Morrell spread his blanket on the ground, made a pillow of his saddle, and helped her to lie down on this improvised bed and relax. When she had regained her composure she rejoiced over her escape: "Death would have been preferable to crossing the mountains with the savages." Then she talked of her experience since her capture at the side of her dead husband. She had been taken over by an old chief who had put her under the care of an "ancient squaw." For the journey into Comanche lands she had been strapped to the back of a mule, to prevent a fall or an escape, and occasionally had been asked by her captors to read from one of the books on Texas law—no doubt a copy belonging to Sam Maverick. While she read, the Indians laughed and hooted, never realizing the extent of their joke.

While Morrell looked after the woman, the Texans had continued their chase of the Comanches. They killed fifty or more and forced the rest to abandon horses, mules, and stolen goods. Finally they broke off pursuit and returned to Plum Creek.

Volunteers continued to come in after the fight had ended. By nightfall Morrell estimated an army of five hundred in the field. Most of the latecomers found it difficult to relax after the anticipation, and many of them stayed up all night talking of events of the preceding days.

One young man who missed the fight was Thomas Bell, the immigrant who had traded Trenton, Tennessee, for Austin, Texas. "I was on my march toward the scene . . . when I heard the fun was all over," he said, "and I had to return mortified before reaching the place."

Morrell, "weary and careworn," rode home, delighted that the Indians had been driven out. Nevertheless, a question plagued him as he traveled. "How long shall these things be?" he asked himself, but no answer came to mind.

31. END OF A DISASTROUS YEAR

After missing the fight at Plum Creek, Thomas Bell returned not merely mortified. He spent seventy cents to send a letter to his relatives in Tennessee about it, and he remarked, "I felt like hiding." This had been his first chance to engage Indians in combat, and he had missed it. But the main reason he wrote home was to reassure his people that he was safe and that the raid, as extensive as it was, was not so large as he knew the magnified accounts in the United States would make it—thousands of Indians involved, numerous towns destroyed, and many persons killed or captured.

Bell suffered from moodiness. Often he could mask it, but not always. In one letter he wrote home, "I can't determine to stay in this country because I don't like it, or at least no part I have yet seen," and in another declared, "I am entirely contented here while I can do as well as I'm now doing. I see no reason why people may not do very well here with industry and economy. . . . I expect to lay hold of anything I can make money or property at. . . . I would scorn to appear before my parents like a great many young men from this country a blackguard or a loafer but with a consciousness of having been beneficial in some way or other to my fellow beings as well as to myself."

But Bell remained consistent in his attitude toward the Republic of Texas government, and especially toward President Lamar. Both were almost useless. At the head of Texas affairs were "the laziest and triflingest kind of men."

Even a friend of Lamar's called his aides impractical "imbeciles" who "regard themselves only in their own counsels." As for the members of Congress, a letter to one of them about this time spoke of the integrity of some: "I am glad you are elected to Congress as that will help you in your speculations."

Of the President himself, Bell said Lamar "cannot see an inch beyond his own nose and is a perfect old granny and all his acts and his course in the administration of the affairs of the nation show [that] he is the dupe of the designing."

Bell was wrong about the President. Lamar could see far beyond his nose, or thought he could. His great fault was that tendency of his to look beyond practicality—a weakness that gave his bitter critic Sam Houston many opportunities to tease and harass him, publicly and privately.

Houston made the most of every chance. Writing from "accursed [Austin], in which villainy has located the seat of government," he summarized the situation as he saw it:

Oh my country! No one can fancy its affliction, and every day only adds to its calamities. The day is not distant when the veil of futurity will disclose scenes of extravagance and corruption that will awaken the most miserable sensations and strike the mind with horror. No patriot can anticipate the future prospects of Texas, without the most acute, and heavy anguish. I have not since the Revolution began, entertained such gloomy hopes for my country. Heretofore God has saved us, and can continue his kind favors, but without them, we are gone. The nation cannot bear the burdens of Taxations, that must be imposed . . . The people are too poor to pay taxes; on oxen, workhorses, and in short everything.

But at a time when the Republic treasury was empty, government salaries were good. The President received $10,000 a year and the use of his "mansion." Annual pay for important members of the Cabinet, like the Secretary of State, came to $3,500; for the Vice-President and the Attorney General, $3,000. Members of Congress received a seemingly exorbitant twenty cents a mile travel expenses and five dollars per diem.

As the criticism of his policies grew, Lamar's health failed, forcing him, near the end of 1840, to ask Congress for a leave of absence that proved to be about three months long. From mid-December, 1840, to March, 1841, Vice-President David Burnet assumed the duties of the presidency—with a fervor that alienated his former friend Lamar. Like Lamar and virtually all other Republic officials, Burnet had become obsessed with the empire dream. As acting president he blustered against Mexico and told Congress, "Texas proper is bounded by the Rio Grande—Texas as defined by the sword may comprehend the Sierra del Madre. Let the sword do its work."

Lamar could not have disagreed with this sentiment, but he brooded over Burnet's presumptuousness in firing some of his own political appointees, and over his poor health, his long-dead wife, and his vicious critics. In the grip of this melancholy he turned to poetry.

> My suff'rings soon, I know, must end,
>   For life is on its ebb;
> The autumn leaves that first descend
>   Will find me with the dead:—
> I wish my fall may be like theirs,
>   From lamentations free;
> I ask no unavailing tears,
>   No friends to GRIEVE FOR ME.

This old sketch based on eyewitnesses' descriptions shows the building where Texas independence was declared March 2, 1836. That day cotton cloth covered the windows against a cold wind.

(University of Texas Archives)

General Antonio López de Santa Anna determined to allow the Texas revolutionists no quarter.
(University of Texas Archives)

Santa Anna, in white trousers, surrenders to a wounded Sam Houston after the San Jacinto battle. This is a section of a painting that hangs in the Texas State Capitol building.

The Alamo lies in ruins in this 1840 drawing.

(University of Texas Archives)

Texas begins rebuilding. This sketch of the 600-ton sloop of war *Austin*, commissioned in 1840, is from a contemporary drawing by Edward Johns, an *Austin* midshipman.

(University of Texas Archives)

Texas Sloop of War Austin

Samuel A. Maverick
moved to San Antonio from
South Carolina in 1835 and
participated in many events of
Republic of Texas history.
(University of Texas Archives)

Mary Maverick, at left,
with Mrs. Jack Hays (standing),
wife of the Ranger,
and another friend.
Mary's hair was lighter in color
than this old photograph shows.
(University of Texas Archives)

Alphonse de Saligny
arrived in Texas
to represent France
as chargé d'affaires in 1840.
(University of Texas Archives)

The French Legation, seen in this old photograph, still stands in Austin.
(University of Texas Archives)

Seventeen men among 176 Texas prisoners from the Mier battle drew black beans —and execution—as punishment for participating in an unsuccessful escape attempt in 1843. The jar containing the beans was held higher than shown here.
(Texas State Library)

Chained Texas survivors of the Mier battle and the black-bean drawing were marched into Mexico for a long imprisonment.
(Texas State Library)

Comanche warriors, fiercely proud, resisted Texas settlers' westward expansion into their territory and continually threatened the capital of the Republic of Texas after it was moved to Austin in 1839.

(Texas State Library)

Frame houses line Austin's Congress Avenue as it appeared in 1844, looking from the Colorado River.

(University of Texas Archives)

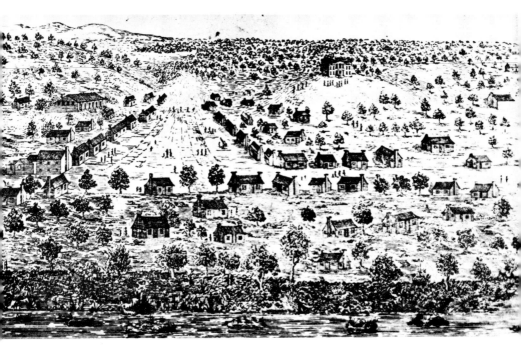

The Republic of Texas Capitol at Austin shows the colors adopted by the Republic January 25, 1839, now the state flag.

(University of Texas Archives)

VIII

VISIONS AND FOLLIES

1841

If there was one man in Texas Sam Houston delighted in berating more than Mirabeau Lamar it was David Burnet, the man who had taunted him about his retreats before the Mexicans five years earlier. With Lamar on leave of absence and Burnet acting president, Houston had his chance. "I can tell you no good news," he wrote a friend, "for we are in a devil of a sweat. We have no defenses for the country, and indeed the means have been so squandered that we are destitute . . . and must by some unforeseen event . . . save the country. The only care of Davy G. is to secure election. This is funny indeed, for he is the most odious man to the people of Austin that I have heard spoken of. . . . Poor dog. Every day has brought new troubles upon him."

The year 1841 also saw a sudden change of administration in the United States, this one permanent. President William Henry Harrison, the Whig, died after a month in office, and Virginian John Tyler succeeded him, the first Vice-President to move up because of a President's death. But Tyler proved to be more of a Democrat, vetoed most of his party's legislation, and eventually broke with the Whigs. In September all of Tyler's Cabinet resigned, with the exception of Secretary of State Daniel Webster, but his nation kept on the move: Charles Goodyear had succeeded in making vulcanized rubber; Captain Charles Wilkes had led an expedition to Antarctica and claimed it for the United States; some three thou-

sand miles of railroad track had been constructed; Dorothea Dix
had begun a campaign for better care of paupers and the insane;
and the first covered-wagon train had arrived in California, traveling by way of the Oregon Trail, the Humboldt River, and the
Sierras. To the north of Mexican-owned California lay Oregon,
which the United States occupied jointly with England, but many
Americans clamored for exclusive ownership.

In faraway Texas, Lamar returned to claim his presidency, but
the troubles increased there—sometimes for ridiculous reasons.
About the time that Lamar's agent James Hamilton seemed hopeful of arranging a five-million-dollar loan in Paris, the French
chargé d'affaires in Austin, Alphonse de Saligny, broke off relations
with Texas temporarily because of what became known as the "pig
incident." Saligny ordered his servant to kill a number of swine
belonging to Austin hotel owner Richard Bullock, because the
animals, allowed to run loose, had broken into Saligny's corncrib
and devoured ears intended for the Frenchman's fine horses. After
losing his pigs Bullock assaulted the servant; Saligny protested;
and Texas tried to placate the chargé, but without success. The
Frenchman demanded his passports and left. Many Texans
laughed rather than grieved. They knew Saligny as a scoundrel:
earlier he had passed counterfeit money in Texas; and before the
pig incident he had moved out of Bullock's hotel in a huff, accusing
the man of charging exorbitant rates, which he refused to pay.

Nevertheless, this left President Lamar without his French loan,
and it left Texas sinking deeper into an economic morass. Lamar
thought he saw a way out of the difficulty, and in midyear he tried
his idea. It would prove to be grasping at a last straw.

32. MINISTER TO THE UNITED STATES

President Lamar could fool himself and maybe some others by
maintaining with deficit financing his ostentatious carriage and the
two-story "mansion" in Austin, but the true worth of Texas money
became evident all too quickly—and nowhere more starkly than at

the Texas legation in Washington. There a representative kept an
office open, precariously. He was Barnard Bee, the former "minister plenipotentiary" to Mexico, who had returned to Texas service
after his visit to South Carolina.

Bee had been given no money to allow him to work effectively
for Texas peace and independence in Mexico—where he had
known that such a path would have to be "paved with gold"—and
now the curse of national poverty haunted him in the United States
capital, where he had been minister since 1838. He shared cramped
quarters with another man in a rooming house at the rear of the
Capitol building, and he avoided diplomatic entertaining. "All are
courteous to me," he once wrote back to Texas, "but having no
command of my salary I mingle as little as possible. It is unpleasant to receive courtesies and not return them, and in debt
I . . . will not go."

In Washington Bee sought to arrange trade agreements with
European nations that maintained representatives there; tried
without notable success to negotiate commercial treaties with the
United States, including a provision that Texas farmers be allowed
to ship their cotton into New Orleans or other ports duty free;
strove to persuade the United States to restrain its Indians from
raiding into Texas or from joining Mexico in an alliance against his
country. Regarding its Indians the United States answered that it
had no legal power to restrain by force their peaceable migration to
another country, and that all it could promise would be to try to
persuade them to stay within the limits assigned. "The Texian
government must, however, be aware of the impediments which the
nature of the Indian character, their nomadic habits, and the
remoteness of the region which they frequent" would pose to any
efforts of the United States to persuade them to comply. These
were empty words of diplomacy. The Texas government knew very
well Indian habits.

One goal Bee did not work for in Washington was annexation.
President Lamar opposed it, dreaming of his empire, and Bee
himself personally opposed it, still believing that the most advan-
tageous route for Texas lay in independence. But he sent back
rumors of annexation he heard in Washington. Once he reported
that some persons there thought that Mexico, "to save her pride"

and to compensate for certain claims, would agree to transfer Texas to the United States.

Bee forwarded to Austin all rumors and speculations. Later in the year he heard that Mexico had ordered two armed vessels from the United States, and he established a primitive espionage network that proved the truth of the story.

In March a new administration, William Henry Harrison's, came into office, and Bee found a new Secretary of State with whom to work—Daniel Webster, former Senator from Massachusetts. Bee expected him to be brilliant in office. He was less enthusiastic about the future of Harrison, and when the President died shortly after his inauguration from exposure to chilling weather during the ceremony Bee commented, ". . . In a little month where was all the pomp—in the grave. Fortunate old man, he could not have selected a better moment. Spared the evil to come, he is literally canonized by the people of the United States."

Bee had attended the inauguration with almost the same consequences, but after resting in bed for a few days he had recovered—in time to attend the funeral of Harrison. After the rites, which were "imposing," Bee felt "everything will go on as commenced," and he returned to work. But his health bothered him occasionally, especially "headache—perpetual headache," which his friend Dr. Ashbel Smith in a letter blamed on immoderate eating and drinking. Perhaps Bee had not avoided all official functions after all.

Despite his disappointments in the city of Mexico, Washington, and elsewhere, Bee remained generally optimistic. "Indeed, with peace with Mexico Texas will be a most inviting country," he wrote, then unconsciously inverted a phrase that would become popular much later: "The eyes of everybody is [sic] upon Texas." But the financial situation plagued him and continually clouded his thoughts. He mused over the problem and decided that the best policy lay in retrenchment—an opinion that coincided with the one held by Sam Houston rather than by his friend President Lamar. Once, in a dark mood, Bee talked of resigning as minister, and several times he voiced a preference for being "a farmer at the head of my family" rather than continuing in political life, a sentiment reminiscent of the period after his failure to secure peace and independence from Mexico.

"I would prefer [the farm] to any political distinction," Bee said, "but until the currency is established it would be ruinous." So Bee stayed on in Washington a while longer and worked to stabilize the new nation he represented.

33. A HOLIDAY MOOD

In San Antonio life became more pleasant for Mary Maverick. Anglo-Americans of affluence moved into town, and social life showed an improvement. Mary's aunt became an across-the-street neighbor, moving with her family into the house where Mary Maverick had witnessed the doctor's ghastly display of Indian specimens. Mary's niece, Annie Bradley, "a lovely girl of 13, very womanly and sweet," attracted a throng of admirers. This was not especially unusual for those frontier days when adolescence was of necessity abbreviated and girls were in short supply. Merchants moved in—"Mr. Wilson Riddle brought his bride out and Mr. Moore his family." A Mr. Campbell brought his wife, and to someone's certain delight her sister came along. A Frenchman arrived with his wife and child, and they were taken into the new society. But mostly the circle was open only to Anglo-Americans. Some Mexicans of social standing had been seen to sneak away from festivities with roast chickens, carving knives, and cakes. One of them, a woman, had eaten so much of a new delicacy called ice cream that she had been seized with cramps. All of the Mexicans, it seemed, allowed their children to play in the nude, a custom that precluded much mingling with offspring of the horrified Anglo-Americans. Considering these things, the Anglo-Americans "never felt like being at all intimate."

On Easter Sunday, 1841, one of Mary Maverick's friends gave a dinner for all Anglo-American families and many of the single young men. After a sumptuous meal the guests, talking and laughing, walked up Soledad Street (where Mary once had seen dead Indians). The very next day, April 12, Mary Maverick gave birth to a daughter, who was named Agatha. Both survived the ordeal of childbirth very well, and Agatha proved to be "very beautiful, a good baby."

Life for the Anglo-American women in San Antonio that spring was leisurely, lazy, and far removed from the worry over economics, politics, and international relations that gnawed at men of government. The San Antonio women delighted in youth, health, and contentment, enjoyed an availability of good books—from their own libraries or borrowed from friends—and surrendered themselves happily to the "fashion of the climate." They took dinner at twelve and napped until three, when they all had a cup of coffee to purge the sleep, then reveled in a cool bath in the San Antonio River.

The bath was a culmination of their hedonistic afternoon. The ladies had persuaded someone to erect a bathhouse at a private location up the river, away from the newly built residences and stores of the growing town. It had been placed between two large trees, "in a beautiful shade," and had been provided with benches and hooks for easy dressing. About four o'clock most afternoons, when the sun had begun to cease its efforts to burn the earth, all the ladies of Mary's social circle and their children and nurses walked in a group to the bathhouse, changed into swimming costume, and splashed, swam, and laughed in the spring-fed water. After that they dried themselves and dressed. One woman always prepared a picnic basket for the group—they took turns at this— and she spread the meal on a table or on the ground. They enjoyed it together while the cool evening came on. "We were all good friends and told each other all the news from our faraway homes and all the happenings at home," Mary Maverick said. "We joked and laughed away the time and were happy and free from care. There were no envyings or backbitings."

Late that spring a ripple of excitement disturbed the serenity. President Mirabeau Lamar and other officials of the Republic visited San Antonio. Citizens gave him a grand ball in the "long room" (reception room) of the Yturri house. For the occasion the building had been decorated with flags and potted plants.

Mary Maverick observed Lamar curiously and closely—and with some amusement. He wore "wide" white pants, short enough to show all his shoe, and he opened the ball waltzing rather awkwardly with the mayor's wife, Mrs. Juan N. Seguin, "who was so fat he could with difficulty get a rest for his arm on her waist and cut such a figure it made us laugh. He was a poet, a polite and brave gentleman, but did not dance well."

Mary saw that the ball had other rustic participants. Three respected gentlemen of the town shared one dress coat among them. They had agreed that one would dance while the other two awaited their turns. While they waited they made faces, shook fists, and watched closely to be certain the dancer did not cheat them by dancing twice in a row. Another singular dancer was a Mexican woman of such glamor that she had received an invitation—an honor that gave her delusions. Dressed in a maroon cashmere, with black plumes in her hair, she looked very handsome and obviously arrogant, until the heat of the evening began to show; then Mary and her lady friends could only laugh at the young woman's haughtiness. Finally, there was the host's wife, who wore a new silk dress so tight that she had been forced to put on corsets for the first time in her life. This tidied her otherwise handsome figure, but it proved disadvantageous in another way. During the evening the woman rushed into her bedroom several times to take off her corsets—"to get breath again," as she remarked to Mary.

Lamar had come to San Antonio to solicit assistance for a bold new venture, one that he calculated would bring much money into the empty Republic treasury and allow for adequate financing of his many dreams. Far to the northwest of San Antonio lay a New Mexican town that offered Texas hope for this wealth—Santa Fe, important because it lay at the southern end of a trail that provided a link and a lucrative trade with the United States. The area around Santa Fe had shown dissatisfaction in the past with the Mexican government, and Lamar believed that the inhabitants still felt that way. By wooing them to Texas and diverting much of the rich Santa Fe trade, Texas could solve her money problems. Furthermore, the southern part of the Santa Fe Trail lay within the area claimed by the Republic of Texas, and Lamar felt obliged to assert that title.

Lamar intended to send a peaceful expedition to Santa Fe. It would have only to explain to the populace its reason for coming, then enjoy a warm welcome from them. No Texan had traversed the vast spaces this expedition would have to cross, but the country was believed to have good water and grass. Only the Indians would pose any threat, but an armed force of sufficient strength to fend them off would accompany the expedition.

Santa Fe, Mary Maverick recorded during Lamar's promotional visit to San Antonio, lay "in northwest Texas."

34. TOWARD A GLORIOUS ADVENTURE

President Lamar had been mulling over the possibility of a Santa Fe expedition for months. Earlier he had sought approval for it from Congress, but it had been rejected. Nevertheless, he had ordered his comptroller on March 24, 1841, to open an account for the expedition, despite the absence of legal authority, and he had sent an agent to New Orleans to purchase supplies. There the agent had met and talked with a newspaperman who would accompany the expedition and become its foremost chronicler—George Wilkins Kendall.

A wandering native of New Hampshire, Kendall had learned printing under Horace Greeley, then after a series of newspaper jobs on the East Coast had gone west to New Orleans, where he eventually founded the *Picayune* with another man in January, 1837. In 1841, when Kendall met Lamar's agent, he was a handsome, restless, witty man of thirty-two, a most eligible bachelor in a city of attractive women, and a fiery advocate of Texas, as were many New Orleans citizens. The year before he had written in his newspaper: "Our Texan neighbors have been talking lately about making a dash into the Santa Fe trade. It will not do for them to waste much time in debating the matter, if they wish to secure this branch of the trade."

Now he would go with the Texans himself, partly to help his health, partly to satisfy his incessant curiosity, and partly to get something interesting to write about. Kendall was forever listening and observing, and when he heard or saw something noteworthy he would pull out of his pocket a small black book and record the information.

The Texas agent lured him into the enterprise with an enticing account of the commercial purpose of the enterprise. The man said Lamar intended to open a direct trade with Santa Fe by a route much nearer than the trail to Missouri. This would be easily accomplished, he said, because intelligence received in Texas pointed to the fact that Mexican rule had alienated nine tenths of all the inhabitants of the region around Santa Fe. He told Kendall the expedition would leave from Austin toward the end of May or the first of June.

Immediately Kendall had made his plans to accompany the Texans. From the Mexican vice-consul in New Orleans he obtained a passport in mid-May to enter Mexico as an American citizen, with plans for a four-month visit, and two days later he took passage on a ship for Galveston. He arrived there May 19, to hear everyone talking about the Santa Fe project. Despite his enthusiasm, he kept some distance between himself and the ebullient Texans. He decided not to join the expedition as a member, but to accompany it as an observer, paying his own expenses. He would leave the expedition before its arrival at Santa Fe, then travel southward and make the leisurely tour of Mexico he had told the vice-consul about. Not until much later did Kendall learn of a Mexican law prohibiting a foreigner from entering Mexico through Texas, and not until he had begun the march toward Santa Fe, he said, did he hear of President Lamar's ulterior intention of bringing New Mexico under Texas protection. Certainly Kendall knew of the military force being planned to provide escort for the merchants—five companies of infantry and one of artillery—but this did not seem extraordinary and never caused him to reflect on the possibility that Lamar might be trying to conquer a territory of some 150,000 inhabitants with an expedition made up of only 320 members. "That an enterprise, so purely commercial in its aspect, was intended for a hostile invasion of Mexico, did not . . . enter the mind of any one at the time—at least not in Texas, where the inhabitants should be best able to judge." Twenty-one ox-drawn wagons carrying supplies and merchandise valued at $200,000 eventually went, attesting further to its commercial nature.

From Galveston Kendall proceeded to Houston, where he found
a company of volunteers preparing for the Santa Fe march. He
bought a horse and struck out late one May afternoon for Austin in
weather that seemed to have been made in New Orleans. The day
was hot and sultry. To the southwest, above the pine woods
through which he rode, he saw rolling toward him a blanket of blue-
black cloud, presaging thunder and lightning and stinging, soaking
rain. He raced the storm to a log cabin where he had already
planned to spend the night and arrived there just before the
heavens loosed a cascade of water. The next day he rode on toward
Austin, across fertile prairies, through corn almost as high as a
man's head, across the Brazos River at crumbling San Felipe,
through shaded Bastrop on the Colorado River, on into Austin.
There he learned that the expedition would not depart for ten or
twelve days. With typical restlessness he struck out for San Antonio, arriving there a short time after Lamar's visit in behalf of
the expedition.

These preliminaries served to prepare Kendall better for the
long ride to Santa Fe. He became inured to traveling horseback in
rainstorms, although in the past he had sought shelter when
showers fell. He learned to pack into camp only the good meat of a
slain deer—about one-fourth of it—instead of the entire animal,
which provoked rough laughter among the old hunters with him.
He taught himself to fall asleep on rough ground, wrapped in cold,
damp blankets, rather than go without sleep, and to get this rest
while hearing nearby howls of wolves that had been attracted by
the deer meat in camp.

Kendall observed the experienced frontiersmen with him and
tried to emulate them. Then one night shortly before the expedition
was to leave he ruined much of his record of accomplishment by
losing his way and walking over a precipice while heading for a
swim in the Colorado River near Austin. His right foot struck a
rock, and he felt acute pain shoot up his spine. He could not walk,
could not even ride a horse, but Kendall was too valuable a man to
lose. President Lamar gave him a covered Jersey wagon and a two-
mule team for the trip. With Kendall would ride another invalided
man, José Antonio Navarro, William Gray's roommate at Washington-on-the-Brazos during the drafting of the 1836 independence

declaration. Navarro had been chosen as one of the four civil commissioners of the expedition. Texas officials anticipated that his ancestry would bring them a warm welcome in New Mexico.

The final few days in Austin proved hectic. Wagoners looked over and mended wagons, volunteers cleaned firearms, last-minute additions checked in—all while Kendall lay helpless in a hotel room, receiving President Lamar and other well-wishers. Lamar presented him a letter describing him as a "guest" of the expedition, and Kendall kept it with his passport to avoid forfeiting his claim as an American citizen.

By mid-June the main body of the expedition had left Austin and encamped about twenty miles north—near Kenney's Fort, a simple outpost on the south side of Brushy Creek consisting of two or three log cabins surrounded by a stockade. There they were joined in a few days by the last detachment to leave Austin, including Kendall and Navarro in the Jersey wagon. Accompanying this group was the President himself, who gave a remarkable display of frontier democracy one noon by unsaddling and staking his own horse along with the rest of the men, then cooking his own meal with them in the cool shade of a grove. After that Lamar saddled and mounted along with the others and rode on across prairies described by Kendall as "rolling and beautiful," broken only by wooded streams. Late in the afternoon they reached the encampment on the Brushy, and the next day Lamar, full of hope, addressed the men, then returned with a small group to Austin. The members of the Santa Fe Expedition devoted some time to reloading wagons before striking out northward toward Santa Fe and fortune.

The journey would be made across country no one claimed to know. As Kendall pointed out, the only concrete bit of knowledge anyone possessed was that Austin lay in such-and-such a latitude and longitude and Santa Fe in another. What rivers must be crossed, what dry wasteland might be encountered, could not be imagined. Still, no one fretted over this ignorance. The Austin *Sentinel* guessed that the route would cover 450 miles through "rich, rolling, well watered country" and that a military escort of fifty men would have been sufficient for protection against Indians. Everyone, in fact, foresaw a pleasant journey, a hunting expedition—a lark. Every man present had been attracted by the thought of adventure and the possibility of financial gain. Every man had volunteered. Within the expedition a band had been organized to provide music during the outing.

Early on the morning of June 19 officers shouted commands to two companies of infantry, about eighty men, sending them out first as an advance guard. Then the wagoners yelled orders and curses to their oxen, and the loaded wagons rumbled and creaked, single file, after the infantry. Following the wagons came beef cattle, driven by another infantry company given this unpleasant task, then the rest of the expedition—a company of artillery with a six-pounder cannon and two more companies of infantry, acting as a rear guard. Commanding the military force was Hugh McLeod, the man who had acted as a commissioner before the Council House Fight had broken out.

Somewhere in all that crowd rode Kendall and Navarro in their covered wagon, banging over rocks and rough places (despite the general levelness of the route) in a manner that could only have sent more jabs of pain into Kendall's injured foot. But from the first he recorded details. On the very first day many young oxen became troublesome and upset a number of wagons, leaving drivers snarling and cursing. Already the venture had appeared to be something other than a joyful excursion, but tomorrow must certainly be better.

Kendall lost no enthusiasm. He supported the enterprise, supported Texas, supported Lamar—all somewhat blindly, as later appeared. Convinced of the logic and the value of the expedition, he wrote, "With the proofs General Lamar had, that such a feeling existed in New Mexico, he could not do other than give the people of Eastern New Mexico an opportunity to throw off the galling yoke under which they had long groaned. Texas claimed as her western boundary, the Rio Grande; the inhabitants within that boundary claimed protection of Texas. Was it anything but a duty then, for the chief magistrate of the latter to afford all its citizens such assistance as was in his power?"

35. INTENDING TO SHINE

Far removed from the clatter of the Santa Fe Expedition, the itinerant Tennesseean Thomas Bell had found his niche, or thought he had, after his bacon selling in Mississippi and his house building in Austin. Bell had moved to Rutersville, a new town six miles northeast of La Grange, where he had used his self-study background and inherent inquisitiveness to form an attachment with Rutersville College. He had been added to the faculty there the year before.

The school had been the dream of a serious, studious Methodist churchman named Martin Ruter, who had come to Texas after San Jacinto as a missionary, but with broader visions of establishing a university that would become the "Athens of the South" and enable young Texans to equal his own educational accomplishments, which included earning a Doctor of Divinity degree from Transylvania University in Kentucky. Rutersville College requirements seemed substantial enough. Terms for admission to the classical course called for a knowledge of "the English Language, Davies Arithmetic, Davies Algebra to Quadratic Equations, Ancient and Modern Geography, Latin and Greek Grammar, Caesar's Commentaries, Cicero's Select Commentaries, Cicero's Select Orations, the Georgics and Aeneid of Virgil, Jacob's Greek Reader or St. John's Gospel in Greek."

In 1841 the college had been open for a year, claimed an enrollment of one hundred students and a faculty of four besides Bell, and granted Bachelor of Science and Bachelor of Arts degrees. All this program was conducted on a shoestring campus that did not, at the time, even include a main building. But the ability to see greatness beyond present paucity was common to many Republic of Texas inhabitants. Thomas Bell told people that Rutersville College "cannot fail to become one of the best institutions of the country." The college was improving, Bell said proudly, and it was gaining credit in different sections of the country. No other institution in the region could rank with it.

He intended that it should do as much for him as he for it. He would devote six hours a day to work at the school, and the rest of the time he would give to his own education. "I don't intend to quit study until I can attain a respectable standing in the literary world," he said. To gain the solitude necessary for this endeavor he would build a one-room house—much preferable to living in an uncle's overcrowded rooming house near the campus. In his own house he could keep a library, and he would never allow the books to gather dust. But he would not become a complete recluse. Rutersville, being a college town, afforded excellent society. Three churches gave him a chance to sample and choose a denomination—from among Baptist, Methodist, and Presbyterian. He voiced a preference for Presbyterian even though his college had a Methodist background.

Better yet, a young lady of Rutersville had attracted his attention and admiration, causing him to think of marriage. Until he found a bride, Bell reasoned, his life would remain mostly empty, no matter how much he devoted himself to study.

Bell's affiliation with the college proved mostly pleasant and beneficial. He enjoyed breathing the clean campus atmosphere, unavailable elsewhere in tumultuous Texas. The May Day celebration especially delighted him. Young ladies of the college crowned a queen; several speeches commemorated the event "in a splendid manner." Then everyone repaired to a home near the campus for tea, conversation, and "a pleasant evening in a company that would do credit to any country or town as young as Rutersville." Bell wrote home proudly that those who thought all Texas a degenerate society should come to see the difference for themselves. Anyone who would move to this part of the Republic would have to be of the "true grit," Bell said, but then he remembered other people and added, "There are some of the scrub breed here as well as anywhere else."

Even placid Rutersville held vicissitudes for Bell. Occasional Indian alarms sent him out on exhausting pursuits with other volunteers; if a man did not "volunteer" on these occasions he was considered a coward or a scab and usually did not stay long in a community. Not that Bell was reluctant to go—he was as "keen for a row" as the rest—but he found some of the Indian fighters, especially the regular troops, to be men of unbelievable depravity, and he did not relish their company. He found it difficult to understand how a man could go into a fight so "unthoughtful" as to ignore his wickedness in the face of possible death.

Other troubles beset him. Rutersville College operated mostly on a Methodist prayer, and Bell found himself three hundred dollars short of pay at the end of one term. Never at any time was he certain of receiving his salary. Furthermore, sickness occasionally laid siege to the countryside—especially during summer, when the land lay stifled by the sun's heat, without even a puff of breeze to rustle leaves. Finally, the instability of the Republic, especially its economy, bothered him, as it did everyone. Texas treasury notes were worth very little—"going at 4 for 1" in late spring—but currency was so scarce that most people around Rutersville did business by trading.

None of these troubles sent Bell reeling home. Such a retreat he persistently refused to make, no matter how low his mood or his fortune sank. He took still another personal inventory, and he decided his prospects for success in life seemed as bright in Texas as anywhere, and his actions were always characterized by honesty and uprightness. He felt he had won the esteem of most people who knew him, and he was certain he had become so attached to the country and its people he had no desire to return to Tennessee.

One summer day in 1841 he paid a dollar and a half to post a long letter to his brother James in Trenton with this message for relatives and friends at home: "You may tell them that I write like I intended to shine sometime if it is somewhat late in life though I do not know if it is any too late."

36. PAYING FOR A MISTAKE

About the time that Thomas Bell posted his expensive letter home, men of the Santa Fe Expedition rested on the bank of "Nolan's River" north of present Waco. Somewhere near there the adventurer Philip Nolan had been killed in 1801 by Spanish troops who pursued him during his unauthorized mustanging expedition, having suspected that he was not really looking for horses at all, but was instead mapping the country for United States conquest.

Surely few of the Santa Fe men knew anything about Nolan. Those who did would have been too weary to tramp around the countryside looking for the forty-year-old remains of Nolan's fort, even if they thought any trace could have been found. By that time the men had come to realize that their journey would be something more than a lark. They had occasionally endured the thirst of dry camps that made sleep nothing of the luxury tired men should expect. They had been forced to hack out a path through a dense wood belt around the Bosque River, then to dig an incline for the wagons in the steep riverbank. They had endured many other hardships, and in Kendall's case this included being jolted, bumped, and jerked along ground increasingly eroded.

But the awakening to reality had come slowly. At the first camp out of Kenney's Fort some men had enough energy left at the day's end to fish for trout and catfish in the San Gabriel River while waiting for supper. When the cattle arrived at camp, a fat animal was singled out, shot, and butchered, and the meat was doled out to hungry men who boiled it or roasted it on spits over a fire, then devoured it with only salt, coffee, and sugar to round out the meal. On that first night out small groups had gathered around campfires and exchanged stories of their experiences fighting Indians or hunting buffalo. After an hour or so everyone except the men on guard made his bed by picking a soft place on the ground and rolling up in a blanket under the stars. Even reveille the next morning sounded "cheering."

On the second day out the expedition had rolled on for an easy twelve miles, then had camped under thick clouds that hid the stars and later sent down thunder and lightning but surprisingly little rain. On the third day the men had made more smooth progress over treeless prairies. They sighted buffalo in the distance and killed a few for supper, temporarily relieving a strain on the beef supply, which had been depleted by the departure delay and the heavy ration—three pounds a day for each man.

The buffalo also provided variety. That night men feasted on choice cuts and on tongue, marrow bones, and other delicacies. The next day they moved on to the banks of Little River. There, on the site of an old Ranger fort—probably the one that had been linked by patrol with the post at the falls of the Brazos—the expedition halted to bring up more beef cattle. This required five days, and during that time the men fished and hunted, lounged and slept, but grumbled all the while about the inactivity and the seed ticks. Except for those pests, the location struck Kendall as being one of singular beauty. A two-mile-wide belt of trees, some containing "delicious wild honey," shaded a fertile bottomland bordered by rich prairies that attracted buffalo and deer. Bear and ferocious Mexican hogs lived in the bottoms, and fish abounded in the river.

On the second night in this wild paradise a man shot himself to death with his rifle, alarming the entire camp. It was only one of many suicides in the Republic of Texas, to which many men had come in an attempt to leave problems elsewhere.

Two hours later, after the camp had settled down again, a guard brought everyone to his feet with a shout, "Who goes there?" He followed this challenge with a rifle blast. Most of the others armed themselves and prepared to repel whatever attackers lurked in the blackness of surrounding woods. Then came an explanation. The "attackers" actually had been one man, a member of the expedition, who was returning to camp after looking for, and finding, a missing horse. The man had not answered the sentinel properly— Texas volunteers were rarely known for their adherence to military formalities—and the guard had sent a shot in his direction. After the second alarm the night passed serenely, and the sleep lost was no nuisance—the men could nap during the following day, since they were forced to wait a while longer. The worst loss during this period was the military commander, Hugh McLeod, who returned to the settlements for a time to recuperate from an ailment diagnosed by one of the men as "too much whiskey."

Finally, one evening toward the end of June, more cattle came in and the men learned that they would renew their march on the following morning. They all greeted this information with cheers. The people of Santa Fe were waiting, including the señoritas of the place, and what señoritas were not affectionate? Their rewards would be great.

So President Mirabeau B. Lamar's Santa Fe Expedition started moving again, and once more the men saw buffalo grazing in the distance—almost anywhere they looked. Toward sundown they saw another sight that vanished from the Texas scene not long after they observed it—a drove of mustangs paying them "a flying visit." They first saw the animals when about half a mile distant. Many men mistook them for Indians—"when seen on a distant hill, standing with their raised heads toward a person, and forming a line as is their custom, it is almost impossible to take them for anything but mounted men," Kendall said. But when the horses had come near enough to satisfy their curiosity about the intruders, they wheeled and galloped off, "their long, thick manes waving in the air and their tails nearly sweeping the ground." Such scenes had attracted the daring Philip Nolan to Texas—and had resulted in his death. The Santa Fe men seemed equally entranced by the vast country.

But after that the expedition grew less of a pleasure jaunt. Sweating, cursing men were forced to dig out a road for the wagons through gullies and creeks. Even this exhausting labor did not prevent breakdowns and overturnings—they averaged about one a day. The swearing that ensued was described by Kendall as the most awesome he had ever heard. "I asked one of [the drivers], just as he had finished a long and most horrid oath . . . why he uttered such profanities. His answer was, they saved much whipping, and . . . his oxen drew much better than with the common kind of swearing."

The July sun burned more fiercely from a cloudless sky when, one day, the expedition began crossing a dry prairie. That evening the men dropped to still-warm earth tired, hot, sweaty, and thirsty, but with no water to drink. The last drop had been emptied from canteens around noon that day. Visions of cool drinks haunted Kendall all night long. The very next day rain poured from a black storm that gave forth startling bolts of lightning and crackling thunder, but the welcomed moisture brought discomfort too. In camp that night a rattlesnake sought shelter in Kendall's tent from the wet ground. Kendall felt the snake crawling over his covering blankets, but he lay motionless, fearing that any movement would cause the rattler to strike. Eventually he did risk covering himself, head and all, under his blanket, and he remained still until daylight, when he and his companions discovered the visitor had left.

Two days after that they encountered the almost vertical banks of the Bosque River, where they were forced to dig a makeshift road with "labor incredible." Even after that exhausting effort each loaded wagon was sent down the steep incline held back by ropes and by locked wheels to prevent a head-first tumble, then on the other side was pulled up by a team of twenty oxen toiling amid a din of whipping, cracking, yelling, and cursing. Dealing with the Bosque required most of one day. Then a few days later the expedition found another river to cross—the Brazos, rimmed by more high banks and bedded in quicksand.

Beyond the Brazos lay "Nolan's River," and beyond that a rough belt of prickly brush and stunted trees called the Cross Timbers. In these badlands the Santa Fe Expedition was to flounder about for almost two weeks.

The Cross Timbers sapped much of what patience was left to the men. They found the country baking in a prolonged drought. The many deep, "almost impassable" gullies they encountered held no water. Rocks and stones covered hills, and nearly everywhere they found their way blocked by tough, spiny vegetation—impenetrable areas of briers and thorny bushes, groves of blackjacks and post oaks. The only way to get through was to hack out a path, which the men did "half choked with thirst." Animals suffered, too. The oxen, worn from travel and lack of water, tugged at their lines dispiritedly. In the midst of this earthly hell, on July 27, someone calculated latitude and longitude and found that the glorious Santa Fe Expedition had progressed about two hundred miles in five weeks.

But spirits soared after the expedition struggled out of the prickly clutches of the Cross Timbers onto a level plain and camped near a thirst-quenching spring. Each man cooked his beef ration on a spit, with nothing else to eat, "but keen appetites supplied bread, vegetables and seasoning." After the Cross Timbers had been traversed the worst part of the journey seemed to be over. To the west and northwest as far as the men could see lay smooth prairie. Twenty miles farther on, according to calculations, the Red River cut through this flat land, but expedition leaders decided against getting any closer, choosing instead to take a course roughly parallel to the river and thus avoid the gullies and ravines that would surely be found closer in.

July had come and gone. Early in August, six weeks after departure, Kendall's injury had healed sufficiently so that he could abandon the wagon and ride horseback. His right foot still would not bear much weight, but traveling became easier for him.

They knew where they were now and where they should be going. To the north they could see a distant belt of woodland running nearly parallel to their western course. This would be the timber along the Red River—and a Mexican member of the expedition, Carlos, a native of Taos who had trapped along the river and knew it well, declared this was so. Because of his knowledge the command moved him to a spy company, for scouting ahead.

They decided now to cross the river and travel along the north bank. As they approached, they caught glimpses of Indians, but they encountered no resistance.

"Red River" certainly matched its name, as a member of the expedition described it. The water was reddish and salty, and it was bordered by rich red soil that seemed especially suitable for corn, which the Indians had planted on both sides. At the point of crossing, the bank-to-bank width of the river was about seventy-five yards, but this was summer and the water did not cover the entire bed.

The Santa Fe Expedition had encountered the river at the location of a Waco Indian village—explaining the earlier sightings. But by the time the Texans arrived, the Indian population—three or four hundred—had fled. The men curiously poked around the village while encamped there, but they were under strict orders not to destroy anything. A twenty-nine-year-old Irishman who had volunteered for the expedition in San Antonio about the time President Lamar visited there walked around the village and recorded what he saw—twenty-five or thirty round huts, about sixteen feet in diameter. He looked into one of the larger huts, located in the center of the village, and noticed benches arranged around the circular wall, some broken pieces of red crockery, and a few pumpkins and squash. He hoped to find a supply of corn from the fields they had seen along the river, but the Indians apparently had cached somewhere every last ear they had gathered.

The Taos native with the expedition looked over the surroundings and pronounced this the Red River. "We had no doubts," Kendall wrote. After the expedition had crossed the stream and struck out westward again along the opposite bank, the men noticed more Indians observing their movements from distant hills, but still they were not attacked. Probably the sight of the six-pounder cannon had something to do with their reluctance, Kendall thought.

Along the north side of the Red River travel was easy at first, although the banks were so steep in places that the river could not be reached. On the opposite side of the river they could see a broken, hilly region, and they gave thanks silently for being able to detour around such rugged country. Somewhat disturbing was the realization that the course along the river ran a little south of west, not the direction they needed to follow to get to Santa Fe, but they reasoned that the river would soon turn northward, and in any event since they knew their general location their eventual arrival at Santa Fe would be easy to manage.

By August 6 Kendall found he could ride without pain, although he still walked only with difficulty and needed help mounting his horse. He joined a spy company, satisfying his craving for more action, more excitement, and something more to write about. He saw Indians often. They were the old shadowers from the Waco tribe, and Kendall guessed they were looking for a chance to stampede the horses and cattle or to collect a few scalps from stragglers. He kept alert to avoid a sacrifice from his own head, but one day while scouting miles away from the main party he became lost—and discovered the true definition of that word. "Lost," as it referred to this New Orleans journalist alone on the vast expanse of Southwestern desolation, meant something beyond the usual concept. It meant loss of presence of mind, of reason, of self-confidence. In this country it could have meant also loss of scalp, but some luck helped Kendall to avoid that. From a ridge he peered around the horizon and saw a rapturous sight—tiny specks winding through a distant valley. He galloped back to the expedition.

The country became rougher. Water and grass dwindled. The beef animals lost weight, which meant that the ration would have to be cut. Sugar already had given out, and coffee was near the bottom. Nevertheless, hope did not subside, because the expedition seemed to be making good progress. The Taos native acting as guide declared he knew this country very well from trapping excursions. He estimated the New Mexican town of San Miguel to be seventy-five or eighty miles distant. That would be the first settlement. August had not even reached its midpoint, and the miles had rolled by, after all, faster than the men had expected.

Expedition commissioners discussed the situation and decided to send three men ahead to San Miguel for supplies. This advance party would take along provisions for three days, would travel only by night and lie concealed during the day to avoid Indians. Kendall saw a chance here for more action, excitement, and topical material, and he thought of volunteering to go as a fourth man, but others dissuaded him. The three men left without him.

For the others came more torturous travel across harsh, rugged country thinly covered by grass so dry now that it crumbled underfoot. The days were dry and hot and of interminable length. Twelve jolting miles across brown gulleys and gulches was a good average for the creaking expedition. Withered men endured frequent dry camps. Parched mouths craved a gourdful of cool water more than anything else. Then some men caught a glimpse of water at the bottom of a steep bluff. Was it real? Scores of horsemen pitched over the precipice nearly head first and tobogganed toward it. Noisy, greedy slurps: brackish water.

Some men forgot the lessons of the wilderness, gulped it down anyway, and fell sick. Others took just enough to wet their lips and throats, and all night long suffered thirst even more agonizing. But wait! Far to the west, illumined by the morning sun—blue tops of mountains that the Mexican guide Carlos identified. Carlos knew where he was; he was close to home. One of the officers had begun to doubt him, guessing that his declared "Red River" actually was the Wichita, too far to the south now for comfort, but the men still believed Carlos. They had to have something more than brackish water for sustenance.

What seemed like an ultimate calamity came at about the middle of August. A fire that streaked across the prairie almost with the speed of burning gunpowder separated the expedition and destroyed several wagons. Kendall described the aftermath:

Daylight the next morning disclosed a melancholy scene of desolation and destruction. North, south, and east, as far as the eye could reach, the rough and broken country was blackened by the fire, and the removal of the earth's shaggy covering of cedars and tall grass . . . laid bare, in painful distinctiveness, the awful chasms and rents in the steep hillside before us, as well as the valley spreading far and wide below. Afar off, in the distance, a dense black smoke was seen rising, denoting that the course of the [fire] was still onward.

On August 15 the Mexican guide Carlos and another man disappeared from camp. Too many men had been pressing Carlos for information that he could not provide. Apparently he had realized for some time that he was lost, but he did not dare admit this to the men. Nearly everyone now became resigned to the fact that the expedition had not been traveling up the Red River toward the destination, but had instead been toiling along the valley of the Wichita River, wasting hundreds of hard-earned miles going southwestward. No San Miguel would be found seventy-five or eighty miles away; no provisions would be rushed out anytime soon. The three men sent forward for help had not even been heard from.

But the Santa Fe Expedition had gone too far to turn back now. The only hope lay in pursuing the "melancholy journey." Some men who refused to face reality still hoped that the vanished guide from Taos might return with an explanation for his absence and lead them on to a nearby San Miguel, but no such delusion fooled the expedition command. On August 17 a detachment of fifty men rode northward under orders not to return until the elusive Red River had been located beyond question.

"No one knew where we were," Kendall said. Observations were of little help. Most of this country was mapped insufficiently or not at all. Anyway, the calculations might prove to contain as much human error as had the guide's declarations. Remaining food came under strict rationing; an assistant surgeon died of a liver ailment; in the distance, west and north, loomed forbidding hills to be crossed. Few men of President Lamar's Santa Fe Expedition would have renewed their contracts this August 17 had they been given a choice.

After that the days dragged into weeks. Hunger and thirst became more acute. Indians killed and mutilated men caught away from the main body. Wagons bumped along behind debilitated oxen. No Red River had been reported as having been found, but the expedition proceeded in a northwesterly direction. Then it came upon a steep elevation onto the Llano Estacado (Staked Plain) that posed for the wagons an insurmountable barrier as far as men could see. There, at the foot of this phenomenon, popularly known today as the Cap Rock, the Santa Fe Expedition came to a halt, on Quitaque Creek in present Motley County. The military commander had no other choice than to divide his force and send one group on to New Mexico to contact the inhabitants and to bring assistance. A hundred men on horseback rode westward across the many miles of the Llano Estacado, an almost level plateau where surface water was even scarcer than it had been, on toward the distant mountains and settlements of New Mexico. Kendall accompanied this group. Behind them, the rest of the men, with the wagons, settled into camp at the foot of the Cap Rock.

Kendall felt the journey would never end. Once in the mountains, the men encountered chasms and cliffs that forced them to make many detours, although they almost dropped from hunger. Discipline vanished. Men wandered away looking for plums, grapes, and berries, but eventually the will to survive brought them back together. Numbers seemed to mean strength, even as weak as they all were. Someone killed a skunk and ate it; then the men decided to butcher one of the weakest horses. Kendall said, " . . . in less time than it takes me to tell it his hide was off and his flesh distributed." It was eaten half cooked and without salt. After the meal they spread their blankets in a dry ravine and tried to sleep, but a cold mountain wind prevented even this brief escape from torture.

Weak and unrefreshed, we arose in the morning—breakfastless and desponding, we mounted our horses, and once more resumed our gloomy march. Our course was southwest, and in the direction of what appeared to be a passage through the mountains; but after travelling some six or eight miles we found our . . . progress cut off by high and precipitous ascents. To

return was our only alternative, and at noon we again found
ourselves near the point whence we had started in the morning.

Thirteen days after they had left the wagons they encountered a
group of Mexicans returning from a trading expedition with the
Indians. They showered them with questions—but without getting
many answers, for the Mexicans were almost as isolated as they.
The traders did share a taste of barley meal and the information
that San Miguel was seventy or eighty miles farther on, beyond a
stretch of sheep country and a small village that would be found
ahead. After a night's sleep Kendall and his companions hired
three of the Mexicans to accompany an expedition member to the
wagon camp and to guide the people there into the settlements.
Then Kendall and the others rode on, and as soon as they found
sheep and shepherds bought twenty head of the animals, butchered
and roasted them, and feasted until some of the men made themselves sick. From the shepherds they learned that New Mexico had
heard of their impending arrival and was awaiting it with belliger-
ence, not happy expectation at all. The three men who had been
sent out so long ago to find San Miguel had been arrested and were
being held in Santa Fe by Governor Manuel Armijo, who had
spread word among his people that the Texans intended to kill
them and to burn their houses.   °

Nevertheless, Kendall and four other men made plans to hurry
on ahead of the others to San Miguel, and one man optimistically
took along some copies of President Lamar's message of hope to
the people of New Mexico for distribution among them. But when
they came to the first settlement they realized the effectiveness of
Armijo's campaign—people fled at their approach. After traveling
two more days, and when within three miles of the long-sought
town of San Miguel, they found themselves suddenly surrounded
by about a hundred soldiers, roughly dressed but well mounted and
obviously sincere in their work. Their commander asked the five
men if they were from Texas. Someone answered yes, and the
commander bowed—politely, Kendall thought, but soon after that
the man forced them to surrender their arms and made moves as if
to execute them on the spot. "I thought of home, relations,
friends, in the fleeting moment which passed," Kendall said. But

the commander eventually settled for marching them to San Miguel and there through the plaza into a building, where they were herded into a small room. That night they were served a skimpy meal of tortillas and weak mutton broth; then they lay down without blankets on a cold dirt floor, chilled by a wind blowing down from nearby mountains. But they had suffered this hardship only a short time before a woman of San Miguel sent them a buffalo skin and a blanket. Kendall bought another blanket with his own money, and the five prisoners made a bed with these three pieces.

The next day they began a trip to Santa Fe, afoot and closely guarded by their captors. Many miles down the road they were startled by the blasts of a trumpet announcing the approach of an important person—Governor Armijo himself, a stocky man about six feet tall, with military bearing in every inch. Armijo rode over to them, reached down and shook each man's hand, and asked his business. One of Kendall's companions, a uniformed Army officer, answered that they were merchants from the United States. Armijo grabbed the man by the collar of his dragoon jacket, pointed to one of the buttons decorated with a single star and the word "Texas," and asked, "What does this mean? I can read—*Texas!* You need not think to deceive *me:* no merchant from the United States ever travels with a Texas military jacket."

Governor Armijo ordered the escort to return the five men to San Miguel. He was told that they had already walked ten leagues that day, but he replied angrily, "They are able to walk ten leagues more. The Texans are active and untiring people—I know them. If one of them pretends to be sick or tired on the road, shoot him down and bring me his ears!"

The escort turned Kendall and his four companions back toward San Miguel, but Kendall's old injury had flared up. His ankle ached; it was badly swollen. Governor Armijo had gone on, however, and the escort proved to be less demanding. Kendall was allowed to pay for the privilege of riding on a donkey.

At San Miguel the New Mexicans locked the prisoners in a small room near the soldiers' quarters. From a barred window Kendall saw Armijo's retribution commence. A Texan he could not identify because of bandages covering the man's eyes was executed against the wall of a nearby house.

A horrible death it was, too! [The] . . . executioners led him
to a house near the same corner of the square we were in, not
twenty yards from us, and after heartlessly pushing him upon his
knees, with his head against the wall, six of the guard stepped
back about three paces, and at the order of the corporal shot the
poor fellow in the back! Even at that distance the executioners
but half did their barbarous work; for the man was only
wounded, and lay writhing upon the ground in great agony. The
corporal stepped up, and with a pistol ended his sufferings by
shooting him through the heart. So close was the pistol that the
man's shirt was set on fire, and continued to burn until it was
extinguished by his blood.

The victim proved to be one of the three men sent from the
expedition long ago to find San Miguel. All three had escaped after
having been apprehended, but had been recaptured. This was the
second of the three to be executed. Later Kendall witnessed the
execution of the other man.

Mexican troops rounded up the rest of the Santa Fe men with
the assistance of the Texas Army officer who had declared to
Governor Armijo that he was only a merchant from the United
States. Armijo sent that officer as a truce emissary to the others,
who had evacuated their camp at the foot of the Cap Rock and had
managed to reach a point just outside San Miguel. The officer
persuaded them to surrender their arms, saying that Armijo had
four thousand troops available in the vicinity—and thereafter the
man was considered a traitor by most Texans.

In early fall Kendall and the other Santa Fe prisoners commenced a march on foot from San Miguel to the city of Mexico, an
ordeal not finished until midwinter, 1842. Most of that time Kendall continually expected orders for release, but each ensuing day
brought only disappointment. He felt his country had failed him,
but he could rationalize the neglect: "The fault lies not with the
people of the United States, but with the *rulers;* for the fact is
notorious that a fear of losing political influence has induced those
in power to sacrifice the independence and jeopard the honour of
the country on more occasions than one." Kendall was to remain a
captive until April, 1842, when orders finally came for release of
the prisoners.

Lamar's vision of a lucrative slice of Santa Fe trade thus vanished—but, back in Austin, Lamar himself had disappeared from the political scene. His old enemy Sam Houston had been elected president again, having won over the despised David Burnet in a campaign characterized by great vulgarity.

In a December, 1841, message to Congress Houston captured the mood of the time: "It seems that we have arrived at a crisis in our national progress, which is neither cheering for the present nor flattering for the future. I heartily regret that truth will not allow me to approach the Congress with the usual felicitations of the present and prospective happiness. The time has arrived when facts must be submitted in their simplest dress."

In Austin, Sam Houston could claim political satisfaction with words, but in Mexico miserable men paid for Lamar's folly.

IX

REPUBLIC IN FLAMES

1842

Americans continued to look westward in 1842, but not really to Texas, its slaves, and its other problems. During the year an expedition under John C. Frémont left on the first of his explorations of what is now the western United States, this one into the unmapped Rocky Mountains. Frémont actually had his eyes on the Pacific Coast, although California and much of the adjoining Southwest were owned by Mexico, of course, and England had that claim on Oregon. But who knew what the future might bring?

This same year a treaty with England defined the northeastern boundary of the United States, which had been in dispute, and brought peace to that area. But it also ended American hopes of liberating Canada—and it did nothing for the friction with England over Oregon.

In the United States proper, temperance movements flourished, including the Washingtonian Temperance Society, with a claimed half-million members, at whose meetings former drunkards described their experiences before and after taking the abstinence pledge, in a sort of mass therapy. In Texas, a good candidate for that society endured frustrations that would have led a less determined man back to the anesthesia of the bottle.

Sam Houston began his second term as president with his usual willingness to go more than halfway toward peace. But it seemed that the further he went, the more elusive peace became. After the arrival of information about the capture of the Santa Fe Expedition an angry Texas Congress retaliated by passing a bill extending the western boundary all the way to the Pacific Ocean, including lower and upper California. Houston vetoed it as a "legislative jest," but Congress overrode him. A few weeks after that—early in March—Mexico compounded Houston's problems by sending a raiding party into Texas, infuriating citizens and forcing Houston to do something about it. He issued a declaration of a naval blockade of Mexican ports on March 26, then sent the ships to New Orleans for refitting and waited for seething Texas to calm down. He vetoed a "war bill" giving him dictatorial powers and the authority personally to lead an army against Mexico. This action brought a compliment from his old friend Andrew Jackson, who said, "By your veto you have saved your country, and yourself from disgrace. *Stand on the Defensive.*" But Houston infuriated many Texans by his veto; they felt that the hero of San Jacinto was a weakling. In September Mexico sent another army into Texas, compelling Houston to make a more drastic show of retaliation.

Domestic problems did not afford him any tranquillity, either. He wanted to move the capital out of Austin, a town he never liked, and this issue dominated much of his second administration. It brought him abuse from irate residents of what was then known as western Texas—around Austin. One man wrote him:

We did heare that you was goin to move the seat of government and the publick papers and that you swore you would do it and then when you come to Austin and found out the boys would not let you do it you sed you never was goin to move it. Now Sam you told a Dam lie for you did promise the people in Houston that you would move it . . . the truth is that you are afeard you Dam old drunk Cherokee. . . .

37. A NEIGHBORLY FIGHT

Texans often were as busy fighting among themselves as they were battling Mexicans and Indians. At home they fought verbally—in their shacklike Hall of Congress, for instance, or with fatal lead, as in the case of a long civil conflict known as the Regulator–Moderator War that had broken out two years earlier in the present East Texas counties of Harrison, Panola, and Shelby, all bordering Louisiana.

The real reason for this conflict antedated the Republic of Texas. Three decades earlier, following the Louisiana Purchase, the United States and Spain had tried to agree on a boundary between Louisiana and Texas. But agreement had proved to be impossible, and representatives of the two nations had worked out a compromise to avoid armed conflict: the designation of a neutral ground, with the western boundary at the Sabine River. Spain and later Mexico refused to permit any settlement of their Texas territory within twenty leagues of the Sabine, but people came anyway, most of them Anglo-Americans from the United States. Neither Spain nor Mexico cared to go to the trouble and cost of permanently expelling these people, but neither did they recognize them as citizens. Consequently the inhabitants became accustomed to making their own laws—and since many of them had been troublemakers in the United States before they moved into what became a haven for the lawless, justice was a rare circumstance. The concept of it differed from person to person.

Even after the formation of the Republic of Texas the inhabitants of this area had insisted on administering their own affairs, but they had split into groups. In 1840 shooting had broken out after a murder that had stemmed from a quarrel over forged land certificates. Brought to trial in a Republic of Texas courtroom for the killing was a man who was already a fugitive in the United States, but he won acquittal after a combination of travesties, and upon his release he organized a band of thirty men, called Regulators, to enforce his own idea of justice, which was generally the opposite of what law-abiding people expected. To counter this the Moderators were organized, but for months they were outnumbered and outgunned. At the height of the conflict crops went uncultivated, men were killed in ambush, prisoners were hanged without trial. The feud roared beyond control of the weak Republic of Texas government, and many people suffered.

The war inexorably affected everyone who lived in the area, and this included Harriet and Robert Potter. Harriet, who had thought life idyllic on Potter's Point overlooking the blue lake, changed her mind early in 1842. With her husband absent much of the time on business trips to Shreveport or to Austin, where he represented two counties in the Texas Senate, she had been left with the management of the farm, assisted mainly by her son Joe, whose father was Harriet's first husband. Harriet had been alone even when a daughter of Robert Potter's was born to her during her first year at Potter's Point. Her husband happened to be in Shreveport on business.

So once again Harriet had been left by a husband to manage for herself, but this time it seemed different. Robert Potter was attentive when at home. Not until later did she learn that he enjoyed the company of another woman in Austin.

Early in February, 1842, Congress adjourned, and Potter returned to his home and to his wife on Caddo Lake—but no longer to tranquillity. Harriet later told his story:

With his interest in politics, law, and East Texas real estate, Potter had become involved in the Regulator–Moderator War as a Moderator and had found a formidable adversary in a hard fifty-five-year-old man named William Pinckney Rose, who was, like Potter, a native of North Carolina. A leader of the Regulators, Rose had insisted on dealing out his own brand of law and order, which earned him various nicknames—"Old Rose," "the Lion of the Lakes," and "Hell-roarin' Rose." But it had also won him some friends who considered him a patriot and a statesman. Everything depended on which side a man supported—and on which side supported a man.

Soon after Potter returned from Austin he collected a group of seventeen Moderators to help him arrest "Old Rose" and to see that the man got a trial and punishment for alleged crimes ranging all the way to murder. Well armed, the Moderators rode toward Rose's farm, but the man saw them coming before they saw where he was—in a field, with several of his Negroes, cutting and burning brushwood. Rose fell to the ground and ordered the Negroes to cover him with brush. Potter and his men looked around for some time, then were prevailed upon by Rose's son—"a nice young man . . . not at all like his father"—to leave. The son said he would persuade his father to surrender himself for trial. Potter dispersed his men and returned home in early-evening darkness.

When Potter arrived home and told Harriet what had happened she begged him to get his men together again and have them wait in the house, because she felt sure "Old Rose" would come after him. Potter laughed and answered that Rose would not be able to collect enough men until morning for an attack, even if his son failed to persuade him to surrender. Then Potter went to bed, weary from the day's activities. Late that night Harriet heard their dogs barking outside the house. More apprehensive than ever about Rose, she tried to rouse her sleeping husband, but he asked her not to bother him.

Potter's confidence was misplaced. Immediately after he and his group of Moderators had left Rose's farm, "the Lion of the Lakes" had summoned men to help him get rid of Potter. A request from Rose was not one that could be ignored, and the summoned men appeared quickly. During the night they surrounded Potter's house and waited, while the tired head of the household slept on inside. The barking dogs eventually fell silent again.

Morning dawned. It was March 2, 1842—exactly six years after Robert Potter had voted for the declaration of independence at Washington-on-the-Brazos. But this morning he appeared something less than a heroic man. He slept late, while his wife and the Negroes began preparing for breakfast. She sent a boy outside to grind meal, and when he failed to reappear soon enough she sent someone else to look for him. Several minutes later she dispatched an old Negro whose usual job was tending the hogs. Then she went herself. In the back yard she caught sight of the old man, heard the crack of a rifle, and saw him fall. Men leaped from hiding and tried to grab her, but she broke from their grasp, ran back into the house, and slammed the door.

Potter slept no longer. "What does that mean?" he asked.

"It means that the house is surrounded and we will have to fight or die."

"Where are all the men?" Potter demanded, referring to the slaves.

"I suppose the men are all killed. They have just killed one."

Potter decided his only hope for escape was to flee the house. Harriet begged him not to go, and their young daughter began screaming her protest, but Potter took a rifle and prepared to run. Apparently he thought of some final words for her, possibly about the other woman in Austin, because he said three times, "I want to tell you something." But Harriet could only repeat her pleas for him to stay—"We can defend ourselves. I'll stand by you as long as we both live. If you'll just kill Old Rose . . . the difficulty will be at an end."

Potter ignored her. He peered through a crack in a back wall of the house and saw a number of men waiting there. His best chance seemed to be to bolt out the front door for the lake, where he might put to use his excellent swimming ability. Harriet heard him say something like "They can't hurt you anyhow," then saw him run out the door and sprint across the yard. From around the house some of Rose's alert companions fired six times at him but missed every shot.

Near the front-yard fence stood two surprised men, both of them recipients of help given by Potter in times past. He glanced at them, looked back toward the house, and called out to Harriet, "Why, these are my friends."

"No, they're not friends," she yelled back. Potter leaped over the fence and ran on just as the two men raised their rifles to fire. From behind the house Harriet heard others yelling like Indians as they also shot at Potter's retreating form.

Potter vanished over the cliff and raced down the steep path toward the lake, with Rose's men not far behind. At the bottom he placed his rifle against one of three magnificent cypress trees Harriet especially admired and dived into the water.

At the house Harriet Potter heard the tumult but could see nothing. As if in a trance she walked out the door and stood peering toward the lake. She was there when Rose walked up, leveled his rifle at her, and ordered her to go back inside. She refused, and he repeated his command—just as another man appeared, walking up the pathway that led from the lake. He had the temerity to ask Rose, "Why are you abusing Mrs. Potter? She's never done you any harm. Come on; let's go. We've done what we came to do."

Harriet did not believe the man. She felt certain that her husband had escaped and that they were merely trying to frighten her. But this was not so. Her husband, the man William Fairfax Gray had predicted years earlier could only float in troubled water, had been shot in the back of the head while swimming for his life on Caddo Lake.

None of the beauty of Potter's Point remained for Harriet after that. She spent much of the rest of her life trying to forget it. Rose never stood trial for the death. The Regulator–Moderator War was to rage on for two more years before the Texas government could end it with a large militia force and mediation of a peace treaty between the two factions.

But perhaps the greatest tragedy for Harriet was that still another man had failed her. Robert Potter had seemed to her to be the epitome of gallantry and nobility. Some time later she learned the truth. In Austin he had signed a will that left Potter's Point to the other woman whose company he had enjoyed; and in still another disappointment the Texas Supreme Court declared her marriage to Potter invalid.

38. INVASION

On the opposite side of Texas, in the western settlements, people had something else to think about besides fighting their neighbors. There, on the extreme frontier, they heard with increasing frequency rumors of invasion from Mexico.

Exposed San Antonio, with its Alamo still in visible ruins, heard the talk with particular alarm. The Ranger Captain Jack Hays kept spies out constantly far to the west, where Mexican intruders would first appear, but his men saw only a lifeless expanse of chaparral country.

Nevertheless, Mary Maverick heard alarming reports almost daily. "All fall and winter of '41 and 2 rumors of invasion in force reached us from various persons. Sometimes friendly Mexicans came to warn us and to beg us not to stay and be butchered, for the troops coming would be vindictive and cruel." Informed persons like Mary knew Mexico had many problems of its own, however, and they doubted the ability of that nation to raise an adequate force to reconquer Texas. But as the winter of 1842 began to give way to spring Jack Hays heard reports that convinced him the Mexicans had indeed mustered a force on the Rio Grande with the intention of invading Texas.

Mary Maverick knew this, but she thought it likelier that the invading force, if one existed, was only a band of robbers who would not venture in as far as San Antonio. Nevertheless, Hays insisted that she and the other Anglo-American women take their children eastward to some place of safety. Mary packed a few necessities, buried some valuables under the floor, carried a few other cherished possessions to the residence of a Mexican woman friend for safekeeping, and departed in the company of her husband, who planned to return as soon as he had placed his family comfortably with friends. Mary herself expected to be absent only a short time.

The date was March 1 when Mary Maverick joined the second "runaway," this one more reluctant and leisurely than the flight that had preceded Santa Anna's invasion in 1836. Many other men besides Sam Maverick accompanied the group, planning to return to San Antonio as soon as they had their families settled. Coming spring had greened the grass and brought forth blooms. "Strange that we refugees should be a happy crowd, but so it was, so it always will be with youth and health," Mary said.

At a large farm home near Seguin she and her children, along with other refugees, were received with "true Virginia hospitality," and Sam Maverick returned to San Antonio. After the first night Mary and two other women insisted on moving themselves and their children out of the crowded house into a blacksmith's shop nearby. There they erected a shelf to hold perfume and a borrowed mirror, brought in flowers, and made themselves at home. But the very next morning at three o'clock a loud rap startled them out of their sleep, and a solemn male voice announced from outside the door, "Ladies, San Antonio has fallen."

They had never anticipated such a development. As they lay

silently reflecting on this appalling news the cold darkness seemed to close in on them. One of the women rose, lighted a candle, and cried in the flickering glow. Another fell on her knees and began counting her beads. A "shaking ague" gripped Mary, and she could not talk for the chattering of her teeth. In dark recesses of the room the children awoke to this grim scene and cried.

Later that day they heard the complete story. General Rafael Vásquez with about six hundred men had appeared on March 5 outside San Antonio and had demanded its surrender. The few Texans there had chosen to flee rather than to fight. Still later Mary heard even more ominous reports from people fleeing eastward: that Vásquez' force was only the advance element of an army of thirty thousand men, bound precisely in her direction.

Then the awful picture began to fade away. Her husband arrived to take her and the children on to Gonzales, and soon after he appeared came word that General Vásquez, threatened by a growing army of Texas volunteers, had begun a withdrawal to Mexico. The raid had been nothing more than a plundering expedition after all, but it had frightened the entire area into pell-mell evacuation.

The apprehension did not vanish. No longer did people in the west presume the Mexicans could not launch an invasion. Sam Maverick returned to San Antonio, but not with his family. There he found their home on the corner of Commerce and Soledad broken into and plundered. Everything of any value had disappeared. He decided to move his family even farther east—to a place on the Colorado River, near La Grange. There he bought land and arranged to build a house. Until its completion Mary and the children could live at the nearby home of an affluent friend. Meanwhile, Maverick's law practice still required his occasional presence in San Antonio, but until the safety of that town seemed better assured he would travel there alone.

39. A TARDY VOLUNTEER

Gloom also pervaded the Rutersville sanctuary of studious Thomas Bell. On March 7, 1842, he had begun a letter to his father: "The dark storm of war is gathering thick and murky on our western frontier." That same day, one hundred miles southwest, Vásquez had begun his withdrawal from San Antonio, but Bell was not aware of this development until later. Instead he heard daily, almost hourly, reports of the Mexican invasion delivered by fast-riding horsemen. Bell had been nearly as appalled as had Mary Maverick to hear of the fall of San Antonio, "without a gun being fired on either side."

The invasion had come as a surprise, Bell wrote in his letter, but Texans were making every preparation to meet the enemy, whose numbers were said to be twenty-one thousand men in three divisions. Probably these soldiers would overrun much of the country before they could be stopped. "Ruin and devastation will be the inevitable consequence wherever they march." Despite this emergency the Texas government—which continued to disappoint Bell even though Lamar had given way to Sam Houston—had issued no instructions of which Bell was aware, but he wrote that he had decided to ride on the following morning for the weak, retreating Texas Army and would probably reach it day after tomorrow. With him would go most men in Rutersville, and every male college student over the age of fifteen. "The chances of war permitting you will hear from me again soon."

Bell laid down his pen and began getting his things together. He left the letter open on his table. Later his uncle found it there and added a few paragraphs about Thomas, but deferred mailing it to Tennessee until word came of his nephew's fate. "We hope the storm will soon blow over and Thomas will return to College Hill," the uncle added.

About three weeks later Thomas himself returned from the army. He began the letter again and explained that the Mexicans had conducted their raid mostly to deceive and unsettle the Texans, retreating before troops could be assembled for a real show of force. But the raid had evoked a reaction that went beyond nervousness, Bell said. Many Texans who had opposed carrying the war into Mexico were incensed "at such an outrage" and now favored offensive military operations to force an acknowledgment of Texas independence or even to conquer the enemy's country.

Accordingly, an army would be raised in the next few weeks to invade Mexico, Bell predicted, and if as many as five thousand men joined in the effort they probably could fight their way clear to the city of Mexico. Should the invasion take place, Bell expected "to make one of the number."

40. AN IMPATIENT MIDSHIPMAN

At New Orleans, a restless midshipman aboard the Texas Navy flagship *Austin* rankled under inactivity. Young Andrew Jackson Bryant, who had come to Texas from Maine with his father, Charles G. Bryant, surveyed the armament aboard his 600-ton sloop of war—it included twenty 24-pound guns and two 18-pounders—and wrote his mother and brothers in Bangor: "We have been here a long time whereas we ought to be down the coast whipping the Mexicans. . . . We would sweep the Gulf."

Young Jackson Bryant possibly inherited his love of action from his father, a man of about forty with an ardent military temperament and a great sympathy for rebellions against autocrats. Four years earlier Charles Bryant had crossed the border from Maine into Canada to help fight in a revolt against English power, and after its failure he had been captured, tried, and sentenced to death. Friends helped him to escape, and he fled first to Maine, then—to avoid extradition—to the Republic of Texas, where he arrived in January of 1839 with his eldest son. He left his wife and four other sons in Maine.

In Texas Charles Bryant had placed his son in the Texas Navy as midshipman. There the boy could have board, room, and education—a great consideration for a man without money—and could learn discipline and integrity. But there his son grew restless with the inactivity.

Jackson Bryant's father had seen more action against the Mexicans than he had, but even Charles Bryant's experience had not been extensive. When news of the Vásquez raid on San Antonio had arrived in Galveston, Bryant was just beginning business with a partner. He volunteered at once for military service, along with every other male worthy of the designation. "All was hurry and confusion, all business stopped at once, nothing was heard but the

drum . . ." Charles Bryant had been promoted to lieutenant of his
company, then to adjutant of the battalion, but he and the others
missed the satisfaction of engaging General Vásquez' troops. After
seven weeks he returned to his home in Galveston, to discover that
his housekeeper had absconded to the United States with every
possession of value except for his clothes. He had lost four hundred
dollars' worth of property.

In New Orleans the Navy Jackson Bryant served in was in
approximately the same financial shape as his father. It was one of
the few holdovers from the Lamar administration, and appropria-
tions for it had just about vanished. Sam Houston never exhibited
any affection for or appreciation of a fleet, even though his old
friend and mentor, the man for whom Midshipman Bryant was
named, Andrew Jackson, advised Houston at the time of the Vásquez invasion scare, "Mexico can never reach you with a formidable army as long as you have command of the Gulf."

It was Lamar who had begun rebuilding the Texas Navy after it
had passed out of the picture in 1837. Between March, 1839, and
April, 1840, seven vessels had been commissioned: the steam
packet *Zavala*, schooners *San Jacinto*, *San Antonio*, *San Bernard*,
brigs *Wharton* and *Archer*, and sloop of war *Austin*. Lamar, to his
credit, had appointed Navy officers on merit rather than for political considerations, and he had chosen as commodore a twenty-nine-
year-old former United States Navy lieutenant, fiery Edwin Ward
Moore, who had quickly disposed of several Mexican ships and had
helped Yucatán briefly in its rebellion against the centralist government. But now, with Sam Houston again President, the Texas
Navy was without a sponsor. Most of the vessels remaining in
commission were laid up at New Orleans. Commodore Moore
begged, borrowed, and used his own money to keep the ships afloat
and refused to take his abbreviated fleet to Galveston, where
President Houston probably would have seen to it that the vessels
went out of commission.

So Andrew Jackson Bryant chafed aboard Moore's flagship
Austin at New Orleans. His pay of eighteen dollars a month presumably accumulated on the books, because he never received any
money. Jackson's father had put him in the Navy with that purpose of teaching him some discipline and integrity, but the work-

aday naval routine was not to Jackson's liking at all. It was galling, and he showed his distaste by rebelling. News of his insubordinations quickly reached his distressed father in Galveston.

"Be a good boy, do not disgrace yourself or your father," Bryant pleaded, but without effect, as other letters indicated:

. . . I was mortified to learn from Lt. [William Tennison] that . . . you had not been attentive to your studies, and that he had found it almost impossible to get you to study at all—how can it be possible that you should have so little pride and ambition as not to improve every opportunity that is set before you to inform yourself in the duties of your profession and acquiring a general education [?]—Jackson I am pained to the heart with the fear that you are so [wedded] to indolence and folly as to grow up without an education, and without forming habits of industry . . . and integrity. . . . You cannot conceive of how much misery you have caused me by telling me of your disgrace—to be suspended from duty for disobedience of orders is disgraceful—how can you have . . . forgotten the advice I have given you so often—to be obedient and diligent in your duty—modest and unassuming in your manners [?] . . . I fear Jackson that the most of your difficulties in the navy are caused by your own faults—you must change your manners towards your messmates before you can be liked, you are entirely [too] arrogant and dictatorial in your manner to make friends with those with whom you are associated . . . —I fear you spend too much of your time in trifling and play . . .

Jackson wanted to go home to Maine, or to get leave from the Navy and enroll in school in Galveston, or to do almost anything besides study and salute and endure the boring routine of a war vessel in port. All this discomfort was compounded by the extreme poverty of the Texas Navy. Midshipman Bryant even lacked shoes and adequate clothing. His family certainly could not help him financially—they hoped that he might help them. In Maine his mother could scarcely get enough food to feed herself and four children, and in Texas his father struggled to support himself and rarely could spare any money even to send back to Maine.

So Jackson continued going through the motions of daily ship-board routine, which started for most men at four o'clock in the morning, even in port. Shortly before that hour—eight bells of the midwatch—drum and fife roused the sleeping men, then the notes of reveille blasted them out of their hammocks, in time to hear the eight strokes of the ship's bell. If all that noise failed to propel them into the day's activities, the notes of the boatswain's pipe and his gravelly shouts, echoed by his assistants, certainly would—"All hands! Up all hammocks."

The midshipman of the watch reported eight bells to the senior duty officer, then clambered down ladders into a steerage compart-ment that had been spared the previous noise, shook his sleeping successor, and bawled, "Eight bells! I'll thank you to relieve me."

On deck, sailors trudged sleepily up from the berthing space below, each carrying his hammock, rolled and lashed. A quarter-master stowed the bedding in "riprap" fashion on the hammock rail. That night the sleepers would at least enjoy aired bedding, if not feathery comfort.

Next the sailors turned to holystoning the deck. They wet it down with water, poured on buckets of white sand, and scoured it with scrubbers. Then they washed off the sand with more buckets of water and squeegeed the residue by pressing and pushing a "nautical hoe" carrying two blades of strong leather in place of a metal blade. After that they gave the deck a final swabbing, then went on to other chores.

Just before eight o'clock in the morning occurred another in a series of reports up the inevitable chain of command. The quarter-master of the watch saluted the duty midshipman and said, "Eight bells, sir." The midshipman reported this information to the officer of the deck, who always replied, "Report it to the commodore, sir." When the commodore heard it he invariably ordered, "Make it so, sir, and pipe to breakfast." Finally, the officer of the deck made it so by ordering the bottommost link in this chain, the quarter-master, to strike eight bells. At that time other men hauled down the night pennant and raised the jack from the bowsprit and Texas colors from the gaff, all simultaneously. Then came breakfast.

About the only lighthearted break in this routine came when grog was distributed, with the sailors always lined up on the port side of the main deck. Otherwise most days passed with great austerity, exemplified by an event at ten o'clock in the morning. At that time the first lieutenant appeared on deck for a meeting with the ship's surgeon, who held in his hand a small square of white paper that had been rubbed around the interior of the cook's pots. If the first lieutenant saw the paper at all soiled the cook was given lashes at the gangway. But the officer usually saw a white piece of paper.

For most men shore leave was scarce. The only chance to sightsee around New Orleans usually was from the deck of their ship, for two reasons: rarely did the men receive any pay to spend ashore (Texas sailors did not even get the land certificates given to Texas soldiers for three months' service), and their officers feared desertion. It was no wonder that under these conditions a mutiny occurred—on board the *Austin*'s sister vessel *San Antonio*. Some members of the crew, led by a marine sergeant, armed themselves and attacked the officers, killing one and locking the others in the wardroom. After that they fled ashore, but most were quickly captured in New Orleans by United States authorities and held for the punishment they eventually received.

Jackson Bryant never resorted to such an extreme, but he yearned all that spring and summer to get away from the life. "Kiss my dear brothers for me," he wrote home, "and dear mother I wish I could be home to kiss you."

41. ANOTHER INVASION

Toward the end of June Sam Maverick found it necessary to return to San Antonio; an impending session of court required his presence there. He planned to travel with four other men—including his slave Griffin, who was then to return to Mary Maverick's temporary lodging in the home near La Grange with any household goods that might be salvaged from the residence on the sunny corner of Commerce and Soledad.

Mary and a few others rode for six miles or so with the departing men. She deplored the necessity of saying goodbye again and could not refrain from telling her husband about her feeling. Mary heard him say before he left, "Almost you persuade me not to go." But he rode off.

Griffin returned some time later, but Sam Maverick remained in San Antonio, living in the now lonesome house. The court began its business on Monday, September 5, and the presiding judge wrote in his diary on that day, "No invasion expected." Before the court was the case of Shields Booker versus the city of San Antonio over an allegedly unpaid fifty-peso fee. Maverick was arguing Booker's case.

Six days later, on Sunday morning, September 11, the second body of Mexican troops in six months entered the town, entirely unexpected—as the judge had indicated—despite the frequent invasion alarms.

Thick fog obscured a rising sun when the first word of attack came. Sam Maverick helped to rally the fifty or sixty Anglo-Americans in town against what they supposed at first to be a gang of bandits. From the vicinity of his house he and his companions maintained a steady fire for a few minutes. Then the fog lifted, and they saw that they were surrounded. Under a truce flag appeared a Mexican colonel, who conferred with Maverick and the others. They learned then, Maverick said later, that they had been firing at troops of the Mexican Army. More than a thousand of them, under the command of a French soldier of fortune, General Adrian Woll, had entered the city. Maverick and most of the other Anglo-Americans, all civilians, surrendered. A few men fled from San Antonio and carried across Texas the news of this latest invasion by Mexico. Again volunteers swarmed toward the town eager to fight.

Near La Grange, Mary Maverick heard of the calamity and immediately sent Griffin back to San Antonio with a thousand dollars in gold belted around his body to buy her husband's release. Griffin expressed eagerness to go. He told her that his master always had treated him more like a brother than a slave, and that he would do anything to help Mr. Maverick. Griffin joined fifty San Antonio–bound volunteers under the command of a man named Nicholas Mosby Dawson and was killed, along with most of the others, by Mexican artillery in the "Dawson Massacre" after the group had been cut off while trying to reach Texan forces engaged against Woll's army on Salado Creek six miles east of San Antonio. The artillerymen had ignored the Texans' white flag.

At noon on September 15, while Woll still held the town, Sam Maverick and his fellow prisoners began a long march into Mexican captivity. But they left behind a note regarding their kind treatment by the Mexican population of San Antonio. "We do hope . . . should this place again fall into the hands of Americans, that for our sake the Mexican population here will not be in any way disturbed or injured, either in person or property."

Maverick was allowed to write his wife during the journey into Mexico, and he was careful to write only cheering news. He said he felt certain his imprisonment would be brief. He urged her to be lively, to keep her spirits up, and to get daily exercise by horseback riding. As for himself, he expected to have plenty of exercise, fresh air, fine scenery, and meat and bread, which would see him safely through his "pilgrimage." "I have nothing, my love, worth writing, only to say that I have confidence in you to do with yourself and our precious little ones what shall appear to you for the best, and that I have good confidence in our meeting again before long."

Only when he referred to Griffin's death, about which he had been told, did he show much emotion. He wrote: "Oh, God forgive me, I am horrified at the death of . . . [Griffin]. Poor, brave boy. I mourn over thee . . . I owe thee a monument, bronze, and a constant tear for thy valor and thy fidelity. This, my love, is the hardest stroke of fortune that has yet fallen on us. It afflicts me most of any." But then he changed his tone, spoke again of seeing her soon, and concluded, "In the meantime . . . kiss my daughter and sons . . ."

Mary Maverick was better suited psychologically than most women to follow her husband's advice about keeping spirits up. Outwardly she seemed to do this, but her hidden emotions were different. "No one can imagine how dreadful this was to me," she wrote. Furthermore, she was worried about her three-year-old son, Lewis, who was seriously ill with typhoid fever at this time. Lewis had lost so much weight that his joints began to look disproportionately large, but he recovered, although for a time he could neither stand nor walk.

Eventually other letters arrived from her husband. Reassured, she moved into her recently completed house near the friend's farm to await Sam Maverick's return.

Her home was a log cabin consisting of a large room sixteen by eighteen feet and a smaller room for a kitchen. Nearby, a shed had been built for the cook, Jinny, and her children. In the yard grew a giant oak tree, which afforded good shade. Soon Mary's brother came, built a cabin near hers, and helped her milk the cows and tend the twenty-six-acre farm. Physically, they "began to be quite comfortable, considering the state of the country," but the mental anguish seemed overpowering. Mary thought of Goliad, the Alamo, and other dreadful places and events. "It was almost a constant dread on my mind to hear any day that our poor prisoners were murdered."

42. COUNTERATTACK, CONFUSION, CAPITULATION

Soon after Sam Maverick and the other prisoners had been marched out of San Antonio toward Mexico, General Woll and his troops followed—on September 20—faced with growing threats from the aroused Texans. President Sam Houston, forced out of his pacific policy by the Mexican incursions, had ordered two regiments of Texas militia to San Antonio, where these men were joined by many volunteers.

This time the men did not all disperse and go home after the intruders had departed. Instead they demanded vengeance. On October 3 Houston selected a circumspect former merchant, General Alexander Somervell, to take command of the militia and the volunteers and to invade Mexico—if success seemed likely, Houston added. Privately Houston still doubted the wisdom of offensive operations against Mexico, even in retaliation, and his choice of this particular officer operating under these particular orders showed that reluctance, but not for an angry public to see.

One of the volunteers was Thomas Bell, recently instructor at Rutersville College. His career had been interrupted, and he had decided "to make one of the number" against Mexico, as he had said earlier he would. The college owed him $454.91 for his teaching but could not—or did not—pay him. Bell filed suit to collect the amount in Fayette County District Court. With that matter pending, he enlisted in a volunteer company on October 17 and left Rutersville to fight.

For more than a month he waited around San Antonio with all the other men while a slow-moving command assembled supplies and ammunition, organized the expedition, and waited out unseasonably wet weather and a cutting north wind that brought early cold to the country and caused one entire regiment to ignore their orders and to return to the warmth of home firesides. Not until late November did the army move across the chaparral country between San Antonio and the Rio Grande—seven hundred troops apparently on their way to teach millions of Mexicans a lesson. They took with them two hundred pack mules and three hundred beeves. The men left first; then the General and the artillery followed, on November 25. The scene impressed tenderfoot Thomas Bell all the more because he was a member of this mighty force: ". . . long lines of mounted infantry wending their way over the grass clad plains of Texas, with banners waving proudly to the passing breeze and arms . . . [challenging] the civilized world to produce their equal." Every person in Texas seemed capable sometimes of ranking the new nation with the likes of the Roman Empire.

Most of the men had left their homes for army duty in waning summer or early fall and had brought with them only light clothing, but that November they marched into icy weather. For a while the cold rain continued, leaving soldiers drenched and shivering. They took advantage of a break in the weather to kill some deer that abounded in the region, and from their skins the lucky hunters fashioned warmer clothes. At one bivouac, said a member of the expedition, the camp looked more like a tanyard than an army setting.

On the Medina River they camped for two nights and a day awaiting the arrival of General Somervell and the artillery. The General came with an idea of surprising the town of Laredo, on the Rio Grande. To accomplish this he decided to send the artillery back and turn the army's march southward toward the Laredo road, which happened to take the expedition through a post-oak bog that held men and animals in its grip for three days. Men could walk on the drenched surface well enough, but the animals sometimes sank through the sod into a quicksand almost up to their bellies, while men yelled curses at the elements, the country, and General Somervell, and sought to extricate the animals. After two days in the bog the expedition had progressed five miles toward its surprise raid, and men and animals had become scattered across the countryside. At night the men built campfires and talked politics or gave impromptu theatricals; sleeping on the soaked ground was almost impossible. The wet wilderness became known as "the bogs of the Atascosa" and "the devil's eight leagues." None of it enhanced General Somervell's reputation as a military commander or a geographer; one volunteer called him "a perfect old Grannie . . . no more fit to command . . . than a ten-year-old boy."

After the expedition finally found firmer footing twenty men left and returned home. The others went on and captured Laredo December 8 without resistance—but also without surprise: the Mexicans had heard of Somervell's approach and had withdrawn a small infantry detachment located there. Instead of preparing at once to cross the Rio Grande and to strike Mexican towns along its west bank, however, General Somervell tarried outside Laredo, gathering some supplies for his men. He ordered them into camp a few miles downriver from the town. The next morning some of the men returned to Laredo and plundered it.

This shocked Thomas Bell, a young man who still held an exalted view of fighting for ideals. "Many things were carried into camp by the robbers, which were immediately taken from them and returned to the owners that evening. [Laredo] situated as it is in Texas and its inhabitants not making even a show of resistance to the entrance of the Texans, it was nothing less than downright robbery to make booty of their property."

Another member of the expedition had a more graphic description of the looting.

A great number of the men went into houses & stores and took a great many such things as they could lay their hands upon &

took them by force & carried them off by violence, breaking down doors, opening boxes, & trunks & taking off blankets wherever they could find them, even from the beds of the women, leaving them to weep the fate of their unhappy lot. The lateness of the day was the only thing that put a stop to this state of things, together with the order to move to a new camping place.

At this juncture the Somervell expedition against Mexico began to go to pieces, to Bell's dismay. The plundering of Laredo gave some men an excuse for deserting and returning home; they declared they could not conscientiously support a venture that resulted in such lawlessness. But one member of the expedition saw another reason for these men straggling off: "I never knew a man truly anxious to meet the enemy [to] turn back under any pretence whatever. . . . Those I have observed with the most bloody mottoes painted upon their caps were the last to prove them true."

The day after Laredo had been plundered Somervell put the entire project to a vote. He formed his men into ranks and told them that every man who wanted to carry the fight across the Rio Grande to the enemy should step to the right, and all who wanted to return should move to the left. If a majority still wanted to continue he would lead them.

Thomas Bell and more than five hundred others voted to go on, but 185 men expressed a desire to return home and were allowed to leave. Somervell took the rest of his dwindling army down the Rio Grande, forced the town of Guerrero to surrender, and ordered residents to supply a specified quantity of provisions. But on December 19 Somervell began to foresee disaster and ordered his men to commence a withdrawal home, by way of Gonzales.

This command infuriated the aggressive members of his stumbling army. About 310 of them, including some officers, refused to obey the order, "not by any means satisfied with what had been thus far effected," said Thomas Bell, "which was nothing more than striking a panic into this part of the territory. . . . Having entered the army and marched here with the expectation of meeting the enemy in battle, and having been thus far disappointed, it was thought not at all improper to remain awhile longer, and at some favorable opportunity give the tawny sons of Montezuma undeniable proofs of what they might expect to receive at the hands of Texas . . ."

Some three hundred men would do all this. They elected as their commander a native Virginian who knew the Rio Grande country: William S. Fisher, a tall man, educated and intelligent. Then they set out southward down the river toward the Mexican town of Mier, in three groups: a small, mounted spy company on the west bank; the main army, marching down the east bank; and a flotilla of four boats, manned by forty men, in the river.

The Rio Grande surprised some of the men, who had envisioned it as a nearly dry stream full of rocks and shoals. When they saw the river that December it was wide, deep, and swift, reminding at least one man of the Ohio. From the chaparral-covered east bank men of the main body looked down from cliffs across a fertile lowland that lay on the other side of the river and extended westward into the country they hoped soon to penetrate.

When the main body reached a location on the river opposite the town of Mier the men halted while the spy company reconnoitered along the west bank. After the scouts had returned, their commander reported to Fisher that Mexican troops were assembling along the river, and he advised against trying to cross. Fisher refused to consider this, and the scouts left the expedition and returned home. Hurriedly designated substitutes replaced them. Not all Texans were rash after all.

Bell approved of continuing. He had come this far in anticipation of a fight, and he hoped not to miss one as he had done at Plum Creek. Some of the officers impressed the men as lacking capacity, but this was excusable to Bell, if not to the wary members of the departed spy company. "Texan officers are generally called to command, not for any skill they possess in the art of war; but for their undoubted courage and respectability as citizens at home, and, therefore, cannot be expected to possess that artifice and intrigue in that most dreadful of all arts . . ."

Two days before Christmas Fisher crossed the Rio Grande and entered Mier. He found it undefended, marched his troops into the public square, and demanded of the alcalde that the town provide his army with "all the government stores of every kind, including cannon, small fire-arms, powder, lead munitions of war of every kind, tobacco, &c.; also, 5 days' rations for 1200 men, to wit: 40 sacks of flour of 6 arrobas each, 1200 lbs. sugar, 600 lbs. coffee, 200 pairs of strong coarse shoes, 100 pair of do. pantaloons, and 100 blankets." After receipt of these stores even Fisher planned to take his men back home and to tempt fate no longer.

The alcalde apportioned this requisition to his dismayed citizens and promised delivery at a designated point on the Rio Grande on the following day. To make certain of receipt the Texans took along the alcalde himself when they recrossed the river. On the other side they built campfires for warmth against a cutting norther, slept, and the next day moved on to the location designated for delivery. There they waited—and waited.

That morning, the twenty-fourth, the Mexicans had captured one of their men while he searched the west bank for horses. He happened to be carrying a pocket journal that described the size and character of the expedition, and his captors passed on this information to General Pedro de Ampudia, who had arrived in the vicinity with an army of several thousand soldiers.

The Christmas gift from Mier never arrived. On the morning of the twenty-fifth a captured Mexican told the Texans why. General Ampudia had intercepted the supplies and had refused to allow their delivery. Bell heard also that the captured Mexican reported the presence of only three hundred men in the opposing army. Fisher and his men decided to go into Mier after the goods—"entirely ignorant of the approach of the overwhelming army," Bell said.

On a cloudy, chilly Christmas afternoon 261 Texans and the carefully guarded alcalde crossed the Rio Grande, leaving behind forty-two men as camp guards. Bell went with the invasion force, in a company commanded by Captain William Eastland. The importance of the occasion, the irony of the date, and Bell's previous studies to achieve a "literary standing" combined to carry him far away in his prose: "Just as the joyous laugh of the giddy and the gay was merrily ringing throughout all Christendom, rejoicing in the festivity of the day, or the pious prayers of the humble and devout Christian were ascending to the throne of the Most High for the reign of peace and good will among the sons of fallen man; at this very time two races destined never to be friends were pre-

paring to embrue their hands in each other's blood, and glut that
hellish vengeance, whispered in the ears of mortals by fiendish
devils only."

In the Battle of Mier the Texans would prove to be as appalling
with firearms as Bell had been with words. By five o'clock that
afternoon the last of the attackers had crossed the river, intent on
vengeance for a number of grievances and on getting the promised
supplies. At seven o'clock, when about a mile outside Mier, they
met a Mexican picket guard that opened fire. The Texans halted
atop a hill overlooking a small, swift stream that curved toward
them. The night grew even darker when a drizzling rain commenced. This pitchness provided a good screen from the Mexicans—but nothing else in the way of comfort. Men sat in the misty
cold and protected their weapons as well as they could while their
leaders groped for the best way into town.

One officer found a passage, with a little help from the reluctant
alcalde, and led the men down an almost perpendicular cliff, sliding
most of the way, then into thigh-deep water of the stream, where
they struggled against the strong current. Somewhere nearby the
stream roared through a rock-strewn rapids, and the Texans
reached the opposite bank before Mexican soldiers heard them
coming. The Mexicans fled toward town, hurried along by a fusil-
lade of a hundred or so unanswered shots. About this time the
alcalde bolted in the darkness and ran for home, too. The Texans
followed steadily, and soon they entered the suburbs of Mier.

But there they became targets of persistent artillery fire from
cannon set up to rake the street along which they advanced. Twice
each minute grape and canister came crashing toward them. They
learned to time the shots, however, and took refuge until the
cannon fired; then they leaped out and blasted away at the
artillerymen.

The drizzle continued, putting some rifles out of order, but the
Texans had taken possession of a row of stone houses, and they
used this shelter to fix weapons in flickering candlelight, and to sit
out the cannon blasts and the rain. Many men remained in these
houses until daylight, since they were unable to see much in the
darkness. But not everyone was so fortunate. The men outside
settled down in such shelter as they could find. Bell observed their
composure in the midst of war and was astonished:

The enemy . . . kept up a constant fire both of musketry and artillery, directed at the position of the Texan force, who with careless indifference common to volunteers of their race in times of danger, were coolly waiting for the approach of day to begin the contest in earnest—Some of these dare devils were talking over their domestic affairs at home with as much composure as if in the house of a friend . . . others were deeply buried in the arms of Morpheus . . .

Daylight brought exposure to reality. The Texans looked around them—at buildings of stone and cement, with flat roofs rimmed by parapets and with yards surrounded by stone walls—and realized for the first time the advantage and the strength of the enemy. Mexican soldiers crowded housetops and streets—their heads and shoulders appeared when they aimed and fired. Bell gawked and "began to be sensible of the fearful odds that opposed [us]," then dug in to fight. That was what he had come for—but not really under these conditions, outnumbered nearly ten to one and now cut off from retreat by cavalrymen and an artillery piece placed at a point across the stream they had forded during the night.

They fought with a ferocity that won them the label of "devils" from the Mexican General Ampudia. Their accuracy seemed uncanny. Within an hour after daylight Mexican artillery had been silenced. Dead men lay all around the guns. Bodies also covered the housetops, and virtually all of them were later found with bloody, jagged holes in heads and shoulders. By midmorning many Mexican sharpshooters were trying another method of fighting. They kept their heads down, well protected, while they pushed their muskets over the walls and fired at random. But not all of them chose this way out. Some Mexican soldiers charged down streets several times, trying without success to dislodge Fisher's men. Only occasionally did any Texans fall, but time worked against them. The rapid firing caused Fisher concern about his supply of powder and lead; and the lack of rest, food, and water began to tell on him and his men.

Exhaustion and an agonizing wound finally defeated Fisher. During one Mexican charge a ball tore off his right thumb, and he began vomiting from pain and shock. Under these conditions he received a truce flag sent by Ampudia after the General had observed slackening Texas fire and reasoned that it meant a weakening of Texas will. Bell saw the white flag and guessed, as did many other Texans, that the Mexicans intended to surrender.

A combination of factors worked to bring a surprising capitulation from the Texans: Fisher's wound; the hunger, thirst, and weariness of his men and their precarious situation; and the fact that the visitor bearing the truce flag was a Texan himself, a man who had fallen prisoner earlier in the day. The man reported that General Ampudia had available to him more than three thousand soldiers, that he would give the Texans a one-hour armistice, and that at the end of that time he expected them to surrender—otherwise he would see that every one of them died.

Bell and the rest discussed their predicament, "surrounded as [we] were by an enemy ten times [our] number, who was now well acquainted with [our] small force and its precise position, [our] stock of ammunition nearly exhausted, and four miles to march before [we] could reach the [Rio Grande], the whole way liable to be exposed to the attacks of the Mexican cavalry and probably when [we] reached the river no means of crossing it would be at hand." But there were men who did not want to surrender, and some proposed trying to break out of Mier and run for the river. Others suggested this would mean leaving the wounded to the Mexicans, and everyone knew how merciless the enemy could be.

For almost an hour they talked, without reaching any decision. Then Fisher left them, to speak personally with General Ampudia under a truce extension. He returned about fifty minutes later, formed the men by companies in the street, and addressed them. Bell reported hearing him say something like this:

"I have known General Ampudia for years—know him to be an honourable man, and will vouch for his carrying . . . out [his promises]; that if you are willing to accept these terms, you will march into the public square and give up your arms, or prepare for battle in five minutes; that, in any view of the case, your situation is a gloomy one, for you cannot fight your way out of this place to the Rio Grande short of a loss of *two thirds*, or perhaps the *whole*; but if you are determined to fight, I will be with you, and sell my life as dearly as possible."

His speech persuaded the men to surrender. Bell and most of the others walked disconsolately toward the square, where they surrendered their arms. But some men broke up their weapons rather than give them away whole, and some threw them to the ground.

The men were crowded into small rooms in buildings near the square. Later Bell heard the statistical results of the Christmas fighting: twelve of his comrades killed, twenty-three wounded; six hundred Mexicans killed, two hundred wounded—by their own admission. He also heard a disheartening rumor: had the Texans not accepted Ampudia's surrender terms, Ampudia was ready to give up Mier and to pull out rather than suffer any more casualties at the hands of those devils.

43. AND MORE FIGHTING AT HOME

Texans continued to fight among themselves while the prisoners at Mier prepared for what would be a long walk into captivity. In time the Mier men would hear of the latest Texas feud and presume that civil war had broken out at home.

It began with President Sam Houston's removal of the capital from Austin. The raids into nearby San Antonio had given him an excuse for arbitrarily moving the capital, first to Houston, then to Washington-on-the-Brazos, where the House of Representatives met in the old "Declaration of Independence Hall" and the Senate in a room over a tavern. The move infuriated residents of the Austin area, and many of them echoed one man's comment, "God send [Houston] would at this moment sink into endless sleep . . ."

Houston had not been able to move the government archives, and Austin residents swore he never would be able to get them. A government without its paperwork, even in nineteenth-century Texas, was only half a government, and the Land Office in particular suffered. On December 10, 1842, Houston secretly ordered two trusted men to organize an expedition "as if for an Indian excursion" to get the archives and bring them to Washington-on-the-Brazos.

While [the archives] remain where they are, no one knows the hour when they may . . . be utterly destroyed. They are constantly liable to attack and destruction by the enemy. . . . You are acquainted with the condition of things at Austin, and the exaggeration of feeling pervading those who are directly interested in that place . . . Do not be thwarted in the undertaking. . . . Threats have been made that if the archives are . . . removed, they will be in *ashes*.

The expedition might as well have been aimed for the interior of Mexico. But by noon on December 30 Houston's operatives had succeeded in loading the most important papers and books into the wagons. They were even contemplating a successful completion of their mission when a group of Austin citizens, including a woman of the community, appeared with a cannon stolen from a government arsenal and opened fire on wagons, men, and the General Land Office building, yelling, "Blow the old house to pieces." Eight shots of grape rained down before Houston's men could begin a retreat.

The wagons clattered up a road northward toward Kenney's Fort, not southeastward in the general direction of Houston's new capital, but the government men had good reason for taking this devious route: they would avoid the area around Bastrop, which Austin residents patrolled to see that no government property passed outbound from their town. The ruse failed to work. After leaving Kenney's Fort the next morning the government men and the archives wagons met an artillery piece planted squarely in their road. An Austin patrol angrily repossessed the archives, "unreserved in their threats against the person and life of the Chief Magistrate of the country." They returned the papers to their town and stored them in a house on Pecan Street, now East Sixth.

"What the result may be," Sam Houston's man in Austin wrote him, "Providence alone can determine."

Sam Houston's popularity headed for a sharp decline, but some staunch supporters still stood by him, like the man who observed, "They commenced a crusade against Old Sam—they wanted to *ruin* him and so bitter is their enmity that I do believe they would prefer the ruin of their country to its salvation through his means."

Houston himself never doubted that history would vindicate him, even in his most unpopular decisions. The rambunctious Republic of Texas could not be administered by a milksop any more than an unruly child could be kept in line by a vacillating parent. The criticism reminded Houston of Lear:

The little dogs and all,
Tray, Blanch, and Sweet-heart, see, they bark at me.

X

THE PRISONERS

1843

Noisy and crude Texas certainly was. So was the United States, as visitors from Europe remarked. Noisy: the clamor of "Dixie" composer Dan Emmett's minstrel-troupe performances in several Bowery theaters during the year. Crude: the violence that ensued after an announcement in July by Mormon leader Joseph Smith that a divine revelation sanctioned polygamy. Smith was killed in Illinois the following year, and two years after that the Mormons would seek their peace in Utah.

But the United States had refinements: the writings of Emerson, Longfellow, and Whittier; the first use of anesthesia for an operation; and, in fact, much celebration of the nation's very noise and crudeness in art and literature, giving to both an originality, a vitality, and a distinctiveness that often set them apart from European forms.

Texas had little more than Sam Houston, and his popularity continued its decline. The editor of the Houston *Morning Star*, a supporter on most issues, thought of the many Texans who had been taken prisoner and of the administration's procrastination in devising means of helping them, and on June 3 he commented: "It is the duty of the President of the Republic of Texas, also to request powers to interpose their authority, and require Mexico to respect them as Texans, and not as rebels or banditti. We have long been waiting for President Houston to make some effort of this kind. . . . But we have waited in vain."

About that same time another Texas expedition fell apart. This time President Houston could blame no one except himself for authorizing it. He had given a man named Jacob Snively permission to raid along a portion of the Santa Fe Trail claimed by Texas; the expedition members and the Texas government would divide the spoils equally, and Houston would thus exhibit some more retaliation against Mexico for the recent incursions. But when the expedition arrived at its destination, delay and dissension divided its ranks; then a force of United States dragoons dispersed them, declaring that the Texans occupied land belonging to their country.

Other troubles for Houston came from the Texas Navy, whose commodore ignored his orders; from the Regulators and Moderators of East Texas, who continued to wage a civil war that blighted a large area; and from Houston's many political opponents, who spoke of impeachment so that Vice-President Edward Burleson could succeed him.

But Houston worked in ways unknown to many Texans. He could have said, as he did before San Jacinto, "I consulted none—I held no councils of war—if I err the blame is mine." With the aid of friends in the English diplomatic service he arranged a truce with Mexico—proclaimed on June 15—that he hoped might lead to peace negotiations. With the help of Indian Commissioner Joseph Eldridge he arranged a treaty with some of the wildest Texas tribes. Through clever flirtation with England he inspired the United States Secretary of State to press for annexation of Texas.

Despite these political maneuverings, the most dramatic events of 1843 Texas occurred outside the Republic. Mostly they concerned the Texas prisoners.

44. A MARCH INTO MEXICO

On New Year's Eve Thomas Bell marched the first twenty-five of what were to be fifteen hundred winding miles into Mexico with the rest of the Mier captives. All were heavily guarded by their captors.

Many Mexican officers had wanted to execute these Texans, especially after they had devoted one entire day following the battle to supervising the lowering of dead soldiers by rope from Mier housetops. But Ampudia had overruled them, and five days after Bell and the rest had been locked in crowded rooms following the fight they began a march along the Rio Grande toward Matamoros. Most of them possessed nothing more than the clothes they wore. Ampudia had ordered their baggage brought from the camp on the Rio Grande—from which the Texan guard had fled after hearing of Fisher's surrender—but the same soldiers who fetched the gear also stole most of it.

Bell and his hapless companions walked in double-file order down the center of a dirt road, closely surrounded by Mexican troops "with burnished steel bristling." To the front and rear he could see large detachments of soldiers and lumbering cannon. On each side a flank guard brandished bayonets fixed and ready to spear any man stupid enough to try to break away. That first day prisoners were not permitted to leave the column even for a drink of water, nor were they allowed to stop and rest aching muscles and sore feet, which caused them almost as much agony as did their parched tongues. Being held in those cramped rooms for five days had not allowed any preparation for such exertion.

At the conclusion of the first twenty-five tormenting miles they reached a small river and in darkness camped on a bank opposite the town of Camargo. Guards doled out half-boiled beef and water. Bell ate and drank mechanically, then lay down on cold ground with only black sky for cover on a frosty night. Thus he greeted the new year.

Sleep was not possible without blankets, but the Mexican soldiers had taken every one worth stealing. Bell rose and spent the rest of the night trying to keep warm at one of several brushwood fires, listening to his companions "cursing their hard fate." When the fires burned low, men raked away coals and lay in the warm ashes.

The next day, January 1, 1843, was not without a New Year's Day celebration, but it was all Mexican—the first of many on this journey. Early that morning guards herded their prisoners back to the road, escorted them across the river into the attractive town of Camargo, and marched them down narrow streets and around the military square to the ringing of bells, the firing of guns, and the loud vivas of most of the three thousand inhabitants. Then the prisoners received a little reward, like circus animals that had performed well: their rations and a night's sleep in comparatively comfortable quarters.

They covered ten more miles on the following march to a rancho, where quarters deteriorated to a cowpen—the first of many used to hold them during their long march. At first their bed of manure, old and new, shocked them, but eventually they learned to laugh at it. A few stouthearted prisoners even flopped down on all fours, bowed their necks, pawed the dirt, and made bull sounds, while their captors stationed outside the fence stared curiously and perhaps envied their survival ability. A few nights later, when a sheep pen served as their prison, the same comedians bleated.

Reynosa greeted them with great rejoicing. Triumphal arches fashioned from reeds, flowers, and bright cloth decorated the streets. From the arches hung colorfully decorated signs bearing various mottoes like "GLORY" and "HONOR." As the glum prisoners marched toward the inevitable public square, women cheered from open windows and housetops, men shouted, Indians yelled, and "church bells clattered as if they would be tossed from their axles."

Twenty-five miles more on January 6. Under other circumstances the journey might have been enjoyable. Bell, with his farmer's eye for fertile earth, admired the scenery—fine mesquite grass blanketing a beautiful, rich land that pastured large herds of horses, cattle, and sheep. But human inhabitants were few. Those Bell saw were mostly herders quartered in small, isolated houses.

That night Bell and his companions found themselves lodged in another cowpen, this time up to their ankles in wet manure. From across the fence an escaped Negro slave stared at them, shook his head sadly, and said, "Aha! White man, dey cotch you now; dey gib you hell."

Several miles outside Matamoros crowds flocked out to meet the victorious Mexican soldiers and their captive "barbarians," as the citizens called them. Army wives and sweethearts came with the throng, seeking their men. Many of them learned then of the awful toll the Texans had taken. Some women cried, others consoled, but the rejoicing exceeded the lamentation.

Among the lamenters was Bell, but he kept his head up and his eyes and ears open.

Streets and houses were filled with spectators, come to witness this triumphal entry. The windows were adorned with fancy goods of various colors and the balconies swarmed with Mexican beauty and fashion to overflowing. The streets were ornamented with arches of flowers, hung with silken hues of various sorts, under which the victorious army passed leading its conquered victims . . . in moody silence . . . [before] the taunts and hisses of the multitude, whose fury was only kept under by the bayonets of the soldiers.

Up one street and down another the prisoners marched, to give citizens a chance to jeer. Then they were taken to comfortable quarters, where they remained for four days.

Many prisoners hoped that they might have to march no farther than Matamoros; General Ampudia had implied that they might expect this. But on the second day of their stay in Matamoros they learned that orders had come for their delivery to the city of Mexico, many hundreds of miles away. Early on January 14 Bell and the other prisoners moved out again, in double file and guarded by an escort twice their own number, "wending [our] way towards the interior of the enemy's country." Another, smaller group consisting of ranking officers and several boys had left on horseback two days earlier under separate guard.

Away from the valley of the Rio Grande the land ceased to appeal to Bell. Between Matamoros and Monterrey, the next major destination, the country was mostly barren and uninhabited, except for occasional lush river valleys where grew oranges, vegetables, and sugar cane. During the two-week journey the prisoners slept outside every night but one, and they talked of escape without having a real chance to try it.

Near Monterrey scenery improved. They saw many clear streams, some neatly cultivated fields, and lofty mountains. But this brought Bell more gloom by reminding him a little of home, and his depression increased when he and the others tramped into town. The delighted citizens celebrated wildly.

The people in this whole portion of Mexico having been thrown into the utmost alarm by the intelligence of the appearance of a Texan army . . . on the Rio Grande . . . were . . . intoxicated with joy at their downfall. But the Mexican authorities treated [us] well while [we] remained here, and the foreign citizens supplied [our] wants . . . with many things . . . necessary to . . . comfort and health. Many were without shoes and were furnished with either shoes or sandals and many other articles of clothing.

From Monterrey to Saltillo they traveled along a winding valley road paralleled by high mountains, past Indian villages whose occupants stared wonderingly at the strange prisoners. The view should have been striking, but one of Bell's companions remarked, ". . . we being generally hungry, thirsty, and tired had no taste for the beauties of nature." Still, the marches were more comfortable than others had been, because the Mexican officer in charge allowed them to rest frequently.

They spent one day in Saltillo, located in the mountains. Gardens, orchards, and fields irrigated from springs provided food —wheat, barley, and Indian corn. They found bread plentiful and cheap. Prisoners who had money were allowed to buy provisions. Women brought cooked foods to sell—beans, meats stewed with red pepper, sheeps' heads roasted under a covering of earth, and a sweet gruel made of water, cornmeal, and sugar. Dishes like these could make a banquet for a prisoner whose traveling ration had consisted of a pint of boiled rice in the morning and a few ounces of biscuit and boiled beef in the evening.

At Saltillo five Texans captured with Sam Maverick at San Antonio were added to the ranks of the Mier prisoners. On February 7 they commenced their torturous march again, this time for San Luis Potosí, southward across bald brown mountains where water was scarce and brackish and the sight of other human beings rare. By this time many prisoners showed signs of sickness and exhaustion, but they were forced to continue. The weakest men were given donkeys to ride or were laid in carts, where the sun seared them and aggravated their fever and thirst. That night one man deliberately poisoned himself in camp and died. Others,

almost as desperate, sought a better bargain. They polished plans
for the escape that had long occupied their thoughts and talk. But
such an attempt could mean suicide. Under any circumstances it
must begin by suddenly attacking guards and wrenching away
their weapons for use in the break.

On the eighth, after an early start, they tramped on for twenty-
four miles, roasting in a natural oven, craving water they did not
get. On the ninth they endured more of this, then that night saw
that they were once again destined to endure more time in a
cowpen while guards kept watch from outside the fence. No chance
for an escape there.

All day February 10—another hot, dry march—they talked
quietly among themselves about charging their guards at the very
first opportunity. They were now in mountains that would afford
hiding places, and if they did not try their luck soon they would be
so far into Mexico they would have no chance of ever finding their
way back to Texas. They quietly elected an escape commander—
Ewen Cameron, a tall, sturdy, light-complexioned Scotsman from
the Highlands and a popular officer. He would give a signal for a
charge whenever he saw an opportunity. Perhaps it would come
that night.

After a twenty-mile hike through desert country, the prisoners
reached a small village hugging the banks of a stream named
Salado. There the guards escorted them to a well where they were
allowed to drink their fill of brackish water before being herded
through a wide door of a rectangular building into an open courtyard surrounded on all four sides by solid walls. But not even this
fastness was their bedroom for the night. The guards escorted them
across the courtyard and through a narrow entrance into an empty
stable yard. There they were to sleep. Close by, locked in an adjacent room, they discovered Fisher and the other officers who had
been escorted out of Matamoros two days ahead of them.

Most of the men dropped wearily to the ground, exhausted by
the day's march. But they talked late and longingly of trying an
escape here. Some wanted to try to overpower the guards at the
quiet hour of midnight, but one of the officers in the adjacent room,
Thomas Jefferson Green, advised sunrise instead, when the horses
would have been gathered nearby for the day's march and would

be easier to seize. Some men argued against attempting any escape at all, declaring they had come too far into Mexico for successful flight back, but others silenced them with persuasion, and the vote went for an effort to escape. Once free, the men would force their way into the room where Fisher, Green, and the several others were locked up and liberate them.

Then came a long wait for sunrise. Despite the approved plans some men watched for a chance during the night for an earlier attempt, but none appeared. They saw to their dismay that the sentinels had been doubled and that they seemed to be more watchful. Either the excessive talk had aroused suspicion—although the guards could understand no English—or one of their own comrades had given them away.

In the nearby room Fisher and the other officers were awakened in predawn light and sent off on their day's march forty-five minutes early. Usually they could expect a departure time of half an hour after sunrise, but this morning they were up, fed, and escorted out before dawn.

For the others came more waiting. Bell peered around him and saw sentinels watching the prisoners closely. He saw stacked near a wall some distance from the stable-yard entrance the extra muskets belonging to the guard, bayonets fixed. At this entrance he saw two sentinels, and on a wall surrounding the yard four more. Ewen Cameron, the designated leader, also studied the situation, from a position near the entrance. But everyone tried to hide his excitement. The prisoners ate breakfast and pretended to prepare for another day's march, all the while awaiting Cameron's signal.

At a moment when the sentinels seemed to relax, Cameron raised his hat with a little flourish and shouted in his Highlands brogue, "Now, boys, we go it!" He seized the musket from one soldier at the entrance. Other men sprinted through the opening and overpowered the other sentinel, while still others clambered up the wall after the four frightened soldiers there. Most of the rest ran for the muskets stacked near the entrance, then opened fire on approaching soldiers attracted by the disturbance.

Some distance away, on the road leading to San Luis Potosí, Thomas Jefferson Green had caught his first glimpse of the morning sun and had remarked to a fellow officer riding beside him that if "our boys" were going to do anything, now was the time. Just then he heard the first shot and exclaimed, "We have them!" The sound of more firing reached him before the guard commander realized something had gone wrong at the village, halted the party, and sent a lieutenant back for information. Green watched him gallop off for a hundred yards or so, then wheel and race back. The lieutenant could see that the Texans had broken out and had sent the troops fleeing in every direction. By this time Green could see the same thing for himself—as could the guard commander, who ordered the party to go on at a full gallop away from the trouble. On each side of Green and the other prisoners rode cavalrymen carrying lances.

After a gallop of several hundred yards they halted again. The commander ordered Green and the other Texans to dismount, and they stood staring toward the village, speculating on the outcome. Green voiced optimism; Fisher thought the attempt would fail. They saw a horseman riding toward them from the village.

A Mexican lieutenant rode up to the guard commander with orders that soon became known to Green: shoot the Texas prisoners and come at once to the assistance of troops in the village. Green observed the officer preparing to comply with his ghastly instructions and through an interpreter asked frantically whether the commander intended to carry out previous orders from a superior to take them to the city of Mexico or subsequent orders from the colonel at the village, a mere subordinate. Green ended his plea by adding, "We expected we were in the hands of a gentleman and a soldier, not a murderer."

The commander lowered his eyes, hesitated, then rose in his stirrups and ordered his interpreter to tell Green and the others that they were indeed in the hands of a gentleman and a soldier, one who intended to carry out superior orders. The officer ordered them to mount, and together they galloped off toward San Luis Potosí, with the lancers continuing to maintain close watch on them from both sides. Green hoped the escaped prisoners would get horses and overtake them, but nobody came to their rescue.

In the village the Texas prisoners had scattered their enemy and fled, except for about twenty who were ill or too fearful to join in the escape and chose to remain in the compound. Thomas Bell was with the escapees who had made quick work of dispatching the Mexicans. Outside the main door to the building where they had spent the night they had encountered a large group of cavalrymen, but they had sent these men too fleeing for their lives after firing only a few shots. At a safe distance some of the horsemen stopped and watched the Texans, but they did not venture back.

The Texans now prepared to flee. Quickly they conducted an inventory and a casualty count: five dead and five wounded. The survivors possessed 160 stands of arms, about eighty horses, fourteen hundred dollars of government cash, and all the provisions they had been able to find, including water-filled gourds. At nine o'clock 193 men began a hasty retreat toward Texas, several hundred miles distant, along the same road they had traveled from Saltillo. The wounded and the sick rode horseback, others alternated between walking and riding. In the first eighteen hours they covered seventy miles, stopping only occasionally for water and brief periods of rest. Gourds emptied quickly.

About twenty miles outside Saltillo they decided to leave the road rather than risk encountering Mexican troops no doubt looking for them. They traveled dry across barren plains and hills broken only by occasional thickets of thorny shrubs and briers that tore their clothing. Then they struck another road and soon saw in the distance to their left an isolated rancho simmering in the afternoon sun. Parched by thirst, they made for it, but before they reached the place they saw a number of Mexican cavalrymen appear on the roof of the house, prepared to drive them off. The Texans fired a few random shots and traveled on in a direction generally north, across more dry hills and mountains, and stumbled onto a water hole that night. They drank greedily, watered the horses, and went on, "guided in their direction by the stars." But two men left behind at the water hole became lost—or else they deserted, as some of their companions later claimed. Along with the pair went two of the better horses and some valuable provisions. Two days later Mexicans recaptured these two men.

The Texans groped on for the rest of that night, trying to stay clear of Mexican troops. Bell thought they were not succeeding. In the surrounding area he saw the occasional twinkle of lamps, held by what he suspected were Mexican spies keeping a watch on their movements. Possibly the men in the darkness were remnants of the cavalry dispersed at the Salado. Some of those troops who had stayed and watched the Texans from out of range later followed them.

Before daylight one morning two days after their escape, just as the fleeing prisoners completed the descent of a steep mountain, they were startled by the appearance of a Mexican man, whom they detained as a prisoner. About eight miles farther on they struck a road leading east from Saltillo, found water, and encountered another stranger—a horseman who rode up, greeted them in English, identified himself as a resident of Saltillo, and told them that no force of any consequence was in close pursuit. Had they kept to the road originally they would have been safe, he said, and far beyond their present position.

The man advised Ewen Cameron to follow the road they were now on. It would take them eastward out of the country without the necessity of struggling over endless mountains. Then he recommended to Cameron the man who had been taken prisoner earlier —a native who knew the country well and would accompany them along the route he suggested, because "no mercy would be shown by the Mexican government to any who might be recaptured." He said he had sent the man to them himself. Then he left, but the guide stayed.

For the rest of that day they traveled along the road as advised. Once they detoured around a rancho whose occupants appeared from a distance to be hostile. Near another rancho they halted, sent one of their men and the Mexican guide to buy food, then discovered that no rancheros in this part of the country seemed to be friendly. The Texan returned alone and reported that the rancho owners had refused to sell anything and had detained the Mexican guide. But the Texans found consolation within sight of the place—water and good grass, where they stopped to refresh themselves and their horses. Then they struck out down the road again.

As the afternoon sun waned, so did their confidence. Treachery and animosity seemed to prevail everywhere in Mexico—look at the rancheros and the promises of General Ampudia. With darkness came complete doubt among many men. About nine o'clock they stopped for a consultation. Their guide had been a decoy sent to lead them into ambush, many men believed, and the English-speaking gentleman from Saltillo had only posed as a friend.

Cameron spoke against the distrust. Bell and some others also wanted to stay with the road, where travel would be comfortable compared to struggling over rugged, dry mountains. But most men wanted to leave the road for the mountains, for a while anyway. Cameron and the rest reluctantly followed. Bell expressed his disappointment:

Instead of travelling a road that led along the frontier of the Mexican settlements and generally through the valley where a sufficiency both of water and provisions could easily have been obtained, and little or no danger to have been apprehended from any considerable force in this region of the country, [we] imprudently struck into the bosom of a barren and desert mountain, in which neither food nor water could be obtained for man or beast.

So they left the road, and suddenly the words of those who had argued in favor of doing so seemed to carry additional weight. Two or three mounted Mexicans appeared, "yelling like Indians," and fired a few random shots at them before galloping off. But no harm had been done, and the Texans went on a few miles farther. When they came to a grassy plain they wearily stopped for the night. They posted a strong guard to watch for other intruders, but worry did not keep many of them awake. Three days had passed since their flight from the banks of the Salado.

On the morning of the fourteenth they buried themselves deeper in the mountains, but found the travel even more torturous than expected. They dismounted and led their horses, clambered over boulders and up steep cliffs, gained a few hundred yards, then came upon a precipice that could not be scaled. They retreated to find another route. All the while they hoped to sight a cool cascading stream where they could quench their agonizing thirst, but they found nothing except more stark mountains, which soon surrounded them on every side.

In dimming daylight they descended into a ravine that seemed to lead to an open valley they had seen from a summit. They struggled down it until nearly midnight, when they encountered black slopes too steep for either horses or men to descend. Obviously the valley could not be reached from this direction. They halted wearily for the night, safely isolated in a badland where no one else would have been desperate or foolish enough to go. They kindled fires for warmth against the cold night and lay down to sleep, but their craving for water kept them restless.

The next morning Bell grimly studied the faces of his companions. He thought they seemed to be without hope, and for good reason: "perishing with thirst seemed inevitable." Then a happy event turned him from his melancholy. Someone stumbled upon a pool of water nearby, only enough to give every man a good drink and to fill most of the gourds, but it meant life sustained—at least for the men.

They decided to kill the horses and mules, and to jerk the meat. The animals were impossible to keep fed and watered and were useless in these mountains anyway. They stationed a few lookouts on surrounding heights and led the animals into a ravine near where they had found the water. There they butchered them, their favorite mounts included, and virtually admitted their defeat. A man on foot in the Southwestern vastness was a man without much hope. Some of the animals squealed before they died.

The men built fires for drying the flesh. While they waited they made crude shoes from the now useless saddles for men who had ruined their footgear on sharp rocks and were traveling barefoot. Then they divided the meat—ten pounds apiece—and part of the Mexican money taken after the escape. They filled knapsacks with these possessions and went northward across more mountains, with "some men so weak that they were unable to reach camp that night, though only four miles distant." Stronger men gave much of their scant water ration to the sick and weak, doling it out to them a few sips at a time.

By the morning of the sixteenth, after restless sleep at another dry camp, more men began to lag behind. Eleven unable to keep up dropped out—but later reached a settlement, where they were recaptured. The last drop of water disappeared from gourds, and some men tried to slake their thirst by chewing plants and swallowing the juice. Palmetto became popular for this purpose, but it left tongues and throats drier than ever and wracked by a bitter after-taste as well.

Nevertheless, hope rose slightly with the sun on the seven-teenth—sleep and a new day provided an elixir. Not even the sight of a steep mountain ahead proved overwhelming, and when the men reached its summit in midmorning brightness they saw before them a smooth valley, where they were sure they would find water.

The stronger men divided into groups to go ahead, spread out, and search for springs and streams. Meanwhile, a main party of about fifty debilitated men, accompanied by Ewen Cameron, struggled toward the valley, halting every few hundred yards to rest. Not until the following day did these men reach the valley, and when they did they discovered it was only a lifeless, sandy plain, where it seemed now their graves must surely be dug. But some of them still argued about the best course to take for finding water.

Bell looked at his dust-covered fellow marchers in this parade of death. "Their eyes were sunken far back in the sockets and seemed to have lost the lustre of human intelligences. . . . The tongues of some were so swollen that they protruded beyond their lips, and stopped nearly entirely the power of [speech]. Some men had gone [nearly] six days without a sip of water—with only the acrid juices of plants like the Palmetto to moisten their tongues during that time."

In that enfeebled condition they saw far off to their right signal smoke. Someone had found water! Slowly they headed for the spot—hurrying was not possible, no matter how ecstatic the thought of a cool drink. Through late-afternoon heat they toiled. Walking seemed an almost impossible task now, and they threw away their weapons to concentrate on it. Occasionally they sought respite provided by a thorny bush. Across its top men threw ragged blankets and crawled into the shade underneath. They dug into the sand hoping to find cool earth to hold next to throats and stomachs. Then they rose to their feet again and walked on, but some men even now prayed for death to relieve them.

Sunset came, and still they had no water. Twilight—and their swollen tongues were drier than ever. In darkness they arrived at the place where the smoke had been sighted. They found encamped there not happy friends waiting to share a precious drink, but a detachment of Mexican cavalry.

Bell and his companions could no longer endure the suffering. "[We] cared little whether [we] lived or died, and the enemy with their usual treachery and cunning, representing their camp to be almost filled with water induced [us] to surrender without firing a shot. But the water was not there, for the Mexicans themselves had . . . only what they had carried there in gourds about forty miles."

They were prisoners again, with only sips of water for consolation and for survival. The Mexicans marched them for two days to a main camp. "Many . . . [prisoners] were severely lashed by the rawhide whips of the Mexican soldiers . . . for no other reason than that they were unable to [keep up]." But at the main camp they could drink water—doled out by their captors a little at a time, to avoid death. With water to drink the lost freedom seemed worth the cost, for a time.

During the next few days more shriveled men appeared from out of the baked desolation and gave themselves up. Search parties found others and brought them in. But four men miraculously survived in the wilderness and later reached Texas.

By the twenty-second, more than 130 escapees had been recaptured. The Mexicans carefully separated officers from men and completely isolated the escape leader, Ewen Cameron. Then they bound the men in pairs with rawhide strips that chafed their wrists, and marched them to Saltillo, from where they would retrace their route to the Salado, then go on to the city of Mexico.

On following days still other Texans were reunited with this group, so that eventually the Mexicans held 176 men—everyone who had participated in the escape with the exception of ten or so who died or vanished in the wilderness and the four hardy men who managed to reach Texas.

Back they went to the familiar routine of marching by day and sleeping on a bed of cowpen manure by night, but now the ordeal was worse. Only one hand was free, and nights were even more uncomfortable. They were not allowed to stand while camped—for fear of another escape attempt—and they had nothing to keep off the cold night wind, since every usable blanket had been taken from them by the soldiers. Two days out from Saltillo some prisoners succeeded in untying their rawhide bonds, but this only resulted in greater suffering—beatings for the guilty, and the substitution of iron handcuffs for the rawhide strips.

The prisoners arrived again in Saltillo on March 1. There the soldiers paraded them triumphantly before pushing them into crowded, filthy, bug-filled rooms, where they stayed three weeks. Finally, on the twenty-second, they were sent out on the road again, weak, sick, and with hope snuffed out—"almost without blankets or clothes, and numbers were destitute of shoes or sandals . . . the blood often trickled from the feet of these poor fellows as they crippled over the sharp stones that gashed them at every step they took." On the way Mexican officers periodically examined the irons, and they ordered the sick handcuffed, too. The Texans guessed that an even harsher future lay ahead.

On the twenty-fifth, about two o'clock of a searing afternoon, they approached the village on the Salado where they had escaped more than a month earlier. As they neared the outskirts they saw a whirlwind sucking up dust from the dry earth and sending it in a spiral into the air. The sight seemed to emphasize the uselessness and the desolation of their lives now. Some men also looked upon it as a bad omen.

45. THE TORTURES OF WONDERING

For months gloom also had possessed two young lovers separated by a thousand miles and an infinite uncertainty. In Texas Mary Maverick grieved for her absent husband. She was twenty-four, the mother of three children and now carrying a fourth, but she called herself "almost a child in experience."

Mary faced each day with that dread of hearing that Sam and his fellow prisoners had been murdered, yet because of his request—"don't fail me in the . . . trial which you will have to brave without me"—she forced herself to assume an outward appearance of hope, cheer, and expectation of the best. "[But] how could I? . . . I, a stranger in the land, my husband a prisoner in the power of a cruel and treacherous enemy . . ." From the depths of Mexico— from a bleak prison there—she occasionally heard from Sam Maverick. Only then could she feel true hope. It usually flickered for a while before despair snuffed it out. Then only another letter could rekindle it.

In the prison of Perote, built in mountains south of the city of Mexico, two visions kept hope alive in Sam Maverick when the cold night winds whined their melancholy—the knowledge that his friends were working for his release, even with General Santa Anna himself, and the thought of seeing Mary again.

Maverick and the other San Antonio prisoners had reached Perote December 22, 1842. There they had been chained by twos and crowded into two damp, dismal cells for a time until their captors put them to work. But Maverick contended the Mexicans had imprisoned him without reason or right, and he refused to work for them. For this impertinence he was locked in a dungeon in the very depths of Perote, threatened with death, and given only enough food to sustain his miserable existence. Then he was released and, in a sort of compromise, made overseer of other prisoners at work.

The torture of wondering about his family in Texas equaled that of prison existence. Although his captors allowed him to write home occasionally, he had not heard a word from Mary. "Are you . . . in good health? Are my precious children alive and well? Great God, how I have longed to know these particulars, and from the silence prevailing for six months I am almost afraid something unpleasant has occurred."

Only at night did release from his torment come—in dreams that were strangely pleasant.

Instead of facts (such as our situation) reflections, memories . . . and dreams have occupied my soul. In spite of my former indifference of dreams they now occupy me much and are in fact the most interesting events of my life. Hardly a night now passes but it presents the most vivid pictures of events and scenes connected with the past. They are all pleasant and happy scenes but in no point of view are they so gratifying to my constant heart as the fact that you, my dear Mary, are always there. Sometimes I have dreamed of my anxiety to recommend myself to the unmarried Mary, and saw her as I first knew her, but more often and otherwise I have dreamed of my sweet Mary amidst scenes and in rooms and places which I knew in youth . . . even in childhood. . . . How strange that here in Perote . . . vagaries of a dream should become the deep mystery and enchanting beauty of poesy, for how just and true it is that thou, my good angel, shouldst be the principal personage in every agreeable scene of my life, *though many years* before we met.

Another dream—a waking one—helped Maverick endure the loneliness: he still expected his friends to obtain his release. But for six months now he had anticipated his freedom and had been consistently disappointed. From the city of Mexico he heard frequently from the United States minister there, General Waddy Thompson, of his own home town of Pendleton, who sent cash loans to buy the few prison comforts available to men with money. Thompson expressed optimism about an early release. He said he had talked with Santa Anna, and the Mexican dictator seemed agreeable.

But the days dragged on, and Maverick remained in Perote. With every letter to Mary he spoke confidently of freedom soon, then when he wrote her the next letter it too was posted from "accursed Perote."

Finally orders came for his transfer to the city of Mexico. On the morning of March 22 Maverick and two other prisoners also ordered there mounted horses and began an escorted ride northward up a winding mountain road. Santa Anna wanted to question them and, Maverick suspected, lecture them before allowing them their long-sought release.

On the afternoon of the twenty-fifth—when the Mier prisoners were being herded back into the village on the Salado—Maverick waited impatiently for the termination of this visit to Santa Anna. Monopolizing his thoughts were Mary and the three children— maybe there were four by now. Or maybe some awful calamity had claimed them all; one never knew in those hazardous days. But

Maverick could not allow himself to reflect on such a grim eventuality. Instead he concentrated on concluding the visit to Santa Anna's satisfaction as quickly as possible so that he could "fly to the little cabin on the Colorado."

46. A LOTTERY OF DEATH

For the Mier prisoners all flight assuredly was over. Their Mexican guards pushed them triumphantly into the same enclosed yard from which they had broken out at sunrise six long weeks before. This time no relaxed sentinels could be seen. Guarding them now were many soldiers, with muskets ready and eyes clear, looking down from atop the wall surrounding the yard. The 176 Texans, still bound in pairs, no longer had potential for escape, as their wan appearance showed. But their guards were giving them absolutely no chance.

Shadows had lengthened as the sun dropped in the west. This gave some relief from the heat, but the prisoners were allowed no time to enjoy it. Soon after arriving they were ordered to stand in formation on the very spot where their escape had commenced. Then came a delay. The waiting became tense. Obviously their captors were preparing some sort of ceremony. Thomas Bell looked around, saw bristling weapons everywhere, and feared the consequences.

A gaudily uniformed officer appeared before the prisoners and read an order from General Santa Anna, which was translated by an interpreter recruited from among the prisoners. Every tenth man who had participated in the escape was to be executed. But this awful sentence nevertheless represented leniency, the officer added, because the order as originally written had called for the execution of all 176 men. The magnanimity of the Mexican government had shown itself.

Bell heard the words with an inexpressible horror, but he said nothing. Most of his companions also remained quiet. Around him he heard only "stifled murmurs." At least the executioners would not have the satisfaction of hearing wails from their victims.

The number to be executed had been reduced, but there would be no other commutation. The punishment was to be carried out at once; the victims would be determined by a lottery of death. The sun set on this melancholy scene, as if planned that way.

Bell looked, listened, and prepared to submit to fate. He observed its coming. A Mexican officer poured 159 white beans into a clay jar, then seventeen black beans. Each prisoner would draw one bean from the jar; white meant exemption, black meant death. The officer gave the jar a little shake, but not much of one. The first man to draw would be the escape leader, Ewen Cameron, and his captors secretly meant for him to draw a black bean.

Bell heard Cameron's name called, and the Scot stepped forward quickly with the man to whom he was bound. "Well, boys, we have to draw—let's be at it," he said. The officer held the jar high so that Cameron could not see it; he and the other prisoners would have to reach above their heads to draw. Cameron thrust his hand resolutely into the jar below the level of the black beans and drew out a white one. Was there no way of defeating these Texans?

The man chained to Cameron pulled out a white bean; then two others drew exemptions. Next Bell heard his company commander's name called and watched the officer, Captain Eastland, reach up into the jar and draw out the first black bean. Another man who drew black held up the bean between thumb and forefinger and remarked to his companions, "Boys, I told you so; I never failed in my life to draw a prize."

Not all the captors enjoyed the Texans' misery. The governor of Coahuila, Francisco Mexía, had refused to obey a prior order from Santa Anna to execute all 176 men, and some officers who presided at the ceremony already had expressed their disapproval. Now some of them wept.

Slowly and in pairs all 176 men stepped up to draw "unflinchingly" as their names were called. Bell drew a white bean, then watched later as the seventeen losers were freed from the men to whom they had been bound. They were taken to a nearby room, where a priest waited to hear confessions and last requests. Only two or three men chose to speak to him, and one prisoner declared resentfully, "I confess not to man but my God."

A few other prisoners were allowed to talk with the condemned men. The Texan who had so casually announced at the lottery that he always drew a prize requested now of an acquaintance, "Say to my friends that I died in grace . . . They only rob me of forty years." Then, to make certain his executioners would not be able to rob him of anything else, he took off his clothes, which he knew would have been removed from his body by some covetous soldier, and prepared to die in his underwear. He gave his outer clothing to a friend. Captain Eastland emptied his pockets of all his cash and handed it to his brother-in-law, who seemed happier to get the money than he was sad about the execution (he later remarked cheerfully that he had "made a raise").

In the fading glow of after-sunset came the time for a last meal. Most of the condemned men had no appetite, but one of them demanded his food—a "little fellow . . . [always] full of hell and jolly as could be." An exempted friend was with him and later wrote a recollection: "Says I, 'goodbye, Henry [Whaling], old boy, I am mighty sorry.' He says, 'Wash, it is all right; we'll all go . . . this is only the beginning,' and he says, 'I'm going to take a good square meal . . . and satisfy myself for once; I've been hungry for a long time.' " Then he ate a bowl of mutton stew.

Death came in the gloom of twilight. Ewen Cameron implored Mexican officers to shoot him and spare the seventeen, but they did not consider his request.

Thomas Bell heard rather than saw what happened after that. He and most of the other exempted men were separated from the execution site by a ten-foot stone wall; only one Texan, the interpreter, was allowed to watch. The condemned men were escorted to the place in two groups, of ten and seven men each, while a shrill fife and a dismal drum played a melancholy Dead March. The prisoners were tied, blindfolded, and seated on a log laid parallel to the stone wall, and there they waited for the firing squad to end the misery of suspense. Absolute silence followed, so that on the other side of the wall Bell could hear the signal tap ordering fire. Muskets roared; men shrieked and groaned. But not all of them died, and the firing continued for ten minutes or so before silence returned. Atop the wall, a Mexican sentry was so sickened by the scene below that he reeled and nearly fell off, but his comrades caught him.

Bell heard around him "low and angry murmurs" and many vows of vengeance. Later he also heard a sequel to the ghastly story. One Texan was lying severely wounded in the bloody heap of bodies, conscious all the while, and after dark he struggled to his feet and staggered out of the yard. He was discovered quickly and given a *coup de grâce*.

For the other prisoners life would go on, and they could only endure it. Many of them believed that their own executions would soon follow, and in the same terrible manner, but they refused to give their captors the satisfaction of seeing consternation. They tried to sleep that night, but many of them remained awake.

The next morning Bell and the others were roused, fed a singularly unappetizing breakfast, and escorted out of their prison yard—bound again for the city of Mexico and an unfathomable fate. Their guards deliberately led them past the execution scene, and they saw the mangled bodies of their comrades still lying where they had fallen in the twilight of the evening before. On the stone wall Bell saw spattered blood that had dried during the night.

Beyond the village the Texans were taken into more grim wasteland—desert plains and barren mountains—that matched their "melancholy reflections." They rarely saw any other people, and when they did they were repelled by the sight of them: half-starved women and dirty children, all covered with vermin. They were the families of wretched Indian men who worked as slaves for the wealthy owner of some hacienda. These Indians lived in crude huts made of stakes driven into the ground and roofed with straw, bark, or palmetto leaves.

The prisoners endured more heat and dust, more brackish water and thorny shrubs that reached through their ragged clothes and tore their skin. They saw prickly pears used as hedges, so impenetrable that no large animal could pass through them. They suffered through more miserable night stops and exhausted sleep, and more gawking inhabitants. Then they found a better land: fertile valleys, large towns, and, all around them, green mountains that sent down streams of good, clear water. They saw the grandeur of San Luis Potosí, a mile-high city dotted with colorful domes, and found a cool, dry climate—delightful relief from the desert. On toward the city of Mexico they traveled, and the landscape did not change much. They ate fairly well—boiled beans and tortillas—and enjoyed fresh water. At one village a man of great civility donated twenty-five hundred dollars for their welfare and gave every man a good blanket. But then their captors demanded the forfeiture of another life.

On the evening of April 24 the prisoners approached a village near the city of Mexico and saw on its outskirts another whirlwind, reminding them of the massacre on the Salado. They marched on into town and were locked up for the night in cramped, stuffy rooms. About eight o'clock guards came with orders to get Ewen Cameron and the prisoner interpreter. Where the two men went or why no one knew until about noon the next day, after they had left the village and marched on to another small town. There the interpreter and his guards rejoined them, and the interpreter reported that Cameron had been shot by order of Santa Anna, who obviously feared the Scotsman's leadership ability and his popularity among the men.

The interpreter also reported Cameron's final acts of bravery. The man's last request was to remain untied for the execution, and this was granted. His last words were, "Never be persuaded out of your own judgment."

Most men thought they knew what Cameron meant. Had he relied on his own reasoning and intuition during the escape he would have kept to the road and would not have been persuaded to go into the mountains, where the escape attempt disintegrated. But perhaps Cameron's last words reflected other disappointments. One would never know now. A firing squad "discharged a volley of musketry" at Cameron, and he fell to the ground, far from his native Highlands.

47. HOLDING THE REINS

Cameron's staunchness was not a universal quality in the Republic of Texas. That spring of 1843 Charles Bryant continued to worry about the shabby naval record being compiled by his midshipman son Jackson, serving aboard the flagship *Austin,* which was still laid up at New Orleans.

Bryant had just heard about Jackson's latest infraction of regulations, and he was greatly distressed.

I am sorely afflicted about your troubles in the Navy [he wrote]. It is certainly your own fault that you are continually getting into hot water. I am mortified that you should not have had more dignity than to use profane language, especially when in the performance of your duty on deck . . . You had better try harder in [the] future to govern your passions and recollect that you are only a Boy yet and if others do not treat you with proper respect in regard to your rank as you are entitled to be regarded your best remedy is to bear with the indignity until you have a proper opportunity of bringing the offender to justice before the proper authority. . . . I beseech of you now to become at once a man and an officer.

But Midshipman Andrew Jackson Bryant was not the only transgressor in the Texas Navy. Commodore Moore was faced with a great morale problem. His ships had lain helpless in New Orleans for months now when they should have been on the Gulf fighting the enemy. Everyone, Jackson included, realized this, and pride among the men of the Texas Navy was almost as scarce as pay.

Only the mighty effort of Commodore Moore kept the fleet intact. Midshipman Bryant knew something of this ordeal, but not until later did he become aware of the whole story. Moore (who had never received any pay for his service) spent his own money, then borrowed, to keep his ships afloat. At home, Moore's endeavor won no sympathy from President Houston, who of course never believed in the necessity of a navy in the first place, and who hated Moore for his independence.

An occurrence that Jackson Bryant and even Commodore Moore did not know of until later exemplified the hostility of Houston toward the Navy. In January of 1843 the President had approved congressional passage of a secret bill to sell the fleet, and he had appointed three commissioners to travel to New Orleans to effect this. Even at that time rumors of Mexican invasion were again flying across Texas, but Houston felt confident of defeating any such attempt through the use of an army, although some of the rumors said the invasion would be launched from the Gulf. Santa Anna's government was in the process of quelling the rebellion in Yucatán, and as soon as he succeeded, it was said, he would have this army transported by sea to Texas and reconquer that place.

Residents of Texas coastal towns listened to these rumors with great anxiety. Among them was one of the commissioners named by Houston to sell the fleet. He refused the appointment, but he did not divulge Houston's plans regarding the Navy, and the public remained largely ignorant of them.

Moore knew more about the plan than Houston thought he did, and the commodore worked against time to get his ships to sea. The best chance for raising money was from the rebellious government of Yucatán, and Moore offered to rent his fleet out for operations there, as had been done during Lamar's administration. Acceptance brought immediate cash of more than seven thousand dollars from Yucatán and donations totaling ten thousand dollars from New Orleans merchants, who continually worked for Texas independence and more trade outlets—and in this case for a return in prize money that Moore hoped to get.

Moore bought ammunition and supplies for a three-month cruise, then recruited men. This was no easy task, because the Texas Navy had earned a reputation for poverty. Eventually, however, Moore manned his ships with a rough crew of men who had no better place to go, and he prepared to sail for Yucatán. Then the two commissioners arrived in New Orleans to sell his tiny fleet.

At almost the same time came orders for Moore to report to President Houston at Washington-on-the-Brazos. Moore realized that these orders had been intended for delivery long before, so that he would be out of the way when the commissioners arrived. But Sam Houston's craftiness failed this time: the orders had been delayed somehow. They had come on the same steamer as the commissioners and had arrived shortly after the appearance of the two men.

Moore fumed. He told the commissioners who had come to take his ships, "You don't get them. . . . I have the reins in my own hand and I intend to hold them." Two vessels, *Austin* and *Wharton*, were indeed prepared to sail, and their readiness impressed even the commissioners, who had expected to find rotting hulks instead of warships capable of attacking an enemy. Aboard the *Austin* were 146 officers and men, aboard the *Wharton* eighty-six—only thirty or so short of complement in each case.

One of Sam Houston's agents then began to waver. James Morgan, a coastal resident, earlier had voiced concern over a possible invasion of Texas from the Gulf of Mexico, but he had concluded that Santa Anna did not have the manpower or the ships. Now he began to wonder again. He had heard the rumors coming out of Yucatán and had heard about the operations there of a Mexican fleet of three steamers and five sailing vessels. After he boarded Moore's flagship *Austin* to accompany it to Galveston, where Moore finally had agreed to take it, he and Moore heard from the captains of two American vessels recently returned from Campeche in Yucatán that the Mexican General Ampudia of Mier fame was indeed embarking troops for a sea invasion of Texas—at Telchac, 150 miles northeast of Campeche, aboard a new ironclad steamer named *Montezuma*. Furthermore, Ampudia was said to be telling the rebels of Yucatán that they had lost the money advanced to Moore and the Texas Navy. Moore had been bribed and was not coming to their aid, Ampudia said.

That news changed James Morgan's mind about carrying out Sam Houston's order. He approved Moore's suggestion that the Texas ships go to Galveston by way of Yucatán, and specifically by way of Telchac, where they would try to attack the powerful *Montezuma* by surprise, then take on the rest of the Mexican fleet later. It would be better to fight there than off the Texas coast, Morgan thought.

I felt justified . . . The fact was, I found our vessels in such apple pie order—the officers so anxious to proceed on the Cruise —such bully crews: and knowing if the vessels did go into Galveston Harbor they would never come out again as *Texas* vessels—if at all—considering still farther that many of the Officers had never recd one cent of pay for the last two years— and if the navy was laid up or sold they probably never would—

That now an opportunity offered to do something for themselves & their adopted Country—a full stop was to be put to the expedition & close it at Galveston—For these & other *still more cogent reasons,* I concluded to stretch my authority as Commissioner, a little, and authorize Com. Moore to go ahead: believing we could visit the Coast of Yucatan & accomplish every object we had in view, in 20 or 30 days . . .

It took a dedicated man to cross President Houston like that, but Morgan was convinced of the propriety of his course. He realized fully his danger, for he knew Sam Houston—and even if he had not known him, he would have known the man's temperament through a proclamation that Houston had given him along with the orders to sell the fleet. Morgan showed the proclamation to Moore and told him its purpose: had Moore refused to give up his ships to the commissioners and taken them to sea instead, President Houston would have released the proclamation, which declared Moore a pirate and called on the ships of any nation to bring him to justice. Now Moore was sailing with his ships—but with the approval of Houston's commissioner.

Jackson Bryant was eager to go. He had endured too much day-to-day boredom, as he had made his father and others know. Of what use was a ship stuck in port or a midshipman without a job of any significance, without a complete uniform, without money or shore liberty? Aboard the *Wharton* the midshipmen had become so weary of the tedium and so ashamed of their appearance that they had resigned *en bloc,* but Commodore Moore could not afford to lose any more people and did not forward the resignations to Texas.

Bryant had stayed on the *Austin* Christmas and New Year's. His dissatisfaction had become so great that his father had written him a suggestion to ask for a leave of absence—he would put him in school somehow—or, if that failed, to offer his resignation, "provided the navy is not going to sea. If the ships are about to go to sea you had better go with them—it wouldn't look well to desert your post in that case."

Now, with the *Austin* bound for action, life would be different, and it even offered small rewards. The crew of the United States sloop of war *Ontario* manned the yards and gave the Texas sailors aboard the *Austin* and the *Wharton* three cheers as they passed close aboard on the night of April 15, 1843. At the mouth of the Mississippi dense fog forced Moore's two ships to anchor until the evening of the nineteenth, when they sailed for Telchac and whatever glory might await them there.

Aboard the *Austin* a midshipman serving with Bryant described their departure and indicated the excitement they all felt. "We left the Southwest pass at night, a moonless night, as black as a crow's wing. . . . The first lieutenant took charge of the deck and wore ship. The breeze was light, and the motion of the vessel scarcely perceptible. When I turned out in the morning the ship was under a cloud of canvas. The ocean was blue, the sky was blue . . ."

The midshipmen could be lighthearted, but the commodore still had his problems. The *Austin* carried eight men accused in the mutiny that had occurred aboard the *San Antonio* the year before. They could have been tried earlier, but Moore had avoided that. No need to hamper recruiting with such unpleasantness; enlistments in the Texas Navy were hard enough to get anyway. But now Moore had his men—although a hard group—and the mutineers had been tried soon after the *Austin* left New Orleans. Announcing findings and punishing the mutineers might serve to give the newcomers a warning regarding discipline.

After leaving the mouth of the Mississippi safely behind him Moore had all hands called out to hear the findings and the sentencings of the court: one man acquitted because he had testified against the other seven, one man sentenced to fifty lashes but pardoned, two men sentenced to 150 lashes, and four men to be hanged. The last punishment was awesome even to Moore, who had never before even witnessed an execution.

The lashes seemed ghastly enough to the young midshipmen. Bryant's companion who had described the *Austin*'s departure also recorded details of the whippings. The first man thus sentenced was "served up at the gangway, naked to the waist." The boatswain unlimbered the nine cords of his "cat" (so named because of the resemblance of its scars to scratches) and delivered the first blow, which brought a red tinge to the man's back. Additional lashes spread the color; further blows turned the man's back into a purple mess from which the blood flowed. After the boatswain had laid on the one-hundredth lash the ship's surgeon decided the man could stand no more, and he was released.

The hangings left everyone depressed. At noon on the twenty-sixth, while nearing Telchac, the *Austin* hove to, and all hands were called for the executions.

There was not a man of the whole crew on board from the boatswain down who knew how to make a hangman's knot, which of course was affected ignorance. [A. G.] Gray, the first lieutenant, who was a thorough marlinespike sailor, exclaimed in a mildly sarcastic tone, "I'll show you how to make a hangman's knot!" which he did. The four lines from the weather and lee yardarms, led through blocks to the deck, were "married' . . . and passed through leading blocks aft to and around the main-mast and forward to a point under the yard. One half of the crew were to walk aft with the line, the other half to walk forward. The officers were all on deck, each with side arms. The prisoners were brought forth and the ropes were passed around their necks. The commodore gave the signal, a shot from the bow gun, and the crew started on their death march. The four [men] were raised to the yardarm, and must have been strangled in the ascent; for they neither struggled nor made the slightest motion.

For an hour afterward the dead men remained dangling; then a work detail lowered them and gave them to their messmates to prepare for burial. The surgeon read a funeral service over them, and they were sent to the depths of the Gulf.

The *Austin* and the *Wharton* sailed on for Telchac in a light wind. Commodore Moore hoped that the executions would have inspired awe and instilled determination among his rough crew to serve well in the battles sure to come. But when he arrived at Telchac on the afternoon of the twenty-seventh he discovered that the armed steamer *Montezuma* had left. He learned that it had joined the other ships of the Mexican fleet.

48. LETTERS AND PROCLAMATIONS

In Texas, Andrew Jackson Bryant's father had followed the news of the *Austin*'s sailing from New Orleans with anxiety. He knew the purpose of Commodore Moore's departure, and he hoped to join a Texas vessel also bound for Yucatán, so that he could be near Jackson in what would surely be a time of peril. But Bryant could not arrange transportation, and he was forced to remain in Galveston, wracked with worry over what might happen to the son he had put in this situation. He could only write letters. "God I trust will hold you safely in his hand and grant you a safe return to your anxious parent, may you be crowned with laurels and your actions greeted with applause by your superior officers."

Charles Bryant was aware of another distressing development, something unknown at the time to either his son or Commodore Moore, aboard the *Austin*. After the sailing of the *Austin* and the *Wharton* from New Orleans, President Sam Houston, furious at the rebuff, had released his proclamation declaring Moore a pirate. Bryant read the text: Houston declared that Commodore Moore had been ordered to sail for Galveston three times, and three times he had disobeyed orders. "This government will no longer hold itself responsible for his acts upon the high seas. . . . The naval powers of Christendom will not permit such a flagrant and un-exampled outrage, by a commander of public vessels of war, upon the rights of his nation and upon his official oath and duty to pass unrebuked."

The proclamation evoked smiles abroad, but it angered many Texans, especially residents of the coastal communities, and it infuriated Bryant. From Galveston he wrote his son that Houston would "do well to keep his head out of this place for some time," and that "should the comadore be so much in luck as to take one of the Mexican steemers he may be the next President of Texas if he wishes—but God grant he may not be so unfortunate as to be taken by the Mexicans." If that happened, Bryant feared, Moore and all of the officers would be hanged, on the strength of Houston's proclamation.

Bryant and many others despised the President, who seemed to sabotage every move made by countrymen who wanted to take the fight to Mexico. Only recently, Bryant heard, Houston also had disavowed the Mier prisoners, in a letter to the English chargé d'affaires in Texas. The contents had leaked out: "It is true that the men went without orders; and so far as that was concerned, the Government of Texas was not responsible; and the men thereby placed themselves out of the protection of the rules of war." Houston added an important qualification to this sentence that most people never knew about: "But the Mexican officers, by proposing terms of capitulation to the men, relieved them from the responsibility which they had incurred; and the moment that the men surrendered in accordance with the proposals of capitulation, they became prisoners of war, and were entitled to all immunities as such."

Bryant and all Texas knew also that Houston was engaged in some dubious dealings with perennial enemies, the wild Indian tribes as distant as the present Texas Panhandle. Houston sent a two-man commission into the Indian country to invite the chiefs to a conference at Bird's Fort (near present Arlington) with the idea of arranging a peace treaty that would establish a line of demarcation for the benefit of both Indians and Texans, and this was accomplished later on in 1843.

To the further annoyance of many Texans, the President also displayed his affinity for Indians—in remarkable contrast to his harsh treatment of Commodore Moore—in a letter to a friendly Lipan Apache chief that was written about the same time as his piracy proclamation against the commodore. In it Houston expressed profound sympathy over the death of the chief's son, Flacco, who had been recently killed, apparently by Mexicans. In the letter Houston also showed that Mirabeau Lamar was not the only important Texan with a feeling for poetry. Houston wrote:

> My Brother:
>   My heart is sad!
> A cloud rests upon your nation.

Grief has sounded in your camp;
The voice of Flacco is silent.
His words are not heard in council;
The chief is no more.
His life has fled to the great Spirit,
His eyes are closed;
His heart no longer leaps
At the sight of the buffalo.
The voices of your camp
Are no longer heard to cry
"Flacco has returned from the chase."
Your chiefs look down upon the earth
And groan in trouble.
Your warriors weep.
The loud voices of grief are heard
From your women and children.
The song of birds is silent,
The ears of your people
Hear no pleasant sound,
Sorrow whispers in the winds,
The noise of the tempest passes,
It is not heard.
Your hearts are heavy.
The name of Flacco brought
Joy to all hearts.
Joy was on every face,
Your people were happy.
Flacco is no longer seen in the fight,
His voice is no longer heard in battle,
The enemy no longer
Makes a path for his glory.
His valor is no longer
A guard for his people.
The might of your nation is broken.
Flacco was a friend to his white brothers.
They will not forget him;
They will remember the red warrior.
His father will not be forgotten.

We will be kind to the Lipans.
Grass will not grow
On the path between us.
Let your wise men give counsel of peace,
Let your young men walk in the white path.
The gray headed men of your nation
Will teach wisdom.

Thy brother,
SAM HOUSTON

Now here was President Houston, the Indians' friend, calling his senior naval officer a pirate. The irresponsibility of this seemed blatant, but Houston had logical motivation. He needed to avoid conflict at this time for several reasons, and Moore was about to frustrate him. Houston always had believed that Texas could not win an offensive war against Mexico, and at this very time he was listening to a truce proposal brought from Mexico by a Texas prisoner, James Robinson, the former lieutenant governor, who had been released from Perote by Santa Anna to deliver this message: if Texas would accept return of Mexican sovereignty, Mexico would assure Texas autonomy. The proposal was ridiculous, and everyone knew that Robinson had instigated it himself to win release from prison as the deliverer of it, but Houston wanted to turn it to advantage if possible. Furthermore, about this time Houston was engaged in tricky maneuvering involving both England and the United States, working one against the other, and he hoped it might lead finally to either of two eventualities: England's persuading Mexico to recognize Texas independence, or annexation by the United States. Wedges used by Houston in this work were England's fear of United States expansion, and United States aversion to English influence in Texas. For these dealings too Sam Houston needed tranquillity, and in the maneuverings directly involving the United states he perhaps needed weak Gulf defenses, to elicit concern and help from the United States Navy. Moore had upset the status quo, and Houston fumed—as he would have done anyway had Moore merely defied orders, with nothing else involved.

Charles Bryant saw displayed only Houston's extraordinary temper and egotism, and in his letter to Jackson he added: "Houston will do all he can to have you taken and sacrificed, but be not alarmed—his reign is short in my opinion. I believe brighter days are about dawning on Texas." Bryant concluded his letter with the usual exhortations about manliness, manners, duty, industry, and learning. Especially did Jackson need to devote attention to his writing—"you must not take example of me writing letters to you"—and he urged his son to watch his spelling and his use of capital letters.

49. MEETING THE DEMANDS

The Mexican Navy had been of greater concern to Jackson Bryant than either Sam Houston or spelling errors. After Commodore Moore missed the *Montezuma* at Telchac he searched for the enemy ships and found them. On April 30 and May 2 he led the *Austin* and the *Wharton* into engagements that proved to be minor and inconclusive insofar as battle results were concerned, but heartening to the Yucatán rebels and actual turning points in the young life of Midshipman Bryant, who left puerility behind with the New Orleans tedium and met the demands made of him.

Sam Houston's wayward naval commissioner, James Morgan, had observed Bryant and other *Austin* midshipmen in combat, and he wrote home in a letter:

> I could not imagine more coolness & determination than was displayed by the Officers & crew in the fight—all appeared delighted & the young middys & powder boys made a perfect Jubilee of the affair! For my own part I had much rather been at a feast—For d—— me if I saw any *fun* in it! I summoned up courage enough to keep on the deck during the action to be sure & like a frightened child who will make a noise to keep fear away—I huzzaed for Texas most of the time as loud as I could howl: but I could not help bowing instinctively to the enemy's 68 lb shot as they came over my head . . .

In the same letter Morgan expressed concern about his relations with the President: "I expect 'Old Sam' will *'hang me'*—for I have travelled out of the course his instructions dictated. But . . . we have played h-ll with the enemys arrangements and calculations in this quarter . . ."

Moore waited now at besieged Campeche and wanted to raise still more hell with the Mexican fleet standing offshore. He hoped to engage it in a situation where he could use the wind to close the enemy quickly—scurrying through the area commanded by their longer-range guns and working into a station where his short-range superiority would tell. For days he sought to do this, unsuccessfully. When he tried to approach the Mexicans, the enemy commander, preferring not to fight, would send his sailing vessels far out of range and back his steamers into the wind, where Moore could not go. At army headquarters in nearby Lerma, General Ampudia observed these actions with disgust and taunted his naval colleague, who finally stayed to fight on May 16 when Moore once again ordered the *Austin* and the *Wharton* out of Campeche on an early-morning breeze. Ashore, thousands of residents watched from vantage points on a high wall surrounding the old part of town and from church towers and the tops of hotels and suburban houses. Most of them cheered for the Texans.

When the Texas ships had ventured into range, the two Mexican steamers, *Montezuma* and *Guadalupe,* fired their big guns. Moore answered, but the range and the wind, which died about midmorning, worked against him. Furthermore, some small Yucatecan gunboats that were to have joined in the fight never did so—with one exception—despite repeated signals from Moore to attack. Shot from the enemy's sixty-eight- and forty-two-pound cannon slashed through the *Austin*'s rigging and rained down on deck. Jackson Bryant's fellow midshipman who had so carefully described the voyage to date also recorded the experience of facing enemy cannon.

One sees the flash of the gun, then hears the whistling of the ball, and then the report, the ball out-travelling the sound. After a little study of the coming balls one could determine very nearly where they were going to strike. Two of them I shall always remember. Of the first one I said, "This is going to pick a man from my gun's crew." It struck just under the port between wind and water. As it was jammed between two of the timbers it was found impossible to drive home a shot plug. The other shot . . . struck the deck of the to'-gallant forecastle directly over my head (for I was at gun No. 1) and tip-tip-tipped overboard, simply denting the planks.

When the Mexicans came near enough the Texans pounded them, too, and in one salvo brought down the *Guadalupe*'s flagstaff and colors, to Texas cheers. Then, shortly after noon, Moore had his chance. The wind freshened, and he took advantage of it to send his ship slithering between the *Montezuma* and the *Guadalupe*, from where he poured destruction on the two enemy vessels from both broadsides. Dead and wounded littered their decks.

Midshipman Bryant survived all that action unharmed and unyielding. Others had not proved so staunch—including one man who had fled to the hold, where he cowered while his shipmates fought. An officer ordered Bryant below to get the man, and just as Bryant came back on deck with him a ball crashed into the side of the *Austin*, sending off a hail of splinters that struck Bryant's knee and leg. He bent over and grabbed his injured leg just as another ball struck, this time hurling a shower of splinters that pierced his right hand. Nearby, one man was killed and seven others were wounded by the same hits.

Bryant was out of action, painfully, after that, but not out of the battle. Enemy shot continued to whistle over his head and to plummet into his ship, but gradually the firing fell off as the Mexican ships withdrew. The *Austin* followed for a while, but gave up the chase and counted casualties: three dead and twenty-two wounded. Aboard the *Wharton*, Bryant heard, two men had been killed when a gun captain fired his piece while it was being loaded.

Montezuma was reported to have lost forty killed and wounded, *Guadalupe* more than a hundred. Neither ship would be taking any invasion army to Texas soon, if that had been their plan, but the man who had been responsible for preventing it was considered a pirate by his government.

The very next day after the battle Bryant asked another midshipman to write to his father for him. He dictated the letter, which contained an account of his wounding. About the same time, unknown to Jackson, some officers of the *Austin* also wrote letters home describing the battle and praising the actions of some individuals aboard ship. Among the persons they mentioned was Jackson Bryant, the once obstreperous midshipman, whom they complimented for valor under fire and patience during suffering.

50. FREEDOM FOR ONE CAPTIVE

On the banks of the Colorado, across that river from La Grange, Sam Maverick had rejoined his family on their twenty-six-acre farm. He found waiting for him a new daughter, Augusta, who had been born the same day, March 30, that General Santa Anna finally had freed him from the confines of the city of Mexico. On April 2 he had left for Veracruz and passage home, where he had arrived May 4.

The reunion had been rapturous, although Mary Maverick had been very ill for days after the birth, and the baby had become seriously ill herself when a week old. But by the time Sam Maverick arrived they had recovered. Maverick himself arrived in "splendid health and happy as could be."

Only one matter troubled him much. He felt sorry, and rather embarrassed, about having left so many comrades in prison in Mexico. Whenever he talked with the families or friends of these men, Mary said, he felt "almost ashamed."

A letter from a former fellow prisoner blackened his mood further. Written from Perote April 15, it described stricter measures in force at the prison—a doubled guard, chains fastened tighter to ankles, and more punishment for mischievous prisoners, especially for those who tried to make themselves comfortable by slipping out of their irons. Maverick's fellow prisoner had been among the troublesome group, and his captors were making him suffer for it: "Here I remain with the heaviest pair of [chains] that the castle can afford, hard rivetted to my ankles. I am writing you with my legs folded under me as well as my irons will permit, so . . . you must look over bad writing."

The more the prisoner thought about it the more he fumed. "If Texas remains quiet after this she will without doubt become almost a baron [*sic*] wilderness. I never will raise a gun in her defense again. When I fight for her again it will be for revenge and not for Texas."

Maverick was forced to agree, on the basis of his own experience. "I am ashamed of the miserable position in which I think Texas now stands. With abundant native strength and resources and, I think, valor to boot we have permitted the best opportunity of relieving ourselves to pass by whilst we stand until we have almost become palzied in the cringing attitude of beggers."

51. BUILDING A ROAD AND HOPES

Deep in Mexico, in a former powder mill converted to a prison, Thomas Bell and the other Mier prisoners heard about Commodore Moore's spectacular activities on the Gulf, and Sam Houston's bitter reaction to them, and they voiced among themselves strong support for Moore. Virtually all of the prisoners echoed the Perote captive who had written Sam Maverick about his disillusionment with Texas. Here they were, helpless in enemy hands, and apparently rejected even by their own President, who had termed their expedition unauthorized. Yet they had fought for Texas as well as they knew how. What kind of a government was that? What kind of a man was Sam Houston? "God forgive him for I fear I never can," said one captive. Many of the prisoners around Bell vowed never to fight again for Texas, or to fight only for revenge, as the Perote man had said he might.

Since May 12 Bell and the others had been working on a road leading to Santa Anna's residence at Tacubaya, in hills overlooking the domes and towers of the city of Mexico. They had been given "gay and jaunty" prison uniforms, which at first had provoked roars of laughter from the men for whom they were intended. The clothes—overshirt and trousers—were made of coarse flannel alternately striped red and green. When some prisoners hesitated to dress in such gaudy apparel they were prompted with bayonets. Then they were paired off; ankle-chained by twos; given crowbars,

axes, shovels, mauls, and bags for carrying sand and stones; escorted to the construction site; and put to work under the supervision of some very ugly felons recruited for that purpose from
Mexican prisons. The convicts had orders to whip anyone seen
malingering.

Nevertheless, the work progressed slowly. The prisoners exerted
only enough energy to avoid the lash. Their job was to bring sand
and stone for the road—enough to make a layer one foot deep.
They carried it in the bags furnished, threw it on the road, and
pounded it with heavy pestles to make it firm enough to support
the carriages that would pass over it. One of Bell's companions
wrote in his diary, "[We are] doing the work of asses."

They worked, rain or sunshine, from 7 A.M. to 5 P.M. six days a
week on a diet of one pint of gruel and a piece of coarse bread in
the morning, a few ounces of boiled beef and five ounces of bread
at noon, and a dish of boiled beans at night. Soon after supper each
man spread his rush mat on the brick floor of his cell and slept,
exhausted by the day's work, halfhearted though it usually was.
The next day the grim cycle started again, with the only change
being the substitution after a few weeks of Mexican Army personnel for the convict overseers.

Bell described the work.

The greater part [of the Texas prisoners] with sacks on their
backs were marched about half a mile and ordered to fill them
with sand and stones, and thus for several months . . . a chain
gang might be seen, consisting of about sixty in number, in
double file with a chain uniting each file, daily trudging the same
road with a slow and even pace; laden with [sand and stone],
and a file of Mexican soldiers . . . on each side . . . Others
were employed in digging up the ground with heavy iron crow
bars, while others leveled it with wooden shovels and laid a
pavement of stones. Various other employments . . . followed
. . . such as culling stones and beating the sand and stones until
a road was graded.

But the men continued to carry as little sand as they could get
away with, then managed to spill much of it before reaching the
road. Fatigue overtook them frequently throughout the day. They

stumbled to the ground under their burdens, and got back on their feet slowly. Many seemed to be utterly stupid. They had to be shown what to do and how to do it more than once by their guards. Illness was common, and the prison hospital overflowed with Texans suffering from a variety of ailments—none of them easily perceived or diagnosed.

At the end of two months the Texas prisoners had completed only one hundred yards of the road: they had adapted admirably to the *mañana* concept. But then their captors instituted some subtle methods of persuasion. When an officer observed a prisoner working well, he rewarded him by taking off his chains; and when an officer saw a man obviously loafing, he punished him severely. Road construction proceeded a little faster after that.

Throughout this period of captivity Bell and the rest heard rumors alternately optimistic and dismal. Once they heard that they had been sentenced to work for life on a road leading to the Mexican Pacific Coast, and that this was only the beginning of that long stretch. But most rumors were hopeful, and this kept spirits up—even if it also led to disappointments.

What could be more appropriate, the prisoners reflected, than for Santa Anna to make the magnanimous gesture of announcing their release on his birthday, which they mistakenly thought to be June 13. As the day neared they all grew hopeful. They stared at his house with this anticipation in mind. Occasionally they even saw the man, but not often—and whenever he left his residence he was escorted by many well-armed dragoons, who were always on guard around the house.

June 10 passed, then June 11. Expectation grew. Even the Mexican officers were telling the Texans they could expect liberation soon.

June 12. One of Bell's fellow prisoners wrote in his diary that every man was anxious to see what tomorrow would bring.

June 13. The same man wrote, "Nothing transpired this day but the clanking of our chains." But wait! Maybe tomorrow. It was a feast day—Corpus Christi.

June 14. No announcement of liberation—"all conjecture being at an end." The prisoners determined not to build up false hopes "on every trifling rumor." They refrained for a while.

Nine men tired of waiting for release escaped at various times. Santa Anna freed a few others, including a teen-age Texan he adopted and sent to school. He also released the boy's father and brother. Some men died. But for Bell and the rest life went on as it had done for interminable months: ". . . resistance was in vain [and] nothing remained but to endure . . . with as much patience as possible, since by resisting, and . . . dying, no good could possibly be gained . . ." Texas was a life away for Bell.

New hope came with the approach of July 4—perhaps Santa Anna would use that day for his announcement. But the only word from him that day, Bell wrote, was this terse declaration: "For the respect I have for American Independence I allow you to celebrate the day."

The women of Tacubaya helped. They prepared dishes for the prisoners, who were formed at noon on the Fourth and marched to the shade of a grove of ash trees, where they found tables spread and ladies smiling. After feasting and toasting they turned to political talk. They commemorated United States independence in speeches and resolutions, voted rejection of the peace proposal carried to Sam Houston by James Robinson, upheld Commodore Moore and the Texas Navy, and condemned President Houston vehemently. They all agreed Texas should prosecute the war "she is now engaged in"—but few really believed she would.

After that interlude the prisoners were put back to work, and for two more months they endured the physical and mental torture they had come to associate now with life. Bell had "got fleshy" the year before and had weighed as much as 160 pounds, but now he lost weight, strength, and health. Then the work was completed— "and a fair road it is," one prisoner said proudly. They had built a quarter-mile stretch of all-weather surface extending from Santa Anna's residence down an incline toward the city of Mexico.

But the prisoners received no reward. In the early part of September they learned they were to be taken to the prison at Perote, there to join other Texas captives. On September 12 they began this part of their long march.

52. A LAST GOODBYE

In Galveston, Texas Navy veterans of the sea fighting off Yucatán had received a cold acknowledgment of their return from their President, who dishonorably discharged Moore and two other ranking officers—illegally, as Houston's critics contended—five days after their reappearance in Texas.

But Moore and the others had won acclaim from most citizens. When the *Austin* and the *Wharton* arrived at Galveston, early in the afternoon of July 14, they were greeted by hundreds of people waving and cheering from small boats in the bay and from wharves. On hand was the mayor, who invited Commodore Moore to a testimonial dinner. Moore agreed to go only after surrendering himself to the sheriff and receiving a refusal of arrest because of an absence of instructions. President Houston might consider Moore a pirate, but to these people he was a hero. Galvestonians answered Houston's charges by burning him in effigy, and later the Texas Congress acquitted Moore of the President's charges even though Houston had many friends in that body.

At Galveston many people were solicitous for the comfort of Midshipman Andrew Jackson Bryant and other wounded men. This concern lasted for only a short time. Caring for Jackson soon became the sole responsibility of his father.

About that time Charles Bryant found himself in a financial plight even worse than usual. A combination cedar-cutting and farming venture had just failed and left him in debt, so that he had to sell the timber and his few cattle and hogs at a sacrifice to pay his way out of the disaster. Furthermore, he had not been able to collect some money owed him; and he had sent to his wife in Maine the small amount of cash he had been able to accumulate in months past. But this had been lost at sea when the vessel sank. Worse, his labors had injured his health, so that whatever earning ability he had was impaired. "Fate . . . seemed to take pleasure in blasting every effort . . ."

Now Jackson required attention. For a time it appeared that the young man would lose his injured right hand, but amputation proved to be unnecessary. Jackson expressed gratitude for favors even in misfortune: "I might as well be dead as have it cut off . . ."

A slight turn in Charles Bryant's fortunes helped out further at this time. Some people who owed him money finally paid, and in Galveston he was suddenly able to find plenty of work, although the wages were low—$1.50 a day—and the hours restricted by the periods when he was unable to leave Jackson unattended. But all the worries were worth it for this concerned father: "To make him happy . . . was my chief study." Gradually Jackson's wounds began to heal, and when his father received two hundred dollars in September from a man who owed him money the Bryants, father and son, determined to return to Maine.

Charles Bryant inquired about vessels bound for the East Coast, found none, and concluded to go to New Orleans, where he and his son could more easily find a ship leaving for Boston or New York. He took passage in a vessel called the *Sarah Barnes,* but a stiff norther delayed sailing. The sudden drop in temperature also caused Jackson painful cramps, and Bryant summoned a Navy surgeon, who advised against taking Jackson north until he had recovered. Bryant rejected a suggestion from his son that he go on to Maine alone, and he mailed the two hundred dollars to his wife in a letter sent out of Galveston aboard the same *Sarah Barnes.* In it Bryant told his wife to use the money to bring the family to Texas, but the letter went down at sea with the ship, which sank during another siege of heavy weather. Fate still seemed to take pleasure in blasting his every effort.

Weeks passed, and Jackson seemed again to be mending well; perhaps by spring he would be able to walk "without caution." But Galveston bored him, and he asked his father for permission to go to New Orleans, where he knew a few interesting persons—male and female—whose acquaintance he had made while idling aboard the *Austin* there. One of them, a widow "of high respectability" who kept a school for New Orleans girls, invited him over to make his home with her and her son, a friend of Jackson's. The surgeon agreed that the move could be beneficial—and New Orleans winters were just as mild as Galveston's. Furthermore, Jackson would have some money coming in to help with upkeep. The Texas Congress had voted that "on account of the bravery and spirit displayed by him, [he] is entitled to, and may receive a yearly pension, equal to the half part of a midshipman's full pay, and said pension shall be paid to said Bryant annually, so long as he may continue disabled from the wounds received in . . . action." Half of eighteen dollars a month could not repay him for his suffering, but at least it was something.

After thinking over the propriety of the situation, his father approved the request. Next spring he would follow Jackson there, and together they would leave for Maine. He gave his son thirty-five dollars and saw him aboard the small schooner *Galveston,* whose captain was a friend of Jackson's and agreed to give the young man passage without pay. But soon after the vessel's departure she returned to Galveston; a squall at sea had partly dismasted her. Repairs required two days. During that time Jackson again stayed with his father.

On the last night before sailing Charles Bryant tried to dissuade Jackson from going.

> I had a foreboding of some kind of evil . . . I [reminded] him of the circumstances of the *Sarah Barnes* starting once and then coming back, and afterwards being lost. I told him I had fears of the safety of the *Galveston* as she was a small vessel and . . . [not] safe in a gale. He laughed at my superstitious fears as he called them, said he had much rather go out on the *Galveston* than on one of the large Steam Boats—that the capt of the *Galveston* was a particular friend and would not charge for his passage . . . He hugged me in his arms and kissed me and then said if it was my earnest wish for him not to go he would remain cheerfully, but he could see no reason why he should not go, it would be a saving of the expense of his Board until spring, he could get his clothes much cheaper in Orleans than here and he should enjoy himself much better there than he could here, and he wanted to go—he prevailed upon me with his arguments; as I saw his heart was set on going I consented . . .

So once more Bryant accompanied his son to the little schooner and helped him board. He watched Jackson waving his cap in a goodbye gesture, and he saw the delight on his son's face. Meeting friends in New Orleans again would be pleasant.

Later Charles Bryant heard that wind and sea had claimed still another victim between Texas and New Orleans. The schooner *Galveston* vanished—his son along with it. Sadly he wrote his wife the news, and remarked, ". . . to live is to mourne . . . Blessed is the flower that nicked in the early spring feels not the blast that . . . scatters its blossoms . . ." But surely God had some reason for running his world this way, so with the religious severity of nineteenth-century New England Bryant rationalized this latest tragedy and all his other troubles. "I can realize that . . . these things may be inflicted for my own good, and perhaps a punishment for my sins."

53. CHAINED IN PEROTE

More hopeful in regard to their own punishment were the 120 or so Texas prisoners who had built Santa Anna's road. Despite all the previous disappointments—all those optimistic predictions that had turned sour—Thomas Bell and his companions listened to still another rumor while they marched under heavy guard through high, rugged mountains along a road leading from the city of Mexico to the prison at Perote, which lay on the route to Veracruz. The talk said that upon their arrival they would be released. Even the United States minister to Mexico concurred in this belief, they heard, so it had substance.

The journey proved to be as uncomfortable as ever. Rain soaked and chilled them. The night stops for sleep included the usual cowpens and barns, and this time a hog sty. The rations left wrinkles in their stomachs, and sometimes they bedded down for the night without any meal at all. The scenery was at times imposing, but Bell could not enjoy it. Pine-clad mountains surrounded them, and in the distance towered snow-capped peaks. Below lay occasional fertile plains nurturing carefully cultivated fields.

But the picturesqueness vanished with the vegetation. On September 21 the prisoners arrived at their destination, a barren region, but they were full of hope for prompt release. They saw in the distance a town that their guards identified as Perote, and about a mile away, on the left side of their mountain road, a rambling old castle, with grim portholes and dark-mouthed artillery, that served now as a prison. Originally known as the Castle of San Carlos, it had been completed by the Spaniards seventy years earlier. As Bell drew nearer he could appreciate the strength of the construction, but he wondered about the usefulness of erecting such a fortification in this wilderness. Bell did not know the original purpose—to guard the route from Veracruz to the city of Mexico.

Around the twenty-six acres of the compound ran a moat, dry and sandy when Bell saw it, about sixty feet wide and ten feet deep. Across the moat lay the prison, built in quadrangular shape with projecting bastions at each corner. The outside walls were made of stone, and Bell later learned the awesome dimensions: thirty feet high, fourteen feet thick at the base, and ten feet at the top.

Across a drawbridge they clattered, through an archway into the prison, where about seventy other Texans already were held. Bell saw mounted along the walls many cannon—six- and nine-pounders—and directly ahead an expansive parade ground surrounded by several buildings. He learned that the post was manned by detachments of artillery, cavalry, and infantry, and he discovered that these troops were to be their guards—for the prisoners were not going to be released. Still chained in pairs, they were assigned to large cells—thirty men in each—located in the interior of the main wall. After Bell had been escorted to his grim quarters with the others in his group he peered around, with growing despair, and saw stone walls, a rough floor of cemented stone, a lofty arched ceiling, a thick wood door—quickly locked behind them—that opened onto the stone hallway, and, built into that door, a small, grated window. He heard that, incredibly, sixteen Texas prisoners had escaped from this place not even three months earlier by patiently hacking into a wall with primitive tools they had been able to sneak into the cell. Some of the escapees had been recaptured, but others of them—including the officer Thomas

Jefferson Green—had succeeded in reaching Texas, where they at once launched a castigation of President Sam Houston.

But to Bell "no way of escape seemed left here, for a sentinel was placed at the door with a loaded musket, to watch every movement of his charge inside, through [the] grated window . . . and by the light of a taper kept burning the whole night . . . nor was it until next day that [we] were allowed to crawl from this living grave, and view again the bright and lovely luminary of Heaven, for about three hours at noon and then retire again to this charnel house . . ."

The first night was especially uncomfortable. The prison had been built in treeless hills at the foot of a mountain range, and down its slopes blew a frigid wind that numbed the Texans, who had for beds only thin blankets and a hard, cold floor. Soon dampness compounded the discomfort—this being a rainy season—and to the prisoners warmth seemed something that had been left far behind in Texas with family, wives, sweethearts, and friends.

Nor did the food provide much comfort. Provisions were issued to the prisoners and prepared daily by their own appointed cooks, camp style: bread made from coarse brown flour, about twelve ounces daily; a small portion of potatoes every day; twelve ounces of beef at noon, with the water in which it had been boiled mixed with a few vegetables in a sort of soup; a pint of boiled onions; a pint of weak coffee for each man morning and evening; and once a week, for variety in diet, tripe with potatoes.

After a few weeks the rigors of diet, weather, bad air, poor sanitation, and chained confinement began to tell on the already weak men. An epidemic they called *"vomito"* swept through their ranks and brought death to many. Early in October the sickness sent eighty-six Texans to the hospital. More than twenty died—some raving mad, others entirely motionless. They were buried, without coffins or ceremony, in the moat, except for the few who had accepted the Roman Catholic faith.

One of Bell's fellow prisoners who fell ill described the torment as he lay helpless and virtually unattended on a hospital bed of straw. "That disease! how can I find language to describe it? . . . I lay in the Hospital thirty days, and fourteen days of that time entirely insensible to all earthly things, even to suffering itself. On partial recovery from this Sensless state, or Stupor, and before I had regained my intellect, I imagined myself many, many miles away from misery, among friends! But Alas! I lay on a Sick couch . . . and Oh! Such Sickness—Such misery! . . . Give me death in any shape, Save me from that disease!"—yellow fever.

Even then many prisoners did not give up hope, although only eighteen of them escaped the ravages of *"vomito."* On October 7 they heard the cannon booming a salute of twenty-one guns for Santa Anna, who was traveling from the city of Mexico to his country residence near Jalapa along the same road down which they had marched. The inevitable rumor spread: Santa Anna would order their liberation as he passed Perote. But instead of that generous gesture he gave orders to put the prisoners to work and to keep them closely guarded.

Even after that some prisoners found satisfaction. The painters, carpenters, and blacksmiths among them were set to work at their specialties, unchained and receiving daily wages. But most of the prisoners worked in irons at dreary tasks: sweeping filth from prison grounds, carrying garbage, hauling sand for repairs to prison walls. Occasionally the chores were more demanding. During one period, when rock was needed for prison repairs, twenty Texans were yoked daily to a cart that they were forced to pull four miles to a location where they loaded it with stone. Then they pulled it back to the prison.

Bell reflected bitterly on his misery, and on the comforts being enjoyed by more fortunate people in Texas and in the United States. He knew that some of them were taking for granted a good life. He himself had been guilty of this, although his life never had come close to affluence.

You pampered sons of freedom, Bell mused. How great would be your indignation were you forced to work like slaves, and chained all the while.

XI

END OF THE REPUBLIC

1844 to February, 1846

The annexation question occupied much of the last year of Sam Houston's presidency and virtually all of the abbreviated term of his successor, Anson Jones, who became President in December, 1844.

For Houston the issue became especially frustrating. In April, 1844, John Tyler's new Secretary of State, John C. Calhoun, a friendly Southerner, drew up an annexation treaty with the Texas representatives in Washington, James Pinckney Henderson and Isaac Van Zandt. The United States promised military and naval protection to Texas in the interim; Sam Houston withdrew his peace negotiators sent to Mexico following the truce; and because of all this Santa Anna declared hostilities resumed. But when the treaty came before the United States Senate for a vote, nervousness about the approaching presidential election and violent opposition to slavery by Northern senators defeated it, thirty-five to sixteen. Sam Houston vowed never again to be so embarrassed, and he redoubled his efforts to get help from England and France in obtaining recognition from Mexico. Both nations expressed eagerness to assist, since neither wanted any United States expansion. This display of friendliness with European powers, especially with England, alarmed officials in the United States and brought about a review of the annexation question.

Another consideration in the change of attitude was a new spirit of nationalism brought on by the desire to expand westward—the spirit described by the term "manifest destiny." On one day alone—May 22, 1843—more than a thousand immigrants had left Independence, Missouri, for Oregon. There the growing numbers of settlers clamored for local government, drew up a state constitution, and hoped for positive action soon by the United States, where many people were demanding an Oregon boundary as far north as 54 degrees 40 minutes.

Impending United States action westward became evident in the presidential election of 1844. The expected candidates, Whig Henry Clay and Democrat Martin Van Buren, both opposed Texas annexation—at least without Mexican consent. Clay won his nomination, but Van Buren, a New Yorker, lost out among the Democrats, who unexpectedly nominated James K. Polk of Tennessee in the first convention ever reported by telegraph—from Baltimore to Washington.

Polk ran on an expansionist platform—occupation of Oregon by the United States alone, and annexation of Texas. This stand united Western and Southern voters, and Polk won election. Another factor in his victory was the old hatred and distrust of England—in regard to Texas and Oregon, of course. As for Texas, the worry over England's intentions proved more powerful than the concern about admitting another slave state, and it was actually the United States, not Texas, that instigated the successful final move toward annexation, during Anson Jones's term as President of Texas.

Later Houston explained his foreign-policy tactics that had confused and angered so many Texans: "I did direct our minister at Washington to withdraw the [1837] application of Texas for annexation and commenced paying court to England and France, for reasons that public policy has heretofore forbade an explanation. . . . If ladies are justified in making use of coquetry in securing their annexation to good and agreeable husbands, you must excuse me for making use of the same means to annex Texas to Uncle Sam."

54. AN ADAPTABLE MAN

Moses Johnson, a young physician and surgeon, seemed at first to be still another unlikely immigrant for the Republic of Texas. Nine months of medical study at Woodstock, in his native New York, had earned him the right to practice medicine there—and had won him an excellent recommendation from teachers as a student of "moral worth": "We know of no one we can more highly recommend . . . We believe his ardent devotion to his profession will assure success for him." Furthermore, he held a commission in the New York militia. With these connections and support he surely could have stayed in his home state and enjoyed a successful career. But Moses Johnson was restless and inquiring, and word of the formation of the Republic of Texas, freedom's newest bastion, had fascinated him. He had felt a compulsion to see it for himself; so several months prior to May 9, 1838—when the Republic of Texas issued him a permit to practice medicine and surgery—he, his wife, and their two children had moved to Texas, settling originally on the coast.

Johnson had moved on from there to the newly designated capital of Austin, where two other characteristics of his personality had become evident. The young doctor had shown himself to be a gregarious and an adaptable man, one who seemed to fit in easily anywhere, even on a raw frontier. In December of 1840 he had been elected mayor of the town for a one-year term. Only the Texas climate—the torrid summers and the changeable winters—seemed hard for him to adapt to, and his health often suffered.

By 1844 Moses Johnson had become well acquainted in Texas. His professional background had brought him into close contact with Ashbel Smith, Anson Jones, and other medical men prominent in Texas affairs. Furthermore, his own brief political career had introduced him to most other influential Texans and had helped him to prosper in other ways. He bought some large tracts of farmland and several slaves—more evidence of adaptability, because he came from a region and a family that were abolitionist in sentiment.

Johnson's pretty wife, Olivia, was much less adaptable than he. She did not like Texas—the weather and other discomforts, the crudeness, the instability. To relatives in Illinois, Massachusetts, and New York she wrote letters exhibiting some self-indulging complaint, and she found sympathy. From Knoxville, Illinois, her brother Edson Huggins replied, "I know how I felt when I was [in Texas]. I always felt as though I was not at home. I was always discontented, but I hope you are more contented than I was. If you ain't I should advise you to leave there as quick as possible if you want to get away as bad as I did. I know you will leave as quick as you can get away."

Edson had stamped the Texas dust from his shoes; nothing there for him, even with a sister for company and consolation. He had returned to Illinois, married a fair girl of seventeen, "one of the best of women," and found plenty of work. His recent venture now faded into only a bad memory. He wanted no more of Texas, not even as a companion state in the Union. He continued his letter: "I want you should get out of Texas, and I think sooner the better, but you have a right to do as you think best. As for Texas being attached to the United States I don't think it will, but I don't know, for there is a great deal said about it in Congress and in the states also. . . . Fact of it is we have got slaves enough and don't want any more . . ."

But Olivia's husband, Moses, obviously felt differently about that, and in those days marital bonds generally superseded any others. Moses Johnson moved again, and his family went with him, to the town of Independence. From there he observed the fascinating, fermenting developments of 1844 Texas. Nearby, in Washington-on-the-Brazos, was the capital of the Republic—although the archives remained in Austin, jealously guarded by those irate citizens. Nearby, too, was the spacious home of Anson Jones, a physician like himself, and the friendship with Jones proved especially rich. Jones, as President Houston's secretary of state, was deeply involved in Houston's intricate maneuverings with several foreign countries to obtain recognition of Texas independence from Mexico or annexation to the United States. Momentous times lay ahead, Moses Johnson realized, and he would be well located to observe them.

55. A TIME OF WAITING

In the prison of Perote, Thomas Bell recuperated from the dreaded *"vomito,"* heard more rumors of impending release with increasing disbelief, and observed the brutalities of his captors and reflected on his reaction to them with some concern.

His worry evolved from his religious background. He hated the Mexicans, yet he could still admit that for a man like himself who professed to be a Christian "it is morally wrong to cherish a hatred and thirst for vengeance upon a people, for the wrongs practiced by their government."

Bell realized that not all Mexicans were despicable, but sometimes he had to force himself to remember that. There was, for instance, the man who kept a tiny grocery store in the castle and allowed small sums of credit to Texas prisoners who had no money. This category included Bell. There were also several Mexican officers who treated the Texans more gently than their orders implied that they should. Finally, there were the many generous, sympathetic Mexican women, whom Bell revered in his ostentatious rhetoric: "O! woman . . . ever ready to administer the balm of consolation to the sorrowing and relief to the destitute . . . heal the wounded, soothe the dying . . ." But too much Perote life was controlled by men like the commandant, who watched prisoners at work from the windows of his office and punished any idler by ordering him sent immediately to the isolation of the *calabozo,* and by guards who whacked prisoners with swords and clubs.

Bell tried to acknowledge the goodness of his captors when he saw it, despite his natural reluctance to do so. He found it almost as difficult to avoid bitterness toward people at home. Sometimes in his frustration he could hate them as heartily as the Mexicans.

I do not blame the Mexicans for taking and keeping us prisoners [he wrote his father in March of 1844], but I consider they are wrong for making us labor and more than that for starving us as they frequently have done; though we have enough to eat now we still do not get what the government allows us for rations, and of clothes and blankets our supply is scanty. Allowance is given [out] and many are almost without clothes and entirely destitute of blankets, and our countrymen have as yet afforded us no relief. It would seem that they [have] forgotten that we were captured fighting in a cause in which they are equally or more interested than we, a common cause in which all should unite if not with their service, at least with their money. . . . [But] Texas can never repay me for the suffering I have underwent in her service for the last fourteen months. . . .

Winter of 1843–1844 ended at Perote with the Mier prisoners more dispirited than ever and without the usual hope of impending release. In the city of Mexico the United States minister persuaded Santa Anna to release the rest of the men captured with Sam Maverick at San Antonio during the raid by General Woll, and the gates of Perote opened for those lucky Texans on March 24. But they closed again, and when they would reopen for any more liberated men was a desponding question for those left behind. The prisoners talked desperately of escape as the only way out of their misery. If they failed in that attempt the death they could expect would be preferable to their present situation anyway.

Bell learned later that some men had done more than talk about escape; they had begun working toward it—in the very cell from which Thomas Jefferson Green and fifteen other prisoners had dug their way out the previous July. How the second group of prisoners finally managed to break out made an almost incredible story.

After the earlier escape the Mexican commandant had instituted rigorous inspections of each cell at irregular times throughout the day—whenever guards threw open a door suddenly and walked in. They always inspected walls carefully to assure themselves that no more Texas devils were making a secret excavation, and they inspected prisoners' chains to be certain they were properly secured. But they always ignored the floor, and this gave the prisoners in Green's old cell an idea.

They asked permission to cover the expansive stone floor with boards. The rough surface made rest impossible, they complained, especially since the only padding between body and stone was a blanket. The Mexicans magnanimously granted permission, as was their occasional inclination, and the Texans began their work. After the wood surface had been laid and fixed they used a piece of tin to saw a trapdoor through a section of the new floor—fitting the opening so well that inspecting officers never noticed it, even though they often stood on it. Then they worked themselves out of their chains (which was often possible when no guards were around to interfere) and began digging a narrow tunnel underneath the trapdoor, using sharp sticks and small knives on the stone-and-concrete floor and working by night after the surprise inspections had ceased. The floor was about ten inches thick, but once they were through that barrier digging became easier, in relatively soft earth. All of this refuse they spread evenly under the boards covering their vast floor, so that inspecting officers never noticed any tilt or gradual rising of the boards toward the level of the elevated cell door. The officers never even realized that any prisoners had squeezed out of their chains; by morning the chains would be reaffixed.

For six weeks the Texans worked in secret, not telling other prisoners of their project. The Mexicans certainly never knew of it, either, although a candle sent flickering light into their cell every night and a sentinel stood constant guard just outside the door. Inside, the prisoners posted watchers of their own, worked exceedingly silently, and created covering noises whenever occasion demanded, and they were able to dig a small tunnel vertically under the floor, then horizontally under the main wall and into the bottom of the moat outside.

On the day that Santa Anna freed the rest of the San Antonio prisoners the Mier prisoners in Green's old cell talked over final plans of how they would make their own exit. With a touch of irony, whether planned or not, they chose the night of March 25, 1844, for their escape—the first anniversary of the drawing of the black beans on the Salado. Sixteen men squeezed through the tunnel and into the dry moat, where they quickly separated and hurried away in the darkness. They left behind in the cell ten men who chose to stay in Perote rather than run the risk of fleeing anywhere from deep in the mountains of Mexico. These men had decided that liberation might yet come, although the escape of their fellow prisoners would surely hinder it. Nevertheless, they gave the sentinel no warning of what was happening, and by morning some of their former companions had managed to obtain horses or mules and to put as many as forty miles between themselves and the dismal prison of Perote.

As soon as the astounded Mexicans realized that sixteen more of their prisoners had escaped they burst into furious activity. An officer of the guard, a fat man the Texans had nicknamed "Old Guts," roared in Spanish, "My God! Sixteen missing! O villains!" He reared back—as he often did, seemingly to maintain his equilibrium and offset the great weight in front—and the look on his face and the laboring of his mighty stomach, "like a bellows," indicated to some amused Texans that he foresaw his own impending imprisonment in some gloomy dungeon.

Quickly the cavalry rode forth to round up the escapees, but all of the horsemen returned that evening and reported seeing no trace whatever of any of the sixteen men. Furious officers wanted to execute the ten men who had stayed in the cell for failing to inform authorities of the escape, but the commandant stopped that, despite the evidence of his previous harshness. He arrested the most vociferous officer for neglect of duty. The commandant wanted to know how that numbskull could have failed to notice chained prisoners digging constantly for a period of six weeks; and he did not punish the prisoners who stayed behind.

In the city of Mexico General Santa Anna heard about the latest escape with incredulity and fury. He wrote the United States minister a complaint about the escape "abusing the generous confidence of my government." Bell heard that Santa Anna had already written an order for the release of all prisoners, and that when news of the escape reached him he held a lighted cigar to the document until it flamed up, then remarked to an aide, "That is the way I'll liberate them."

At Perote the remaining prisoners endured restrictions more severe than ever. One Texan wrote home that the Mexicans now believed them capable of escaping in an envelope. Bell, who had heard about the escape with as much surprise as anyone else, wrote:

The chains of all the captives were examined daily after this event, to see that they were not cut or broken and . . . the rooms occupied by the Texan captives were divested of every thing but the naked walls, and these scrutinized with the utmost caution by the Mexican officers, to see that no holes could possibly exist through which a Texan might squeeze his magic body. Every aperture made by rats or mice . . . was eyed with distrust and suspicion; every mat and blanket had to be removed and the walls and floor sounded to find whether they were hollow or not, and every other precaution taken to prevent a recurrence of what had lately happened.—And for a short time after this, a stricter watch was kept over [us] during the night, and all were ordered to observe perfect silence after eight o'clock, P.M., but this was only enforced a few weeks, for they found it a difficult matter to shut the mouths of these captives until overpowered by sleep, [when we] retired of [our] own accord.

Eventually eight of the escaped prisoners, chained and heavily guarded, clanked back across the drawbridge into the prison. The other eight men managed to reach Texas or the United States, and one of them accomplished this in a manner as bold as the escape: ". . . he hired himself on board a Mexican war steamer, then bound to the United States; which landed him at Charleston, S.C., without the officers or crew being aware of his having escaped from one of their own prisons."

The excitement caused by the latest break died slowly at Perote, but eventually the prison returned to its clammy normalcy, and again the Texans endured the usual dreary routine—eating, working at menial chores, sleeping, most of that time in irons. Whiling away leisure time proved almost as dreary as doing the monotonous work required of them. Some prisoners picked lice from their bodies and matched the fastest specimens in impromptu races. They drew a charcoal circle on a board, turned the lice loose on a spot in the center, and declared as winner the louse that first crossed the circle.

Others preferred more conventional entertainment: card games, writing letters or diary entries, mending clothes, fiddling and dancing—usually to the popular tune "Nancy Rollin"—during the brief periods when irons were removed, or reading the latest newspapers from the United States or Texas, the most recent at least two months old. Five violins had been made in the carpentry shop by prisoners, and there were many fiddlers to play them.

Their life was dreary, but humor rarely forsook these Texans. To survive the ordeal of Perote prisoners had to have more mental than physical stamina. An ability to see the humorous even in their dismal situation was essential to this makeup. Thomas Bell observed his comrades and remarked, "A spectator casually to have viewed the mirth and merriment sometimes enjoyed by the captives would have supposed them very contented and happy with their manner of life, had not a nearer inspection . . . convinced him otherwise."

Spring gave way to summer, but by night the chill mountain wind still whined through the prison, and the captives' treatment grew worse than ever, so that again they talked of escape as the only way out of their predicament. "They treat us so bad lately," one of Bell's companions wrote, ". . . . [I] apprehend that we will charge them . . . and take the castle . . ." The very next day an officer whaled a Texan with his sword for refusing to work, then locked the man in isolation. Nevertheless, the United States minister was quoted in newspaper accounts about this time as saying that the Perote commandant was an honorable man, and that no doubt the prisoners were receiving good treatment. "I believe [the minister] would sooner take the word of the Mexicans than ours," said an angry Texan.

Rumors brought more bad news. Negotiations between the United States and Texas in regard to annexation had taken a favorable turn, and the prisoners heard that Santa Anna had said that as soon as word of annexation came United States legation personnel could pack up and leave the country. A prisoner wrote, "If this is the case, which we have no reason to doubt, we [are] in here during the war, as the saying is." But other prisoners saw hope in the situation. Surely Santa Anna would not risk war with the United States, and they would be released.

The next few days and weeks brought no annexation, no liberation—no change at all except for another rumor. Santa Anna's "birthday," June 13, was again impending, and renewed speculation about liberation spread throughout the compound. Once more Mexican officers assured the Texans they could expect release—

something the officers themselves hoped for, having become weary
of serving as guards. Once more the prisoners became convinced
that a favorable turn in their fortunes was near, but once more
they were disappointed. No news of release came.

After that disappointment most men gave up all hope of liberation and concentrated again on plans for escape, but on July 4
came another one of those odd interludes enjoyed even by Texas
captives in Mexican prisons. The commandant issued a no-work
order, gave permission for his prisoners to celebrate the day of
American independence, and allowed them to buy the ingredients
for a party: mescal, eggs, asses' milk, and a loaf of sugar.

One of Bell's fellow prisoners described the festivity:

> Our boys prepared for a big spree, we got some eggs and liquor
> to have an egg-nogg tonight; a Dutchman by the name of [Wil-
> liam] Miller, a rather eccentric character, went round to the
> soldiers' wives and procured some 10 or 15 dresses to have a ball
> at night,—we was locked up at 5 o'clock into two rooms, as we
> had two fiddles, and we commenced and such another time we
> had of it,—I never see before, there was scarcely a man but what
> was drunk, we kept perfectly good order the whole time, and
> between 9 & 10 o'clock we retired to bed, being too much corned
> to continue the ball any longer.—

On the following day guards saw the strange sight of prisoners
working under the effects of a mass hangover, but it wore off as the
day wore on. That night the Texans returned to their recently recommenced nocturnal labor—chipping away at the stones and
cement of their cells while watching the sentinels who guarded
them.

They had been able to smuggle into their cells small hardware
items from which they contrived tools for removing stones from the
walls. During the day they were able to camouflage their work with
stolen putty so well that it escaped the scrutiny of the inspectors,
who had once more lapsed into a casual attitude. Bell observed the
work with amusement:

> [It] was effected by working a small part of every evening at
> twilight, before the candle was lighted, while some were em-

ployed in sawing the cement that surrounded a large stone at the
further end of the prison, the remainder were fiddling, dancing
and kicking up a row, to divert the attention of the sentinel
stationed at the door, and allay suspicion in the minds of the
guard, who thought . . . [the Texans] were the most happy,
jovial and contented set of fellows on earth; when they were at
that very time executing a work that would have sent half the
Mexican officers in the castle to prison for life, had it been
accomplished.

But the job never was finished. In August the United States
minister visited the prison with fresh information about the possibility of liberation. He heard from the captives about various plans
for escape, and he advised delaying all of them. Another break now
would disrupt his touchy negotiations with Santa Anna. The prisoners agreed to put their projects in abeyance, and again the time
began to drag. Bell and the others numbered the hours and days
with impatience, "and every post arrival [was] listened to with
breathless anxiety and interest."

Toward the end of August came word of the death of Santa
Anna's wife, at the age of thirty-three. Texas prisoners knew her
by reputation as a woman of simplicity and compassion; it was
said she had interceded in their behalf on several occasions. Now
she had helped them again, the prisoners heard, for shortly before
her death she had asked her husband to set them free. Whatever
the truth was, a letter did indeed arrive at Perote about mid-
September announcing liberation for all Texas prisoners. As this
news spread throughout the old castle, Bell said, it was greeted
with shouts and cheers.

The day set for release was September 16, 1844, the anniversary
of Mexican independence. But the captors had one last punishment
to inflict. Although most prisoners had risen before daylight to
begin gathering their meager possessions and tying them in knapsacks and blankets, they were forced to wait until midafternoon for
orders to form on the parade ground. There they stood in double-
file order another half hour before being escorted to the commandant's office, where each prisoner was asked to sign a pledge
never again to fight against Mexico. After that each man received

one dollar for expenses to Veracruz—where ships waited—and a passport. Then all prisoners were ordered to form again on the parade ground.

At five o'clock all the remaining prisoners of the Mier expedition, about 110 men, lined up once more. Near them they saw in full dress the seven hundred officers and men of the artillery, infantry, and cavalry units stationed at Perote. Overhead, clouds dimmed the fading afternoon light.

The commandant instructed that the entire group, soldiers and prisoners, render a cheer in Spanish: "Long live the President of the Republic of Mexico." Bell followed orders, but gave his cheer halfheartedly, as did most other Texans. One prisoner nearby more nearly moaned his lines than yelled them. Then, released at last, Bell and the other Texans "sprang like wild beasts from a cage . . . and although a heavy shower of rain was falling, not one stopped [for] shelter [in the prison]. . . . As [we] left the castle gate-way the battery guns opened with their last deep and solemn roar, in commemoration of Mexican Independence, and the chapel bells jingled their parting Vesper . . ."

Bell made a quick calculation, another of so many done during his imprisonment. He and his companions had been held in Perote for about a year, and had been absent from their homes in Texas more than two years. He probably could have given the exact number of days and hours.

Ironically, Bell's tardy benefactor, Santa Anna, suffered anguish of his own soon after this. In December the Mexican Congress deposed him, as a result of another of the endless domestic quarrels that left Mexico continually unsettled. José Joaquín Herrera succeeded Santa Anna, only to be deposed himself a year later and succeeded by Mariano Paredes y Arrillaga. None of the changes were to make any lasting difference in the Mexican attitude toward Texas, and Bell could be everlastingly thankful for getting his freedom when it came.

56. REUNION IN TEXAS

The approach of winter, 1844, found Charles Bryant very lonely, cold, and poor. With his son Jackson dead he had lost his only close relative within a thousand miles. Furthermore, with the disappearance at sea of the *Sarah Barnes* carrying the letter containing his two hundred dollars he had lost the chance of bringing the rest of his family to Texas, at least for a while.

The summer had been especially hard, and he had been barely able to earn enough to pay his room and board. But that fall he had happened upon a money-making possibility—a small grocery and oyster business, in partnership with another man. If they could stay open through the winter Bryant believed they might have a bright financial future. If that happened, he wrote his wife in Bangor, he could send some money. "God knows I'd do something for you if possible."

But some people in Maine did not believe Bryant. His extended absence from his family and his continued failure to send for them caused acquaintances in Bangor to talk about many obvious possibilities. It also brought Bryant a deluge of plaintive letters from kinfolk at home. Bryant's sister Martha wrote:

[Sarah] has suffered very much, her health and spirits are broken and she appears to me about worn out with cares, troubles, and toil. . . . I feel as if you should make an effort to come home—your children need you in every respect—I do not know what she will do—Your family reside near us in a very poor tenement—but it was the best [Sarah] could get . . . for . . . 79¢ a week. You can earn a livelihood here as well as you ever did and certainly you have suffered enough in that vile Texas.

In other letters relatives reminded Bryant that his wife had been forced to support herself and four sons for five long years now, that she had remained faithful despite his long absence, that he should return to Boston or New York if not to Bangor, but if he did not come back she was ready to join him in Texas anytime he could send for her and the children.

One letter, from his sister Welthea, was especially moving. In it Welthea told about the successful effort of the Bryants' young son Martin to avoid a hungry Thanksgiving. "Mart," an intelligent youngster who was often lost in thought, was sitting in quiet reflection shortly before the holiday, his feet propped warmly near a stove, when he suddenly broke the silence.

"Well, ma," he asked, "what are you going to have for Thanksgiving—anything?"

"Why, I don't know, my son. You know we are poor."

"Well, will you prepare [a dinner] if I . . . get the things?"

"Most certainly I will, but what can you do?"

"Well, I've been thinking . . ."

Mart bundled up in his warmest clothes and walked over to Aunt Martha's. There he casually remarked on the number of chickens that he saw she had and added that he wished his mother had only one. Aunt Martha immediately caught three chickens for the boy to take home. Mart answered innocently that he had not meant he wished his mother had one of those particular fowl, just a chicken, but Aunt Martha insisted he be off with the gift.

At home Mart's mother questioned him anxiously about the three chickens. Where did he get them? Had he stolen them?

"I guess I think more of [myself] than to steal," he replied. Then he told his mother how Aunt Martha had given him the chickens.

The next morning Mart walked over to a neighbor's house and noticed a number of dressed geese awaiting the oven. He looked at them, then at the neighbor, and remarked that his mother had some nice chickens for Thanksgiving dinner, but that he did not like chickens so much as geese. The neighbor picked up a goose and handed it to him with the comment that he should be suited this time.

Mart delivered the goose to his mother, then visited the house of

another neighbor, a man who raised turkeys. With his usual innocence he engaged the man in conversation, then mentioned the
chickens and the goose his mother had for Thanksgiving dinner.
But was it not customary, Mart asked, to have turkey that day?
He added that his papa used to buy one for Thanksgiving, but his
papa now was far away in Texas, as everyone knew. The neighbor
offered him one of his fine birds, but Mart answered that his
mother could not buy one—that they would have to get by with
chickens and a goose. The man insisted Mart take the turkey as a
gift, and he did, with thanks. The Bryants dined exceptionally well
on Thanksgiving Day.

In Texas Charles Bryant read that story with emotions unre-
corded. Perhaps coincidentally, he wrote his wife soon afterward
that she should come to Texas with the boys, and all Bangor
seemed to be gladdened, especially the relatives. His sister Welthea
wrote him immediately of Sarah's preparations for the trip—"a
proof sufficient to [you] and us and everyone else and I rejoice in
it as it is a most powerful refutation to the scandal which has
sometimes since prevailed against my *brother dear*. . . . I trust
you appreciate her worth." But the letter was not entirely a happy
one, because in the immobility of that day a move from Maine to
Texas was likely to be forever, and Bryant's womenfolk had been
close—"like a sister to me," Welthea said of her brother's wife.
Sarah Bryant's endurance of "many heavy trials" had endeared
her even more.

Bryant's sister Louvisa wrote a similar letter. She fought sleepi-
ness to stay up late on the night of January 9 to write it—"probably the last night your family will ever be in Bangor"—then in
the early morning hours went over to Sarah's to help her complete
packing for the long trip to Portland, New York City, and Galveston.

Bryant read those letters about the same time he welcomed his
wife and four sons to Texas. The sea that had taken his son Jackson now brought him new life.

57. COMMITTED TO HISTORY

The New York native Moses Johnson had an opportunity to observe closely the last days of the Republic of Texas through his friendship with his fellow physician Anson Jones, elected President in late 1844.

Jones had succeeded Sam Houston, who gave up the reins reluctantly. In his valedictory to the Texas Congress Houston sought to chart the course he had decided that Texas should take after the United States Senate had rejected the Texas annexation treaty, and he also corroborated, perhaps unintentionally, what many people had been saying about him all the time—that he was an underhanded man.

"I have now no reason to conceal the convictions of my judgment or the feelings of my heart," Houston declared to the assembled senators and representatives. ". . . If we remain an independent nation, our territory will be extensive—unlimited. The Pacific alone will bound the mighty march of our race and our empire. From Europe and America her soil is to be peopled. In regions where the savage and the buffalo now roam uncontrolled, the enterprise and industry of the Anglo-American are yet to find an extensive field of development."

But this time the mighty persuasive powers of Sam Houston did not sway his listeners for long. Despite the recent rebuff by the United States Senate and some ensuing goodwill from England (which aroused various suspicions in the United States), the overwhelming sentiment in the Texas Congress and throughout the Republic was for annexation, if it could be arranged. Joining the Union would solve most Texas problems—would ensure stability, enhance prospects for trade and prosperity, and enable Texans to live without fear of reconquest by Mexico. The people waited to hear what Anson Jones would say about annexation.

But in his inaugural address President Jones said nothing on the subject. Apparently he too supported the idea of a continued

Republic of Texas. Certainly he had in the past. In his 1838 diary he had written, on August 26, *"How glorious* will Texas be standing alone, and relying upon her own strength." Furthermore, Sam Houston had been able to pass on to Jones a better legacy: some prospect of peace with Mexico and the Indian tribes, increasing immigration, improved financial conditions through good crops and the subsequent collection of taxes. It seemed that Jones intended to use this improvement to further his own dream of empire. He named his Cabinet, and five days after inauguration he appointed Moses Johnson treasurer. Then Jones quietly devoted himself to the duties of administration.

Weeks passed—months. Anson Jones remained silent on annexation, even after expansionist James K. Polk's election as President of the United States on a platform of adding Texas to the Union, and after outgoing President John Tyler, recognizing this mandate, had won approval for a proposal of annexation by joint resolution of Congress. Furious Texans assumed Jones intended to sabotage this opportunity of joining the Union. They burned him in effigy and threatened to throw out his government.

But all the while Anson Jones was working quietly—somewhat like Sam Houston—to give Texans a choice they had so long wanted: recognition of independence by Mexico, and a genuine opportunity to establish a firmly founded Republic of Texas, or annexation. Jones deliberately delayed consideration of annexation until England and France, working feverishly against it, could persuade the Mexican government to recognize Texas independence with the hope of thus preventing acquisition of the country by the growing power to the north.

By June the opportunity had arrived. President Jones presented Texans a choice of peace and independence or annexation. He called the Texas Congress into session for a decision, and its members chose annexation overwhelmingly, then censured the President for his delay. Jones also called the Convention of 1845 to vote on annexation and, if that was accepted, to draft a state constitution. Its delegates echoed the members of Congress: they voted for annexation and drafted a constitution, then a few delegates sought to remove Jones from office at once. This lame-duck President certainly was not wanted.

Moses Johnson observed the dissatisfaction and heard the insults with much sadness. As a member of the Jones administration he could see for himself the man's dedication and capacity, and this inspired Johnson to more diligent work of his own as treasurer.

In 1845 Jones moved the capital back to Austin. Moses Johnson complied dutifully, although he would have preferred giving up the job and remaining with Olivia in their home near Washington-on-the-Brazos. Johnson set up his treasurer's office in the two-story Austin residence he still owned, and he moved the official desk, archives, and safe into his house as he had done at Washington-on-the-Brazos. Such devotion prompted Olivia's sister in Illinois to write in a letter, "I should not like to have that iron chest in the house that I lived in, especially [in Texas] where the people would as soon kill a man as a chicken." But nobody bothered the safe, which must have been almost empty anyway.

The town was empty, too. Without Olivia, Austin was not the pleasant place Moses Johnson had known in previous years. "[It] is to me . . . dull . . . at present, but the people are very friendly and inquire very particularly for you." The late summer was exceptionally hot, "enough to roast eggs," and the mosquitoes were bad.

Johnson found their residence in need of repair, and he devoted himself to bringing it back to its former state. He fixed the fence, repaired leaks in the roof, put his manservant Cambridge to washing the interior "upstairs and down." To avoid the mosquitoes that swarmed on the first floor, he slept upstairs, which for some reason the pests ignored.

His family might as well have been a thousand miles away. When he failed to hear from Olivia he began to imagine all kinds of sicknesses that might have incapacitated her, and he wished he could be at home to treat her. Leisure left him too much opportunity to create these calamities in his mind, so he strove to fill in the off hours. Twice he drank so much brandy he made himself sick. "I have stopped now," he wrote Olivia. ". . . I expect if it didn't make me sick I'd drink frequently—I don't know what else to do." He went bathing often in the Colorado River—"the water is so clear and the banks so clean that I live to get into it." He accompanied ten or fifteen "ladies and gentlemen" to a picnic on nearby

Mount Bonnell—"you need not begrudge my going . . . for I am inclined to the blues." He sought the company of friends—"time goes dreadfully slowly. I am getting impatient. If I could see you but one moment to get one kiss . . . I could remain the time out quietly. . . . I cannot express to you how much I suffer. It does seem to me that I shall endeavor to avoid leaving all I love very long soon again."

Then, abruptly, his duties ended. In September a fire swept through his Austin home and burned the treasurer's office. But a Republic of Texas treasurer was no longer needed anyway—no more than a president was needed. On December 29, 1845, Texas formally became a state in the Union, and on the following February 19, at noon, cannon boomed a salute as the ceremony at Austin celebrated the changeover of jurisdiction. "Thank God we are now annexed to the U. States and can hope for home and quiet," Mary Maverick wrote—somewhat prematurely, for after annexation came the Mexican War and United States expansion westward all the way to California. Even as the cannon boomed their salute at Austin, United States Army troops commanded by General Zachary Taylor prepared to march for the Rio Grande from Corpus Christi, where they had landed on President James K. Polk's orders to defend Texas against Mexican assault in the wake of annexation. Some of these United States troops later would be attacked by Mexican soldiers on the east bank of the Rio Grande in an incident that was to bring on Polk's much-disputed "American blood [shed] upon . . . American soil" call to war (eventually to be formally declared May 13, 1846). American critics of Polk and the Mexican War repeated the claims by Mexicans that the Nueces River, not the Rio Grande, was the traditional boundary of Texas, and they contended that Polk could not legally or ethically call the east bank of the Rio Grande "American soil."

So quietude hardly prevailed, but Mary Maverick was right in a way: annexation did indeed lead to a period of stability in Texas that would not have been possible under the government of the Republic of Texas.

With cessation of the Republic there passed into history heroism sometimes unappreciated, cowardice unerasable, wisdom occasionally unrecognized, follies uneradicable. Into history passed the people who made it: Dr. Joseph Henry Barnard, Barnard E. Bee, Thomas W. Bell, Charles G. Bryant, Andrew Jackson Bryant, William Fairfax Gray, Dr. Moses Johnson, George Wilkins Kendall, Samuel and Mary Maverick, the Reverend Z. N. Morrell, Harriet Moore Page, and thousands of others.

Anson Jones, the last President, sent them all on their way at the noon ceremony in Austin. Up went United States colors, and Jones declared, with emotion that brought tears to the eyes of some listeners, "The Republic of Texas is no more."

EPILOGUE

Ten of the twelve major characters used in telling this story of the Republic of Texas lived to be aware of annexation.

Joseph Henry Barnard, the doctor who left his medical practice in Canada for Texas and arrived in time to witness the massacre of James Fannin's men at Goliad, later bought a ranch about five miles from the site of the battle on the Coleto, where he and the others had surrendered to General José Urrea's Mexican army. He married in 1838, served as a member of the House of Representatives in the Eighth Texas Congress, ranched near the old battle site, practiced medicine, and surveyed professionally. He died in 1861 while on a trip to Canada and was buried there. His wife died six years later.

Barnard E. Bee, the South Carolinian who came to Texas at the age of forty-nine and visited Mexico for President Lamar in the unsuccessful attempt to secure recognition of Texas independence, never favored annexation. After it came he moved back to South Carolina for good—in 1846—and died there, in Pendleton, seven years later.

Thomas W. Bell, the young introspective Southerner who joined the Mier expedition and spent a year imprisoned at Perote, resented what he thought to be Texas indifference to the Mier men, and upon his release he eschewed the Republic and returned to Tennessee to teach school, although he later returned to Texas at least once on a visit. His disaffection perhaps was partly appeased when he heard that the bones of the men executed on the Salado were exhumed after the Mexican War and brought for burial at a place now known as Monument Hill, near La Grange.

In Tennessee Bell visited the young widow of a prisoner who had died at Perote October 13, 1843, during the *"vomito"* siege. Later Bell wrote a book about his experiences and gave a copy to the widow, Mary Asletha Willis. This book found its way to the Earl Vandale Collection of the University of Texas Archives. Inside is this inscription following Mary Willis' name: ". . . a young widow of a Mier prisoner (O. R. Willis). Thos. W. Bell was waiting on him, and took his messages the night he died in the prison. When the prisoners got home Thos. Bell met, and married Mrs. Willis, who brought up a large family and died in 1897 at Wrightsboro, Texas, aged 73 years. Thos. Bell died in Dyer Co., Tenn., 1871. He was born in 1815." Just before his death Bell had made plans to move back to Texas, to Gonzales County. His widow later made the move, and that was where she died.

Charles G. Bryant, the man from Maine who placed his son Jackson in the Texas Navy as midshipman, moved to Corpus Christi after the arrival of his wife, Sarah, and the four boys. Later they had a fifth son—whom they named Edwin Moore Bryant, apparently after the Texas Navy commodore—and a daughter, who gained some standing in Texas poetry as Welthea Bryant Leachman. Early in 1850, Charles Bryant, a major in the Texas Rangers, left Corpus Christi on a horseback business trip to Austin. On the morning of January 12, at a location near the head of Corpus Christi Bay, a party of marauding Indians attacked, killed, and robbed him within the sight of several persons who had hidden in chaparral. Thus his wife, who had struggled five years in Maine for existence during his absence, again was forced to rely on her own resources. Bryant later was buried where he fell by other Rangers. One of them cut a lock of hair and brought it to Sarah Bryant, who misplaced it "after looking the first time at it" and never saw it again.

Andrew Jackson Bryant's disappearance aboard the schooner *Galveston* in 1844 already has been recorded.

William Fairfax Gray, the Virginian who looked continually for a good business deal, even around what became a few days later the San Jacinto battlefield, eventually brought his wife to Texas.

She echoed the feeling of a great many immigrant wives—"it requires an effort to wear the appearance of cheerfulness." Later Gray served as clerk of the Texas House of Representatives, in 1837; as secretary of the Senate, in 1838; and as clerk of the Texas Supreme Court, shortly before his death. When at home in Houston he enjoyed browsing in his 250-book library, relaxing by playing the flute, and furthering his knowledge of law, religion, and philosophy. He died in Houston April 16, 1841; his wife died in Houston ten years later at the age of fifty-one.

Moses Johnson, the New York physician appointed treasurer of the Republic of Texas by Anson Jones, died of yellow fever at Lavaca in 1853. Surviving were three children and his wife, Olivia, who never shared his enthusiasm for their adopted Texas home.

George Wilkins Kendall, the New Orleans journalist who accompanied the Santa Fe Expedition, lived more exciting days after that adventure. His book about the expedition, first published in 1844, went into seven printings before 1856 and was reprinted again in 1929 and 1935. Kendall covered the Mexican War as a correspondent, married Adeline de Valcourt in Belgium in 1849, and bought a ranch in present Kendall County, Texas, in 1857. He died there October 21, 1867.

Samuel A. Maverick, the South Carolinian who chose San Antonio for a new home, finally took his wife, Mary, back there in 1847, after having evacuated her and the children before the March, 1842, raid by General Rafael Vásquez. But life in San Antonio never was the same. Mary Maverick wrote that the town was "terribly changed": it was dirty, dusty, and hot; sickness was common; and they found their home in disrepair, the garden gone, and the fence down. But the Mexican woman to whom Mary had entrusted valuables before the Vásquez raid returned them when Mary moved back five years later.

After lengthy membership in the Texas Congress and the state legislature Sam Maverick died, in San Antonio, September 2, 1870. Survivors included Mary and seven children; daughters Agatha and Augusta and a tenth child born in 1857 had preceded him in death. After burying her husband, when Mary was going through some of his valuables, she discovered a strip of green muslin—a piece from the dress she had been wearing when they first met. Ten years later, on October 24, 1880, Mary Maverick completed her "Recollections assisted by notes taken at the time," now kept in the University of Texas Archives. She died in 1898.

Z. N. Morrell, the Baptist preacher who could substitute rifle for Bible when he thought the occasion demanded, outlived his wife and all four of their children. His wife's death in 1844 no doubt was hastened by the capture in San Antonio by General Woll of a son, A. H. Morrell, and the young man's lengthy imprisonment after that in Perote, then the death of their eldest daughter. "My cup was full of sorrow," Morrell said of the years following his wife's death, but he never gave up his church work. After striving to convert Texans during the ribald Republic days, he went to Honduras late in life on the same mission, but with disappointing results. He died in Texas December 19, 1883, at the age of eighty.

Harriet Moore Page, the pretty young woman from New Orleans who found a good life for a time at Potter's Point on Caddo Lake, finally found a man who could be trusted: Charles Ames, whom she married August 23, 1842, in Clarksville, Texas. "He had not an enemy in the country." After his death she moved back to New Orleans to live with her children. There, at the age of eighty-three, she wrote her autobiography, shortly before her death about the turn of the century.

The three regularly elected Presidents of the Republic of Texas lived out their lives this way:

Sam Houston refused a generalship during the Mexican War, served as United States Senator for nearly fourteen years, then was elected governor of Texas in 1859. In that office he again infuriated his countrymen—by opposing secession. He died in 1863, survived by his wife and eight children.

Mirabeau B. Lamar fought as a lieutenant colonel in the Mexican War, served in the Texas state legislature and as United States minister to Nicaragua and Costa Rica, and married again. He died at his home near Richmond, Texas, in 1859.

Anson Jones, the last President, committed suicide in 1858 after suffering a disability to his left arm and after being twice rejected for the position of United States Senator from Texas.

The people are dead, but in Texas, among a segment of the population, the spirit of the Republic lives on.

CHRONOLOGY OF THE REPUBLIC OF TEXAS

As has been mentioned in the Notes on the Text and elsewhere, different sources give differing dates for some of these events. When that happened the most reliable source was used—or, in a few instances, a consensus.

1836

March

2 Texas declaration of independence adopted by delegates to the Convention of 1836, meeting at Washington-on-the-Brazos.

4 Sam Houston confirmed as commander of all Texas military forces.

6 Fall of the Alamo, in San Antonio, to General Santa Anna's Mexican troops. All the defenders died—probably a total of 183 men.

12 Texas flag adopted; on it is a five-pointed star with one letter of the name "Texas" at each point. Commanding officers also appointed for the four ships of the Texas Navy: 60-ton *Liberty,* 125-ton *Invincible,* 125-ton *Independence,* and 125-ton *Brutus.* Charles E. Hawkins, senior captain, named commodore. By September, 1837, all these ships will be lost in various ways, but not before some successes.

16 Constitution adopted and officers of ad-interim Texas government sworn in, before the convention hastily adjourns in the early-morning hours of March 17: David G. Burnet president, Lorenzo de Zavala vice-president, Samuel Carson secretary of state, Bailey Hardeman secretary of the treasury, Thomas Rusk secretary of war, Robert Potter secretary of the navy, David Thomas attorney general, John Rice Jones postmaster general. (Before that, Texas tried to function under provisional government officials elected by a General Consultation that had met at San Felipe de Austin in November, 1835, and had determined that Texas should be given status as a separate state in the Mexican nation: Henry Smith governor, James W. Robinson lieutenant governor, Charles Bellinger Stewart secretary of state, John Rice Jones postmaster general, and a General Council composed of a total of 39 men who served at various times. In January, 1836, the General Council impeached Smith and named Robinson acting governor, but Smith refused to recognize the action. The provisional government fell apart after that and in effect ceased to function.)

20 James Fannin's Texas troops surrender at the Battle of Coleto; taken to Goliad as prisoners.

27 Palm Sunday massacre of the Texas prisoners held at Goliad; 342 men killed.

April

21   Texans under Sam Houston defeat General Santa Anna's Mexican army at San Jacinto.

22   Santa Anna brought before Sam Houston as a prisoner.

May

14   President Burnet signs two Treaties of Velasco with Santa Anna, who promises never again to fight Texas and to work in Mexico for an end to the war and for recognition of Texas independence. Several of Burnet's Cabinet members violently oppose the treaties, neither of which will bring Texas any advantage.

19   Fort Parker attack and massacre by about 500 Indians.

June

 1   Santa Anna placed aboard Texas schooner *Invincible* at the mouth of the Brazos River for return to Mexico.

 3   Military funeral held at Goliad for victims of the March 27 massacre; General Thomas J. Rusk speaker.

 4   Santa Anna removed from the *Invincible* by demand of an irate mob, including a group of newly arrived Army volunteers from New Orleans commanded by Thomas Jefferson Green and Memucan Hunt.

July

23   President Burnet issues national election proclamation for September; national and county officials to be elected, constitution ratified, and annexation to the United States voted on. Campaigning begins.

September

 5   Sam Houston elected President with 5,119 votes to Henry Smith's 743 and Stephen F. Austin's 587. Mirabeau B. Lamar easily elected vice-president over Alexander Horton. Texans express themselves as favoring annexation to the United States by a vote of more than 6,000 for the move. Only 93 oppose.

October

 3   First Congress of the Republic of Texas meets at Columbia.

21   Vice-President Lorenzo de Zavala resigns.

22   President Burnet resigns after pressure, allowing President-elect Sam Houston to take the oath of office immediately, without further "lame-duck" delay. Lamar also sworn in as vice-president. Houston chooses for his Cabinet Stephen F. Austin secretary of state, Henry Smith secretary of the treasury, Thomas Rusk secretary of war, S. Rhoads Fisher secretary of the navy, James Pinckney Henderson attorney general, Robert Barr postmaster general. (Houston originally chooses other men for attorney general and postmaster general, but neither accepts.) This Cabinet changes —as do later ones—before the President's term is concluded. (A complete list of Cabinet members can be found in *The Handbook of Texas*.) After

Houston's inauguration Congress elects James Collinsworth chief justice of the Republic's Supreme Court, and these four associate justices: Shelby Corzine, Benjamin C. Franklin, Robert M. Williamson, and James W. Robinson, each of whom also presides as judge in one of the four judicial districts. Elected first speaker of the House of Representatives is Ira Ingram of Matagorda. Lamar, of course, presides over the Senate.

November

25   Sam Houston releases Santa Anna, in the company of Barnard Bee, George Hockley, and William H. Patton, to go to Washington, where Santa Anna promises to work in behalf of Texas with President Andrew Jackson. After talks, which serve little purpose, the former dictator, who now has lost control of his government, is returned to Mexico on a U.S. Navy vessel.

December

15   Texas Congress, meeting at Columbia, chooses town of Houston as seat of government until 1840.

20   Tariff Act passed by Congress, to become effective July 1, 1837; taxes on imports—averaging about 25 per cent—to be relied upon as primary means of raising revenue.

27   Stephen F. Austin dies; James Pinckney Henderson succeeds him as secretary of state.

1837

March

3   Texas independence recognized by the United States (after much labor by Texas emissary William H. Wharton) when President Andrew Jackson as the last act in his last administration signs resolutions passed by Congress and appoints Alcée La Branche chargé d'affaires to Texas.

April

17   Texas Navy vessel *Independence,* proceeding from New Orleans, attacked by two Mexican vessels and forced to surrender off Velasco.

May

5   Congress convenes at Houston after a five-day delay for the erection of temporary cover for the roofless Capitol building.

18   President Houston, through the Secretary of War, furloughs Texas Army, except for 600 men, to break up a scheme instigated by army commander General Felix Huston to invade Mexico at Matamoros.

June

9   Congress authorizes paper-money issue, a financial expedient that eventually proves disastrous—but one that will be resorted to again.

11   *Invincible* and *Brutus* depart Galveston on a two-month foray into the Gulf of Mexico, raiding Mexican towns and capturing Mexican vessels.

August

4 Memucan Hunt, Texas minister to the United States, formally petitions for Texas annexation. After a three-week delay Secretary of State John Forsyth replies with a firm rejection.

27 *Invincible* and *Brutus* battle two Mexican ships off Galveston, are eventually lost because of grounding and high winds, leaving the Texas Navy with no ships.

November

4 Bill passed allocating $280,000 for building six ships for a new navy, eventually constructed by Frederick Dawson of Baltimore. The ships and their eventual delivery dates: 170-ton *San Jacinto*, June, 1839; 170-ton *San Antonio*, August, 1839; 170-ton *San Bernard*, September, 1839; 400-ton *Wharton*, October, 1839; 600-ton *Austin*, December, 1839; 400-ton *Archer*, April, 1840. Also to be in the new navy are the decrepit brig *Potomac*, to be bought in early 1838 as a receiving ship, and the steam packet *Zavala*, to be commissioned in March, 1839.

1838

September

3 Mirabeau B. Lamar elected President with 6,995 votes to Robert Wilson's 252. David Burnet elected vice-president over Albert Horton and Joseph Rowe.

October

12 Anson Jones, Texas minister to the United States, withdraws the annexation petition of August 4, 1837, on instructions from President Houston.

December

10 Lamar takes oath as President at Houston, Burnet as vice-president. Lamar chooses for his Cabinet Barnard Bee secretary of state, Richard Dunlap secretary of the treasury, Albert Sidney Johnston secretary of war, Memucan Hunt secretary of the navy, John Watrous attorney general, Robert Barr postmaster general.

1839

January

14 Five commissioners appointed to select a site for the permanent capital of the Republic of Texas.

25 "Lone Star" flag (later the state flag of Texas) is adopted by the Republic when President Lamar signs bill specifying it.

March

29 Detachment led by Edward Burleson encounters a party commanded by Vicente Córdova, engaged in a plot to persuade Indians to raze Texas; kills twenty of Córdova's men, wounds Córdova himself, but fails to capture him. Córdova flees to Mexico.

April

13 Commissioners select as site for the new capital of Texas the small village of Waterloo—now renamed Austin—partly to attract to the Lamar administration voters in the western part of settled Texas, at this time country threatened by Indians.

May

8 Barnard Bee arrives in Veracruz on unsuccessful quest for the Lamar administration for peace and recognition from Mexico.

17 Manuel Flores' men en route with supplies for an Indian uprising against Texas, initially planned by Córdova, are attacked and dispersed by a handful of Rangers led by James Rice. Flores killed.

July

8 Lieutenant Edwin Ward Moore, age 28, resigns from U.S. Navy to become commodore of the Texas Navy, a post evidently promised him in March of this year.

16 Climactic Battle of the Neches in the Cherokee War, undertaken by Lamar; Chief Bowl killed. Cherokees suffer casualties of about 100 braves and are eventually forced out of Texas.

September

25 France signs commercial treaty recognizing Texas independence; Count Alphonse de Saligny appointed chargé d'affaires.

October

17 Government officials arrive in Austin, which formally becomes Texas capital.

December

10 Lamar obtains congressional approval to send another agent, James Treat, to Mexico to seek to win recognition of Texas independence and acknowledgment of a boundary at the Rio Grande by payment of $5,000,000 or through bribery as necessary. This mission fails, although Treat remains in Mexico from the end of December until next autumn. (He was to die aboard ship, en route home, November 13, 1840.)

1840

January

18 Republic of Rio Grande organized by Mexican dissidents led by General Antonio Canales; one of several rebellions by Mexican federalists during Republic of Texas days, but none proves successful.

March

15 Canales' Republic of Rio Grande forces defeated by General Mariano Arista.

March

19 Council House Fight in San Antonio: 35 Comanches killed when fighting erupts between Texans and Indians during truce discussions. Comanches vow vengeance.

May

9 Sam Houston marries Margaret Lea in Alabama.

July

22 New Texas navy provided for in the bill passed November 4, 1837, departs Galveston—leaving *Archer, Wharton,* and *Potomac* behind to protect the port—for rebellious Yucatán, where Commodore Moore is to establish cordial relations on orders from President Lamar, who also instructs Moore not to fire unless fired upon.

August

8 The town of Linnville, on Lavaca Bay, destroyed by raiding Comanches.

12 Decisive defeat inflicted on Comanches at Plum Creek by Texans, forcing the Indians westward.

September

18 James Hamilton, Lamar's envoy to Europe, concludes a commercial treaty with the Netherlands, resulting in that country's recognition of Texas independence.

October

31 Schooner *San Jacinto* wrecked in storm at Arcas Islands, off Yucatán.

November

13, 14, 16 Three treaties concerning trade, navigation, and other matters signed in London. These in effect recognize Texas independence in England, although some delay ensues in treaty ratification and in exchange of diplomatic representatives.

December

12 President Lamar granted leave of absence by Congress to recover health. Vice-President Burnet becomes acting head of state.

1841

February

1 Commodore Moore and the cruising Texas fleet return to Galveston; scant work of note has been done since their July, 1840, departure.

March

22 Lamar, back in office, sends another peace negotiator, James Webb, to Mexico with a "final offer" from Texas: in the event of failure of the mission, Texas will aid the rebels in Yucatán against the Mexican government. Webb too fails, and returns to Texas late in June.

June

19 Five companies of infantry and one of artillery, accompanied by merchants and teamsters—321 men in all—leave encampment near Austin for
Santa Fe, New Mexico, and an attempt to bring that place under Texas
jurisdiction and to get the profits from the lucrative Santa Fe trade. Expedition commander is General Hugh McLeod.

September

6 Sam Houston again elected President, with 7,508 votes to David Burnet's
2,574. (Other figures have been given, but the margin is about the same.)
Edward Burleson elected vice-president over Memucan Hunt.

17 Alliance signed between President Lamar's Texas and the rebelling Yucatán;
Yucatán to get services of Texas Navy for $8,000 a month. All this amounts
to very little, because Yucatán soon renews its allegiance to Mexico—although trouble will in time break out again there.

October

5 Main force of the Santa Fe Expedition surrenders to the Mexicans; other
groups have given up earlier. Captives begin a march into Mexico and long
imprisonment.

December

13 Sam Houston again takes oath as President, at Austin; Burleson sworn in
as vice-president. Houston chooses for his Cabinet Anson Jones secretary
of state; William H. Daingerfield secretary of the treasury, George W.
Hockley secretary of war and marine, George Terrell attorney general. The
duties of postmaster general are shared by the secretaries of state and of
war and marine. Houston also names James Reily minister to the United
States and Ashbel Smith minister to England and France. The inventor Gail
Borden is named collector of the port at Galveston, Thomas William Ward
Land Office commissioner. This same day Commodore Moore sails from
Galveston with *Austin, San Bernard,* and *San Antonio* for Yucatán, as
previously ordered by President Lamar. Sam Houston's recall does not
reach Moore until March, 1842, after which he returns to Galveston, then
proceeds to New Orleans, where the ships lie inactive for months.

1842

January

19 Congress votes economy measures in retrenchment program, canceling
authorization for the attempt to get a $5,000,000 loan, abolishing a number
of government jobs, and cutting salaries of others—even their own (from
five dollars to three dollars a day).

February

11 Mutiny aboard the Texas vessel *San Antonio,* being refitted at New Orleans,
is quelled with help of U.S. authorities; mutineers captured. More than a
year later, in April, 1843, four men will be hanged aboard the *Austin* for
the offense.

March

5 A Mexican army under General Rafael Vásquez occupies San Antonio for two days before withdrawing, apparently to keep Texans on edge and to show them that Mexico has the power for reconquest. President Houston, adhering to his peace policy, refuses to support a retaliatory expedition against Mexico.

26 Sam Houston, bowing to Texas demands for some kind of action against Mexico, orders a blockade of Mexican seaports, but it is a gesture only: the fleet is not available or in condition to support it. The few ships that could possibly operate against Mexico are ordered to New Orleans for refitting, even after Houston's order is announced.

June

27 Congress assembles at Houston, President Houston having ordered the government out of Austin—but without removal of the archives, which he could not effect in the face of opposition by furious Austin residents.

July

22 President Houston vetoes a war bill passed by Congress giving him dictatorial powers to organize an army and attack Mexico.

August

6 Charles Elliot arrives at Galveston as English chargé d'affaires in the Republic of Texas.

September

11 General Adrian Woll, a French soldier of fortune, captures San Antonio with more than a thousand Mexican troops, holds it for nine days.

18 Battle of the Salado, inconclusive, between Texans, led by Mathew Caldwell and John C. (Jack) Hays, and Woll's Mexican troops; 35 of 53 Texans led by Nicholas Mosby Dawson, their white flag ignored by the Mexicans, are killed at a location one and a half miles from the main army while trying to join it, in what becomes known as the Dawson Massacre.

20 Woll begins retreat to Mexico. With his army go, as captives, judge, jury, and three attorneys from a district court in session when he arrived in San Antonio.

28 President Houston, in an attempted compromise on the location of the capital, moves government from Houston to Washington-on-the-Brazos, where he arrives October 2.

October

3 President Houston orders Alexander Somervell to organize and command a punitive expedition against Mexico.

November

14 Congress meets at Washington-on-the-Brazos (not Houston or Austin) on Sam Houston's instruction. Not until ten days later is a quorum finally obtained in the House of Representatives—and in the Senate even later than that.

25 Somervell expedition departs camp near San Antonio for Mexico in retaliation for recent Mexican raids into Texas; about 700 men at its peak.

December
8 Laredo captured by Somervell expedition.

19 Somervell orders his men to return home; about 300 refuse and continue into Mexico as the Mier expedition.

25–26 Texas volunteers of the recent Somervell expedition, commanded now by William S. Fisher, attack the Mexican town of Mier, but surrender and later begin a long march into Mexican captivity.

30 Ranger company under Thomas I. Smith and Eli Chandler retrieves many archives at Austin during secret operation ordered by President Houston and begins withdrawal to Washington-on-the-Brazos, but only after furious Austin residents, who discover the .ruse, open fire with a cannon. On the following day an Austin "vigilance committee" led by Mark B. Lewis recaptures the archives and returns them to Austin, where they stay.

1843

January
16 Congress, in secret session, votes to disband the Texas Navy and sell all the ships, laid up at New Orleans, but this project of President Houston fails.

February
11 Mier prisoners break away from their captors at Salado Creek in Mexico, but most are recaptured.

16 Texas government authorizes the organization of a private force of 300 men, to be led by Jacob Snively, to capture Mexican trade caravans traveling along the section of the Santa Fe Trail claimed by Texas; the government and expedition members will divide the booty.

March
25 Seventeen of the 176 recaptured Mier prisoners who participated in the February 11 escape—one of every ten—are executed at the Salado after drawing black beans in a grim lottery. Following the execution of the seventeen men the survivors are marched on into Mexican imprisonment.

April
19 *Austin* and *Wharton* clear the mouth of the Mississippi River for Yucatán and for battles with the Mexican fleet, despite the January action of Congress ordering sale of the navy. Commodore Moore's purpose: to help Yucatán, again rebelling; to raise money from the rebels and from prizes he hopes to capture; and to get the ships away from Sam Houston.

25 Snively expedition departs.

30 *Austin* and *Wharton* battle Mexican fleet of six ships off Yucatán; action indecisive, as is another fought on May 2.

May

6   President Houston publishes proclamation declaring Commodore Moore and his fleet pirates; asks any friendly nation to capture the ships and to bring them to Galveston. The proclamation, prepared in anticipation of Moore's actions, is dated March 23.

16   *Austin* and *Wharton* engage the Mexican ships off Yucatán. Mexicans withdraw after suffering many casualties.

27   Snively expedition, authorized in February, reaches Santa Fe Trail and Arkansas River, in vicinity of present Edwards County, Kansas. After weeks of waiting, the men find no trade caravans, but encounter a Mexican force of 100 men, of whom they kill 17 and capture 83 (later released), suffering no casualties themselves.

June

15   President Houston proclaims an armistice with Mexico, pending peace negotiations, with English help and assurance. Mexico follows suit soon afterward.

28   Snively expedition, after finding no booty, breaks up into two groups, both still seeking Mexican loot. One group of Texans is surrounded by U.S. dragoons on June 30 and told to leave what is called U.S. territory. Eventually the entire expedition proves a fiasco.

July

14   Commodore Moore returns to Galveston, having heard on June 1 of President Houston's piracy charge. He tries to surrender, but receives a hero's welcome. (Later, in August, 1844, a court-martial clears him of all but minor charges.) The cruise ending this date marks the end of Texas Navy operations, but, because of Moore's work and the departure from Mexican service of recruited English seamen who have become disgusted by the lack of action, Mexico gives up control of the Gulf of Mexico.

August

6   Last remnants of Snively expedition disband, return home.

October

16   U.S. Secretary of State Abel Upshur, after rumors of English inroads in Texas, tells Texas minister Isaac Van Zandt in Washington he would be willing to discuss annexation, but says he cannot promise Senate acceptance. Shortly afterward Upshur is killed in a shipboard accident.

1844

April

12   U.S. Secretary of State John C. Calhoun, from South Carolina, signs treaty of annexation with Texas emissaries James Pinckney Henderson and Isaac Van Zandt, then urges Senate ratification. Calhoun pledges pro-

tection for Texas during the proceedings. U.S. chargé d'affaires William Sumter Murphy brings the treaty to the Texas capital at Washington-on-the-Brazos for signing.

June

8 Calhoun's annexation treaty is defeated, 35 to 16, in the U.S. Senate, on the strength of abolition sentiment. Among senators from states outside the South only three—two from Pennsylvania and one from New Hampshire—support it. Texans are embittered.

August

15 President Houston orders militia into East Texas to quell the Regulator–Moderator War, which has been raging for four years.

September

2 Anson Jones elected President with a total of about 10,000 votes, 1,389 more than Edward Burleson. Kenneth Anderson elected vice-president without opposition.

16 Last of Mier prisoners released from Perote by order of Santa Anna.

December

9 Anson Jones takes oath as President at Washington-on-the-Brazos, Kenneth Anderson as vice-president. Jones chooses for his Cabinet Ashbel Smith secretary of state, William Beck Ochiltree secretary of the treasury, George Washington Hill secretary of war and marine, Ebenezer Allen attorney general. As in the preceding administration, no postmaster general is named. Jones also names James Reily minister to the United States, George Terrell minister to England and France, William Daingerfield minister to the Netherlands and to Belgium and the Hanse towns, which also have recognized Texas independence. Thomas William Ward again becomes commissioner of the General Land Office. Prior to the arrival of Ashbel Smith from Europe, where he has been representing Texas, Ebenezer Allen also functions as secretary of state. Several appointees are holdovers from Houston's administration; Jones foresees the possibility of a short term, with annexation the major consideration, although he does not publicize this.

1845

February

27 U.S. Senate, by a 27-to-25 vote, passes resolution offering annexation to Texas; 14 yes votes come from slave states, 13 from free states concerned about English designs on Texas. Earlier the House of Representatives passed the resolution, 120 to 98, and the Mexican minister to Washington left the United States.

March

1   President John Tyler signs the resolution offering annexation to Texas; two days later, and only hours before leaving office, he sends a copy to Texas and urges quick action by the Congress there.

April

29   A. J. Donelsen, newly appointed U.S. chargé d'affaires in Texas, arrives in Galveston for the primary purpose of urging prompt action by Texas on acceptance of the annexation resolution.

June

3   Charles Elliot, English chargé d'affaires in Texas, returns from Mexico to tell President Jones that Mexico is willing to recognize Texas independence if Texas will reject annexation. England and France have cooperated in urging this agreement on Mexico.

16   Congress meets at Washington-on-the-Brazos until June 28 and hears President Jones submit two possibilities: annexation to the United States or recognition of independence by Mexico. Annexation is unanimously approved, and Jones issues a proclamation for election of members to a July 4 convention to draw up a state constitution.

July

4   Convention of 1845, meeting at Austin, approves U.S. offer of annexation by a vote of 55 to 1, then draws up a state constitution for submission to voters.

October

13   Texas voters overwhelmingly ratify annexation and the new state constitution. Final action by the United States still pends.

December

16   U.S. House of Representatives passes a bill admitting Texas as a state, 141 to 56, despite protests and petitions from Connecticut, Massachusetts, and Rhode Island.

22   U.S. Senate passes the statehood bill, 31 to 14.

29   Texas officially becomes the 28th state in the United States when President James K. Polk signs annexation bill. Republic officials continue to administer the Texas government until February.

1846

February

19   President Jones formally relinquishes control of the government of Texas to Governor Henderson and the United States.

NOTES ON THE TEXT

Further information on the sources appears in the Selected Bibliography.

PROLOGUE

Anson Jones's letter of February 19, 1846, to his wife is from the Anson Jones Papers in the University of Texas Archives, which contains all manuscript material cited herein unless otherwise noted. A common error in some books of Texas history gives the date of the annexation ceremony as February 16. This letter and other documents clearly show otherwise.

The quotation regarding the popularity of titles before names is from Philip Graham, *The Life and Poems of Mirabeau B. Lamar*.

I

INTRODUCTORY MATERIAL

The statement by José María Tornel y Mendívil is from his pamphlet *Relations between Texas, the United States of America, and Mexico*, quoted by Carlos Castañeda in *The Mexican Side of the Texas Revolution*. Some Spanish officials had commented earlier, before Mexican independence, on this Anglo-American tendency toward taking land.

I

For a detailed account of Philip Nolan's activities in Texas until 1801 see John Edward Weems, *Men Without Countries*.

With two exceptions, the direct quotations from Stephen F. Austin in this section are from his letters to Thomas F. Leaming of the following dates (all found in the Thomas F. Leaming Letters and Papers): February 1, 1828; May 13, 1829; June 29 and July 14, 1830. The exceptions are Austin's order to Indian fighters to avoid "offending innocent persons," dated August 22, 1829, to Abner Kuykendall, found in the James Hampton Kuykendall and William Kuykendall Papers; and the statement that Texas was his "mistress," quoted in a letter dated Sept. 25, 1889, from Moses Austin Bryan, Austin's nephew, to Bryan's son Beauregard, found in the Caryl C. Hill Collection. The physical description of Stephen F. Austin also is from Bryan's letter, which was his recollection of Austin recorded mostly for family history.

2

The family from Carthage, Tennessee, who traveled up the Red River to Pecan Point in 1816 was the Claiborne Wright family, whose journey was recounted in a reminiscence in the George W. Wright Memoirs. The Irish trader who arrived with his bride in 1834 was John J. Linn, who told of his experiences in a book, *Reminiscences of Fifty Years in Texas*. The Massachusetts trader forced to man the ship's pumps for his life was Ammon Underwood, who arrived in Texas in April of 1834 after a voyage from Boston by way of New Orleans, and told the story in his journal, 1834–1838, kept in the Ammon Underwood Papers. The man from Maine who lived at the water's edge on Matagorda Bay was Thomas Decrow, who wrote the description (found in the Daniel and Thomas Decrow Letters) to his father in June, 1838—after colonial days but still typical of them. The two men who wrote so glowingly of Texas were Asa Brigham ("superior to any other part of North America"), in a letter dated February 28, 1832, to relatives in Marlborough, Massachusetts, kept in the Asa Brigham Papers; and John J. Linn ("cribs knew nothing of locks") in his book. The quotation about the absence of chivalry in Texas is from an undated letter, apparently from the early 1830s, signed "T. McQueen," found in the Caryl C. Hill Collection. The two Indian stories at the end of this section were told in detail by John Wesley Wilbarger, a Kentucky native who came to Texas in 1837, in *Indian Depredations in Texas*.

A detailed description of life in Texas about this time and later can be found in William Ransom Hogan, *The Texas Republic: A Social and Economic History*.

3

Moses Austin Bryan wrote his son Beauregard (in the letter referred to in the Section 1 notes) about Stephen F. Austin's popularity in the Coahuila-Texas legislature and about the tamed mouse Austin had for a companion in jail. Austin's letter to San Felipe—to the *ayuntamiento* there, dated January 17, 1834—is quoted from Eugene C. Barker, *The Life of Stephen F. Austin*, as is Austin's statement about his love of books. Austin's own description of prison, his reasons for being there, and the good that he expected to result are from his letter to his brother-in-law James F. Perry, May 10, 1834, found in the Caryl C. Hill Collection. The quotation at the end of the section about fighting and whipping Mexico was in a letter written by Ira R. Lewis to Duncan S. Walker, January 26, 1836, quoted in Stanley Siegel, *A Political History of the Texas Republic, 1836–1845*.

The significance of the *San Felipe–Correo de Méjico* sea fight is discussed in Jim Dan Hill, *The Texas Navy*.

The standard biography of Austin, which discusses in detail his activities in Mexico and his imprisonment there, is Barker's book, mentioned above. Barker also edited the multivolumed *The Austin Papers*, in which Austin's correspondence has been collected, but which is not a major reference for this narrative.

II

INTRODUCTORY MATERIAL

The declaration by Santa Anna's aide about troops that had quelled the Zacatecas uprising with such ferocity being sent on to Texas for similar work there is from Andrew J. Houston, *Texas Independence*.

4

This section is based largely on Sam Maverick's 1835 diary entries, in the Maverick Papers, and on Rena Maverick Green (editor), *Samuel Maverick, Texan: 1803–1870*. Maverick was inconsistent occasionally in diary entries, and his material has been corrected, but without changing his story. For example, he wrote on October 27 about the Mexicans positioning a total of twelve cannon, then referred to "the 18-pounder" and "ten smaller cannon." The discrepancy has been eliminated in this narrative. He also wrote of hearing the sounds of the Battle of Concepción on October 27. Actually, skirmishing began that afternoon, when the Texans first took a position near the mission, but the main battle occurred the next morning; Henderson King Yoakum, *History of Texas,* has a detailed account of it, and of the entire siege. Some other supplementary information for this section came from the "Siege of Bexar" entry in Walter Prescott Webb (editor in chief), *The Handbook of Texas.*

Research into the Texan death toll at San Antonio emphasizes the vagueness and inconsistency prevalent in the supposed facts and figures of Texas history. Differences are common; even official reports sometimes are in obvious error; and frequently official reports do not even exist, having been burned or otherwise lost. In regard to the San Antonio death toll, one fanciful story says that only one man was killed—Ben Milam, the man who inspired the attack. *The Handbook of Texas* states that four men were killed, fifteen wounded. Other accounts give still different figures, twelve killed and eighteen wounded being a common count. For this reason approximations occasionally have been used in the narrative—in the case of San Antonio casualties, the reference to "twenty or thirty killed and wounded."

Vivid descriptions of San Antonio about this time were left by William Fairfax Gray, who visited the town and described it in his journal, found in the Earl Vandale Collection; and by an unknown traveler whose account appears in Andrew Forest Muir (editor), *Texas in 1837: An Anonymous Contemporary Narrative*. Both were used, along with Maverick's material, to describe San Antonio here.

The story of the Stephen F. Austin–William H. Wharton feud, which continued during the siege of San Antonio, is from Moses Austin Bryan's letter of September 25, 1889, to his son, referred to in the Section 1 notes.

III

INTRODUCTORY MATERIAL

Yoakum, *History of Texas* (first published in 1855), covers this period in detail, benefiting throughout from the availability of documents that have since vanished. Walter Lord, *A Time to Stand,* presents a factual account of the decision not to abandon the Alamo—despite Houston's orders—and of the subsequent battle.

5

William Barret Travis's statement about the scarcity of volunteers appears as it was quoted in Herbert Pickens Gambrell, *Mirabeau Buonaparte Lamar:*

Troubadour and Crusader, but virtually all of the rest of this section is based on Harriet Ames's "Reminiscences," with some supplementary information used from the "Harriet (Moore) Ames" entry in *The Handbook of Texas.*

6

William Fairfax Gray left a "Journal, 1835–1837," consisting of numerous books, 3½ by 5½ inches, in which he carefully detailed in a small, neat hand his experiences in Texas. Most of the material used here comes from that journal, but some is from William F. Gray, *From Virginia to Texas,* and from the "William Fairfax Gray" and "James Gaines" entries in *The Handbook of Texas.*

7

Joseph Henry Barnard kept a journal, but it vanished long ago. Before its disappearance, however, its contents had been printed in several old books and newspapers, with some minor variations among these sources. Barnard's story, as it appears here, is based largely on his journal excerpt published in Linn, *Reminiscences of Fifty Years in Texas.* Also used as references were J. H. Barnard, *Dr. J. H. Barnard's Journal,* a composite of known versions, edited by Hobart Huson, and the "Joseph Henry Barnard," "John Shackelford," and some other entries in *The Handbook of Texas.*

The other visitor to New Orleans that January 8, 1836—the day Barnard observed the commemoration of the twenty-first anniversary of the battle there—was Andrew Janeway Yates, who wrote about the "spirit in favor of Texas" to an unknown New York resident in a letter dated the following day and found in the A. J. Yates Papers.

8

This section is based entirely on William Fairfax Gray's journal, referred to in the Section 6 notes.

9

Years after this, Z. N. Morrell assembled his recollections in a book, *Flowers and Fruits in the Wilderness* (published in 1886), which is the source for this section. Morrell never again saw his friend David Crockett, who was, of course, killed at the Alamo in March.

10

Gray's journal again provided the information.

11

Harriet Ames's reminiscences, mentioned in the Section 5 notes, served as the basis here. She wrote these recollections at the age of eighty-three, and by that time her memory obviously had dimmed, especially in regard to dates, which she rarely mentioned. Furthermore, her story shows a few inconsistencies and some obvious exaggerations, whether or not intentional. But much of it is reliable, as authentication shows, and those parts were chosen for inclusion in this book.

IV
INTRODUCTORY MATERIAL

"Blue northers" are still a Texas phenomenon, of course, but this description of one is based on an account of a man who observed many of them in the early days of Texas: John Washington Lockhart, in *Sixty Years on the Brazos*. The quotation about "the old blood of '76" is from a letter, Thomas Jefferson Green to Jesse Benton, dated April 4, 1836, found in the Thomas Jefferson Green Papers.

12

Gray's journal was used for most of this, his book (*From Virginia to Texas*) for some. Usually Gray was an accurate recorder, but in his journal he erroneously gave Sam Houston's birthday as March 3, 1793; it was March 2.

The recruiter who wrote of "virgins defiled" was the bombastic Thomas Jefferson Green, in a letter dated March 30, 1836, to Adolphus McCall, in the Green Papers.

13

Fannin's "farewell" letter was sent to Joseph Mims, with whom Fannin had operated a sugar plantation near Brazoria in 1834. It was quoted by Linn in *Reminiscences of Fifty Years in Texas*.

Barnard's experiences in the Battle of Coleto and at the massacre are based on his journal as excerpted by Linn and on the published composite mentioned in the Section 7 notes, but Barnard was not always accurate in regard to some events he only heard about and did not see. For that reason other sources were relied upon for information here: Hobart Huson, *Refugio* (which quotes Shackelford extensively, as well as Barnard and others); Yoakum, *History of Texas* (which also quotes Shackelford, and the Mexicans Santa Anna, Portilla, and Urrea, and still others); Frank W. Johnson, *A History of Texas and Texans;* and *The Handbook of Texas*. On occasion the various accounts differed in minor details; when that happened what seemed to be the most logical was selected.

The terms of surrender at Coleto were as described by Shackelford, in Yoakum's book. Barnard, in his journal, gave them as substantially the same. The two men differed, however, on the number of days to elapse until they and all the others would be given their freedom. Barnard said it was ten days— as used in this narrative—but Shackelford said, "The first words Colonel [Juan José Holsinger, a German soldier of fortune] uttered, after a very polite bow, were, '*Well, gentlemen, in eight days, liberty and home.*' I heard this distinctly."

The Texan who described the Mexican retreat at Coleto as resembling the flight of "a herd of buffaloes" was quoted by Yoakum. The fifteen-year-old volunteer who said, "We was in a great fix to fight," was Benjamin F. Hughes, who left a written record of his experiences. Parts of his account are of questionable accuracy, but obviously not the statement used, nor the fact that his life was saved by Señora Alavez, who was, by the way, identified as the "angel of Goliad" by Texas historian Harbert Davenport after many years of uncertainty. The prisoner who bolted for the San Antonio River and escaped the massacre was Samuel Brown, a member of Ward's battalion, quoted in Johnson, *A History of Texas and Texans.*

14

This section is based on Gray's journal and on his book, *From Virginia to Texas.* Sam Houston's statement about "consulting none" is from *The Writings of Sam Houston, 1813–1863,* edited by Amelia Williams and Eugene Barker. Gray did not mention that the Twin Sisters cannon were aboard the *Flash* when he encountered that ship, but they must have been: the guns originally were shipped to the mouth of the Brazos for transfer up that river to Houston's army, but because of bad weather they were carried back to Galveston, then to Morgan's Point aboard the *Flash,* at the time Gray met that vessel. From there they were transported to Sam Houston. (See "Twin Sisters" and "Flash" entries in *The Handbook of Texas.*) Neither did Gray mention that Harriet Page was aboard the *Flash,* but he did state that the Secretary of the Navy (Robert Potter) was aboard, as were a "number of ladies from the Brazos whose husbands were in the army." Comparing that with Harriet's own story makes it clear she was there.

Some people said and some still say that Sam Houston had no plan during his long retreat. Houston said later he had intended to seek sanctuary near the United States if necessary.

Details concerning the Texas Navy when Gray visited the ships at Galveston Island can be found in Hill, *The Texas Navy.*

15

The source is Morrell, *Flowers and Fruits in the Wilderness.*

16

This is based mostly on Barnard's journal in Linn and the published composite. His quotation, " 'Twas whispered," has been corrected. He wrote it: " 'Twas whispered in heaven, and muttered in hell,/And echo caught softly the sound as it fell." The tenth edition of *Home Book of Quotations* (New York: Dodd, Mead, 1967) notes that this should be credited to Horace Smith—not to Lord Byron, as is commonly done, and as Barnard did.

The quotation about Santa Anna's lack of hospital facilities, "not as bad to die as to come out wounded," is from Lord, *A Time to Stand.*

Barnard, apparently writing afterward, and from memory, said the burial ceremony at Goliad was Wednesday, June 5. Thomas Rusk in his official report (printed in Linn, *Reminiscences of Fifty Years in Texas*) gives it as June 3.

Barnard was wrong on two counts: the ceremony was June 3, and June 5 was not a Wednesday. Rusk's speech there was quoted by Linn.

V

INTRODUCTORY MATERIAL

The man who committed suicide was James Collinsworth. He made the statement in a letter dated May 31, 1836, to Thomas Rusk, quoted in Siegel, *A Political History of the Texas Republic.*

17

Most of this section is based on Morrell's book.

Wilbarger, *Indian Depredations in Texas,* gives an account of the Fort Parker tragedy, as do many other sources; the story is widely known in Texas. The baby referred to in this narrative was Mrs. Rachel Plummer's. It was not dragged through prickly pears at the time of the attack on the fort, but six months later. Nevertheless, the brutality was included here as being typical of what Texans were forced to endure at the hands of the Comanches. After the baby was dead the Indians untied the rope attached to it and tossed the remains back to Mrs. Plummer, who said, "I dug a hole in the earth and buried them . . . [rejoicing that] my baby had passed from the sufferings of this world."

18

The main source was Harriet Ames's reminiscences. Other references include the "Harriet (Moore) Ames" and "Robert Potter" entries in *The Handbook of Texas.*

Harriet did not write about the Santa Anna kidnapping, the invasion scare, or Sam Houston's election and inauguration, but she and Potter were certainly aware of these happenings, and they have been inserted here, in chronological order. Yoakum, *History of Texas,* details the events, as do many other books of history.

The farewell note of Santa Anna is quoted from Yoakum's book. The commissioner's news from Matamoros about the impending invasion of Texas is from a letter, Henry Teal to Thomas Rusk, dated June 9, 1836, in the Thomas Byers Huling Papers. The fact that "three-fourths" of the men and boys turned out to "teach the . . . foe . . . a sequel" is from the Ammon Underwood diary for June, 1836, in the Ammon Underwood Papers. The contemporary's favorable description of Sam Houston ("remarkable memory") is John J. Linn's, from his book; the reason Houston gave for allowing his "name to be run for President," from *The Writings of Sam Houston* (but originally in the Houston *Telegraph and Texas Register* of August 30, 1836); the observation of the unwilted observer at Houston's inauguration, from Homer S. Thrall, *A Pictorial History of Texas;* the critical contemporary's unfavorable description of Houston ("consummate actor"), from the Moses Austin Bryan letter to his son first referred to in the Section 1 notes.

19

Virtually all of this is based on Morrell's book.

The lawmaker "so tired" of the town of Houston was Kelsey H. Douglass, as he stated in letters to his wife of September 4 and October 15, 1837, now kept in the Kelsey H. Douglass Papers.

20

Used for this section were the Maverick Papers, especially the manuscript "Recollections assisted by notes taken at the time of Mary A. Maverick's early days in Texas." Other references include Rena Maverick Green (editor), *Memoirs of Mary A. Maverick*, and Green (editor), *Samuel Maverick, Texan: 1803–1870.*

21

Morrell's book was used as the source.

22

Mary Maverick's recollections provided all the material.

VI

INTRODUCTORY MATERIAL

An account of Lamar's election as president and his ensuing administration can be found in Gambrell, *Mirabeau Buonaparte Lamar.*

23

Quotations attributed to Morrell are from his book. The Houston resident who wrote about yellow fever was Milly (Mrs. William Fairfax) Gray, in a diary entry for October 15, 1838, in the Earl Vandale Collection. The man who wrote that Houston "will *use* but not serve" was Barnard Bee, in a letter to Ashbel Smith July 17, 1838, Barnard Bee Papers. The man who spoke of Lamar's election as a result of Houston's not being "godlike" was the historian Herbert Gambrell, whose book on Lamar served as a reference for this section, along with Philip Graham's (where was found the verse written for Emily Goode and Lamar's statement about the poorest citizen deserving security) and *The Papers of Mirabeau Buonaparte Lamar,* edited by Charles Adams Gulick and others. The fellow boarder who described Lamar was Francis R. Lubbock, quoted by Gambrell, who also quoted Lamar's statement on a "cultivated mind." The cost of Lamar's carriage was given by William Bryan in a manuscript dated February 10, 1839, found in the Alexander Dienst Collection.

24

This section is based on Morrell's book, with supplementary information about the Córdova and Flores fights from Yoakum, who erroneously inverted the order of these two events, and from John Holland Jenkins (a participant), *Recollections of Early Texas;* Wilbarger, *Indian Depredations;* Walter Prescott Webb, *The Texas Rangers;* and *The Handbook of Texas.* Jenkins recorded the date of the Córdova fight as March 29, 1839; Wilbarger said March 28. Morrell gave no date.

The instructions to the Indians "to burn [Texas] habitations" is from Yoakum's book, quoting a letter found on Flores' body after he was killed. The quotations in the Andrews-Rice chase of Flores are from Wilbarger, who called the victory second in importance for the Republic only to San Jacinto.

25

The Barnard Bee Papers and *The Handbook of Texas* entry "Barnard E. Bee" were the sources, with two exceptions. The description of bustling Galveston on the day Bee left there is from *The Daily Picayune* of New Orleans, March 29, 1839, in which was mentioned Bee's arrival in the city. The quotation from *El Censor* was taken from Yoakum's book, although Bee himself referred to it. This quotation also has appeared elsewhere. The *Telegraph and Texas Register* of June 5, 1839, reprinted it, as have other publications. Two misspellings have been corrected from the way they appeared in Yoakum: "pedler" to "peddler" and "embassador" to "ambassador."

Letters in the Bee Papers from which the other direct quotations were taken are these: James Webb to Bee, February 20, 1839; Bee to Webb, April 18, May 13, May 16, and May 24, 1839; R. G. Dunlap (the Texan minister in Washington) to Bee, May 17, 1839; Bee to Ashbel Smith, September 13, 1839 (on "sickenings of public life").

26

Morrell's quotations are from his book. The officer who wrote of the Indian depredations that ensued was Major John Wortham, quoted by Yoakum. Another source for this section was *The Handbook of Texas.*

27

Much of this, and all of Thomas Bell's quotations came from the Thomas W. Bell Family Papers, especially from these letters: Thomas W. Bell to James W. Bell (his brother), August 7, November 1, November 18, and November 19, 1839. Another major source was Gambrell's book on Lamar, where were found the quotations about "the seat of future Empire" and the Secretary of State's warning to Lamar.

VII

INTRODUCTORY MATERIAL

Ashbel Smith wrote about the San Luis depression, in 1840, quoted in Hogan, *The Texas Republic,* where also was found the statement about "perfectly ruinous" times—by J. H. Kirchhoffer, in a letter to James H. Starr, January 5, 1841. Bee's remark about bridegroom Sam Houston is from a June 5, 1840, letter to Ashbel Smith, in the Bee Papers.

28

This section is based on Mary Maverick's manuscript of recollections, first mentioned in the Section 20 notes. Additional information on the Council House Fight came from Jenkins, *Recollections of Early Texas;* Linn, *Reminiscences of Fifty Years in Texas;* Webb, *The Texas Rangers;* Wilbarger, *Indian Depredations;* Yoakum, *History of Texas;* and *The Handbook of Texas.*

The quotations from inside the courthouse during the discussion are from Wilbarger, but they have appeared in the same words in many other publications. For the most part, however, the council-house story is as Mary recorded it. She differed slightly, and occasionally, from some other accounts. For instance, one version said that a soldier shot the Indian who leaped on Lysander Wells's horse, and that this incident happened earlier than Mary indicated. Still another story also differed from hers in regard to the turpentine-burned Indian; it said that only one Comanche was in hiding, and that it was in another location. There are a few more differences, but they are minor and do not affect the body of her experiences, even if excitement jarred her observation somewhat. On the other hand, she was a witness to most of the events she described, and many of the other writers were not.

Sam Houston's recollection of the Council House Fight and what ensued is from a Senate speech in Washington of January, 1855, reprinted in *The Writings of Sam Houston.*

29

Morrell's experiences are based on his book. The account of the Indian attacks at Victoria and Linnville is based mainly on the books by Linn, Webb, Wilbarger, and Yoakum, and on *The Handbook of Texas.* The lucky Linnville merchant who passed the Indian encampment at Placido Creek on his way to Victoria under the cover of night was W. G. Ewing, as related by Linn, who also recorded the preceding story of the two men driving freight wagons. The quoted description of the celebrating Indians "dashing about the blazing village" is from Linn, for whom the town of Linnville was named. The observer who waded ashore for a shot was John Hays (not the Ranger)—again, according to Linn.

30

Morrell's book was used for his own experiences, except that his account of the Plum Creek fight is inferior to some others in regard to certain matters concerning terrain and tactics. For that reason this part of his own account has been revised—without changing his personal experiences—after reading Jenkins, Linn, Webb, Yoakum, and *The Handbook of Texas.* Webb in particular has a brief but accurate account of this period of Indian fighting, in *The Texas Rangers.*

One other revision was made in Morrell's story. He said that after finding the wounded Mrs. Watts he saw two other women lying nearby, both dead. The official report stated that the Negro woman was not dead but wounded, and though official reports can be wrong sometimes, one was used in this instance.

To illustrate further the inconsistency particularly common to this period of Texas history: *The Handbook of Texas* mentions that Burleson and his men arrived too late to fight at Plum Creek; but, though delayed, they were there. Jenkins and Morrell, both with Burleson, described the fighting, as did others.

31

The material concerning Bell is from the Thomas W. Bell Family Papers, as is the brief quotation at the end of the preceding section, about Plum Creek. Specifically the letters used were Bell to William A. Bell (his father), July 23, 1840; and to James W. Bell, August 17, 1840.

As for the other notable quotations here: Lamar's impractical imbeciles, Ashbel Smith to Barnard Bee, March 22, 1840, Bee Papers; Congress as a help in speculations, D. W. Huling to Thomas B. Huling, undated, 1840, in the Thomas B. Huling Correspondence; Houston's letter from "accursed" Austin, Sam Houston to Robert Irion, January 27, 1840, Robert Anderson Irion Papers; Acting President Burnet on the boundary, from Graham's book on Lamar, where was found also Lamar's melancholy poem.

VIII
INTRODUCTORY MATERIAL

Sam Houston's remarks on "Davy G." were in a letter dated January 27, 1841, to Irion, in the Robert Anderson Irion Papers.

32

The Barnard Bee Papers provided most of the information, especially these letters: Bee to Ashbel Smith, a letter undated ("all are courteous to me") but probably written in 1841, and letters dated April 25, November 1, and November 20, 1841; Bee to Lamar, September 21, 1841; Bee to John Brower (the Texas consul at New York) September 22, 1841; Brower to Bee, October 2, 1841.

33

Most of this is from Mary Maverick's recollections manuscript, although she did not write in this much detail of Lamar's plans regarding Santa Fe.

34

Kendall's own book, *Narrative of the Texan Santa Fe Expedition,* is the foundation here. Additional references: Peter Gallagher's diary of the Santa Fe Expedition; George W. Grover's manuscript account; Fayette Copeland, *Kendall of the Picayune* (also based extensively on Kendall's book); "George Wilkins Kendall" and "Texan Santa Fe Expedition" in *The Handbook of Texas;* and *The Papers of Mirabeau Buonaparte Lamar.* Another notable book on the

Santa Fe Expedition (Kendall's is emphasized here because he was selected as a character for the narrative) is one by Thomas Falconer, edited by F. W. Hodge: *Letters and Notes on the Texan Santa Fe Expedition, 1841–1842.*

Lamar's order to his comptroller to open an expedition account appears in the published Lamar Papers. The agent Lamar sent to New Orleans was Major George T. Howard. Kendall's newspaper statement about the "dash into Santa Fe trade" appeared in *The Daily Picayune* of August 4, 1840; it was quoted by Copeland.

Kendall gave the departure of the expedition as June 21, 1841. George Grover, another member, said in his diary it was June 20. Both of these accounts were written later, and memory apparently failed. The leading authority on the expedition, the late H. Bailey Carroll, gave the departure date as June 19 in *The Handbook of Texas,* basing it on his research done for a doctoral dissertation.

35

This is from the Bell Papers. Letters quoted are these: Thomas Bell to James W. Bell, May 31, June 10, and July 25, 1841. Other references: "Martin Ruter" and "Rutersville College" entries in *The Handbook of Texas,* and an article by Julia Lee Sinks, "Rutersville College," in the October, 1898, issue of the *Quarterly* of the Texas State Historical Association.

36

The same sources cited in the first paragraph of the Section 34 notes were used here, with emphasis on Kendall's book. Quotations and vital information not from Kendall are these: Gallagher called Hugh McLeod sick from "too much whiskey," recorded the progression of the expedition after five weeks as only two hundred miles, and described the Indian village; Grover described the "Red River"; H. Bailey Carroll, in *The Handbook of Texas,* provided information about the expedition's halt at the Cap Rock. Sam Houston's message to Congress of December, 1841, can be found in *The Writings of Sam Houston.*

The Texas officer sent by Armijo to persuade the other Texans to surrender was W. L. Lewis.

IX
INTRODUCTORY MATERIAL

The compliment from Andrew Jackson was in a letter to Sam Houston dated August 17, 1842, in *The Writings of Sam Houston.* The letter calling Houston a "Dam old drunk Cherokee" is famous in Texas—from John Welsh, a resident of Webber's Prairie (now Webberville), to Sam Houston, dated January 7, 1842, kept in the archives of the Texas State Library.

A thorough study of Texas–Mexican relations of this period and earlier can be found in Joseph Milton Nance, *After San Jacinto* and *Attack and Counterattack.*

37

This story about Potter is based on Harriet Ames's reminiscences, with some additional information from Yoakum and from the "Regulator–Moderator War," "Harriet (Moore) Ames," "Robert Potter," and "William Pinckney Rose" entries in *The Handbook of Texas*. The acquitted man who formed the Regulators was a Kentuckian named Charles W. Jackson. The slain man was Joseph G. Goodbread.

Harriet made the favorable statement regarding Rose's son. She identified the two men standing near the fence when Potter ran out of the house as Sandy Miller and Stephen Peters, and said that Potter had loaned Peters money to make land payments and had also helped Miller.

38

Mary Maverick's manuscript of recollections was the source.

39

The letter referred to—Thomas W. Bell to William A. Bell, March 7, 1842— is in the Thomas W. Bell Family Papers.

40

Most of this is based on the archives collection of Charles G. Bryant Letters, which includes the correspondence of Andrew Jackson Bryant. The Bryants' quotations used here are from these letters: Andrew Jackson Bryant to Mrs. Sarah Bryant (his mother), June 8 and August 9, 1842; Charles G. Bryant to Andrew Jackson Bryant, February 27, June 11, September 14, and December 10, 1842.

Information regarding Charles Bryant's activities in Canada and his arrival in Texas with his son is from John Henry Brown, *Indian Wars and Pioneers of Texas*. The description of naval routine is from an article by another *Austin* midshipman, George F. Fuller, "Sketch of the Texas Navy," in the *Quarterly* of the Texas State Historical Association, January, 1904. Andrew Jackson's letter to Sam Houston about command of the Gulf was dated May 25, 1842; a copy was found in the Jesse Grimes Papers, and the letter is quoted in *The Writings of Sam Houston*.

Detailed information regarding the Texas Navy at this time can be found in Hill, *The Texas Navy*, and Tom Henderson Wells, *Commodore Moore and the Texas Navy*.

41

The Maverick Papers provided virtually all of this information—particularly Mary Maverick's recollections, and letters written or signed by Sam Maverick dated January 21, 1843 (to the Mexican Secretary of State recounting the Vásquez attack and the fact that Maverick thought he and his companions were firing on "a gang of bandits"), September 11, 1842 (urging leniency toward the

Mexican population of San Antonio), and October 6, 1842 (advising Mary to keep her spirits up, and the quotations immediately following).

Rena Maverick Green (editor), in *Memoirs of Mary A. Maverick,* quoted the San Antonio judge, Anderson Hutchinson, on "no invasion expected" and gave information on the case before the court.

42

Thomas W. Bell wrote of his experiences in the Mier battle and as a Mexican prisoner in a book first published in 1845, *A Narrative of the Capture and Subsequent Sufferings of the Mier Prisoners in Mexico.* A first edition is in the Earl Vandale Collection of the University of Texas Archives. Much of this section is based on his book and on the Bell Papers. The book is a frustrating reading experience at times; Bell wrote in the third person, rarely mentioned dates, inverted some order of events, and was sometimes vague and occasionally obviously wrong in minor matters. For that reason additional sources were relied on, while still focusing on Bell as a character and not changing the substance of his story. The other references: James Glasscock's diary (original in the archives of the Texas State Library); Hubert Howe Bancroft, *History of the North Mexican States and Texas;* Brown, *Indian Wars and Pioneers of Texas;* Frederick C. Chabot, *The Perote Prisoners;* James M. Day, "The Writing and Literature of the Texan Mier Expedition, 1842–1844," a doctoral dissertation submitted to Baylor University; Thomas J. Green, *Journal of the Texian Expedition against Mier;* William Preston Stapp, *The Prisoners of Perote;* and *The Handbook of Texas.* Day's dissertation contains many quotations from diaries, journals, and books left by these Mier men: Harvey A. Adams, John Rufus Alexander (the last survivor to die—in 1908), Thomas W. Bell, Israel Canfield, Willis Coplan, George B. Erath, James A. Glasscock, Thomas Jefferson Green, John C. C. Hill, George Lord, Joseph D. McCutchan, William P. Stapp, George Washington Trahern, James L. Trueheart, and William A. A. (Bigfoot) Wallace.

The man who called General Somervell "a perfect old Grannie" was Harvey Adams, in his diary, where also appears the graphic description of the looting of Laredo—both quoted by Day. Fisher's demand for provisions from Mier is as reported by Green—a participant—in his book, as is some other information: the army bivouac looking like a tanyard, some description of terrain and weather en route to Mier, and much recounting of the battle. Some description of terrain and weather also comes from the book by Brown, another participant.

Green was the man who jeered at soldiers displaying "bloody mottoes," the one who was reminded of the Ohio River by the Rio Grande, and the writer who quoted Fisher's advice to his men to surrender—which Bell also mentioned. The Texan captured on December 24 was A. S. Holderman, according to John Milton Nance in *The Handbook of Texas.*

43

This short section is based on various sources: John R. Jones, Jr., letter of December 1, 1842, to Thomas T. Brady about the hope that Houston would sink into "endless sleep," John Rice Jones Letters and Papers; Sam Houston, order of December 10, 1842, to Thomas I. Smith and Eli Chandler to get the archives, in *The Writings of Sam Houston;* Thomas William Ward ("Houston's man in Austin"), letter of January 8, 1843, to Houston about the Austin cannon firing on the wagons, in *The Writings of Sam Houston;* J. H. Kuykendall, letter of August 20, 1843, to James Grant staunchly supporting Houston, James Hampton Kuykendall and William Kuykendall Papers; and Sam Houston, letter of December 21, 1845, to Hamilton Stuart, about the barking dogs, in *The Writings of Sam Houston.* The last quotation is a few years out of place chronologically, but was typical of Houston throughout his political career.

X
INTRODUCTORY MATERIAL

A detailed account of Sam Houston's maneuverings at this time can be found in Llerena B. Friend, *Sam Houston: The Great Designer.*

44

This is based on the sources mentioned in the first paragraph of the Section 42 notes, with emphasis on the book by Bell, supplemented especially by Green's. Bell never referred to the manure in the cowpens that served as overnight jails, apparently believing such information should not appear in print, but Green and others wrote about it, as well as some other things Bell did not mention. Their material has been added to this account and to later sections concerning the Mier prisoners.

Green did not make the march into Mexico in the company of Bell and the rest of the men (he went ahead of them, guarded by a separate escort), but he talked with the men later and in his book provided what is obviously a generally authentic account, although it is packed with fulminations against his enemies.

Bell's companion who had "no taste for the beauties of nature" was James Glasscock. The casualties recorded during the escape on the Salado are Bell's; other accounts show a variety of figures. Bell's book also differs sometimes from other accounts in various minor details. When evidence indicated he was wrong the other accounts were used for those few details. In no instance was the body of his story revised or a direct quotation changed, except occasionally to substitute in brackets the first person for his lifeless third person. When contrary evidence did not disprove Bell his narrative was relied on. For example, Israel Canfield wrote in his diary that during the escape attempt the men left the road for the mountains—which proved to be a tragic mistake—more or less spontaneously, without discussing the move. Bell and others reported a consultation before this was done. Canfield must have missed something, because his account seems illogical on this point.

Green named the four Mier men who managed to reach Texas from the Mexican mountains as John Alexander, John Blackburn, Thomas Cox, and William Oldham. (See the Section 42 notes for more information on Alexander.)

45

Sources here were Mary Maverick's recollections and a letter to her from Sam Maverick, from Perote, dated March 15, 1843, in the Maverick Papers.

46

Again, this is based on the material first mentioned in the first paragraph of the Section 42 notes—with emphasis on Bell's book, as qualified in the Section 44 notes.

Green quoted Cameron's words at the drawing. He also identified the man chained to Cameron as William Wilson, the next two men to draw as William Ryan and F. M. Gibson, the man who "never failed to draw a prize" as J. D. Cocke. Bell named the man who confessed only to God: Robert Dunham. Canfield told the story about Captain Eastland's brother-in-law, and he should have known: Canfield was chained to the man. The story about Henry Whaling was a recollection of George Trahern, quoted by Day; the story of the wounded man in the pile of dead was told by Bell and several others; Bell named him— James Shepherd.

Glasscock mentioned the ominous whirlwinds; Bell did not. Glasscock said the guards came for Cameron and the interpreter about eight o'clock, and he was probably right. Bell said midnight.

47

The letter from Charles Bryant to his son Jackson was dated February 18, 1843; it is in the Charles G. Bryant Letters, which also provided other material used here.

Hill's and Wells's books on the Texas Navy relate in detail the events narrated here.

The commissioner who refused the appointment to sell the fleet was Samuel M. Williams; he had helped to buy it in the first place. The quotation attributed to Moore, "You don't get them," is from Wells's book, as is Morgan's "I felt justified" (written in a letter dated May 11, 1843, to James Reed). The *Austin* midshipman who described the departure ("moonless night") and recorded the naval punishments was George Fuller, referred to in the Section 40 notes.

48

Charles Bryant's letter to his son, quoted here throughout, is the same one mentioned in the Section 47 notes.

The Writings of Sam Houston provides details for this period. In that publication will be found Houston's proclamation against Moore, dated March 23, 1843; his letter to the English chargé d'affaires, Charles Elliott, dated January 24, 1843; and his poem in memory of Flacco, dated March 28, 1843.

49

Hill's and Wells's books provide details of the battles, as does *The Handbook of Texas*. James Morgan's letter is the same one referred to in the Section 47 notes. George Fuller, first mentioned in the Section 40 notes, described the cannon fire. Jackson Bryant's letter, dictated the day after the May 16 battle, is in the Charles G. Bryant Letters. The letters from *Austin* officers praising Jackson Bryant's conduct were mentioned in a letter from Charles Bryant to his wife dated June 8, 1843, in the Bryant Letters; Charles Bryant said he had read the favorable references.

50

The main source is Mary Maverick's recollections. The prisoner who wrote Sam Maverick on April 15, 1843, was R. A. Barkley; his letter is in the Maverick Papers. Maverick's letter about Texas' "miserable position" was to R. N. Weir, August 15, 1843, also in the Maverick Papers.

51

See the first paragraph of the Section 42 notes for references used here. The prisoner who could not forgive Sam Houston was Joseph McCutchan, quoted by Day; the man who wrote of "doing the work of asses" was Glasscock, who also made the June 12, 13, and 14 diary entries and boasted of "a fair road it is." The prisoners' resolution to prosecute the war Texas "is now engaged in" is from Canfield's diary, quoted by Day. Other quotations are Bell's, from his book.

Santa Anna's birthday actually was February 21.

52

Virtually all of this is from a long letter Charles Bryant wrote to his wife much later—on September 25, 1844—kept in the Bryant Letters. The congressional resolution praising Jackson and allowing him a pension was adopted February 2, 1844; it was found in the Alexander Dienst Collection. Chronologically part of the story is slightly out of place here in the section covering 1843, but this was where it fit.

53

Bell's book was the basis, but some information came from elsewhere. Several prisoners' accounts went into the description of Perote, along with an article, "Perote Fort," by J. J. McGrath and Walace Hawkins, in the January, 1945, issue of *Southwestern Historical Quarterly*.

The prisoner who described the ravages of *"vomito"* was McCutchan. The concluding paragraph is a paraphrase of Bell's words, which were—as they often were in his book—ridiculously ostentatious and flowery.

XI

INTRODUCTORY MATERIAL

Some details of this period can be found in Siegel, *A Political History of the Texas Republic*. Another source, although not used as a reference here, is Justin Smith, *The Annexation of Texas*.

54

The Moses Johnson Papers provided most of the material. That source yielded his letter of recommendation, dated at Woodstock May 29, 1834; the permission to practice, signed by Ashbel Smith; and the letter from Edson Huggins to his sister, Johnson's wife, dated October 10, 1844.

55

Bell's book was used as the basis. The story of the prison escape of March 25, 1844, utilized Green's book as well as Bell's.

Green quoted "Old Guts's" remarks after the escape. He also wrote that eight of the men were recaptured later, and he named them; Bell erroneously said seven. But the story about the escaped prisoner who traveled to the United States aboard a Mexican ship is Bell's, as are the rest of the quotations, with four exceptions: Glasscock wrote in his diary on June 8, 1844, about taking the castle, penned the criticism of the United States minister's confidence in the commandant, speculated on being in prison "during the war," and described the "big spree" of July 4, 1844.

56

The Charles G. Bryant Letters provided the material, particularly these: Bryant to his wife, October 1, 1844; Bryant's sister Martha to him, December 12, 1844; from his sister Welthea, December 19, 1844, and January 5, 1845.

57

Sam Houston's valedictory to the Texas Congress, given December 9, 1844, is in *The Writings of Sam Houston.* The August 26, 1838, diary entry of Anson Jones is kept in the Anson Jones Papers.

Details of these days can be found in Herbert Gambrell, *Anson Jones.*

The rest of the material in this section is from the Moses Johnson Papers. Olivia's sister wrote her about "that iron chest" on January 26, 1845. Moses Johnson's quotations (and other information here) are from his letters to his wife dated August 15, 19, 20, 22, 23, 24, 26, 27, 29, and 30, 1845.

EPILOGUE

The Handbook of Texas contains biographical information on these individuals: Joseph Henry Barnard, Barnard Bee, William Fairfax Gray, Moses Johnson, George Wilkins Kendall, Samuel A. Maverick, Mary Maverick, Z. N. Morrell, Harriet (Moore) Ames, and, of course, Sam Houston, Anson Jones, and Mirabeau B. Lamar. Further information about the first nine persons came from their letters or diaries or other archival material, or from the books written by them.

The information on Charles and Jackson Bryant came from the Bryant Letters and from Brown, *Indian Wars and Pioneers of Texas;* on Thomas W. Bell, from the Bell Family Papers and Day's dissertation.

ACKNOWLEDGMENTS

Over a period of eighteen months my wife, Jane, examined holdings in the University of Texas Archives, Texas State Archives, and elsewhere, gathering virtually all of the original material from contemporary diaries, journals, and letters on which this narrative is based. At the conclusion she had accumulated four thousand pages of notes.

Librarians deserving particular thanks are Llerena Friend, since retired, of the Barker Texas History Center; Dayton Kelley, librarian of the Texas Collection, Baylor University; Chester Kielman, archivist for the University of Texas; Dorman Winfrey, Texas state librarian; and Jack Grimes, archivist, Texas State Library.

Also deserving the author's appreciation are two employers, Baylor University and McLennan Community College, Waco, Texas, for encouragement during the writing of this book. My thanks go especially to Professor Hudson Long, chairman of the English Department at Baylor, for arranging a leave of absence from teaching, allowing much time to devote to the book; and to Victor Jeffress, librarian, McLennan Community College.

Michael Korda, William H. Simon, and others at Simon and Schuster helped with interest and advice, and many valuable suggestions came from Mrs. Vera Schneider.

Finally, thanks to our five children, Donald, Carol, Mary, Barbara, and Janet, for assistance ranging from typing to sharpening pencils by the pack.

A SELECTED BIBLIOGRAPHY

MANUSCRIPTS

Material found in contemporary accounts—diaries, letters, journals—was used as the basis for this narrative. In cases where some of this material later appeared in published form, the original version was relied upon. More collections than are listed below were examined; those listed are the papers that proved most valuable in telling the story. Unless otherwise noted, all are in the University of Texas Archives, a voluminous collection.

Harriet Ames Reminiscences.

Archibald Austin Papers.

Barnard Bee Papers.

Hamilton P. Bee Papers.

Thomas W. Bell Family Papers.

Dora Dieterich Bonham Papers.

Asa Brigham Papers.

Guy Morrison Bryan Letters.

Charles G. Bryant Letters.

John Wheeler Bunton Papers.

John W. Dancy Diary, 1838–1839 (copied from original in possession of his daughter, Mrs. Lena Dancy Ledbetter, Austin, in 1933).

Daniel and Thomas Decrow Letters (copied from originals in possession of D. A. Peaslee, Georgetown, Texas, courtesy Frank Caldwell, Austin, February, 1931).

Alexander Dienst Collection.

Kelsey H. Douglass Papers.

George John Durham Papers.

Alexander Wray Ewing Papers.

Samuel Rhoads Fisher Papers.

Edward Fontaine, Biographical Sketch of Lamar (transcript of original loaned by Louis Lenz of Houston).

Letters to William Winston Fontaine from John S. Moore, New Orleans (a descendant of the Bowies).

John Forbes Papers.

Benjamin C. Franklin Papers.

Peter Gallagher Diary of the Santa Fe Expedition.

James Glasscock Diary of the Mier Expedition (original in Texas State Library, copy in the University of Texas Archives).

Milly R. Gray Diary, 1835–1839.

William Fairfax Gray Journal.

Thomas Jefferson Green Papers (photostats of originals in the Southern Historical Collection, University of North Carolina Library).

355

Jesse Grimes Papers.

George W. Grover account of the Santa Fe Expedition (copy in the Earl Vandale Collection).

Caryl C. Hill Collection.

Addison C. Hinton Papers.

Benjamin F. Hughes Papers (copied from original loaned to Texas Centennial Exposition in 1936 by Irving Merry of Joplin, Missouri).

Thomas B. Huling Correspondence.

Robert Anderson Irion Papers.

Brewster Jayne Letters.

Moses Johnson Papers.

Anson Jones Papers.

John Rice Jones Letters and Papers.

James Hampton Kuykendall and William Kuykendall Papers (copied from seventeen manuscript books loaned by the heirs, through the courtesy of J. Frank Dobie, some years ago).

Mirabeau B. Lamar Papers.

Rebecca Ann Lamar Journal, 1838–1840.

Thomas F. Leaming Letters and Papers, 1796–1847.

Adel Looscan Papers.

Maverick Papers, including journals and letters by Samuel and Mary Maverick.

Thomas J. Rusk Papers.

Ashbel Smith Papers.

Ammon Underwood Papers.

Earl Vandale Collection.

George W. Wright Memoirs (transcribed from original by Project 12, Bureau of Research in the Social Studies, University of Texas, June, 1936; signed by J. Evetts Haley).

Andrew Janeway Yates Papers.

BOOKS

Many more books about the Republic of Texas than are listed below have been published. Two notable examples are Paul Horgan's *Great River* and Marquis James's biography of Sam Houston, *The Raven*. A complete list would include hundreds. The following list is a selective one of books that proved most useful in preparing this particular narrative.

Bancroft, Hubert Howe, *History of the North Mexican States and Texas*, 2 vols. San Francisco: A. L. Bancroft, 1884.

Barker, Eugene C., *The Life of Stephen F. Austin.* Austin: University of Texas Press, 1969. (Originally published 1926.)

Barnard, J. H., *Dr. J. H. Barnard's Journal: A Composite of Known Versions of the Journal of Dr. Joseph H. Barnard, One of the Surgeons of Fannin's Regiment, Covering the Period from December, 1835, to June 5, 1836,* edited and annotated by Hobart Huson. Goliad Bicentennial Edition (limited to 333 copies), 1949. (Barnard's journal also appears in John J. Linn's *Reminiscences* and elsewhere.)

Bell, Thomas W., *A Narrative of the Capture and Subsequent Sufferings of the Mier Prisoners in Mexico,* with introduction and notes by James M. Day. Waco: Texian Press, 1964. (Originally published 1845.)

Brown, John Henry, *Indian Wars and Pioneers of Texas.* Austin: L. E. Daniell, n.d.

Castañeda, Carlos M., *The Mexican Side of the Texan Revolution.* Dallas: P. L. Turner, 1928.

Chabot, Frederick C., *The Perote Prisoners.* San Antonio: Naylor, 1934.

Copeland, Fayette, *Kendall of the Picayune.* Norman: Oklahoma University Press, 1943.

Day, James M., "The Writing and Literature of the Texan Mier Expedition, 1842–1844," a dissertation submitted to the faculty of Baylor University, Waco, 1967.

Dobie, J. Frank, *The Flavor of Texas.* Dallas: Dealey and Lowe, 1936.

Encyclopedia Americana, 30 vols. New York: Americana Corporation, 1954.

Encyclopedia of American Facts and Dates, edited by Gorton Carruth and associates, 4th edition. New York: Thomas Y. Crowell, 1966.

Ford, John Salmon, *Rip Ford's Texas,* edited by Stephen B. Oates. Austin: University of Texas Press, 1963.

Friend, Llerena B., *Sam Houston: The Great Designer.* Austin: University of Texas Press, 1954.

Gambrell, Herbert, *Anson Jones: The Last President of Texas.* Garden City, N.Y.: Doubleday, 1948.

Gambrell, Herbert Pickens, *Mirabeau Buonaparte Lamar: Troubadour and Crusader.* Dallas: Southwest Press, 1934.

Graham, Philip, *The Life and Poems of Mirabeau B. Lamar.* Chapel Hill: University of North Carolina Press, 1938.

Gray, William F., *From Virginia to Texas.* Houston: Fletcher Young, 1965. (Originally published 1909.)

Green, Rena Maverick (editor), *Memoirs of Mary A. Maverick.* San Antonio: Alamo Printing, 1921.

———, *Samuel Maverick, Texan: 1803–1870,* a collection of letters, journals, and memoirs. San Antonio: privately printed, 1952.

Green, Thomas J., *Journal of the Texian Expedition Against Mier.* New York: Harper, 1845. (Facsimile reproduction by Steck, Austin, 1935.)

Gulick, Charles Adams, and others (editors), *The Papers of Mirabeau Buonaparte Lamar,* 6 vols. Austin: University of Texas, 1921–1927.

Hill, Jim Dan, *The Texas Navy.* New York: A. S. Barnes, 1962. (Originally published 1937.)

Hogan, William Ransom, *The Texas Republic: A Social and Economic History.* Austin: University of Texas Press, 1969. (Originally published 1946.)

Hollon, W. Eugene, and Ruth Lapham Butler, *William Bollaert's Texas.* Norman: University of Oklahoma Press, 1956.

Houston, Andrew J., *Texas Independence*. Houston: Anson Jones Press, 1938.

Houston, Sam, *The Writings of Sam Houston, 1813–1863*, 8 vols., edited by Amelia W. Williams and Eugene C. Barker. Austin: University of Texas Press, 1938–1943.

Huson, Hobart, *Rufugio: A Comprehensive History of Refugio County from Aboriginal Times to 1953*, 2 vols. Waco: Rooke Foundation, 1953.

Jenkins, John Holland, *Recollections of Early Texas*, edited by John Holmes Jenkins. Austin: University of Texas Press, 1958.

Johnson, Frank W., *A History of Texas and Texans*, edited and brought to date by Eugene C. Barker with the assistance of Ernest William Winkler. Chicago and New York: The American Historical Society, 1914.

Kendall, George Wilkins, *Narrative of the Texan Santa Fe Expedition, Comprising a Description of a Tour through Texas and across the Great Southwestern Prairies . . .* , 2 vols. London: Wiley & Putnam, 1844. (Facsimile reproduction by Steck, Austin, 1935.)

Kennedy, William, *Texas: The Rise, Progress, and Prospects of the Republic of Texas.* Fort Worth: Molyneaux Craftsmen, 1925. (Originally published 1841.)

Linn, John J., *Reminiscences of Fifty Years in Texas*. New York: D. & J. Sadlier, 1883. (Facsimile reproduction by Steck, Austin, 1935.)

Lord, Walter, *A Time to Stand.* New York: Harper, 1961.

Morrell, Z. N., *Flowers and Fruits in the Wilderness: or Forty-six Years in Texas and Two Winters in Honduras*, 4th edition revised. Dallas: W. G. Scarff, 1886.

Muir, Andrew Forest (editor), *Texas in 1837: An Anonymous Contemporary Narrative.* Austin: University of Texas Press, 1958.

Nance, Joseph Milton, *After San Jacinto: The Texas-Mexican Frontier, 1836–1841.* Austin: University of Texas Press, 1963.

———, *Attack and Counterattack: The Texas–Mexican Frontier, 1842.* Austin: University of Texas Press, 1964.

Oates, Stephen B. (general editor), *The Republic of Texas.* Palo Alto, California: American West, 1968.

Ramsdell, Charles, *San Antonio: A Historical and Pictorial Guide.* Austin: University of Texas Press, 1959.

Sheridan, Francis C., *Galveston Island: The Journal of Francis C. Sheridan, 1839–1840.* Austin: University of Texas Press, 1954.

Siegel, Stanley, *A Political History of the Texas Republic, 1836–1845.* Austin: University of Texas Press, 1956.

Stapp, William Preston, *The Prisoners of Perote.* Philadelphia: G. B. Zieber, 1845. (Facsimile reproduction by Steck, Austin, 1936.)

Thrall, Homer S., *A Pictorial History of Texas from the Earliest Visits of European Adventurers to A. D. 1879.* St. Louis: N. D. Thompson, 1879.

Wallis, Jonnie Lockhart, and Laurance Hill (editors), *Sixty Years on the Brazos: The Life and Letters of Dr. John Washington Lockhart, 1824–1900.* Los Angeles: privately printed, 1930. (Facsimile reproduction by Texian Press, Waco, 1967.)

Webb, Walter Prescott, *The Texas Rangers*. Austin: University of Texas Press, 1952. (Originally published 1935.)

———— (editor in chief) and others, *The Handbook of Texas*, 2 vols. Austin: Texas State Historical Association, 1952.

Weems, John Edward, *Men Without Countries*. Boston: Houghton Mifflin, 1969.

Wells, Tom Henderson, *Commodore Moore and the Texas Navy*. Austin: University of Texas Press, 1960.

Wilbarger, J. W., *Indian Depredations in Texas*. Austin: Hutchings Printing House, 1889. (Facsimile reproduction by Steck, Austin, 1935.)

Wooten, Dudley G., *A Complete History of Texas*. Dallas: Texas History Company, 1899.

Yoakum, Henderson King, *History of Texas from Its First Settlement in 1685 to Its Annexation to the United States in 1846*, 2 vols. New York: Redfield, 1855. (Facsimile reproduction by Steck, Austin, 1935.)

MAGAZINES AND NEWSPAPERS

These were used only for certain supplementary information not available elsewhere. Past issues of the *Southwestern Historical Quarterly* and its predecessor, the *Quarterly* of the Texas State Historical Association, contain a wealth of material on the Republic of Texas.

Day, James M. (editor), "Diary of James A. Glasscock, Mier Man," *Texana*, Spring and Summer, 1963.

Friend, Llerena (editor), "Thomas W. Bell Letters," *Southwestern Historical Quarterly*, July and October, 1959, and January and April, 1960.

Fuller, George F., "Sketch of the Texas Navy," *Quarterly* of the Texas State Historical Association, January, 1904.

McGrath, J. J., and Walace Hawkins, "Perote Fort—Where Texans Were Imprisoned," *Southwestern Historical Quarterly*, January, 1945.

Sinks, Julia Lee, "Rutersville College," *Quarterly* of the Texas State Historical Association, October, 1898.

The Daily Picayune, New Orleans, March 29, 1839. (On booming Galveston and Barnard Bee's arrival in the city.)

Morning Star, Houston, June 7, 1839, and June 10, 1839. (On the Bee mission's failure.)

Natchez Daily Courier, February 3, 1837. (On Santa Anna's trip to Washington with Barnard Bee and two other men to meet with President Andrew Jackson.)

Telegraph and Texas Register, Houston, July 17, 1844. (On the 1844 presidential campaign.)

INDEX

D

I

J

K